Larry L. King
A Writer's Life in Letters, Or,
Reflections in a Bloodshot Eye

Larry L. King:
A Writer's Life in Letters, Or,
Reflections In A Bloodshot Eye

Edited by Richard A. Holland

TCU Press / *Fort Worth, Texas*

Copyright © 1999 Texhouse Corporation

Library of Congress Cataloging-in-Publication Data
King, Larry L.
          Larry L. King : a writer's life in letters, or, reflections in a
bloodshot eye / Larry L. King : edited by Richard A. Holland.
          cm.
          ISBN 0-87565-203-4 (cloth : alk. paper)
          ISBN 0-87565-214-X (paper)
          King, Larry L. Correspondence. 2. Authors, American—20th cen-
tury Correspondence. 3. Journalists—United States Correspondence.
I. Holland, Richard (Richard A.) II. Title.
          PS3561.I48Z48   1999
          818'.5409—dc21   99-22568
          [B]   CIP

Design by Barbara Mathews Whitehead
Cover photo by Austin American-Statesman / Larry Kolvoord.
Courtesy Southwestern Writers Collection.

The letters of Larry L. King are reproduced without editing, reflect-
ing his own exuberant spelling and capitalization and his equally exuberant opinions on a wide variety of subjects.

Comments on Larry L. King's Work

"King is one of the finest writers of our time." —*Los Angeles Times*

"One of the best writing men in the land, with more than a touch of Mark Twain in his soul." —*Willie Morris*

"It is clear that King has a natural gift for theater."
—*The New York Times*

"King's strengths are his energy and wit and his integrity not to compromise the fundamentals. He rings an American bell."
—*Norman Mailer*

"He is the Texan with a Mencken touch." —*Newsweek*

"It is my single claim to literary eminence that I came to realize what a good writer Larry L. King is before most other people."
—*John Kenneth Galbraith*

"King can weave together words, phrases and ideas to engross, touch, titillate or outrage the reader." —*The Washington Post*

"He does it all so well. He could make a conservative cry, a liberal laugh. He watches with a perfect eye; he listens with a perfect pitch." —*Jim Lehrer*

"King tells his tales, both funny and sad, with dialogue as hot and spicy as three-alarm chili, and with the indisputable truth of a man who's been there himself." —*The Associated Press*

"Larry L. King writes just like an angel would if it grew up in West Texas and drank." —*Roy Blount, Jr.*

"Aw, shucks, folks. Ain't nothin' to it but talent and clean livin'."
—*Larry L. King*

Also by Larry L. King

NONFICTION

. . . And Other Dirty Stories (1968)
Confessions of a White Racist (1971)
The Old Man and Lesser Mortals (1974)
Wheeling and Dealing: Confessions of a Capitol Hill Operator
(with Bobby Baker) (1978)
Of Outlaws, Con Men, Whores, Politicians & Other Artists (1980)
That Terrible Night Santa Got Lost in the Woods (1981)
The Whorehouse Papers (1982)
Warning: Writer At Work (1985)
None But a Blockhead (1986)
True Facts, Tall Tales & Pure Fiction (1996)

NOVEL

The One-Eyed Man (1966)

FOR CHILDREN

Because of Lozo Brown (1988)

STAGE PLAYS

The Best Little Whorehouse in Texas
(with Peter Masterson and Carol Hall) (1978)
The Kingfish (with Ben Z. Grant) (1979)
Christmas: 1933 (1986)
The Night Hank Williams Died (1988)
The Golden Shadows Old West Museum (1989)

The Best Little Whorehouse Goes Public
(with Peter Masterson and Carol Hall) (1994)
The Dead Presidents' Club (1996)

TELEVISION DOCUMENTARIES

The Clean Water Act (PBS-TV, 1970)
The Best Little Statehouse in Texas
(CBS Reports, CBS-TV, 1981)

SCREENPLAY

The Best Little Whorehouse in Texas (1981)

PERIODICALS, 1964-1998

American Heritage, American Theatre, Atlantic Monthly,
Audience, Book Week, Book World, Boston Traveler Magazine,
Capitol Hill Magazine, Chicago Sun-Times Magazine,
Chicago Tribune Magazine, Cosmopolitan, Country Music,
Dallas Times-Herald Magazine, Detroit Athletic Club News,
Dissent, Dossier, Dramatists Guild Quarterly, Esquire, Harper's,
Harvard Crimson, Holiday, Life, Iconoclast,
Los Angeles Times Magazine, Modern Maturity, New Choices, New
Republic, Newsweek, New Times,
New York Magazine, New York Times Sunday Magazine, Oui,
Parade, Phillip Morris Magazine, Playbill, Playboy, Progressive,
Psychology Today, Publisher's Weekly, Quest, Reader's Digest, Roll
Call, Roundup Quarterly, Saturday Evening Post,
Southern Magazine, Southwest Review,
Southwestern American Literature, Sport, Sports Illustrated, Status,
Story, Texas Monthly, Texas Music,
Texas Observer, Theatre Week, Time, Today's Health, True,

T.V. Guide, U.S. News & World Report, Venture, Washingtonian Magazine, Washington Post Magazine, Washington Sunday Star Magazine, Washington Redskins Game Day, West, Writer's Digest, Writer's Yearbook.

Larry L. King wishes to thank those at the Southwestern Writers Collection, Southwest Texas State University, San Marcos, for their vital contributions to this book in time, talent, and research money: William D. Wittliff and Sally Wittliff, founders; Richard Holland, first curator and compiler of this book; Connie Todd, present curator; and the many good and helpful worker bees swarming the Alkek Library. All letters herein—and many others—are on deposit with the Southwestern Writers Collection as are most photographs used here.

EDITOR'S ACKNOWLEDGMENTS

There would be no Larry L. King Archive at Southwest Texas State University, had Bill Wittliff not brought his vision of a Southwestern Writers Collection to the campus. University President Jerry Supple and Alkek Library administrators Joan Heath and Bill Mears could not have been more supportive of the King archive and this book. The Special Collections staff instrumental in arranging and describing the King papers included René LeBlanc, Gwynned Cannan, Jennifer Peters, David Bruner and Steve Davis. My successor as curator, Connie Todd, has been a help in every aspect.

During the last few years many of the letters in the book became performance literature due to the talent and good ear of actor G. W. Bailey. His performances in San Marcos and as part of Kay Cattarulla's Arts & Letters Live programs at the Dallas Museum of Art brought the letters to life like nothing else.

Mark Busby, director of the Center for the Study of the Southwest at SWT, not only published excerpts in Southwestern American Literature but became a true compadre on the project.

The final mention appropriately goes to my beautiful and big-hearted wife, Cynthia Bryant, who listened to everything three times. Thank you, darlin', you are the very best one.

for

LANVIL GILBERT:

Cousin by blood, Friend by deeds,

Brother in my heart.

— L.L.K.

Contents

Foreword

When I was growing up on a hardscrabble, isolated Texas farm—in the 1930s and early 1940s—I learned, early on, that letters and postcards were vital forms of communication.

In my formative Great Depression years the King family owned no radio, phonograph, telephone or automobile; my siblings being sixteen, fifteen and fourteen years my elders, I had no ready playmate. Neighbors were few, far between and busy with their own agrarian tortures from before dawn to after dusk; not many had either the time or the natural inclination to indulge in amusements or frivolities. Other than grinding work, the main thing I recall is boredom and a loneliness that ached to the bone. My cousin and lifelong "best friend," Lanvil Gilbert, credits "the nurturing of your isolation" with making me a writer. He may be right—I did have ample time to think and to imagine—but I wish I anvil had told me that early, rather than late, since the solitude as I lived it seemed quite without reward or purpose.

One who is raised in such isolation—and who is keenly aware of it—somehow presumes a monopoly. So I was astonished some years later, as a young man newly working in the United States Congress, when a group of we starry-eyed Texas rurals gathered one Saturday morning at the feet of House Speaker Sam Rayburn—by then an old and venerated and powerful man—to hear him say of his own youth on a farm near Flag Springs, Texas: "Sunday afternoons, I would lean on a fence-post by a country dirt road, hoping that somebody—hell, Boys, anybody—would pass by that I could say 'hello' to or even wave to!" And I thought: My God, Mr. Sam, me too! In that moment, I think, I sensed that if Sam Rayburn had escaped his own solitude and gone on to great things, then perhaps even I might eventually amount to a little more than the farm boy, ranch hand, oil-field worker and small-town newspaper reporter I had been. It was, somehow, one of several defining moments aiding my decision to attempt to become the writer I had dreamed of being since age six despite being both a high school and college dropout.

I welcomed everything: thick "Wish Books" from Sears & Roebuck or Montgomery Ward mail order houses in distant cities, seed samplings, political circulars, the magazines *Farm and Ranch* or *Progressive Farmer* to whom I sent, without encouragement, my first ill-formed and derivative essays on raising hogs or growing peanuts or cotton and poems praising bucolic sunsets, creeks or newborn colts. None, alas, assisted my early ambitions to break into public print.

The real magic was contained in letters from kin. My mother's eight sisters—"The Clark Girls" as they called themselves to the grave—were, in my father's words, "Mighty good hands to write." I was entranced as Mama read these letters aloud, marveling at being able to learn news of the outside world and family lore at a cost of only three cents to the writer and none, blessedly, to the lucky recipient: bulletins from Rotan, Burkett, Fort Worth, Trent, Putnam, Galena Park and even distant California—where Tom Mix, Tarzan and my Aunt Dewey lived.

My big brother and personal hero, Weldon, sent intermittent scrawled notes from Midland, where he prospered as a short-order fry-cook at the Piggly Wiggly Store lunch counter, part-time announcer for radio station KCRS and $2-per-game second baseman for the semipro Midland Cowpokes. Sister Libby sent gossipy reports from Kermit, Sundown, Seminole or other oil-patch centers where her husband J.D. moved on short notice as suited the needs of Magnolia Petroleum.

My father's people only infrequently took up the pen and then only as emergencies seemed to dictate. Where the Clark Girls and Sister Libby wrote long-winded if entertaining and dramatic accounts, the Kings owed more allegiance to the economy of words; one must admit, however, they were good at what literary critics call "thematic unity." One old uncle wrote, "Need rain for crops, tho we is all in as good ahealth as can be expected except for our boy Rufus who drownded to death in a stock tank a few days ago." End of report. Some years later another of my father's brothers wrote—in full—on lined tablet paper bearing the rubber-stamped designation "Texas State Penitentiary" and his brand new prisoner number: "Dear Clyde, I do wisht you'd try to get me out as I am not-a-tall satisfied down here."

At age seven or eight I began writing letters of my own. Originally these were short notes to my siblings or Clarkside cousins, appendages stuffed into my mother's outgoing letters. Soon I discovered that unmatched bargain called "the penny postcard," buying two or three almost every time I could accumulate a nickel even should it mean shorting myself on jawbreaker candies or popgun caps. These penny dispatches almost uniformly exaggerated my athletic talents and my devilish way with girls; in so doing, they reflected my life not so much as it was as what I wished it to be.

In time I realized that for a mere copper cent I could advise, chastise or enlighten the high-and-mighty as well as common friends or close kin. Thus did I write F.D.R. of my approval of his "lend lease" program to England in 1940, inform the boxer Billy Conn that he had been "real dumb" in trying to slug it out with Joe Louis in that fatal thirteenth round at a time when he was ahead on points in 1911, clue West Point Coach Colonel "Red" Blaik as to exactly where he might find and develop a certain fourteen-year-old high school football tackle surely qualified to succeed his All-America fullback Felix (Doc) Blanchard three or four years hence, and send to singer Ernest Tubb a couple of sure-fire country-western hit songs I was certain he would gratefully rush to record. None of these targets, alas, proved to be serious correspondents despite my haunting of the family mailbox; much the same might be said, over the next few years, of Washington Redskins quarterback Sammy Baugh, Winston Churchill, the boxer Max Baer, actor Clark Gable and the writer James M. Cain even though I had little doubt that my missives had the potential to much improve their lives. In defense of their not responding, I must wonder whether the postal service really tried to locate recipients whom I could only address to "General Delivery" in such places as London, England and Pittsburg, Pennsylvania, and Hollywood, California. I remain certain that I would have accumulated an impressive group of pen pals had zip codes then existed.

I did receive varied reactions when writing to sources closer to home. At age ten, I advised the coach of the Putnam Grammar School Panthers football team—Mr. Jesse Overton—of the very deep do-do his team would be in on playing the Scranton Grammar School Antelopes, which I had the honor to quarterback; my exact words were "We intend to roll you in the dirt." A couple of weeks later—when, as Scranton team captain I met the Putnam captain, Benny Ross Everett, at midfield for the coin toss—Benny Ross narrowed his eyes and reddened his neck in saying, "Lawrence, you made a dern bad mistake in writin' that ding-busted postcard." Indeed. The aroused not-so-neighborly neighboring town team, to whom we had lost only by a 7-6 score a month earlier, stomped us 47-to-zip amidst many negative comments and rowdy celebrations of intercepting a half-dozen of my passes and sacking me for losses eight or ten times. Down 0-27 at half time, I presumed to deliver a stirring half-time oration until a teammate, Carl William Bailey, said "Lawrence, why don't you just shut up and play ball and quit writin' silly post cards?"

One might presume that I painfully learned, that day, the passions that careless verbiage might visit upon the verbalizer. Not so.

Over the years I have warred by mail with the alleged actor Burt Reynolds, some few professional critics, a couple of other writers, an editor or two and several private citizens who wrote nasty letters about articles or books I had crafted. Early on I vowed never to let anyone abuse me in private correspondence without returning fire. This reaction may in part be assigned to my own volatile or churlish personality, but I have no doubt it was sharpened and honed when I worked in Congress and my bosses—politicians dependent upon the public favor—instructed that when preparing responses to letters from abusive constituents I should, like Christ, "turn the other cheek." I chaffed, cursed and groused under such restrictions. Once free of them, and having become my own man, I sometimes threw caution to the winds when writing to rat-bastard assholes who some-how thought that buying a magazine in which I had an article they didn't like or purchasing a book of mine with which they disagreed gave them the right to piss on my feet without danger of receiving return water.

But don't get the wrong idea: most of my letters have not been mean-spirited, though not a few contain whines, complaints or curses when frustrated in my craft. The majority have been written to relatives and friends—including other writers—to entertain, inform, and occa-sionally even to encourage or inspire. Some were full of mischief, raw jokes, fun and wild exaggerations. Often they served the purpose—at the beginning of the writing day—of getting my creative juices flowing so that when the reluctant flow commenced I could attack whatever article, book, short story or play that had temporarily stayed me. But, mainly, I have always written letters simply because I love writing let-ters and love receiving them. That has been true all of my life, now at the Biblical "Three score years and ten"; I hope the work now in your hands will show my long appreciation of what has become—alas!—a relatively minor form of communication.

I began making carbon copies of perhaps ninety-eight per cent of my letters—excluding longhand efforts, which were comparatively few—in the mid-1950s. This was because, suddenly, I found myself working amidst the politically famous of my time in the United States Congress: Sam Rayburn, Lyndon Johnson, John F. Kennedy, many others who were household names or one day would be. Removed from my isolated West Texas plains and dunes, I also began to meet young writers just beginning their careers: William ("Billy Lee") Brammer, David Halberstam, Warren Miller, Tris Coffin and—a bit later—Willie Morris, Bill Styron, Norman Mailer, Edwin (Bud) Shrake, Dan Jenkins, Larry McMurtry, William D. Wittliff and on and on. I saved their letters to me and mine to them, out of two instincts: (1) I am a pack-rat and always have been, and (2) I sensed or felt or at least hoped that, one day, they might assist a book such as this. Credit me with a sense of history or a run-away ego, and you'll probably be right in either case.

My regret is that not much of my 1950s or early 1960s stuff survives. Not to speak ill of the dead but when, in 1963, I parted from my first wife she celebrated with a back yard bonfire fueled by most that I held near and dear: my personal correspondence, ill-formed early manuscripts, football letter jackets, high school annuals, clippings of my by-lined newspaper stories from New Mexico and Texas, and other such precious trash. With respect to the manuscripts—and perhaps some letters—she probably did me an unintentional favor. Nonetheless, I—and others—in the past few years have attempted to secure from old friends, kin and former associates my lost letters from their end; unfortunately (I think) few among those old sources reckoned my correspondence as valuable or collectible as I did, and so this tome contains only scattered samplings of my Neanderthal period. Only from 1964 on, when I began my freelance writing career following almost ten years as a second-banana politician in Congress, is there any true continuity.

Even then, this book contains less than everything. The Southwestern Writers Collection at Southwest Texas State University, San Marcos, literally has thousands of my old letters on hand: I have heard estimates ranging from 13,000 to 18,000, and one fellow crassly described my correspondence as amounting to "about three hundred pounds"; and obviously, I am neither so famed nor revered that more than a relative handful could make the cut as Richard Holland, curator of the Southwest Writers Collection at the time that outfit claimed my papers, waded through all that chaff in hopes of finding a few buckets of wheat.

I hope, and about half believe, this collection is representative of one American writer in his time and place: his preoccupations, successes, failures, anxieties, frustrations, hopes, fears, dreams, angers and joys. Though I was dead certain in my youth of becoming "A Famous Arthur"—sure to rank with the Old Dead Greats like Twain and Dickens and Fitzgerald and Shaw and O'Neill and Hemingway—I now drink from bitters not all that tangy. On days when the words won't come and I would like to hide under the bed and only my faithful dog Buster looks at me with anything like worshipful eyes, I wonder if I might have been better off had I gone into roofing and shingles.

All the more reason for embarrassments when I read in this book old letters composed in the hopeful white heat of my neophyte years in the wordsmith trade. That younger man seems so arrogantly certain that he will become so great and famous in American letters that he presumes his friends and kin to have little interest in life other than hearing of what he is writing or thinking of his own work or publicity promotions in the most picayune detail. It is, indeed, rather like listening to a boastful barroom drunk. I now apologize both for that youthful exuberance and the overly inflated future I presumed. Yes, I have accomplished thirteen books, eight plays, countless magazine articles, have been anthologized, won some awards and had some satisfactory paydays but, somehow, it falls so short of what was intended that to my ears it all rings a little hollow and tinny and dimestore.

That said, however, the truth is that I have been luckier than most writers—probably luckier than I deserve—and should quit this goddamned whining. I had the good fortune to come along when publishing houses still cared enough for the future to attempt to develop and sustain young writers, when they published books they knew would not make money, when they looked ahead and cared about their product; this is less true in an age where publishing houses are minor offshoots of huge conglomerates and in-house bean counters look only to the bottom line. When I began there were numerous general interest magazines that solicited, nurtured and wanted essays on serious subjects; they were not afraid to let their writers slash and burn or use wit or dark humor like a rapier; now most magazines are celebrity-driven and cower in the dark shadows of "political correctness" and, to tell the truth few—as Texan John Nance Garner said of the vice-presidency—are worth a bucket of warm piss.

I have in my archives at least fifteen partial books and five plays that have not come to fruition, plus God only knows how many short stories or magazine articles: projects abandoned on page three or page 88 or page 127 or page 289 or worse. I frankly don't know if that is typical or atypical, writers not often confessing to others their failures or false starts or died a-bornings. Suffice it to say that I have had far too many, as my letters attest. You will find in this book great and temporary enthusiasms for projects that, in the end, never amounted to a popcorn fart. All part of the daily warp and woof of those of us who live by our wits and imagination, and for whom failure in one degree or another is virtually guaranteed. No piece of writing—one of my superiors in the craft once said—is ever finished; it is simply abandoned out of a realization that perfection is impossible; that includes articles and stories and books and plays that may actually go on to earn plaudits and money. All of which may account for why so many writers drink so much, wear shoulder chips, need mood modifiers, rank themselves in one minute three steps on the ladder ahead of Hemingway times Vonnegut plus Mailer and—in the next minute—pray they will prove to be the literary equal, when all is said done, of Mickey Spillane or Jacqueline Susann.

What this should tell you, Dear Reader, is that I remain serious about my sullen craft and expect to fret and sweat and pound out yarns of one kind or another until Gabriel blows his horn and that sweet chariot swings low. Each new article, book, play, short story—hell, even reprints—gladdens my withered old heart and gives me temporary fresh hope. And I include the writing of letters—a lost art, almost, because, over a lifetime of word strivings on this good green-and-blue earth, I have enjoyed writing nothing so much as letters. One does not have to skate them by picky editors, or reluctant publishers or beg anybody's permission to circulate them, except now and again when my wife-lawyer-agent—Barbara S. Blaine—rips up the occasional death threat or my sly hints of possible future fornications and whatnot, her being narrow minded in certain areas and scared to death of lawsuits unless she is the one bringing them.

Otherwise, writing letters remains a pure joy. And I hope that in these formerly private jottings some of the fun will seep through to you, the reader.

Larry L. King
Washington, D.C.
1999

1

A Prologue in Politics

L arry L. King's first exposure to power politics came at the age of twenty, when he was fired from his first real job. He was a forty-dollar-per-week cub reporter for the Hobbs, New Mexico, *Daily Flare*—"the second paper in a town of 10,000 people"— and after five months was let go for coming dangerously close to libeling a federal judge on page one. Young King vehemently disagreed with one of the judge's decisions from the bench and proceeded to ridicule the judge in print; when a complaint was lodged, King was gone.

Back in West Texas he lasted eighteen months as a sportswriter for the *Midland Reporter-Telegram* until his making fun of local sports teams once again landed him in hot water. After working for radio station KCRS as newscaster and sportscaster, in late 1952 King went to the Odessa American at $100 a week, over twice his wages in Hobbs and Midland. In Odessa he was assigned the police beat and once again covered legal activities. He soon conned his editors into making him the *American's* "political writer," a surprising departure for the West Texas daily that King later described in *None But a Blockhead* as "so rabidly anti-government it never had named a political correspondent." This was a natural step for a young man who at the age of nine had vigorously campaigned for Eastland County Commissioner Arch Bint, and three years later campaigned fields and creek banks for Lyndon Johnson in his unsuccessful Senate race against W. Lee (Pappy) O'Daniel.

During the 1954 16th District congressional campaign the *Odessa American* supported the incumbent Ken Regan. Somehow, perhaps due to his editors' inattention, their young political writer started touting Regan's opponent, State Senator J.T. Rutherford. Of his propensity for personal political loyalty over journalistic indifference, King later wrote: "Purists may charge that I became a propagandist rather than a reporter. Guilty as Thomas Paine, your honor. I lost not a wink of sleep over the ethics of the thing: all was fair, I had heard, in love, war or politics; I took to that credo as unthinkingly as members of the Watergate Gang later would. An impossible objectivity has never been my forte" (*None But A Blockhead*, 1986). When Rutherford upset the incumbent congressman, he selected King from among numerous applicants for the job as his administrative assistant in Washington.

The twenty-five year old was plenty interested in politics but was also aware that compared to Odessa and Midland working in Washington would place him where at least there was some opportunity to make contacts for writing magazine articles or publishing books. Still, when King arrived in Washington in November of 1954 to learn the ropes before Rutherford took office two months later, he lost little time seeking out young men—especially from Texas and the South—who ran the offices and campaigns of some of the greatest and most villainous politicians of the century and some of the most mundane.

He immediately took to the place, joining other administrative aides adept at making political deals; numbers of these new colleagues over future years would go on to become congressmen, senators or governors themselves, or powerful Washington lawyers. King drank and schemed and yarned with them, picking their brains and forming helpful alliances that would last over lifetimes. Within a year King was elected program chairman of the Burro Club—a group made up of Democratic aides to congressmen and senators. He thus controlled who would or would not speak to this powerful insider's group, and gave the nod, variously, to John F. Kennedy, Lyndon B. Johnson, Adlai Stevenson and other would-be presidents from among governors, senators and congressmen; he also attracted Dean Acheson, former President Harry Truman, former Texas Senator Tom Connally, Speaker Sam Rayburn and other elders to Burro Club luncheons or dinners. And he was elected to the board of directors of the Texas State Society in Washington, composed of Texas expatriates who largely lobbied or lawyered and perhaps more importantly included the entire Texas congressional delegation and their wives as active members. King now says, "Yeah, I hit the ground running. Wanted to make my mark."

Once in place in Rutherford's office, however, King quickly was disabused of the notion that he would have time to write imaginative novels or magazine articles: instead, he wrote routine speeches, press releases, and newsletters carrying the by-lines of his boss in twelve-hour days he now recalls as "almost as tough as those in the cotton patch or the oil fields." On weekends, though raising a young family with his wife Jean, he doggedly tried to learn how to write "for real." Indeed, before Rutherford's political career was over eight years later, King had produced two-and-a-half novels, but they proved to be unpublishable.

By the time King was the administrative assistant for Fort Worth Congressman Jim Wright in the early 1960s, he was quickly becoming disenchanted with politics and had seen literary success up close on the part of his dear friend Bill Brammer, who had written *The Gay Place* while he was a staffer for Lyndon Johnson. This is when King became friends with Willie Morris, who had edited Brammer at the *Texas Observer* and, after a stint as a Rhodes Scholar, had joined *Harper's*. Literary success was nearby, and King was stuck in a deteriorating marriage and in Jim Wright's office. In the meantime he had in his hand his first legitimate book contract from McGraw-Hill for a southern political novel.

John Kennedy's death in Dallas led King to perform a "personal inventory" that convinced him that nothing would do but a complete break with job and family. King moved into a rooming house for men that he dubbed "Heartbreak Hotel" and began working on what would become his first book, *The One-Eyed Man*. After ten years as a political worker bee and family man, King shoved aside the past. The brashness of completely starting over at age thirty-five King attributes to his optimism and naiveté about the odds against any free-lance writer making a living. King's years in politics, however, proved to be formative and indeed became manifest in his subsequent career as a writer. His profiles of those in power, including Nelson Rockefeller, John Lindsay, Gerald Ford, Jim Wright, Morris Udall, and LBJ, are written with an insider's sharp eye and ear, and his later comic theatrical output is bracketed by the dancing, side-stepping Texas governor in 1978's *The Best Little Whorehouse in Texas* and the sight of Presidents Johnson and Nixon conniving to bargain their way out of Purgatory in 1996's *The Dead Presidents' Club*.

The King letters that do survive from this period are largely those saved by Lanvil Gilbert, described by King as "more like my brother than not; our mothers were identical twins from the day they were born until their respective deaths." The sense of beginning a new life is very real in these letters as is the vast world of knowledge and influence now available to him. This chapter closes with two memory letters recapturing this time period—one recalling King's first, comic meeting with Harry Truman, the second recalling for his son Brad where he was on the day of President Kennedy's assassination.

—Richard Holland

20 December 1954

Greetings and Best of the Season, Cuz:*

. . . Most of my personal time has been spent buying furniture, renting a place, counting my lack of money and getting my family settled in our new home. My official time has been spent wandering in a daze, down a never-ending line of halls, meeting people, hunting future work spaces and trying to find what makes the U.S. Government click. . . .

I think I will like this business . . . once I get my teeth into it. I've been here for the past 21 days in the office of U.S. Rep. Olin Teague of College Station. His assistant, a fellow named George Fisher, is showing me the ropes, of which there are many, and some of them slippery with the sweat and blood of politics. In addition to myself, Congressman J.T. Rutherford will have an office force of three women, over which I am to preside. My duties will consist of news releases, handling "case" requests from constituents, supervising correspondence, seeing that the boss is comfortable, seeing that visitors from our 16th District are shown the proper respect and routes in Washington, and in general making Rutherford an impossible man to beat come election time.

[The job] carries a starting salary of $8,000 and can go as high as $11,500, which I have been promised if I'm a good boy and don't committ a multitude of political sins. Due to squeezing my nickles until the buffalo humps more—because I won't get paid until February 1— my social and sight-seeing activities have been rather limited . . . and probably will be until the long green starts its seemingly-slow flow— or maybe I should say trickle—into my hands.

I have, however, visited the Capitol, looking under each nook and cranny; wandered through both the Old and New House office buildings; been through the Library of Congress—and you, by the way, would love to work there as a research man, I'm sure—and have explored the entire Capitol Hill District. . . . I got in touch with a guy named John Saunders, who lives in Arlington, and who fought the

Battle of Long Island New York in the Army with me with valor and honor, and he drove us around to points of interest one night. . . .

I have visited each of the Texas Congressmen, including the Senators, and have met their assistants and staff members. They all seem very likeable and sincerely want to help—as you might imagine, the Texas delegation has strong ties. Lyndon Johnson is in my mind one of the top political figures of our day. Whether or not you agree with his policies, as politics they are wonderful and I would hate to have the job of trying to defeat him, ever. And Mr. Sam—Speaker Rayburn—is absolutely God on the Throne. Quite a man and a likeable old gentleman at that.

In spite of all this, life at present is rather lonely. I have never prided myself on being a family man, but I must confess I truly and sorely missed my wife and daughter until they arrived. Now that they are here, life is somewhat more cheerful for me, but I think Jean gets very lonely and blue. Being only six weeks or so away from her second shot at motherhood, and with our finances at low ebb currently, all she has to look forward to each day is some ten hours of a romping, prancing, screaming three-year-old in strange quarters without a friendly face to be found.

It is rather lonely to be alone. But it is far more lonely to be surrounded by semi-familiar new faces and be lonely still. That is the most lonely lonely of them all. To clear the situation I take long and cold walks around the hill, looking at what is immediately before me, not having to speak to those around me. And somehow in this lonely state I find companionship with myself. . . .

This would be a good time, theoretically, for me to write and create. But as of yet I cannot. Everything is too new and I am too busy thinking, watching, and observing. I am looking forward to much material and many writing hours, in spite of two kids, in the future.

I think Mother is coming up here when Jean has her baby in February to spend two or three weeks. All my life I can recall her fondest hope: to see the nation's capitol before she dies. That opportunity is now a possibility. But like so many of us, she now worries about the physical side of things—money, travel, weather—rather

than concentrating on what she had heretofore thought was a dream
come true. . . .

*Cousin Lanvil Gilbert.

May 10, 1961

Dear Lanvil:

Better late than never.

Am submitting to you the first ten chapters of my manuscript.*
The first six of these are being judged in the prospective publisher's
in-house contest, along with the general story plot outline. Which is:
In each of us there is a stream of secret music, or the sound of a different drummer or a river of a certain depth, and whether it is music
or drum tempos or water, it takes a given form because of our experiences. I firmly believe that the boy shapes the man. Therefore, I am
taking the case of an American Turncoat of the Korean War, and
looking first at his boyhood and young adult-hood experiences to see
what shaped him. The portions of the manuscript herein submitted
deal mainly with those boyhood experiences, tho I have not yet completed that. I have written virtually nothing of the actual prison camp
experiences, which is to come—as is the trial, which will be a key part
of my story. And it does not end there. I send him back into the world
after serving his sentence, and we look at how society treats a
Turncoat, and what he thinks of it. I am months away from finishing
this. It does not come easily. Especially the polishing for rewriting. If
and when I sell to someone, somewhere, the pages submitted here for
your inspection may not be found there or may be drastically altered.
Who knows?. . .

Spare me not. Suggest. Criticize. Snort. Cuss. Laugh. Register your
reactions to me honestly. I need help. I need ideas. I need honesty. . . .

*A fanciful, failed attempt at a novel. King as a newspaper reporter had
known and written of Corporal Claude Batchelor, of Kermit, one of twenty-
one American POWs in Korea who had originally refused repatriation during
prisoner exchanges between the U.S. and North Korea.

May 19, 1960

Dear Folks:*

We have been hitting the ball in an effort to adjourn about July 1st, prior to the Democratic National Convention July 11th, and of course I worked night and day getting ready for our trip to Wyoming in behalf of Senator Lyndon Johnson, and got two hours to three hours sleep each of the four nights we were gone. When we returned my work here was behind and I'm just now catching up.

Doesn't look as if I will have much free time from now on until Lord knows when. We are taking this weekend a trip to the Delaware seashore and it will be my last chance to relax. I am probably going to fly to Los Angeles with the Johnson delegation to the National Convention sometime during the first few days of July, and be there ten days to two weeks. Then I suppose I will have to fly back here and drive the family to Texas, staying there most of the Fall. As you probably know now, Dr. Dorothy Wyvell is running against Slick [Rutherford] in November, and while I don't think she constitutes any kind of threat, we will be out around the District as usual. **

Was quite a trip to Wyoming. We stumped the state by small private plane for LBJ, hitting about 30 towns, and going over mountains and canyons that caused a constant air current updraft. This tossed the small plane about quite a bit, as a result of which I spent half of my time losing what I had earlier eaten. We'd land at a town for a meeting, and about the time I'd recovered, I would have to get back in the plane to fly to another town, and it would start all over again. However, the last two days and nights we were in one town (Thermopolis) at the State Democratic Convention, and I felt fine there—except for being tired as the devil. In spite of all that, I enjoyed the change of scenery and a chance to get out of the office awhile. . . .

*LLK's parents, in Midland.
**Rutherford easily won, carrying all but Midland County.

Jan. 16, 1964

Dear Lanvil:

Riding up on the elevator to my office one morning this week, numb and drained from grappling with the midnight woes, I had a quick and burning need to hear from you. Almost immediately I was seized with a great anger that I had not. As if you owed me money and wouldn't pay, had something that belonged to me and wouldn't give it back. The rage was quite genuine, quite complete and behind it thundered the resolve to write you a quite brisk and cutting letter, or even to telephone you a carping message of personal invective. And then, also abruptly, the rage washed itself out as I became smitten by the certain thought that a letter from you would be on my desk. It was. I was delighted, surprised and no end astonished, even though I had expected it to the degree that had it not been there, I am sure I would have been gripped by the black throes. Fearful secretaries would have walked on tip-toe all day around the growling form, hoping not to awaken the sleeping beast. My secretaries are having a lot of days like that lately. I do not think they have healthy enough nerve ends for me to sell another book or bust another marriage.*

Your letter was a tonic. It was almost as if written by doctor's prescription, in that it said some things I have been telling myself in the shapeless void of night, when the glooms overtake me and I must be concerned with Justification. It came at the end of a very bad week in which I had gone through colossal traumas: the bad scene of putting the kids on the airplane (one that, God knows, will play in their little heads how many times?), of selling the furniture in our former house, of having to clean that house and dispose of the familiar items in it. Reminders everywhere in the silent, accusing rooms: a two-year old book written by Cheryl: "My Family, by Cheryl King. . . . This is my Daddy. He works hard and loves us and wants to be a writer, and is a friend of President Kennedy. . ." The discarded worn shirts and blue jeans of little Bradley, a crushed old cowboy hat he loved, an Army truck he brought to me often until he learned my ineptitude at mechanics and so taught himself to repair the faulty wheels. . . . By instinct did he know he must learn to do for himself that which I would prove incapable of doing for him? If so, wish that he learned the lesson large. . . . A pink hair ribbon from a blond pony tail I used to know by soft touch, a miniature metal horseshoe engraved "Kerri". . . the dismantling of bunk beds. . . the bone-sore weariness of scouring and scrubbing and disposing of the evidence of our habitation of the house (you too can scrub away the past with Brillo pads). . . the moving into a new apartment only two hundred yards away from my office. . . the straightening up, the beginning anew, the hours lost at the typewriter, the necessary compromise with all that nagging guilt.

So thanks for what you said.

This experience is a new one. It has taught me things. About the Union of Wives, for instance. At the outset of our split, the wives of my friends remained kind beyond that point which passeth all understanding. They felt (I know in retrospect) that I was making a Grand Gesture, was playing a trombone solo, and as soon as I had captured the attention of the crowd I would put the instrument back in the case and run home, purged of my ills and somehow made a better husband and father for it. They may even have admired the gesture a little, may have secretly wished their husbands had the pizzazz to bring them so painful a gift . . . temporarily, of course. But woe, the script did not have a happy ending. No one meant for me to pack family off to Texas kit and kaboodle, to sell furniture, to end the blessed union, to blossom out in public places as escort to a couple of ladies of mystery. (One is for real, one is a bellcat). Suddenly I had done a Terrible Thing. Suddenly I was a Threat To Security. Suddenly husbands were not to be trusted around Him, and the dinner invitations with all the polite little chitchat about my domestic difficulties, and how it is a shame but I'm sure everything will turn out for the best, came to a screeching halt. Just in time, too. I felt obligated to go and never was comfortable. Example, shrilled during the pie a la mode by six-year-old Joel Raupe: "Mr. King, how come you don't live with Bradley anymore?" Who needs it?

This much more about The Situation, and then no more. (I cannot learn the lesson about how difficult it is for even the most understanding to work up a prolonged interest in the problems of others; in that, at least, I do not deviate from the norm.) Yes, I miss the kids. Hell yes. The hardest thing I shall ever do has been done: putting them on the airplane. The day [was] appropriately cold and overcast, dreary, the wind howling, Kerri crying when a friend hove into view bringing the family for the final ride, Cheryl silent and brave, Bradley (heretofore relatively unconcerned) gripped by deep deliberation which at the last minute broke me in pieces when he burst into tears, threw one short arm around my neck, hugged me like he wanted to crawl inside and begged: "Daddy, *please* go with me," Jean having the bad judgement under the impact of emotion to beg me to reconsider that which has been considered and reconsidered until the mind boggles and the senses fog over; my own shameful breakup, my stumbling blindly away, the tears coming down the face, shoulders shaking. And most incredible of all: Congressman Ralph Rivers of Alaska falling on me immediately, pumping my hand, beaming cheer, apparently *unmindful* of my state, *unseeing*, babbling to me the recollection of how *he* had been for LBJ in 1960 and did I remember the trips he made with me to Wyoming and Colorado in pre-convention 1960, and wasn't our original choice doing a splendid job, simply a marvelous job, oh yes a grand job, under the burden of his new responsibilities? KeeRist! The macabre touch of the early O'Hara.

Well, these scenes proved something, alright. They proved my decision appropriate down at the bedrock. Without that conviction I never could have made it, for I am crassly sentimental if nothing else. I won't say it proved the wisdom of the choice, for actions do not lend themselves to immediate judgement wisdom-wise. But it proved the inevitability. . . .

Book: curve downward, as might be expected, but rising. Editor Bob Gutwillig called from N.Y. yesterday, wailing the blues: Get more copy in. The last chapter you sent doesn't measure up to what has gone before, you are deviating from the story line, tell the goddamn *story*. (My answer to part one: Even the Goddamn *Bible* doesn't swing all the way through, man; have you picked up on the Book of Mark? Slow action, bad plot development, mediocre prose. . . . My answer to

LARRY L. KING

part two: I can't tell the story, for I have lost my outline and *forgot* the goddamn thing.) He had the chillbanes and a vocal spasm. Jollied him into a good humor with broad imitations of Lyndon Johnson, slurs at his Hebrew religion, misquotations from the Book of Job. But apparently the last chapter needs to be re-worked. I admit it, knew it before he told me.

Teacher to pupils in writing class: "Compose a story containing the following elements: religion, royalty, sex, mystery. Little Johnny writes: 'My Lord, said the princess, pregnant again! Wonder who did it?'"

My new apartment is nice. Small by the five-person dwellings I have grown accustomed to, but ample for me. Large living room, kitchen with dining nook I have turned into writing den, walk-in hall closet, bath, small closet. One and one-half blocks from my office door, two and one-half from the shadow of the Capitol dome, three minutes by car from the apartment of Rosemarie (a Greek lady about whom you will hear more in the future, I feel sure),** third floor, automatic elevator, no desk in lobby to provide prying eyes.

I have lately been re-reading old books long enjoyed. They seem better than the new ones. Is it nostalgia? . . . No matter. *Lie Down in Darkness* (a poem of a book, beautiful, recognizing evil for what it really is and locking on beauty and full of so much truth), Eric Sevareid's *Not So Wild a Dream*, Hemingway's *The Sun Also Rises*, Penn Warren's *All the King's Men*, stories by Eudora Welty, some of the brilliantly mad ravings of Mailer in *Adverstisements for Myself*, the great rise and fall of the wonderful prose in The Bible.

I grow weary at 1:45 A.M. and must sleep. Thank God for the weekend coming—a great slice of time to give to my own book. Christ, would I like to accept your invitation to hibernate with you and be closeted with the muse! I need it badly. I think if Jim Wright knew just how badly, he would insist I do it, but of course he doesn't know and I can't tell him. . . .

Do write and much love to you and Glenda.

*King had in September of 1963 sold his novel *The One-Eyed Man*, and a

22

few weeks later left his wife, and would soon leave his job. He has written that the assassination of John F. Kennedy caused him to realize that should he die early and suddenly that he would not have accomplished "any of the things I wanted to do."

**Rosemarie Coumaris Kline became King's wife on February 20, 1965.

April 21, 1994

Dear Jim:*

I am getting so ancient and forgetful that I couldn't recall which of my books the Harry Truman-Craig Raupe story was in.** After more than a fleeting search, I conclude that it's not in any of them. I think I wrote it once in some magazine piece that did not make it to hardcover, I know I've told the story many times and may have included it in my remarks at Craig's funeral. Anyway, here's my recollection of that event:

In the spring of 1956, Harry S. Truman came back to Washington for the first time since he'd left the White House to speak at a Jefferson-Jackson Day Dinner. Craig Raupe read in the newspaper that HST would be staying at the Mayflower Hotel and rushed to me in the kind of trembling, energetic excitement I shall always associate with him.

"King," he said, "I wrote my Master's Thesis on Truman's defeat of Dewey in 1948. I want to present a copy to President Truman, and I want you to bring your office camera to take my picture when I do." It sounded like a good deal: I was freshly 26 and had yet to meet a President or even an ex-President. Craig, I think, was 29 and probably hadn't met one either; we'd both been in Washington only a year as rookie A.A.'s on Capitol Hill.

So, at an indecent hour on a Saturday morning, Craig honked for me in his old green '37 Chrysler—we lived but a block apart in Southeast Washington—and duly washed, polished, shined, and combed we crossed the Anacostia River as pumped up as two young explorers invading uncharted territory. We stopped by Congressman J.T. Rutherford's office where I temporarily liberated his big, bulky

Crown Graphic camera and a dozen flashbulbs. Back in the car to the Mayflower, Craig babbling like a brook. By now it's maybe 8 A.M.

Craig picks up the house phone in the Mayflower lobby, says "President Truman's room please" and within seconds he begins to stutter: "Ah. . .President Truman? Er, ah, my name's Craig Raupe" and he states our purpose, listens a minute, grins, says, "You bet, Mister President! Thank you!" He hangs up the phone, punches me on the arm and says "That was Truman his *goddam*-self! Come on, you sumbitch, he's waiting on us!" So we scurry to the elevator, running high fevers, two young Texas hicks getting to meet the Great Man, and Craig is laughing and pulling his nose as he did when excited and saying things like "I like to crapped when he answered the phone himself" and "Keep your mouth shut and let me do the talking, King, this is *my* deal" and otherwise instructing me as if he fears a boy from Putnam, Texas might embarrass a boy from the big city of Granbury, Texas in the presence of the mighty (which as we shall see, I dutifully did.)

HST himself answered the door, beaming that friendly smile, in shirtsleeves but with a tie on. "You boys like some coffee?" and of course we would, so he picks up the phone and calls room service—ordering coffee for four—and, *very* soon, coffee is there and lo! Mrs. Truman joins us and pours. Meanwhile, Craig is hopping around like a rabbit and talking up a storm while I fiddle with my camera and flash-bulbs. I was not then, nor am I now, a great photographer or a competent operator of any other machinery. My main recollection is that Truman didn't say much, just drank coffee and grinned, while Craig held forth on Democrats, 1948, his Masters Thesis, and God knows what all.

Comes the time for the big picture-taking. I shoot four pictures. To my astonishment, the flashbulbs go off as they are supposed to, Craig and Truman beam at each other as Craig gives HST a bound copy of his work. The job done, Craig begins to thank Truman for receiving him when I say "Wait a minute, Craig! Now make a couple of me and Mr. Truman." Craig gives me a killing look, but grabs the camera. Truman locks arms with me and says "Democrats should lock arms when being photographed so some damned Republican editor can't cut anybody out!" We laugh at that, shake hands with HST and Mrs. Truman and leave. (Male chauvinist pigs that we were, it didn't occur to us to get the former First Lady's picture!)

Craig is happier and higher than an airplane a mile over Denver, spouting a torrent of words and pulling his nose half off. He drops me at the New House Office Building (Longworth, now) and I go to work while he rushes up the street to a photo shop to get his precious pictures developed and printed. They aren't open yet. He waits on the sidewalk until they do open and stays to see the results.

The results are not good.

This I learn when Craig Raupe bursts into my office wild-eyed and mad enough to eat nails, shouting "King, you *son-of-a-bitch!* You sorry *bastard!* The pictures I made of *you* and Truman are perfect! The ones *you* made of me and him are *blank.* Not a goddam *thing* on the film! How'd you screw up, you son-of-a-bitch?"

We figured out that in my excitement I got "buck fever" and forgot to pull a protective plate at the rear of the camera. Forgot it *four times!* And with the plate still in the camera, for reasons still beyond my uncertain expertise, no images are recorded on the film. It was, indeed, blank and as black as Tahiti at midnight.

I don't suppose Craig cursed me more than fifteen minutes, though he came back an hour later to improve his invective, and I had the misfortune to suffer another profane lecture as we rode home after a half-day in our respective offices. I apologized until I turned blue, but to no avail.

I am sound asleep in the dark when my phone rings the next morning at 3:45 A.M. My first thought was that Mama had died. Who the *hell* calls anyone at that hour unless inspired by the darkest of disasters?

Raupe says in a deadly, even tone: "King, you son-of-a-bitch, get up and shave and dress. We're gonna go see Harry Truman again. He takes a walk real early. We're gonna be outside the Mayflower waiting when he comes out. You're gonna have your camera in hand, and if you fuck it up *this* time, I'm through with you." He bangs down the phone. Half-way to the shower the phone rings again; I grab it so won't wake my wife and two babies: "You up!" Craig asks. Well, hell yes! "Just checking to see you didn't go back to sleep. Hurry up, goddammit, we don't wanta miss Truman!"

Truman comes out for his walk at about 5:30 A.M. as I recall. We are waiting along with a couple of Washington newspaper men. Craig rushes up to Truman and says "Mister President, excuse me, but this jackass"—and he gestures toward me—"forgot to pull the plate when he made our pictures yesterday and we need to do it again. Do you still have my Thesis?" Truman says why, yes, he's looking forward to reading it, let's go upstairs and get it. So we traipse to the elevator, go up, Truman immediately produces the document and as they pose Craig keeps up a running chatter of instructions to me: "Don't forget to pull the plate, dammit . . . screw the flashbulb in tight . . . Did you get it? . . .take another one!" and so on. HST seemed rather amused, chuckling, while I felt like the 5th Place Jackass at the County Fair.

We rush to the photographer's place on Capitol Hill. "Craig," I say, "it's *Sunday!* They won't be open!" "I called the dude last night," Craig says. "He agreed to meet me here." We wait and wait and wait. I finally persuade Craig to go with me to a nearby greasy spoon for breakfast and coffee. He darts out the door every three minutes to check on whether the photo guy has arrived. "Goddam it, Craig"—I grumble—"it ain't even seven o'clock! That guy may not show for hours." Craig said we'd by-God be there when he did arrive. We waited only about another 90 minutes.

Now I'm *really* nervous. If the photos are bad *this* time . . . too horrible a thought to be permitted to live, so I wipe it out of my mind. Craig paces like an expectant father, pulling his nose while the photo man does his lab magic, and issuing the occasional threat should I have screwed up *again*—though, if so, I might not be here to tell it!—but this time Craig was handed good pictures; he received them with a great shout, and began pounding me on the back as if I'd scored a winning touchdown. Great, great, *great* was my relief!

I wish we had Craig's version, Jim, bless his old heart. He *delighted* in telling that story on me for the next 32 years—and he *always* told it with more humor and laughter and élan than I can muster.

Damn, but I still miss our old friend!

Always good to hear from you, Jim. Stay in touch. Love to you and to Betty from, your old friend,

LLK

P.S. Jim, the pictures made of me and Truman by Craig did not survive; they perished in a fire. . . . Fortunately, when HST came back to D.C. in 1958, I introduced him at a Burro Club meeting and we were photographed together again and he again locked arms and said that line about "damn Republican editors." Apparently it was a staple with the old boy!

*Retired Speaker of the House Jim Wright of Fort Worth.
**Craig Raupe came to Washington as Jim Wright's first administrative assistant the same year King arrived in town with J. T. Rutherford. Raupe and King remained close friends until Raupe's death in 1988.

March 3, 1992

Dear Brad:

As promised, here's my recollection of that fateful day—November 22, 1963—and the days just before and just after.

First, the reason for John F. Kennedy's trip to Texas: politics, pure and simple. The Democratic Party in Texas was pulling itself apart due to hostilities between Sen. Ralph Yarborough on the one hand and Vice-President Lyndon B. Johnson and Governor John Connally on the other. Yarborough and Johnson had been on opposite sides of the political fence in Texas for years. Yarborough led the real liberal wing of the party; LBJ's camp had some liberals, but more closely aligned itself with the powerful and rich making up the conservative wing of the party. Connally not only was a former aide to LBJ and thus cast his lot with him, but was an ideological conservative.

Yarborough had even considered running for control of the Texas Democratic Party in a precinct fight in 1959, so as to deny LBJ a strong Texas base on which to base his 1960 Presidential campaign. He talked this over with me, and got very angry when I advised against it on the theory that LBJ would beat hell out of him and Yarborough would gain nothing while being seen by many Texans as an obstructionist trying to keep LBJ from having a good Presidential shot. Texans, I told Senator Yarborough, were too clannish for that; they would punish him for trying to stop a fellow Texas Democrat from national honors. Ralph got so upset he banged his desk and said "Well, it's good to know who my *friends* are! You're fired!" I was a bit astonished and said, "Senator, you can't fire me! I don't *work* for you!" He looked a bit confused, then embarrassed, and shook my hand and thanked me for stopping by to see him! (He had *sent* for me; sometimes Ralph was a bit goofy.)

Anyway, when LBJ became Vice-President, Yarborough originally thought that he would benefit: he would become the Senior Senator from Texas, with all the prerogatives accruing to same, including being the patronage chief who decided the people to be chosen for judgeships and other Federal appointments. Much to his shock, anger, and surprise he learned that JFK had promised LBJ that Johnson could have *half* those appointments even though—as Vice-President—he really wasn't entitled to them. This drove Yarborough nuts. He began to snipe at LBJ and John Connally in public to some extent, and cursed them in private.

LBJ, meanwhile, had encouraged Jim Wright on the sly to run for Senator against Ralph Yarborough; I know, because I was Wright's Administrative Assistant at the time. On two separate occasions—each a Saturday morning in 1963—LBJ called Wright's office and had him come to his house. I took the calls. He promised Wright the undercover backing of LBJ's organization and money from his friends, if Wright would run against Yarborough in 1964. Wright was tempted and very much wanted to. I fought against it, telling Jim that even if he won—and that would not be guaranteed—he would alienate the liberal wing of the Democratic Party by trying to unseat an incumbent liberal Senator. *

So you can see the Democrats in Texas were eating each other up. JFK, no fool, decided it had to end. The Texas trip was to force LBJ, Ralph, Connally and their key supporters all to come together in a public display of harmony so as to put an end to the in-fighting and bad publicity about it. (Even so, Connally had to be ordered to invite Yarborough to a planned reception for JFK in Austin—which never came off, due to the assassination—and Yarborough had to be forced to ride in the car with LBJ in Dallas.) The first stop was Houston, which went well, JFK announcing a lot of new money to be thrown into the NASA complex there. Fort Worth was also a success, bringing together all the divergent Demos. Then came Dallas, which was to be followed by the Austin . . . .

Originally, I was scheduled to make the trip with the Kennedy-Johnson-Wright group to Texas. But I got strep throat and was out sick for several days and was still sick when they all left Washington. November 22, 1963 was my first day back in the office after being sick.

I recall reading in the morning papers of how well things had gone in Houston. Jim Wright called me at mid-morning, a quick call between the Fort Worth appearances and the short flight to Dallas, on office business I no longer recall. I do remember he was happy with the way the Texas trip was going and said, "We're looking good down here for next year's election."

I went to lunch at the Democratic Club, a small room in the Congressional Hotel right across the street from my office in the Longworth House Office Building, at New Jersey and "C" Streets, S.E.; my luncheon companion was former Congressman J.T. Rutherford of Odessa, for whom I had worked before his 1962 defeat, at which point I went to work for Jim Wright. I recall that two tables away was Walter Jenkins, a top aide to Vice-President Johnson, who was eating with former Kentucky Senator Earl Clement. House Majority Leader Carl Albert (D-Oklahoma) was also at a nearby table.

Halfway through my corned beef sandwich, I was aware of a commotion at the bar and somebody yelled—with reference to the TV set—"Turn it up!" When the sound got louder I heard from the TV: "President Kennedy's motorcade was reportedly fired on in downtown Dallas. Witnesses said the President appeared to be bleeding from"—

I thought he said—"the *hand*." I said "Oh, thank God!" because a hand
wound wouldn't be too serious. But Rutherford, who had correctly
heard the announcer say "the *head*" looked at me like I was crazy.
When the announcer repeated his words, I then realized he'd said
"the head" and knew it was serious. Suddenly I found myself at the
bar, hitting it so hard my hand later swelled, cursing and—I think—
crying and shouting "They got him! The sons-of-bitches *got* him!" It
was my presumption that some Right Wing nut had shot the
President, Dallas then being notorious as a hot-bed of Right Wing
kooks including John Birchers, H.L. Hunt, General Walker,
Republican Congressman Bruce Alger, and the *Dallas Morning News*.
All were stridently anti-Kennedy.

I looked around for LBJ aide Walter Jenkins and found him gone. I
started back to my office and in the hall saw Majority Leader Carl
Albert, who had run into a larger restaurant room (public) outside the
small Democratic Club restaurant; he was wild-eyed and running in
aimless circles. I was so shocked that that hardly registered on my
conscious mind then, but I can still see it now. When I got to my
office, the staff girls had the radio on; they were white-faced and
shocked. I remember standing in the door of the office, right by the
reception desk, and listening to reports; people were running up and
down the halls like crazed rats. Within what seemed like a very short
time, the radio reports said that two priests had given JFK the final
rites of the church at Parkland Hospital and one had told the press he
was dead. We all started crying. Shortly, I returned to the
Congressional Hotel's Filibuster Room—a cocktail lounge—with Joe
Bailey Swanner, aide to Congressman Clark Fisher of San Angelo.
The TV was on. Everybody was staring at it and drinking madly. Some
were cursing, some crying. Some bastard saw me and Swanner and
said "There are two of those Texas pricks now," and I hit him. There
was a commotion, and I don't remember all the details, except I was
screaming and crying and went back to my office.

Soon I heard on the radio that LBJ had been sworn in on board Air
Force One as President; a bit later that George Reedy, an LBJ aide,
had appeared at the White House, the first member of the new

Administration to do so. I remember thinking "Why, that son-of-a-bitch!" The night before, you see, my strep throat improved enough that I treated it with whiskey at a bar on the Senate side of the Capitol . . . . and Reedy had come over and sat with me in a booth. He had four or five martinis, then disappeared before the check came and I got stuck for his drinks! . . .

By . . . a couple of hours later, I was fielding calls from all over Texas; people somehow thought we'd have information in our Congressional office not available to the public, but in reality we knew no more than we heard on radio and TV. Someone in Jim Wright's District Office called from Fort Worth to tell me to have someone meet Wright at Andrews Air Force Base that night. My sense of history failed me: instead of going myself, I sent Marshall Lynam, and thus missed being on hand in person when JFK's body returned and LBJ made his little reassuring speech to the nation on landing. I saw all that on TV, from Rosemarie's apartment at 1100 6th Street, S.W. a few blocks from the Capitol building. Then I drove back to the office to meet Jim Wright.

On seeing me, he burst into tears and I did too. He kept saying "It was so horrible, so horrible!" After he had calmed himself he said, with respect to Lee Harvey Oswald, "Larry, I am certain in my mind that I have had correspondence about Oswald in the last couple of years. We have to find that correspondence!" It proved not to be in the office. Jim suggested it might be in our storeroom in the Longworth building and insisted I go seek it out. I spent about an hour in that dim, musty storeroom and found two letters from Oswald's mother to Jim Wright. One, from a couple of years before, had asked him to find her a better job than the practical nurse job she then had; Wright had written her a routine letter and bucked her request to the Fort Worth office of the Texas Employment Commission. A second letter from Mrs. Oswald told of her son, Lee, being in Russia but wanting to come home and asking help in getting him home. Wright routinely bucked that letter to the Department of State and, as it turned out, State did make a loan to him to get back to the U.S.—a loan never repaid, incidentally.

Congressman Wright had a curious and momentarily panicky reaction to this correspondence, suggesting that we destroy it. I was aghast. *Why* destroy it? I argued, as did Marshall Lynam, that the thing to do was turn it over to the Press the next day. It was innocuous, it wasn't harmful, why *destroy* it? I still don't know why he reacted that way, but assume he wanted to be disassociated from the Oswalds and felt he might somehow be blamed for helping—indirectly and routinely—Oswald come back from Russia. The next day, Jim Wright did call a press conference and turn that correspondence—or copies of it—over to those who attended. So much more was happening, however, that Wright's revelation got only a few lines in the Texas papers and, I think, no national mention at all. I'm sure, in retrospect, Wright was in shock and not thinking clearly.

By now it was Saturday, November 23rd. I was in the office early; phone calls from Texas were constant; Jim Wright kept trying to get through to LBJ at the White House to see "if I can be of any particular service," but could not reach him and got crabby and grumpy.** He told me to meet a delegation from the Texas Legislature, coming to put a bouquet of flowers on JFK's casket—to lie in state in the Capitol Rotunda—and I met them at the Washington airport in a driving rain and took them to the Madison Hotel. I recall that the delegation included Texas Senators Don Kennard and Babe Schwartz, but I don't remember the House delegates other than Rep. Malcolm McGregor. Anyway, I remember everybody was feverish and crazed and drank heavily. Later that night, the rain had stopped and it had grown extremely cold, I took the delegation to the Capitol and arranged for them to put the flowers on Kennedy's casket. . . .

When I came out of the boarding house at mid-morning, I discovered to my chagrin that my 1962 red Chevrolet coupe had a goddamned flat; it was parked in front of my boarding house. I was clumsily trying to fix it when I heard a cheerful voice sing out, "They got him! They got that Oswald!" I looked up and a black man, bouncing along the street, was wearing a big grin and repeating himself. I said "*What?*" and I remember thinking it was the first smile or grin I had seen since the assassination. And the dude said "Some guy just killed

Oswald! They showing it on TV over and over." I ran upstairs to my room, turned on the TV, and sure enough, there was Jack Ruby killing Oswald—again and again. I thought *Fuck it, I'm not going to work!* (Jim Wright had ordered the staff to work that Sunday "Because Lyndon might need us and we've got to be here to help him.") I called Rosie, who was at her apartment, and had not seen the TV killing. She turned it on, saw it, and then came after me; I left the flat-tire flat for several days. I did not go to work that day, nor did I go on Monday— the day of JFK's funeral—or even call in to the office. Jim Wright was furious with me. But I didn't care. My hero was dead, the dream was gone, I knew politics held no more hope for me. And a few months later—in early May 1964—I quit my job on the theory that if I should die as abruptly as JFK had, that I would not have done any of the writing I had always meant to do.

My final memory of the assassination weekend was of sitting numb in front of the TV, and not really being able to function. Nor did I function well in politics thereafter. It was over.

Best and love,
Ol' Dad

*Congressman Wright ultimately decided he would have campaign finance problems—as well as political problems—should he then run for senator.

**LBJ did not move into the White House living quarters for several days, in deference to Mrs. Kennedy, but did conduct business from the Oval Office.

2

Starting Out

L arry L. King quit Jim Wright's office in the spring of 1964 with no visible means of support, to the polite puzzlement of Congressman Wright and the complete horror of his McGraw-Hill editor Bob Gutwillig. During the summer he accepted the generous offer of his Austin cousins Lanvil and Glenda Gilbert to share their house, where he could write during the day while they worked. Paying work consisted of book reviews and short pieces written for *The Texas Observer* and *The Nation,* whose book-page editor, Warren Miller, had been instrumental in helping King obtain his book contract with McGraw-Hill. Miller managed to pay King $40 per piece from his shoestring budget, a princely sum compared to the $15 available from Ronnie Dugger's *Observer.* Paltry money equaled stylistic freedom, and King's early pieces for these publications show a young writer delighting in the written word. His first published piece for Dugger was a "you can't go home again" meditation concerning Billie Lee Brammer's decision to move back to Dallas, his hometown.

By the end of the summer of 1964, after a painful failed reconciliation with his wife, King retraced his steps and headed back to his adopted home, contradicting his own published advice to his friend Brammer concerning the pitfalls of returning to the past. Now traveling light, he set up shop on the Maryland shore, living on the Chris Craft cabin cruiser belonging to his Washington girlfriend, Rosemarie Kline. Free of rent, King productively wrote and found part-time jobs, the most backbreaking of which was in a construction crew that installed seats in the Naval Academy's new football stadium. (Years later, covering a Navy game for a sports magazine from the comforts of the Press Box, he would claim sudden back pains traceable to old memories.) He finished his first *Harper's* story, an autobiographical piece about life as a congressman's assistant and sent it to Willie Morris for editing. The economic realities of freelance work must have hit home when Morris reported to King that he had been able to talk Jack Fischer, *Harper's* editor-in-chief, up to $400 for the piece from his usual $250; it was published in the January 1965 issue of the magazine.

Larry and Rosemarie married in February 1965, and he seriously took on the life of the East Coast freelancer, adding to his list *Sports Illustrated*, *The Reporter*, *Progressive*, and *The New Republic*. In the meantime, Willie Morris had accepted a second story for *Harper's*. By the end of the spring King had also finished what he considered to be a final draft of his novel for McGraw-Hill. His work still reflected his political background as well as his formative sports writing experiences in West Texas. Book reviewing was still an economic mainstay—in a preface to his wickedly funny review of Hedy Lamarr's *Ecstasy and Me*, King comments on the life of a second-string reviewer:

> America's book-page editors have crowned me heavy-weight champion reviewer of the non-book book. Among the literary giants whose works have been assigned to me for critical

attention are Miss Hedy LaMarr and Lyndon B. Johnson's mother. If anybody ever writes a book called *The Wit and Wisdom of
Benito Mussolini*, no doubt a half-dozen literary editors will strain
their equipment rushing it to me for review.

. . . And Other Dirty Stories (1968)

In his first year as a freelancer, King had brought in a grand total of
$3,500, including the $1,500 advance for *The One-Eyed Man*, yet his
work was appearing where he wanted it to and he had high hopes for
his first novel.

Faced with overlapping deadlines and offers from a multitude of
magazine editors attracted to his published work, King followed the
advice of friends to shop for a literary agent. On the recommendation
of Bob Gutwillig and Willie Morris, King paid a high energy visit to
New York, interviewed three top agents and quickly came to terms
with Sterling Lord, with whom he worked for over a decade.

By the beginning of the summer, King had what he considered a
finished manuscript of his political novel in the hands of McGraw
Hill's Bob Gutwillig, who had promised an anxious King that he
would circulate galleys and perhaps a dust jacket at June's American
Bookseller's Association meeting. When King learned that this did
not happen, he was furious. Soon there was a greater crisis when
Gutwillig announced that he was leaving McGraw-Hill for another
publishing company—New American Library—and that he wanted
King to follow him to the new house. This first required a bit of subterfuge on the part of King, a seemingly innocent request to Gutwillig
to return the manuscript for some fine tuning. The full story of
extracting his contract from McGraw-Hill is told in his Labor Day letter to his Austin cousins.

Bad news came in multiple doses during the early fall of 1965. NAL
delayed publication of *The One-Eyed Man* because a *New York Times*
strike removed primary review and advertising resources. King's
August 31 letter to Sterling Lord indicates the financial perils of living from one freelance assignment to the next with the novel temporarily on hold. Early in the fall, Rosemarie was diagnosed with

breast cancer and after a quick doctor's consultation underwent mastectomy surgery. The operation, occurring only eight months after their marriage, incapacitated Rosemarie through the rest of the fall. Still King plugged away, and in his October 11 letter to Warren Burnett had much optimistic career news. By the end of the year King and Gutwillig were thinking about cutting *The One-Eyed Man* to make it eligible for book club editions.

—Richard Holland

June 8, 1965

Memo from: Larry L. King

To: Robert Gutwillig, Editor

About thirty minutes after I found today that you had not advertised my book at the Bookseller's convention—but had, apparently, at the cost of great effort and expense managed to keep secret its existence—I got a wire from *Commentary* magazine asking me to do a profile about you.

I wired back: BOB GUTTWILLIG IS A BAD JEW. Two hours later I received another wire from them: Love Title. When can we see manuscript?

June 10, 1965

Dear Bob:

In case you corporate wing-dings are still the least bit interested in publishing *The One-Eyed Man*, all re-writes, new scenes and assorted modifications will be dispatched your way by Monday or Tuesday next at the very damn latest.

So much for my responsibility.

A man's legend dying hard, I would give my *AU3 H2O in '64** sticker to make the following witty, charming, and altogether worthy of inclusion in the future publication of *The Letters of Larry L. King* (which some firm considerate of authors someday will make many gold dollars from) or at least tickle the ribs of present readers. Alas and alack, I cannot. Bile wins out. I'm gonna tell it like it is.

I'm pissed. Pissed and hurt and hung-up and a few dozen other choice adjectives, more than half of which will probably be edited out by some goddamn editor.

Time passes. I work a little. Go off to Virginia beaches for several days. Return home for the express by-God purpose of being on hand for whatever promotion we might reap from the American Bookseller's Convention and, witless boy of trusting soul that I am, wait by silent telephone for the call to go into my act. (Remembering that one R. Gutwillig had told me he intended to be here for same). Assuming, mind you, that since my current work had been compared by corporate figures of McGraw-Hill to the Bible, Mark Twain, and even the Sears-Roebuck catalogue, all the enthusiasm fired my way over the past twenty months would culminate in a really grand show at the said convention. She-*it*. Much to my chagrin and surprise and personal pain, it turns out we don't have any inkling at the Bookseller's goat roping that one L. King is, in fact, extant and writing. Not so much even as one filthy postcard. Much less a novel called *The One-Eyed Man*.

This . . . how you say . . . burns my ass? Yas, indeedy. For had I known I was to be ignored worse than Lyndon Johnson in the dear, dead days of J.F.K., I would have put together my own little coterie of fanatics, who would have gone forth—Congressmen and Hill staffers and radio and TV men and newsmen, a circus clown and a few wing walkers—to sing my praises, and claque like they were wired for it while I soft-shoed and yes-mammed and son-of-a-bitched as appropriate until every bookseller in the U.S. of A. would have lamented our small first press run, and maybe tried to buy my offering black-market-wise. But I put blind faith in McG-Hill, and you, Sir. And have experienced humiliation for my pains. Several men who have written lesser books than I—and know it, because I told them so—got feted by their publishers and exposed and advertised, and reporters beat a path to my door asking what I do for a living, and did I not know why my little ole book was not being advertised or even whispered about at said convention? I said no I did not. And then, I fear, unleashed long strings of mystic oaths. My tormentors left perfectly happy. I leave it to the wisdom of the McGraws and the departed ghost of Hill as to how I left. . . .

I'm mad, goddamn mad. Why no advertising? Why months of silence, and "there's no hurry" about my re-writes, and then all this jazz about how "we don't advertise books until we know for sure if they're coming out"? Look, I am trying to support myself, three children by a busted union, and—of late—one unemployed wife on whatever comes from these moving fingers writ. Goddamnit, I have notified your publicity department by curt letter that I would "go anywhere and do anything to sell a goddamn book." I think I have stressed to you my true need to score on this book. And you've said little to throw damp water on my dreams.

If you think the book is no-good or so-so or not worthy of a major promotion effort then send it back—for you are wrong. I have written—and am writing—a hell of a book. It will knock them on their kumquats. It should make me by-God money, and it by-God *will*. Even if it has to come off on the printing press I may install in my basement for the purpose, and pay back my little advance to boot. Come on, now. What gives? What happened? Why the last minute oxelene? (A rustic farm term, incidentally, for bullshit.)

I want to box. Indian wrassle, even. Screw you folk.

A Very Unhappy Arthur**

*An actual "Goldwater for President" bumper sticker in 1964.
**King and his Texas friends had all adopted Billie Lee Brammer's mother's habit of referring to themselves and each other as "Famous Arthurs."

July 13, 1965

Dear Willie Morris, Bud Shrake, and Bill Brammer:
Excuse mass production to announce to the waiting world that

yours truly and bride Rosemarie will fall on N.Y. City come July 21st and Thursday July 22nd, plus maybe a longer period of time if the livin' is easy.

What I have got in mind is an historic drunk involving all salutated and mentioned in this missive to this point, plus whatever funny companions, loving wives and/or girl friends may be willingly coaxed into the fray. The time and the place for this drunk is best left to your collective wills and the destiny guided by Almighty God. Brother Willie Morris marginally being the most reputable among us, I suggest we polarize efforts around him to the extent that he is appointed a Committee of One to check with all hands for the purpose of making whatever logistical and spiritual arrangements deemed necessary to carry out the provisions of this Act.

Let it be understood I am not footing the bill. There is a paucity of cash on hand and a surplus of unsold literary articles in my chest. I will, however, grudgingly bear my share of the pro-rata cost. I would like to hear from everybody interested. Anyone showing the good judgment or gall to plead prior commitments will be excused by notifying me of same. . . .

July 26, 1965

Mr. Sterling Lord
75 East 55th Street
New York, 22, N.Y.

Dear Mr. Lord:

I enjoyed talking with you by telephone this morning, and am delighted that we have reached accord. A couple of matters have arisen since I saw you that I'd like to inform you about in the way of prospective work.

Willie Morris at *Harper's* discussed in general terms with me the possibility of my doing three or four more Washington-type pieces in the months ahead, to go with the two already used by his magazine. He has the notion after they've all appeared they might be published in book form, with a foreword written by someone—perhaps John Kenneth Galbraith. Harper & Row would want to do the book or, in Willie's words, "work out something satisfactory to McGraw-Hill." This of course would be off sometime in the future, and I didn't discuss it much other than to say the prospect sounds interesting. I don't know all the complications involved but thought I'd pass this along for future reference.

Bob Gutwillig told me something in strict confidence which I think you as my agent should know, but it's my judgment we should say nothing to him about it until he says something more to us. The thing is this: McGraw-Hill is considering my novel, along with two others, to receive a $10,000 "house" award. (I am speaking of *The One-Eyed Man*.) Bob tells me $2,500 would be an outright grant and $7,500 would be additional advance royalties against the same book. He says he and [Editor-in-Chief] Ed Kuhn will make the decision, that he is voting for me and attempting to encourage Kuhn to go along. He seems to think the decision would be reached sometime in August, and quite frankly was very encouraging about my being the favorite to get it—though he did caution about the proverbial slip between the cup and lip.

I cannot at the moment find my contract with McGraw-Hill for that novel, nor the later paper I signed getting an additional $2,000 to be applied either against *One-Eyed* or my second novel, at my option. (And naturally I shall choose to apply it against *One-Eyed*.) I've gotten money from them for that book on a least three occasions and—counting the latest $2,000—think I have received $6,000 to date. But it may be $5,000. (Yes, I obviously need an agent!) Could you get Bob to send you an accounting and let you photostat the contract and the later amendment I signed? I think he could do it quicker than I could find all the papers scattered among my souvenirs, since I have moved several times in the last 18 or so months and my things are scattered.

You asked for a recapitulation on what I have received for articles: $600 for the first (January) *Harper's* piece; $700 for the second (August); $100 from *Progressive* for the article on Texas Congressmen to run in September or October; $1,000 for the Sugar Ray Robinson piece to appear in *Sports Illustrated* August 23rd. I have agreed—though not on prices—to do a piece for *Harper's* they plan to run in December. (The one about my old home town in Texas virtually no longer existing and the one about Bob Jones University in Greenville, South Carolina. The latter is unscheduled, as we haven't discussed when I would go to S.C. for a few days to work up the piece.) In mentioning future Washington-type articles Willie Morris and I have discussed a piece on Capitol Hill pages (the very same idea *Topic* magazine proposed to me today) and another on Congressional mail and the Postal lobby. No agreement exists on these, merely informal talks.*

Here are some capsule reports on other articles I have in mind:

My sports-writing days in the flat and arid badlands of West Texas, where local citizenry thinks more of sports than of God. I was chased around my desk and threatened with a physical beating by Zeke Bonura, former major leaguer, then managing the Class D Longhorn League team in Midland, Texas. (Because I wrote that as a fielder "He couldn't trap a fat bear in a phone booth and runs the bases like a man in leg irons." Bonura was then a 260-pound, aging player/manager.) I once, as a newspaper photographer, unintentionally broke up a touchdown pass in the end zone in a state high school play-off game, and a riot almost ensued. I was offered for sale on the public address system by the Midland baseball club "for $1 and absolutely no other considerations" when the floundering franchise was being sold. Parents threatened me because Junior's name was misspelled in the box score. In a touch football game between oil company employees late one summer, I, as referee, got into fisticuffs with Bobby Layne and Glenn Davis—on the same play [and into an argument with a then-young George Bush]. I invented a heavyweight boxer, publicized him, and got him damn near beat to death in his first and only fight. There are other incidents, and the piece also would touch on my very undistinguished record as an athlete in high school, college, and the Military service. Example: Because of glowing sports stories in a Long Island paper about my football prowess with the Signal Corps Photo Center Signalmen, Fordham offered me a "make good" football scholarship. I did not make good. What they didn't know was I had organized the team, coached it, (and therefore could not be taken out of the games)—and then was the stringer who phoned in those glowing accounts to the *Long Island Star Journal.* (*Sports Illustrated,* maybe?)**

The Midland-Odessa (Texas) area is noted for its John Birch hotbed. I lived and worked as a politician among them, trying successively to neutralize, fool and beat them, in my role as A.A. to the Congressman from that district. To keep this short, it would be a kind of "Life Among the Super Americans" thing. . . .

Other thoughts thrown out for what they're worth: How about a piece on the surviving widow of the late Senator Joseph McCarthy? and a nostalgic piece about my father (one-mule farmer, country preacher) called "Dad and The New Deal" . . .***

That will do for now. [Governor John] Connally piece**** follows shortly.

I am eager and enthused about our potential together. Thanks for taking me on. . . .

*All save the postal lobby idea King turned into magazine pieces for *Harper's, The New York Times Magazine,* and *Capitol Hill.*
**Published in the *Detroit Athletic Club News.*
***Ultimately published in *Playboy* as "Remembering the Hard Times."
****Written for the *Reporter.*

July 28, 1965

Hon. Robert Gutwillig
McGraw-Hill Publishing Co.

Dear Bob:

You may be very vexed at this letter, but then you will have to get in line.

I have decided *The One-Eyed Man,* while bordering on a classic, could stand more work. Yas, ah have. And I want to do more work on it—say, three, four weeks or maybe six at the most. I have been sitting and reading over the manuscript, and weeping both at the wisdom and how much wiser I could be if only ah had time. . . .

So, hurry up. Send it back. Love to Harold [McGraw]. . . .

Sept. ??, 1965
(Labor Day, anyway)

Dear Lanvil & Glenda:

I recall very little of what I told you with respect to my proposed move to New American Library from McGraw-Hill. I think I told you it was in the mill, since Bob Gutwillig is moving to a position of great authority and salary at NAL, and wanted to take me along in the package. (I have told it in some quarters that he got a big cash bonus for bringing me over, but this is merely to add to my legend and in no wise represents the truth to the best of my knowledge.) Anyway, the plot was thick with intrigue, under-handed dealings, lies, and poses necessary to spring me loose from M-H so I could take the better offer at NAL. Naturally, I enjoyed all the double-dealing very much.

First, upon advice from a certain editor who shall be nameless, but who tipped me off that he was moving from M-H to NAL three weeks in advance, I wrote that editor a letter asking that he send my manuscript back to me for "re-writes" that were resting heavy on my heart until done, blah-blah. He did, of course, very promptly. This gave us a point in one-upsmanship on them, because now M-H *physically* had no *One-Eyed Man* cluttering up the place.

In due erosion of time, that same editor wrote me a letter of record announcing his departure to NAL. He said this was awfully sudden, and he was sorry he wouldn't be around to edit my book, but he knew I would remain in good hands with McGraw-Hill because everybody staying behind was wonderful and great, honest, strong, and true. Then he bid me fare-thee-well.

Right on cue, I wrote to Mr. Crandall, and among the things I told him were these: that Gutwillig's departure was a shock bordering on the traumatic, that we had worked together on my novel line-by-line and page-by-page from the time he purchased it when it consisted of only 36 pages and a three-page outline, that although Gutwillig recommended strongly that I stay with M-H I just couldn't bear the thought; that this was not to disparage M-H as a publishing house but reflected the fact that my association with Gutwillig had transcended the editor-author relationship to the point that we were fast friends and I sometimes had trouble keeping my hands off Gutwillig's thigh, and that while my book represented to M-H only one of many it would publish in the eons to come, it represented to me a start, a new beginning, a career, the Creation that preceded the Begatting. I said I wanted out of my contract. Now. Soon. Pronto. On the double. I said I would even send back the $5,000 M-H had paid me. I said I knew M-H would want to act as gentlemen, because gentlemen would let me go. I said that if Gutwillig were to be honest he would admit that I was more of a burden than a less understanding editor would wish to carry over the distance.

Harold McGraw read the letter and he saw threats and trouble therein. He called my agent. My agent very cleverly said that I had been his client only three weeks, and he wondered at the wisdom of our pact. He said I was stubborn and temperamental and had chin whiskers and cried a whole lot. He said it would be best to let me go.

Mr. McGraw communed with Mr. Gutwillig. Mr. Gutwillig said he had done his best to assure me that M-H was my best publishing house, but that I was a fellow who would not listen to reason. Mr. Gutwillig told Mr. McGraw that I drank heavily and quit my wife and kids and will not pay my debts. Mr. Gutwillig said I will not write a line when I am unhappy, and am always demanding money in the dead of night in a surly voice, and was altogether crazier than Norman Mailer.

Mr. McGraw wrote me a nice letter saying he sure wanted to be a gentleman, and to do nothing foolish until I heard from him again.

I wired McGraw: Thank you for your letter. If you chiselers don't release me by Thursday I am coming in with both guns blazing.

Mr. McGraw called Mr. Gutwillig in, showed him the telegram, laughed and said wasn't it a funny joke? Mr. Gutwillig in soothing tones said he hated to say so, but it probably wasn't a joke. Mr. Gutwillig said he had heard dark rumors of how back in Texas I had done violence on a fellow or was it two fellows?

Mr. McGraw called my agent, who confirmed Mr. Gutwillig's suspicions that it wasn't a joke, but he said he didn't *really* think Mr. McGraw needed any police protection. After all, this was 1965. And New York wasn't Texas.

Mr. McGraw then asked Mr. Gutwillig to bring the manuscript of *The One-Eyed Man* to him for his personal review. Mr. Gutwillig coughed discreetly and said he thought he had mentioned that Mr. King took it back a few weeks ago for re-writes. Mr. McGraw did not say anything, though he seemed to study it for the longest time.

The following day I wired Mr. McGraw: Re my previous telegram. Today is Wednesday.

Early the next morning Mr. McGraw called my agent to say they were releasing me upon payment of the $5,000 I owed, and would the agent mind terribly much telephoning Mr. King right now and telling him, because M-H wanted to operate as gentlemen.

This date $5,000 was delivered to my agent from sources I do not wish to question, and was in turn delivered to M-H. There followed a ceremonial tearing up of old contract.

On Wednesday, two days hence, there will be signed in New York between an agent representing yours truly, and B. Gutwillig representing NAL, a two-book contract with fresh money.

I reckon the moral is: it either pays to lie, or to have an agent. . . .

I wonder how crazy Norman Mailer *really* is? . . . .

August 16, 1965

Dear Warren:

I want to bring legal action against the *Austin American-Statesman* newspaper, published in Austin, Texas, as a result of a libel that paper printed linking me to an alleged 'smear campaign' on Gov. John Connally of Texas. This libelous account appeared in the newspaper issued Sunday, August 15, 1965. From the copy of the paper I am enclosing, you will see the story in question was very prominently displayed as the "banner" story. It was written by one Sam Wood, Capitol Correspondent for the *American Statesman.*

The clear (though erroneous) conclusion is reached in Mr. Wood's story that a profile story I did on Governor Connally for *Reporter* magazine was designed to 'tarnish the halo' of the Governor. It also intimates that I have conspired with a member of Senator Yarborough's staff, certain 'liberals' and another magazine writer to 'plant' an unfa-vorable story on the Governor in a national publication. This is a whole lie.

We can prove the following:

(1) I was asked by Meg Greenfield, Washington editor of *The Reporter* magazine, to write a profile on Governor John Connally of Texas. The idea was not my own nor that of any personal acquaintance of mine. I must assume on the facts that the idea was Miss Greenfield's, or that of one of her superiors.

(2) That I did not therefore lend myself to any effort to 'smear' Governor Connally, but received a normal assignment in the course of my work as a writer.

(3) That, subsequently, I agreed to do the piece and in so doing contacted numerous people, *including Governor Connally,* in an effort to get a well-rounded picture of him for that purpose. The Governor and I exchanged letters, and he answered in writing numerous questions I had put to him in an effort to secure information.

(4) That the piece was turned in to Miss Greenfield acting as an agent for *The Reporter* and that subsequently I was asked to do re-writes to conform more with the normal style of that magazine.

(5) That I performed the re-writes, but further were asked and that I conferred several times by telephone, and at least once personally, with Miss Greenfield. That, ultimately, I reached the conclusion that the editing and requested re-writing had changed my writing style so much as not to reflect the quality of work I wished to see appear under my name and that I requested the piece be returned to me, and *not* appear in *The Reporter.* (This certainly shows I was not trying to 'plant' any propaganda piece.)

(6) That, subsequently, the Connally piece was returned in accordance with my wishes and,

(7) That after rewriting it more to conform with my original version and my writing style, I placed it in the hands of my literary agent, Mr. Sterling Lord, 75 East 55th Street, New York, 22, N.Y. for sale about 10 days ago.

I feel very strongly that this reckless, inaccurate article cannot be allowed to stand unchallenged. My only income is from my writing. I have sold articles and stories to such magazines as *Harper's, Sports Illustrated, Progressive,* and *The Texas Observer,* as well as a book to the McGraw-Hill Publishing Co. Currently, my agent has in hand outlines of several articles I propose for other national magazines. The insinuation by the Austin newspaper that I am irresponsible enough to enter into a 'smear campaign,' to be a 'hatchet man' or to 'plant' stories has done harm to my professional reputation and I fear it will adversely affect my earning power as a professional writer.

While I have been interested in Texas politics and am generally known as a 'liberal,' I have not entered into any conspiracy to smear Gov. Connally or anyone else. If any 'smearing' has been done (and I maintain it has) it was done to me in the August 15, 1965 issue of the *Austin American-Statesman.* And that is why I ask you, as my attorney, to initiate legal proceedings so that I may gain redress for damages.

I shall forward to you correspondence bearing on this matter between myself, Miss Greenfield, Governor Connally, and my agent. I shall also send a copy of the story as it ultimately was returned to me—after having been set in print at *The Reporter*—upon my request. . . .*

---

*Burnett, a noted West Texas trial attorney, recommended not suing on grounds that should a jury find against King, such a verdict could be construed as saying that perhaps he was a "hatchet man" and that such a designation would not help his career as a fledgling political writer. He further advised King to take deep breaths, have a few drinks, and relax.

August 31, 1965

Mr. Sterling Lord
The Sterling Lord Agency

Dear Sterling:

For some time I have felt with the late Herbert Hoover that "Prosperity is just around the corner." Ole Herb proved to be monumentally wrong, and in the absence of a fleet miracle* I shall match his record.

Is there any damn thing happening at all with the various pieces I've sent you, or the two outlines? Also, how about that Hubbell Robinson TV deal I asked you to check out?

I would, in fact, appreciate a run-down on exactly where the pieces I've sent you have been, what the reaction has been, where they are now and your appraisal of them. Since they obviously aren't being snatched up like hotcakes, I'd like your frank appraisal on each of them as to whether you think they might make it if re-written or whether you just don't consider them salable.

I'm sending along the outline for the Gerald R. Ford piece for *True*.** You'll note I've attached a request that a decision be promptly given, because Congress is going to be adjourning soon and I'll need time to make interviews while all the pertinent parties are in handy appointment. I just don't feel I can spare the time for the interviews until I know for a certainty that I have the assignment.

There is a check in sight from *Harper's* as soon as I get the piece on my old hometown to them,*** but other than that the cupboard is extremely bare. I grow morose and all hung-up when the only sound is the disconcerting one of dollars rapidly spilling out of my extremely modest bank account. Get out there and sell the product, fellows, even if it means a moneyback guarantee and double Green Stamps.

Flatly,
LLK

*That is, his ship coming in.
**Subsequently published, this piece mildly speculated that Ford might one day become president.
***"Requiem for a West Texas Town."

October 4, 1965

Mr. Willie Morris,
Harper's Magazine,

Will-ey:
That "Requiem for a West Texas Town" is a fine piece, and I don't

see how any editor who pays less than $3,000 for it will be able to sleep nights. . . .

O.K. re taking the quote from "Scarlet Ribbons" and using it under the title. I think its a good idea. Are you having this piece illustrated?

Re my updated biog., here goes: I was born in a manger, and lived to be 32 years of age. . . .

I'll attach one.

Sterling Lord has remained ominously silent when I bug him about bugging you about money, and please remitting. I do hope the two of you will begin to show a joint and immediate concern about my financial well-being. Since you are obviously getting the story at such bargain prices, no matter what you pay, I know you will prominently use my good name on the December cover.

Our trip southward has been postponed until roughly October 20th-25th on account I am snowed under finishing pieces for *S.I.*, *True*, *Book Week*, and *Esquire*. Sure is nice to have work. Then, too, Miz King has got to be cut on by way of surgery later this week and will need a few days to mend her flesh. We'll probably be in N.Y. just before we leave. Chill a bottle of your very best wines. . . .

October 11, 1965

Mr. Warren Burnett
Attorney-at-law

Dear Edsel:

I doubt there is a news stand or drug store in the whole of the 16th Congressional District tinged with enough communism to sell *Progressive* magazine, so I'm enclosing the October issue in which I defamed the Texas Delegation through telling the truth. . .

Please tell Miss Emma that we appreciate the fine gesture in sending those nice flowers to my lady in Doctors' Hospital. This whole incident is one bordering on the traumatic, and somewhere the Gods of Former Wives are laughing fit to bust a strut. Rosemarie is amazingly cheerful, though in dark moments she broods over an obvious loss of feminine equipment. It is those dark depressions, which the mind simply must boil up now and again, that I dread in the future. We had, as I'm sure you know, planned to do some traveling beginning—and again let us add a dash of irony for spice—about the time her malady was discovered, and travel surrendered to the knife. She seems as despondent over the postponement of plans as over the physical infirmities, though she is being told that "with luck" she can travel in six to eight weeks. Probably, however, she cannot. The doctor "thinks" he got all malignant matter, but is the first to admit there's no way to know in the absence of post-operative examinations and possible treatment extended over a long period of time. I am making arrangements through Congressional sources to have her submitted to all cancer tests known to the National Institute of Health as soon after her recuperation as possible. All one can do is curse the Gods and smile in public. And wait. . . .

Professionally, perhaps by way of showing that nature does not intend to heap too much of what makes the grass grow green even on the most tempting target among us, everything is great. I next appear in December *Harper's*. I have just reviewed four books for *The Nation* and one for *Book Week*, which appears in the *N.Y. Herald-Tribune*, *Washington Post*, and *San Francisco Chronicle*. I have sold a second piece to *Sports Illustrated*, and a piece to *Esquire* that is now in the writing. I am also working on a political profile of the GOP leader in the House, Gerald Ford, for *True*, and will fly with him tomorrow to Gettysburg, Pa., for a political to-do that I'll make the center-piece of the profile. I have informally agreed to do a piece for February *Harper's*, and for January *Progressive*, and there's a new magazine here called *The Washingtonian* with monthly columns by Art Buchwald and Howard K. Smith—and which may begin a monthly column by Larry L. King if we can get together on content and money in current negotiations. I am also talking with one Bobby Baker about doing a "tell all" (or *almost* all) piece "as told to" to me. *Life* and *Look* tell my agent they'll buy in a minute at top dollar if he agrees to go. I haven't decided if he's really serious, or just using it as a threat to cause not-too-subtle pressures on the Grand Jury now considering his past perfidies . . . .*

This has gone on too long and too much about one L. King, but at the hazard of boring you I'd add this footnote: you can't believe how the word is out among publishers, editors, writers—the whole literary crowd—that I am a "hot property" type and bells are ringing in my name. Johnny Carson's show** has inquired re: an appearance about the time *One-Eyed* hits; some similar show in Chicago has made similar overtures; I have been on TV and radio in Washington until it's getting to be old hat, and my agent is in the lovely position of turning down work from low-pay mags or rejecting overtures for me to "ghost" books for various public figures. I don't know exactly how it happened, but I am not the holder of the indoor record for modesty, and I must admit to many kicks. When RM gets straightened out, we must celebrate in style through a trip with you and Miss Emma to some spot where the wine flows and the dice click. . . .

---

*Baker's lawyer Edward Bennett Williams would not permit the Baker article. A dozen years later King wrote Baker's best-selling biography, *Wheeling and Dealing*.

**The *Tonight Show* later rejected King as a guest because he had first gone on the Dick Cavett Show.

October 31, 1965

Mr. Warren Miller
The Nation

Dear Giver-of-Angst:

Well, your kind letter of rejection closed me up like a winter tulip. All that saved me from total trauma was your $25 check (which I almost sent back because the pride gorged my throat, but good sense and the bill collector prevailed in the end) and the fact that *Book Week* carried a review today that I did on LBJ's Mama's Family Album. Oh, rejection! Oh, pain! Oh, shat!

I, being new at this racket, would like to know what I done wrong? I am sure I done wrong, because you folks are not do-wrongers without cause and you love me and all that stuff. But the review missed, and I want your expert advice why. I think maybe it was because I tried to concentrate on the book, instead of just using the book as a showcase to say shitty things about Sen. Joe McCarthy. If that is the case, then I have scrapped integrity for all time. . . .*

Your Crushed Compadre

*King had written a review of a book by Senator Charles Potter (D-Michigan) about hearings leading to Senator Joseph McCarthy's 1955 censure by the Senate.

November 22, 1965

Mr. Robert Gutwillig
New American Library

Dear Bob:

I'm enclosing the negatives of the two photos from which you are to choose the dust-jacket photo for *One-Eyed Man*. You have brightened our Soap Opera lives by pledging to use the creditline "Photo by Rosemarie King." ("Look at it this way, Hunny. We haven't lost a tit; we've gained a creditline. . . .")

I am puzzled to some extent about exactly how we are going to conduct the necessary cuts in *One-Eyed*, feeling that the telephone isn't exactly the most perfect instrument for that purpose, though this should not be construed as criticism against either Alexander Graham Bell or Don Ameche. My best suggestion is that you get on the airey-o-plane and come somewhere to meet me at a time and place to be dictated by circumstance.

In Christ's Name, A-Men. . .

3

Making It

Sterling Lord called King in November 1965 with the excellent news that the Literary Guild Book Club had picked up *The One-Eyed Man* and that he would have $10,000 front money within a month. Cash in hand, Larry and Rosemarie spent over four months in Sarasota, Florida, living in a glass house on the beach. Sarasota was chosen because New College had offered King a job there teaching—the job failed to pan out, but the beach and sun were restorative, and King soon fell in with Sarasota's literati, who included McKinley Kantor, Borden Deal and John D. McDonald. Although he enjoyed spending some time with a congenial group of his "literary betters," King's gamesmanship, honed in Washington, asserted itself. He says, "Probably I used techniques learned in the political arena, both for fun and for practice. There is a gene in me always demanding to be in charge."

The first full month King and Rosemarie spent in Sarasota coincided with *Harper's* publishing King's first breakthrough piece, "Requiem for a West Texas Town." It was the first extended opportunity for King to write about his West Texas roots, and the response on the part of readers was tremendous. King's mood in Florida was upbeat, even when Gutwillig flew down and they spent days cutting *The One-Eyed Man* to comply with a length acceptable to the Literary Guild.

King's mention of "Clark guilt" in the letter to Lanvil and Glenda refers to Lanvil's and Larry's mothers who were Clarks and twin sisters and apparently had cornered the market on Protestant foreboding and dread. This quality passed down to the younger generation in some form, usually manifesting itself after a "sinful" episode (such as writing truthfully about a hometown!).

After finishing revisions of *The One-Eyed Man* with Gutwillig, King was in a heightened state of activity through the spring and summer, anticipating publication of the book as well as its promotion. As early as the March 11 letter to his old friend Ben Peeler, King had begun to formulate an extravagant book party for himself, although publication date was almost three months away. The manic enthusiasm of his April 8 letter to Gutwillig did nothing but alarm the editor, who with NAL was working with a modest publicity budget. The last section of the letter describing efforts on the part of Morris Udall and Jim Wright and the hiring of a jazz combo to be called "The One-Eyed Men" were in earnest and must have reinforced Gutwillig's perception that he was not in control and that the plans did not really resemble the normal booksigning event for a first novel. King's letter dated April 27, responding to Gutwillig's request to trim the guest list to 150, pushed Gutwillig to complete exasperation, and he let King know in a strongly worded letter that once again he had overstepped his role.

Gutwillig's efforts to cut the size of the party totally failed. Some 350 eating and drinking guests attended along with book dealers and various media people on June 6. Among King's expected friends from Texas who did not attend were Warren and Emma Burnett, whom

King then drafted to host an Odessa party for him during his Texas tour for the book. King planned his book events in Odessa, Midland, Abilene, Fort Worth and Austin with military precision, and, at the height of civil-rights tensions in the Deep South, was at least jokingly nervous about a book event in Greenville, Mississippi. He was still a first novelist with a promising but just beginning reputation as a New York journalist, plenty of debts and a wife with a serious illness.

King's growing position with *Harper's* was evident in his invitation to Willie Morris' "southern dogwood party" on the weekend of May 6–8. His report to Lanvil and Glenda on the dinner party with the Morrises, C. Vann Woodward, William Styron, Robert Penn Warren and their wives is an unusually fresh report on the beginning of a life in the literary fast lane.

"Bob Jones University: the Buckle on the Bible Belt" was written in Florida and drew a number of strong responses to *Harper's* and to King. Some were from fundamentalists, including Dr. Henry Grube, founder of the Greystone Bible Church in Mobile, Alabama. Sarcastically calling King a "genius" for coming so close to the truth yet missing it, he added that he was a 1931 graduate of Bob Jones University and a member of the Swamp Angels football team and signed his letter: Henry Grube, *Romans 8:28*. David Halberstam, wrote on Paris Bureau *New York Times* stationery:

"Dear Peckerwood,
I was just thinking about you when I got a copy of that free book; thinking of you, because by chance I had bought (of all things) a copy of *Harpers* and the Bob Jones piece was very good, and seemed to me to be very well written (if you like Baptists). The *Harpers* said that you had become a literary lion, and then the next day what happens but a free goddamn copy of your book (mounting your affluence), and to prove it all, a beard which would be the pride of any Rabbi in Poland, if there were any left. . . ."

Halberstam had just been joined in Paris by his new wife, a Polish movie star, whose life had been complicated by Halberstam's having been ejected from Poland as an "enemy of the state" for his critical *New York Times* dispatches. Halberstam's bride spoke little English and had difficulty finding film work in the U.S.

At the end of the summer, King was putting final touches on what would become a signature *Harper's* piece, "My Hero LBJ," his first cover story. He had now reached a point in his quickly developing career where book publishers and editors other than Bob Gutwillig were making offers.

— Richard Holland

January 9, 1966

110 Beach Road
Siesta Key
Sarasota, Florida

Dear Willie:

Charley Odom, late a grocer of Putnam, Texas ("She's about dried up and blowed away") is dead. Charley kicked his way to Glory on the streets of Abilene, Texas. Heart attack. Nearest I can pinpoint it, Charley checked out about the time Jan. *Harper's* checked in at the news-stands. I am Southern and know the guilt of Faulkner, Styron, our Ole Confederate Grandpappies and our Dear Mothers, and so I know what happened. Charley dressed up in his best pressed khakis and buttoned his shirt at the collar, and caught the Greyhound to Abilene to buy *Harper's* so as to know the glory of his name in print. Charley wore himself to a frazzle walking around looking for It and finally found It and had to pay seventy-five cents for It besides, and then ran his eager eyes down the column and THERE IT WAS! By God! His name! In print! Charley Odom! Me, merchant of pickles and salesman of baking soda! Charley started running up the street toward the Greyhound station, waving the article over his head, no doubt, and yelling to be heard in Putnam, and fit to bust something. And his heart went *zing! zank! zonk!* and Charley fell, the treasure in his hand, his bones turning to dust and clay like the Good Book promised, and Jesus swung down and called him Home. And now I have got Charley Odom's blood on my hands. No, there is no use to argue: the evidence is there, and I always knew no good could come of semi-educated men telling all they know in print. Charley will never hear T. Texas Tyler again, nor Ernest Tubb, and all the songs of all the angels will not suffice (no, not even the wailing ghosts of Patsy Cline nor Jimmie Rodgers nor Hank Williams serenading Charley in Heaven). Charley has et his last T-Bone and trumped his last trey. Catch me before I kill again.

I'm about half-finished with the Police Reporter draft.* I would be through, but goddamned editors have been bugging me at *True* and *Sports Illustrated,* and Gutwillig is sore because I haven't progressed to his satisfaction in my Work-in-Progress for him, and I keep making galley revisions for *The One-Eyed Man* because I see the Pulitzer and Nobel and Literary Guild and Truman Capote all beckoning me right out Yonder; and then to top it off I have got involved writing a weird piece about my War Experiences, which occurred in a theater every Saturday afternoon during World War II, when I parachuted into Occupied France with Alan Ladd, spent thirty seconds over Tokyo with Dana Andrews, and hit enemy beaches with Pat O'Brien from Catalina Island to the Yellow Sea.** Besides that the ex-Mrs. King is out of work and creating new money demands on me for my three children, and rent is high here, and we own an expensive boat and I am near-broke again, and altogether headed toward being another Bill Brammer, only taller. . . .

*An article based on King's earlier experience as a newspaper reporter in Odessa, where he attended murders, car wrecks, robberies, assaults, and the courtroom trials of his felonious neighbors.
**Published in *Harper's* as "The Battle of Popcorn Bay."

Siesta Sand Apts.,
Sarasota, Florida
Jan 9, 1966

Dear Lord and Lady Legg:

Enclosed find my check for a considerable sum, in payment of legal services rendered.

How I came not to take the New College job has nothing to do with my sordid past. My soiled reputation, I think, would have worked to my advantage had I taken the job. All the boys wear beards and the girls patterned stockings (thought on two occasions I saw a reversal in these roles) and go round damning Lyndon and Viet Nam and Jesus Christ. I rejected the job because that grand mansion they wanted me to live in was—though admittably spacious and once grand—rotting unused in a jungle full of scorpions and serpents and booger bears. I think too much of my wife—and of her husband—to live in such primitive diggings. (When I reported this to my editor in N.Y., he was so smitten with visions of a place too low for me to live in that he flew all the way down here to see it, stayed four days, and got drunk with me several times.) . . .

Midnightish
Saturday
January 7th or 8th, 1966

Dear Lanvil and Glenda:

Bob Gutwillig returned to New York at noon today after we had labored four days on final galley-proof editing of *The One-Eyed Man*. I have never worked harder, at least since I got out of the cotton patch or maybe politics. We hit it for six, eight and ten hour stretches, pausing only to eat and defecate (which I have begun to suspect have some correlation) or to mourn work remaining.

I think we improved the book immeasurably in this final cutting. We went far beyond that which the Literary Guild Book Club had requested and I am satisfied the actions were wise. Gutwillig came with cuts he wanted to make, but did not dare, fearing my wrath and,

I suspect, bruising my ego to the point it would put my new novel in jeopardy simply because I would get the *angst* and no longer produce. A few months ago, even weeks, he would have been correct. Somehow, though, as we stooped to the task I happily became All Pro; the work seemed to be that of an utter stranger, the words less precious than they seemed when coming from my typewriter in the hot flash of creation. I even found myself grumbling at the "author" in the removed person: "Why do you suppose that sumbitch wrote *this* crap?" greeted many gray gobs I had once presumed choice selections in the hymn of American Letters. Cutting a sentence here, a paragraph there, a half-page here, or re-writing a slumgullion stew of a sentence, we performed, I think, a miracle. I learned something I would not have earlier believed: that every word of my prose isn't Sacred or Anointed (though I seem to have forgotten the lesson in the third or fourth sentence of this paragraph.) Anyway, I am vastly pleased. . . .

Your comments on the Putnam piece very effectively massaged my egos and extended my ids. It is not altogether as I wished—but then nothing is. I suppose if I write until the earth comes to claim me back that I shall never see my work in the awful finality of public print without crying internal tears over what I failed to do to make it better, or seeing some place that I missed a perfectly obvious boat. In Putnam's case I would—if I could do it over—include something more about the fascination of its graveyard. I tried, but it did not come off, and so I cut it of my own volition. (My Clark genes tell me It Was For The Best; that somewhere inside me a story or article on death or cemeteries or family plots is brewing, and that Nature and God conspired to save the waste of that material until it could be put to better use.)

As to the "inherited guilt" fear that most Putnamites and *all* relatives would disown me once the piece appeared—well, I will not give up the luxury of my misery until I have been personally reassured by all bloodkin and a mass meeting of Putnam citizens that Everything is Forgiven. (Mother did not help. Her "We enjoyed the Putnam article" [period] seemed only to be a loving mother's way of telling the gentle lie when the hard truth wouldn't help.) The rest of her letter was pure Clark—weepy and imagining woes and calling all to Repent without telling us what we should Repent *about*—so that I tossed in my sheets *certain* that some line or word or perhaps misplaced comma in the article was responsible for her agitated state. Quite naturally I was disappointed when most of this torture vanished with a new day. . . .

Fuck Happiness.

There was, though, pleasure in the article for me: your comments did the most, though I was cheered by a friend who works for Senator James Eastland of Mississippi (and who happens, despite this, to be wise and good) and who judged it "the best yet"; also, Gutwillig's report that he had lunched with no less than three *Saturday Evening Post* editors all of whom gave rave notices to it. Believe me it is not just a swapping of compliments when I tell you that the line you got off when we (and our respective fathers) visited Putnam ("Somebody's sawed the top off Harper's Hill") was put to noble purpose when I purloined it, and that the theft of the concluding lines from one of your old letters gave me the most perfect of conclusions.

It is altogether wonderful here in Florida. I may have mentioned that the sea crashes up to our back door (literally; I am saved only by a small retaining wall three-feet high, non-swimmer that I am, and by the fact that I chose a *second story* apartment) and that seagulls fly at eye level as I look out the glass-enclosed elevated sun porch where I work, and that we have had days of 81 and 83 and like that when it comes to degrees.

If Hugh Hefner is a philosopher, then I am too, and my recent thoughts have dwelled on the balance of the good in this particular life I now lead as opposed to the bad. The Good is the luxury of not being at anyone's beck and call for a daily work schedule, and in having time to think and reflect so that what I try to commit to paper makes more sense, say, than the average *Dallas Morning News* editorial; the Bad, if there is any, lies in the nagging worry that maybe—just maybe—this withdrawal from the mainstream might dull whatever perceptive instincts one has. I am, for example, getting to be so much of the hermit that I almost refused to answer the door when the Special Delivery Man came with your letter today. I growl about having to eat in a restaurant where neckties and coats are considered necessary equipment, and—through Rosemarie's promotion—have picked up some fans down here that I bolt and run from because I don't want to be *bothered*.

I am sitting here googly-eyed and abstracted and staring long moments into the dark outside, and cannot see through it. It's time for bed. We're staying here for at least another month, at this same address. So write. And again thanks for—well, all that flattery and the juice that helps keep the battery charged. . . .

January 26, 1966

Dear Sterling:

Herbert Gold, agent for actor Dan Blocker, traced me here today and asked for clean proofs of *The One-Eyed Man*. You will note my response and action per the attached copy of my letter to him.

I think we might have something here, and would want us to be particularly alert to opportunity. As I'm sure you know, Dan Blocker has played "Hoss Cartwright" on the TV show *Bonanza* for 10 years. It has been rated at or near the top in audience viewing for that entire time.

Gold tells me confidentially that this may be Dan's last year with the show, and that they are searching for a movie script to star him. They propose to put some of Dan's money in it, produce it with (I think he said) Paramount or Columbia, and take a slice of the film profits. They've looked at a dozen scripts, and can't find anything they like. Dan read only a couple of pages of Governor Cullie Blanton's dialogue a couple of years ago, and has been fascinated since. If he likes the entire manuscript, it might be interesting and profitable for us.

I'm sure Herb Gold will be in touch with you and/or Cindy after they've read the proofs. Though we may be a long way off from any firm deal, please remember in any future negotiations that I'd like a job at big money helping to adapt *One-Eyed* for the screen.

A couple of things you should know for purposes of any future contact with Gold or Blocker: Dan Blocker and I are old Texas buddies of many years standing, and of course you have heard me "speak highly of him." Gold and Blocker also learned, through a friend in Washington, of Literary Guild's interest. He made some mention of their being excited and impressed because it is a "Literary Guild selection." I did not tell him, nor did I think it's necessary for anyone to volunteer, that at the moment it's an *alternate* selection.

Gutwillig tells me that Literary Guild will decide whether to boost *One-Eyed* to its main selection in (as I recall) the first or second week in February. Is there any way they should be advised of the movie possibilities, perhaps so as to influence (or at least not harm) their upcoming decision?

What is life without plots?

Schemingly yours, . . .

Feb. 17, 1966

Dear Lanvil & Glenda:

Wait a minute! Don't write Willie Morris a "thanks-but-no" letter! Write Willie Morris a "I am flattered and want to do it" letter. Even add that you aren't sure you can find the time, energy, formula, or whatever—but that you will try, and if the trying comes to anything you will get back in touch. *Please* do it that way. Leave the door open. If you then do it—as I am sure you can, and have a sneaking suspicion based on some Mystic Faith that you *will*—then everything comes up roses. If you try writing for *Harper's* or it doesn't come off or you never get around to it, then the thing can die a natural death, and in due time, I can lament The Loss (and would mean it) to Willie, and he will feel sorry for me and commiserate to the extent of buying me a free drink, so *some* smidgen of good will will have come from it, at least. . . .

When I read of how you can't do it, your crying about subject matter, lack of form, etc., I am inclined to think on horseshit. Especially am I inclined to think on horseshit when you say, apparently without tongue in cheek, that you "fail to see how pure reminiscence could interest an editor for a second." To give you but a few of countless examples, let us begin (as Willie Morris did in the letter I sent you) with mention of Mark Twain's *Life on the Mississippi,* proceed to a recent article you claimed to be moved by called "Requiem for a West Texas Town," consider Bruce Jay Friedman's "A Mother's Kisses," consider Willie Morris's in-progress work on life in Mississippi (already chosen by H-M Co. to receive its annual $10,000 House Award or Fellowship or whatever they call it). . . . all the kick everyone is on now re Batman, World War II, High Camp. Man this is the *Age* of Reminiscence! What better time than now?

Glenda, give him a choice: either get to work writing, or lose 85 pounds under penalty of having certain favors withheld, or under threat of other special torture. It is in your hands, so to speak. Kick the hell out of It if It won't cooperate. We will make It happy if we have to kill It.

Now for Sarasota happenings. The first time I saw MacKinley Kantor,* maybe a month ago, I called at his home here on Siesta Key (a really lovely place, right on the water, all glass and that indoor-outdoors look, palm trees, manicured grass, isolated, acres of ground) in response to his invitation responding to my earlier note asking if I could call. He met me at the door, big and surly looking, glanced at his watch and said, "Well, you're nine minutes early." I used up most of the nine minutes apologizing. In his study, hung with pictures of Himself and Literary Greats, and framed covers of his old magazine pieces (until then we thought Rosemarie had invented the idea) there is a big fireplace, and over the fireplace hangs a gaudy red, white, and blue sign, spangled with stars, and the sign says: FUCK COMMU-NISM.

Well, MacKinley Kantor and I have been buddies since. I have got drunk at his house, and he here at our quarters. He is the most reactionary man I think I've ever met ("I'm a child of the 19th Century, I don't like this one"), and at the same time one of the most delightful drinking companions. He has a song that lasts for a solid hour, of his own composition, about how he hates tourists and what all they do. It is lewd, vulgar, and a side-splitter, because it is obviously so true. . . .

Each Friday the Literary Establishment of Sarasota lunches together at The Plaza here: it is an old, graceful restaurant, with something of Paris about it, I am certain, though the only Paris I have ever been to is in Texas. But it feels like Paris. Mac Kantor explained to me, very carefully at that first meeting, that I could come to the luncheon as his guest *once*; that if I were asked back a second time, then I could continue to come so long as I felt "the members welcomed me," but if I misjudged and came when they had decided I wasn't welcome, I would be *asked to leave*. Rather cruel, yes. Snobbish no doubt, and even petty and silly. But it's intrigue and conflict, and I like that next to my loving wife (and maybe beer) better than anything in the world.

I showed as his guest for the first luncheon. Present: Mac, myself, Borden Deal (*The Loser, Dunbar's Cover, The Tobacco Man, A Long Way to Go, The Innocent Breed*; in short, 11 books in 11 years, plus 400 short stories, never a non-fiction article), Joe Hayes (*The Desperate Hours*), Alden Hatch, biographer (*Mountbatton's* his latest), John D. McDonald (54, count 'em, 54 mystery novels), David Weiss (Hell, I don't know what all: Literary Guild novels twice, Broadway play, musical comedy, Hollywood film scripts); Nick Kenny (corny old poet of 30 years ago on old *N.Y. World-Telegram,* and I blanched when we were introduced, for I thought Nick Kenny was dead), a run-of-the-mill retired railroad man who has written two or three novels that didn't make it, Jim McKague. Two other new guest writers other than myself. After before-luncheon drinks (beginning at 1 P.M.) and lunch and one after-luncheon drink, the other two guest writers (I didn't get their names in the confusion) were formally told by their sponsors that it had been "a pleasure to have them there" and they were given handshakes of obvious dismissal. They left in a shambling sort of way. I sat wondering what to do. Decided, "Hell, this is poker. I'll stand pat. Let Mac Kantor make the bet." When they had shambled out, Mac said, raising a glass in a toast: "Gentlemen, I propose we invite Mr. King back next Friday." Borden Deal said, "Second the motion."

Everybody said "Hear Hear," and I was informed I should buy a round of drinks in celebration, and did. Came the next week. Everything lovely. Obviously was expected to come back the third week: remember the rule, "so long as I felt the members welcomed me."

Hell, I wasn't *about* to play by their rules. Between that luncheon and the third one, I pointedly entertained Mac and got drunk at Borden Deal's house by invitation. Friday, I didn't show. Wondered how long it would take them to solicit me. (They'd bragged, you recall, or at least inferred, that they didn't really want to attract new members, or hangers-on, or whatever). One hour after the luncheon MacKinley Kantor called to ask, "Where were you today, Boy?" Casually, I said, "Mac, I worked late and just flat overslept, and to tell you the plain truth I'd about half forgotten about the luncheon." Borden Deal woke me up the next morning with same question. Gave him the same answer. I am going back this Friday (tomorrow) of course, and am now secure in the knowledge that I Have Won Again. God, I love contests. . . .

*Pulitzer Prize winner in the 1950s for his Civil War novel, *Andersonville*.

Feb. 17, 1966

Dear Willie:

I don't expect you to read every letter Lanvil Gilbert writes me, but this one is his reaction to the prospect of his writing something for you and I know you'll be interested.

Unless I am inordinately biased, his two pages explaining why he can't write for *Harper's* is good enough to sell to *Harper's*. I told him so in a letter today, and told him to goddammit write you and say he'd try and then, dammit, to *try*.

I continue corresponding on this subject at the hazard of seeming pushy, but I do it only because—at least much *more* because—I think he has boatloads of talent than because he's my cousin and favorite person. If you agree he's worth trying to save, could you quicklike drop him a note of encouragement or some such—busy as you are. He doesn't know I'm sending you the enclosed letter. If, however, you wish to mention it should you write him, feel completely free to.

This is the last time I'll bug you on the subject. I feel an obligation, however, to make at least one final effort to get Lanvil Gilbert to produce. If I can, it will be as great a contribution as I shall ever make to the hymn of American Letters. . . .

P.S.: Ex-Supt. of Schools R.F. Webb of Putnam, mentioned in "Requiem For A West Texas Town," died of a heart attack last week. That's two by the same route since the article appeared. Omens are all about.

March 1, 1966

Mr. Dan Blocker,
^c/o Herb Gold,
9034 Sunset Blvd.,
Los Angeles, 69, California

Dear Dan:

I am pleased, flattered, and excited at your interest in seeing the proofs of *The One-Eyed Man.* I am equally abashed and no little miffed that I've been unable to jar proofs loose and get them to you. I want to explain the situation so you won't think the lack of action is because of any lack of interest on my part.

Let me preface the explanation by saying that you *will* get proofs, and I am *hopeful* it will be within the next two weeks.

I suppose you've found in your business that every time you sign a new contract, or introduce a new force, into a situation you lose some control over your time, talent, and yourself. Baby, in this goddamn writing game that goes in spades.

Basically, my hands are tied on getting proofs to you until Literary Guild Book Club gives the O.K. This applies not just to you, but to anybody. Contractually, I find that I'm prohibited from sending proofs out or having my agent send them out until Literary Guild and my publishers, New American Library, have "coordinated" activities involving editors, advertising executives, P. R. men, the art department, and everybody else. I am such a rookie I do not profess to know all the reasons, but I have checked with writer friends (as well, of course, as my agent) who tell me there's damn little I can do but go along with them, shout when I'm mad, and keep goading them to hurry. It's simply a matter of my prose being put into the great grist mill, and varied Gods must grind it mysteriously fine.

One of the hangups is that Literary Guild keeps changing its mind about the month they want to release the book itself—it was May, now July, vague rumors of September. That is supposed to be settled for good and all any day. Then the final mysterious "coordinating" will be accomplished, I am repeatedly told, and proofs will go out to you shortly thereafter—which is translated to mean "in about two weeks."

I'm embarrassed that my enthusiasm for having you play Governor Cullie Blanton, coupled with my asbymal ignorance of how many people get involved in handling a property like this, caused me to innocently assume I could just snap my fingers and get proofs to you when I want to. Consequently, I over-promised myself when I told Herb Gold three or four times that the proofs would be on their way "immediately." For this I'm sorry. Know that I do my best.

I *am* excited over you in the role Governor Blanton. He is a merry, mercurical rogue one minute, a raving nutbuster the next, a sly old fox in the next moment. He is the total good politician, and he knows how to use every motion known to man. I hesitate to say that the role has the range of *Othello,* but I am tempted to say so. As I've told many, including Herb Gold and maybe you, Dan Blocker was in my mind every time Cullie Blanton uttered a word or crossed the stage. Additionally, I will crassly and commercially, admit that in writing many scenes I was thinking how it would "play" on the screen. So there is action, and variety. (Christ, if I could get this printed as a review . . .). Admitting to certain biases, I think you'll see potential in the role. So please don't get too impatient and buy somebody else's property. Proofs will be a-coming. . . .*

*Nothing ever came of Blocker's interest. Many years later King's friend

Sander Vanocur, while visiting the famed movie director John Huston in Mexico, found a copy of *The One-Eyed Man* inscribed to Blocker in Huston's library. Huston could not recall how he came to have it but speculated that Blocker or Blocker's agent had sent it to him to see if he might be interested in making a film of the book. When Vanocur asked Huston had he read King's book, he said "If I did I don't recall it."

Sarasota, Florida
March 9, 1966

Dear Sterling:

Here's the *Sports Illustrated* re-write on the sports writing dodge. Perhaps this will reverse the recent trend.

Gutwillig and I talked at great length and with wracking sobs last night. He jangled my juices with atypical joy by mention of various promotionals and so forth we are to plot when we return to Civilization, and pledged to get me $500 right soon to meet current obligations. We are leaving for Washington March 16th, though I hate to leave my new job here at the gas station. . . .

April 8, 1966

Hon. Robert Gutwillig
Editor, New American Library

Say, Darlin'. . . .

About my Washington whiskey drink selling *One-Eyed Man*. . . .

Right after they present my Cadillac, but before my two-hour speech of acceptance, entertainment will be laid on. Festivities will open with a roll of drums, at the conclusion of which Congressman Joe Pool will be shot out of a cannon in his Batman Suit into what he thinks will be a protective net. Liberals, however, are going to strike the net at the last minute so that Joe gets the Batcrap knocked out of him. Whereupon six Southern Congressmen will attack and gang-bang Miss Black-and-Tan Washington of 1966, in spotlights of alternating colors, until upon hand signal Chief Justice Earl Warren bursts upon the stage to rescue her in as symbolic a presentation of the last decade as one could wish. Southerners will boo loudly and throw their bourbon glasses. A riot will be averted when the band plays "Dixie." As the mutiny stills, we will throw the Southerns a sop by letting George Lincoln Rockwell* ride on stage in spurs, astride a nekkid Rabbi. Congressman Gerald Ford will speak on the subject, "The Flying Saucer Gap" at the conclusion of which Rockwell will take charge of a book-burning featuring all the Principal Selections of Literary Guild for the current year. A gospel quartet composed of Marlon Brando, Senator Hickenlooper of Iowa, Katherine Ann Porter, and Willie Morris will render "The Old Rugged Cross" while Ralph Ginsburg is nailed to one by the Supreme Court of the United States.** All members of the Hebrew faith will rise under the direction of Mitch Miller to sing, "Let My People Go, Already." The United Nations will play the Kennedy family in ice-hockey. Rev. Billy Graham will announce that all Baptists who have married Catholics are to be ex-communicated. Enter, Famous Arthur Larry L. King, Center Stage, Spots Up, Martial Music, carried on silk pillows by 50 Vestal Virgins. Preceding the processional, Congressman Mo Udall of Arizona, Congressman Jim Wright of Texas, and Mr. Bob Gutwillig, Editor, New American Library, will strew roses and exotic scents. After my two hour acceptance speech, Mr. Ed Kuhn, High Official in the New American Library, will give me a gunny sack full of $1000 bills and announce NAL's construction of The Rosemarie King Rest Home for Tired Writers' Wives. All join hands and sing "Hail to the Redskins." Benediction by Rev. Norman Mailer, who will then box ten rounds with himself.

(Door prizes: A gold-plated dust jacket of *The One-Eyed Man*, symbolic of the one-millionth copy given away free by the Famous Arthur's wife; Original contract between Larry L. King and McGraw-Hill Publishing Company; two weeks of free tours in Washington Wax Museums; John F. Kennedy's assassination shirt, and a life-sized statue of Truman Capote that glows in the dark.)

Well, maybe it won't be all that flamboyant but it is now laid on.

Hons. Udall and Wright understand they are to allow use of their names on invitations and are ready to reserve the hall. (Downtown

National Capitol Democratic Club free.) The jazz quartet is ready to toot as "The One-Eyed Men" and wear eye patches. Whiskey is being set aside. To you shall come a list very shortly of the invitees: names, addresses, titles, and/or positions. . . .

Goodnight, Sweet Prince. . . .

*Rockwell was the self-proclaimed head of the American Nazi Party.
**Ginsburg had been sentenced to prison for publishing pornography; King and others considered him a political prisoner jailed for leftist beliefs.

April 25, 1966

Dear Cousins:

Paranoia, anyone?

No, your letter didn't stick in the mail chute. You have earned your spurs as a True Clark for good and all with this exhibition, and when I got your postcard out of the mailbox this morning I whooped and gurgled so that parents took their children by the hand and old ladies looked the other way. I was having very much fun over your particular mental processes until Rosemarie, who has an abiding preoccupation with Truth, pointed out that I once had spent the whole weekend fretting because a fat letter I had mailed my folks was *surely* stuck in the mail chute; I did not hear it go down and know that it stuck between the second and third floors! As the separate sons of identical twins, should we report this to medical scientists?

Don't think I told you how well *One-Eyed Man* figures to sell among the Clark sisters: Mother wrote for the publication date because Aunt Bessie and Ida Beth wanted "to be the first ones to check it out of their local library." That will make the royalties roll in, won't it?

Did you read that my friend Warren Miller died? It happened while we were in New York last weekend. Lung cancer. He woke up unable to breath at 2 A.M. and horrible drowned in his own fluids. Age: 44. Bob Gutwillig had told me a month ago that Warren had but a few weeks to live. It seems that he had an operation for a tumor about a year ago, they found he was long past the saving point, sewed him back up, and gave him about the year he consumed. Warren didn't then know it: I saw him a few months ago, and had no idea of his condition. Only his wife and Gutwillig knew. For the last couple of months he had been in the hospital getting blood transfusions and all the pain-killing dope they could shoot into him. Less than a week before his death he was sent home to die. This shook me very badly. He was one of the Good Ones. . . .

Gutwillig sent proofs of *One-Eyed* to about ten authors. At this writing he's heard from three. (Point: to get usable quotes for ads, possibly for dust jacket.) Robert Penn Warren wrote that "from the opening paragraphs, it seems your author has been writing in my sleep"; promised to finish reading and get back to Gutwillig with his comments soon. David Weiss wrote: "*The One-Eyed Man* is dramatic and moving . . . The characterization of the Governor, Cullie Blanton, is a reader's delight: fascinating and yet always fluctuating in the infinite variety that is man. Larry L. King has written a fine book: powerful, pungent, and provocative. A vivid experience." Borden Deal wrote the following mish-mash, from which we conclude that he does not like the book: "I read Larry King's first novel with considerable interest. The American political scene, from the insider's point of view as Larry King knows it, is a fascinating novelistic area."

The weekend of May 6th-7th-8th, Rosemarie and I are to be guests at Willie Morris's country place a couple of hours out of New York City along with the Robert Penn Warrens, William Styron and Ralph (*Invisible Man*) Ellison. I am all a-twitter and hope I pull no literary blunders in the presence of such talents. A full report to you shall follow.

Had a productive trip to N.Y. Jim Atwater, editor of *Sat. Eve. Post*, had telephoned me in Florida asking if I might discuss some sports work with them. (On the basis of the *S.I.* Sugar Ray Robinson piece.) Jack Fischer at *Harper's* was an absolute delight. He asked me to come by and filled me with so much praise that I will need no pep pills for two or three weeks. He's very much pleased with Bob Jones U. piece (firmly scheduled for June) and asked me to do one on William Buckley, the Rightest in residence of New York City. Am lining up to interview him and folks who know him; will spend several days in N.Y.

City soon for that purpose. That's four pieces I owe *Harper's* they are taking my war experiences piece ("The Battle of Popcorn Bay"), another on my police reporting days, and one on New College. Fischer had recently returned from Amarillo. Said several people who knew Putnam (or towns like it) had been moved to tears by "Requiem for a West Texas Town."

Making a snap review of our past correspondence, I see that I have spoken only of Successes. One would think that Failures have never entered my door. Well, they have. For the record, let me tell you about them. One, the Connally piece, never found a home after I got stubborn over the version *Reporter* wanted to print and said "No." Subsequently, it was rejected by *Sat. Eve. Post, New Republic,* even *Harper's. Esquire* had me re-write the Life Among the Super Americans piece three times and *still* turned it down, paying only the guarantee. *Sports Illustrated* had my sports writing days piece for weeks, finally asked for a re-write, I did a sloppy job and they paid the guarantee but will not publish it. It is painful to dwell on such things, but now my soul is free and purged of guilt. . . .

April 27, 1966

Dear Bob:

Stipulating that you are busy with Senator [Thomas] Dodd and Maud Shaw,* further stipulating that you have been through recent traumas, and additionally you have other things to worry about, I make the following personal declaration:

I have about decided to hell with any *One-Eyed Man* promotion party . . . I'm just tired of the hassle. I don't have it in me to fuss with Jay Tower or you or anybody else over the guest list. It's not worth the hack, and is turning into a burden when it should be a pleasant experience.

To trim the guest list to 150 from my standpoint would force me either to eliminate (1) many personal friends and relatives or (2) the Washington officials and publicity outlets that would get us in the papers, on radio and TV. I simply can't do the former because of personal considerations and the feelings of friends and relatives. (Of which there are 23 in the latter category.) To do the second makes the party void of any purpose. So rather than have a half-assed thing that isn't personally satisfying, I think I'd rather forget it.

At the hazard of stating information you already know, let me point out that I've cooperated every possible way in an effort to get the book off the ground. You said get a hall for the party at a reasonable rate: I got the best, free. You said come with a gimmick. I got politicians and a national political club to promote a political book, and came up with the band angle at virtually no cost. Additionally, I've met with your sales people and agreed to visit every book store in Washington to seek window displays—and this at my own initiative. I've told your people I'd go anywhere, sing any song or dance any step to sell books. I wrote the dust-jacket blurb, furnished free pix for dust-jacket and ads, went over the book in line-by-line editing with you. All this was based on the assumption that NAL is as interested as I am in seeing the book sell. If we have to squabble over a hundred people at a party, however, then apparently I was wrong and I therefore withdraw from the field.

So advertise or don't advertise as you please. I'm not disposed to knock myself out and wind up on the short end, or having to fight and scrap. The book will apparently be lost among the hundreds that spew forth, so I am planning to get a gig and write in my spare time. It's the only way I can make it. And it at least shouldn't be any more aggravating than this. . . .

*A politician and a nanny to the JFK children, each of whom had recently committed what King called "non-books."

May 9, 1966

Mr. Robert Gutwillig
New American Library

Dear Bob:

Robert Penn Warren wants to come to my book party, but I told him you said too many people had been invited already. Before I could stop her, however, Rosemarie did invite the William Styrons and they are coming. I apologize for this. . . .

I got a letter from a fellow the other day and he signed your name to it, telling me that I should go sit in the back of the bus. That's what they told Rosa Parks, too, and look what happened. . . .*

Your friend,
Martin Larry King

*A sarcastic response to Gutwillig's stern letter to King pointing out his unrealistic expectations as a first novelist.

Editor's Note: Through Willie Morris, King also was beginning to be introduced to the New York literati. The following letter, written to his Austin cousins, describes a trip to Morris's country home for a southern-boys weekend where two of the other guests were his literary heroes Robert Penn Warren and William Styron.

May 9, 1966

Dear Lanvil & Glenda:

We motored up to Willie Morris's country place in Putnam County, N.Y., about 30 miles from Hyde Park, with Willie, his wife, son, and dog Friday afternoon. Friday was given to drinking in front of the fireplace in Willie's 130-year old house, recently renovated and full of rustic charm, sitting on a hill overlooking a picture-book valley full of old barns, church spires, and vague, misty hazes. Saturday we mowed

3000 acres of lawn, give or take a few acres, did a little incidental beer drinking and primped for the party.

It was to have been a "Southern Dogwood Party," Willie pridefully owning the largest dogwood tree above the Mason-Dixon line, but there was still a wintry look on the hills and trees, with no sign of dogwood blossoms. This proved a minor handicap. We took up the slack by eating a purely Southern dinner: ham, black-eyed peas, green salad. There was good wine, fine cigars, smooth brandy, and wonderful conversation.

Robert Penn Warren was there (and writer wife Eleanor Clark) and William Styron and C. Vann Woodward. Ralph Ellison did not make it. Herewith my impressions.

"Red" Warren was very much as I expected him to be: courtly in the gracious, Old South way that is a mixture of instinct, training, humility and quiet confidence. He looks his 61 years, no more and no less. The hair is reddish and the complexion decidedly so. The face is full of strong lines and wrinkles. There is a sort of country squire aura about him, in the best sense, but underneath it is the faint hint that he is slightly On Guard against something: when Willie's wife, Celia, opened a conversation, "Mr. Warren, there are three questions I have always wanted to ask you," he took on a faint, haunting look in the eyes and knew he was meant to suffer unless he came up with something quick, and he did, by taking her elbow and saying smoothly, "Fine, but before you do I'd like to take a tour of this fine old house." It worked. He got the tour and he got out of having the questions put.

I cued in from that and bit back some questions I would have liked to ask, but the evening was far from a shutout. At dinner Warren asked me questions about my background, my work, and the like. We established common ground in the conventional ways: politicians we have known, the mutual friendship of Tommy Thompson (editor of the Amarillo newspaper), and I then said kind things about his work. I told him that my favorites of his books included *Flood, All the King's Men, World Enough and Time*. He beamed what appeared to be a sincere beam, commenting that of all his books "Those are the ones I feel personally closest to." He volunteered the information that *Wilderness* was the only book he has done that gave him little or no satisfaction: it missed, he said, because he set out to do one thing and did another. (He did not elaborate on this and since I had him talking I didn't break in to ask questions but let his story roll on.) He spoke of his difficulty with the short story: can't write them, he said. Thinks no more than 10 Americans can or ever could. Eudora Welty is his choice as the best; perhaps the only natural short story writer in America. (He thinks it an "unnatural" art form for most and that you are either born to it or you are not, and doubts that truly fine short story writing can be taught or acquired beyond a small point) . . . .

At one point, when he was quizzing me on my hopes and dreams, I made the statement (defensively, perhaps, because of his scholarly accomplishments ranging from being one of the Fugitives at Vanderbilt U., studying at Oxford, teaching at Yale) that there are many books I would like to write but that "I have little formal education and feel so goddamned *ignorant!* There's so much I just don't understand." Warren's comment: "Well, if you did understand—and that's to say if you *thought* you understood very much about anything—I doubt whether you'd be very successful at the creative processes. I've always found that I write to learn as much as I do to tell or instruct. I don't think a writer is really having a creative experience when he merely tells: there should be in his work a great seeking." At this point I mentally deshod him and kissed his feet.

Warren signed a copy of *Flood* that I had taken along "with warm regards." I did not get to talk to his wife too much. She seemed altogether charming and quite aware. Frankly, I avoided talking to her except in groups because I've read none of her books and felt that I might transmit my damnable ignorance. . . .

One more thing about Warren: Rosemarie proved that he can be embarrassed—though there was no call for his being embarrassed. I think I'd written you that he has galley proofs of *The One-Eyed Man* and had written Gutwillig that from the opening paragraphs "It seems your author has been writing in my sleep." Rosemarie told him that Gutwillig showed us the letter. He blushed, ducked his head and said,

"Well, I certainly hope you will forgive me for it." We protested: it was, we felt, the greatest possible compliment. He muttered apologies that he hadn't had time to get back to the galleys because of his own work but would do so now that he's met us. Then he rushed on to get away from the subject but was so truly embarrassed that he quite pathetically stammered over the first few lines, and I inserted a couple of comments to get us over the bump. He was, I think, most grateful.

William Styron is a different breed. He is, in fact, a great deal like me except he is handsome, rich, and of proven talent. What I am saying, really, is that he is more of our generation, less a legend, and I approached him with far less awe. (Thinking on it, it seems to me that Warren's manner does not let you drop the awe but actually causes it to build a little; Styron, on the other hand, is so comfortably old shoe and so full of the same hidden fears I know that he discourages any awe-building.) Styron is strong with ego, you sense, and I am told by Willie Morris that this is extremely true. Not that he put it on display; somehow you know it's there and intermingled with the fears. He has not scored a major success since *Lie Down in Darkness* (1954), his subsequent work, *The Long March*, getting so-so reception and his latest, *Set This House on Fire*, being something of a disaster.* He badly needs to have another critical success and his hopes lie in a fictionalization of the Nat Turner rebellion in Virginia in the 1830s. I've read excerpts from the *Paris Review;* it will not be the disaster that *Set This House on Fire* was, and will, I think, be quite good: I don't think it's going to be any *Lie Down in Darkness* though. He simply set himself too high a standard with that first great work.

There was about Styron, too, a sort of seeking of acceptance with us. Warren did not show that because he does not have to. Styron feels that he does. We talked little about our work, in contrast with conversation with Warren. We more nearly talked about our experiences: boyhood, the South, and such. We both drink with both hands and he has a mad-cap streak, too: at an uncertain hour he sought me out to listen to some 40-year old records of old hymns on a hand-cranked phonograph, during which he would quote the Bible and snatches of obscure poetry some of which I suspect he wrote himself.

Styrons live in Roxbury, Conn., about 50 driving minutes away from Willie's house. He telephoned back to ask for me upon arrival home (4 A.M.? 5A.M.?) to say that he'd gone through his mail when he arrived and found there a manuscript of *The One-Eyed Man* mailed to him by Gutwillig. He would, he insisted, begin reading at that very moment. (Seeking of acceptance comes to the fore.) Yes, he would begin it then and plunge right on through to the end before his eyes closed. He did not, I am certain, because by this time he was dog-drunk and sleepy and I imagine he hung up the phone and went straight away to bed. In my own stupor I generously told him that he didn't have to read it right then: just do it the first thing when he woke up.

Rose Styron is a delight. Beautiful, charming, and incidentally awfully rich. Was most eligible rich Jewish girl in Baltimore when Southern Boy Styron married her. Baltimore's Jews disapproved to a man, to say nothing of the women. Her people knew vaguely that Styron is supposed to be a well-known writer, but are said not to be interested enough to read his books. They claim they'll come to my book party here June 6th. She has done a couple of children's books and some poetry. She's 38, he's about 41. Styron inscribed *Lie Down in Darkness* for me thus: "To Larry King, the best writer and Southroner they ever was. Peace." I would put more faith in the inscription had he ever read a line I've written. He is, incidentally, looking forward to the BJU piece in *Harper's,* as he has an abiding interest in Fundamentalism, was exposed to a lot of it in his youth (and at Davidson, where he first went to school.) Willie told him of BJU piece, and he'd seen the plug for it in current *Harper's*. I think we'll be friends as time goes on: drinking companion types, and will blurt out one day our fears and vital secrets.

With C. Vann Woodward I drew almost a blank. At the outset of the party, before things were rolling and inhibitions had been laid aside, I spent fifteen tough minutes trying to talk to him. He tried, too, but we couldn't find much to sustain us. Then he startled me, at party's end, by giving me a good-night handshake and saying, "I had really hoped to talk to you more, but you seemed to have been pretty well monopolized by Red Warren and Bill Styron." What he was really saying, I guess, was that I had monopolized *them* and didn't pay him much attention. I just stood there with my hand a captive in his own and mumbled awkward things about how we'd no doubt have the opportunity to know each other better at a later date, or some such inane thing . . . .

I must get to work on work, but wanted to get these impressions down while they were fresh. Oh, a couple of nights before we went up, Eudora Welty read two of her short stories at a do here and we attended. Enjoyable, yet disappointing; she seeks to run from the public and as soon as the reading stint was over she plunged off-stage. She was dragged back for questions, but was so reluctant that nobody asked any of consequence. Got her to autograph a volume of her stories, Rosemarie got in a quick plug for *One-Eyed* (Mrs. Welty saying graciously she'd be on the look out for it) and everybody went home. . . .

*King later recanted these "youthful opinions" after re-readings of these works, although *Set This House on Fire* in particular was flogged by the critics.

––––––––––––––––––––––

May 29, 1966

Dear Lanvil & Glenda:

Thirty-one months after I sold *The One-Eyed Man*, after all that sweat and work, and hopes and dreams, the first published review today—in *Book Week*, published here and in San Francisco.*

It was a disaster.

Not because I want to circulate it, and not because I'll derive any pleasure from it, but largely because you can't hide forever and also because I understandably didn't feel like buying an extra copy of so catastrophic a review, I send along a reproduction of it as follows:

All the King's Horses

[*The One-Eyed Man.* By Larry L. King. The New American Library

320 pp. $5.95. (Reviewed by R.Z. Sheppard, assistant editor of *Book Week*)]

"Mr. King is, among other things, a contributing editor of the *Texas Observer*, a liberal periodical which is often a burr under the saddles of high-riding Texas politicians. Perhaps the best known writer of what has loosely been called the *Texas Observer* crowd is Bill Brammer, a former Johnson aide who turned his political experiences into a first-rate *roman à clef* called *The Gay Place*. It starred Governor Arthur (Goddam) Fenstemaker, a sympathetic mixture of shrewd intelligence, cornpone, and pragmatic good will, qualities so recognizable as belonging to The Man Himself that Brammer hasn't been seen at an LBJ barbeque since his book was published in 1961.

"Now Mr. King, who has been an administrative assistant to two Texas Congressmen and plumped for Lyndon Johnson's Presidential nomination in 1960, attempts to turn the lead of political experience into the gold of fiction. The result is something less than 10-karat: a static, often pretentious, and derivative assemblage of cliches which at times reads as if Mr. King were parodying Robert Penn Warren and even Brammer himself ("Maybe I knew . . . that at some sweet time and at some gay place we would make it.") But mostly it reads like imitation James M. Cain: 'The old wheel of fortune keeps spinning in worn grooves and the X of chance falls wantonly on the squares, and about all any mother's son can do is ride with the play. . . . Only the historians don't dig it. . . . So before they rip it up and go labelling it pure grade-A History, and wrap it in the clear cellophane of hindsight, I want to tell it like it was.'

"That's from the lips of the narrator, the familiar shopworn ex-newspaperman turned political press agent and hatchetman. His yarn has to do with the efforts of Governor Cullie Blanton to convince his Southern state (unidentified) that the North won the Civil War and it is necessary to accede to a federal order to integrate the state university. Blanton, too, is a sympathetic mixture of shrewd intelligence, cornpone, and pragmatic good will, although he is too composite and exaggerated to resemble the living.

"The highpoint of the book is Blanton's politically suicidal speech in which he attempts to awaken his legislature to the realities of the 20th century. But to get to this tough, moving message the reader must be prepared to wade through far too many swamps of local color, hoked-up dialogue and bargain sentiment."

Ouch!

It hurts, let me tell you, to be branded a Public Failure.

As clinically as possible, let me set down for the record my emotions from the first terrible moment.

Numb and horrified, first. A state of shock to the point of paralysis. I just couldn't *conceive* of it having happened to me after all those years of hope and toil. Humiliated. Oh, so *very* humiliated. Physically ill. Truly, gagging physically ill. All those emotions in about that order, each state lasting a few minutes in its turn, and then mingling or interchanging so that I seemed to be experiencing all those emotions at once in different parts of the brain and being.

What did I say? "Oh, shit!" was perhaps my longest comment for ten minutes. A four-letter word meaning fornicate was popular, too, repeated as a sort of profane prayer.

As soon as I could recover enough to make sentences, I thought of the fact that I am to review a book (ironically for *Book Week*) within the next two weeks, and I told Rosemarie: "I'll not review it. Not because I got a bad review in that publication—but because I don't ever want to make a guy feel like I feel now." Two minutes later I changed my mind: "No, I'll review this one book *because* it's for *Book Week*. I need to prove to *Book Week* readers that, this review of my book aside, I can write. But after that, no more reviews. Ever." (I mean it too. It's too much responsibility for me. It's too much like playing God. I never knew that until last night, midnight.)**

We decided that we would arise at dawn, sneak out of the apartment, go to the boat on Chesapeake Bay and hide for two or three days. Not answer the phone. We didn't—I got to sleep around 5 A.M., woke at 9:30, read the terrible thing (it had been telephoned to me at midnight, when I was on the verge of sleep, by a well-meaning friend who had not read it before calling: just saw it and called by impulse and then got all hung up when she saw what we were into, and I was making little wounded sounds over the phone, I recall) again. Our phone has not jingled once at 2 P.M. I conclude that all the world loves A Winner.

After the call I prowled and smoked and drank three beers in about fifteen minutes and got to having fantasies: maybe, hopefully, the world's biggest newspaper thief would come in the night and steal every paper in Washington, save the one the lady called me to read. For a while I thought chances of this were at least fair: maybe even money. Somehow, all papers would be magically transported away and No One Would Know.

But this morning, there was *mine*, evilly looming in front of the door, and up and down the hall there were others, and some were gone from in front of the doors, which meant people had them and it was Too Late.

Last night I thought, "I'm Dead. Publication date is still *three weeks* away, the advertising campaign *not even started* and I'm dead. Fantastic!" I thought of how this will hurt my party crowd. The word of mouth will go around this week, and everybody will turn thumbs down and my book is dead. (I don't feel very much different about it right now.)

Then I thought of how it will affect the immediate future and the long range. Will NAL throw up its hands, write it off, cut down on the ads? Does this not weaken my position with them on the book-in-progress? Will I have to give up writing full-time and take a job? I called Gutwillig at his weekend place on Long Island around noon, read him the review. He's in a state of shock. "Catastrophic," he said. "That ruins us in Washington." He's trying to think of whether there's a way to regroup.

I couldn't believe all that—couldn't afford to believe it. So I grasped straws: re-reading the laudatory quotes from William Styron, David Weiss, Richard Condon, Virginia Kirkus. Thinking of Gutwillig's enthusiasm and faith in the book, the fact that it *is* after all a Literary Guild alternate selection for August. Could so many be so wrong? Could R. Z. Sheppard know that much more than all those good brains? Could all the signs toward Success—now so familiar to me that I had come to believe that Failure was as impossible as victory by Monday in Vietnam—be that far off and that wrong? What in God's name was the matter with an industry that was so inexact a science after all these years?

I began to hate Mr. Sheppard in a way that even I cannot describe. Outrage. Bitterness. Vile. Bile. I began to pick his review apart.

Cliches? Too many swamps of local color, hoked-up dialogue and bargain sentiment? Well, politics in the South is a matter of local color, hoked-up dialogue, bargain sentiment. Witness Pappy O'Daniel, John Connally, Lurleen Wallace; a million, billion more. Had I not lived through much of this book in actual experience? Yes, so is not cliche another word maybe for "truth"—for "the way it is"?

But how to communicate that to the reader poisoned by Mr. Sheppard's review?

The Governor "too exaggerated to resemble the living"? How about Lyndon B. Johnson saying, for example, to a reporter as recently quoted in a book: "Why do you come to see me, the leader of the Western World, with a chickenshit question like that?" How about Uncle Earl Long cursing on the House floor and going on that crazy trip across Texas and New Mexico, wearing pillowcases over his head and making obscene gestures to reporters while standing stark nekkid in his hotel room? How about George Wallace bumping bellies with a Federal Marshall in the schoolroom door? How about Huey Long, Alfalfa Bill Murray, Ma & Pa Ferguson, oh Christ, a billion? Were they anything but *exaggerated*? But did they not live?

Yet, how tell the readers out there? I can't reach them!

That's when I guess I hit the lowest point. So helpless! So frustrated! So goddamn powerless! Like Henry Cooper, bleeding at the hands of Cassius Clay, and unable to do anything about it. No doubt Henry was thinking, "Look, folks, I knocked him down [in the Olympics] in 1963. He was out. The bell saved him. If it had happened 10 seconds earlier, I would have won. I have *proved* I can punch. If you'll just give me a minute to get the blood out of my eyes, I'll show you! Look! Please! . . ."

But they stopped the fight, of course, and Henry couldn't get any-body to listen because The Verdict Was In.

So's mine, for the moment.

Today I am trying to recover by getting interviewed for *Roll Call* read by the 7,000 or so people on Capitol Hill, to be published next Thursday, in which I point out that four of five pre-publication com-ments have been good. Then quote from Styron, Weiss, Condon, Virginia Kirkus. Maybe it will help. Can't hurt. Something's gotta be done.

We can't end not with a bang but with a whimper. Not now. Not after all this.

Peace. More when I am sane.

Book Week also was published by the *New York Herald Tribune* and was a Sunday book review supplement in Washington, Chicago and San Francisco.
**This vow was later broken, oh, no more than maybe 100 times—LLK

June 9, 1966

The Warren Burnetts,
Route 1, Box 516,
Odessa, Texas

Dear Warren & Emma:

I truly do appreciate your coming to my Drink-A-Book. More than that, I doubly appreciate your letting me know exactly when I could expect you. For the sake of your Precious Children, I will say nothing harsher than that.

Had a note today from Justice W. O. Douglas, regretting that he had not been present to see "you, Warren Burnett and your book." Frankly, I did not like the order of listing too much. It are a good thang the Justice aren't got to campaign for high office. . . .

My Precious Children are here for a month. On July-The-Oneth I am starting the long drive to bring them back to Texas. Then follows two, three week promotional tour of Texas for the book. Dates being firmed up within 48 hours.

Now for the pitch. I will be in Odessa-Midland promoting from about July 5th to July 9th: book store autographs, radio and TV. Since you didn't come to my party, I am going to give you the opportunity to throw one for me at your very own home. Select your date: July 5th through 9th. Or we can make it continuous.

I are going to promote definitely also in Austin, Fort Worth, Dallas, Houston. Probably Abilene, possibly El Paso. Also swing back for a big party doens and promotion in Greenville, Mississippi, where young Hodding Carter will roll out the red carpet. TV and radio dos start here immediately. Taping for Canadian Broadcasting Company tomorrow. Numerous Washington TV and radio shots upcoming between now and July 1st, plus same in N.Y.

I are not got anything dirty to say about you standing me up here until I see you in person. I keep thinking how I drug my Raggedy-Ann self, sweet wife and tired old car down to your moment of glory in your own home climes and how you didn't reciprocate. I figure you can have a party for me there for a little less than $25,000.

Yours In Christ,
Larry-The-Stood-Up

P.S. At least Reagan Legg sent a telegram!

June 9, 1966

Mr. William Styron
Roxbury, Conn.

Dear Bill:

I got through my party without upchucking on any booksellers, critics, or myself. In public, anyhow. Long 'bout seven P.M. I raised my glass in toast, which was in secret response to your own pledge to do same at that hour. . . .

Sure enough, it was a good blast and we missed and yearned for you, though the extra $3 cost might have driven the NAL's past the jumping off point in that they had authorized me to invite a mere 150 persons and I went and invited 350, and asked everybody to bring somebody else besides, so instead of them getting out for $29.17 they got out for around oh, three four thousand dollars. This has made their executives hostile and has put my agent on Defense.

Two purty good thangs happened re my book lately. One: *Publishers Weekly* said a whole bunch of sweet thangs. Two: John Kenneth Galbraith authorized a quote which said, among other things, that *"One-Eyed Man* is the best political novel since *The Last Hurrah."*. . .

Fellow named Irv Goodman with Literary Guild, told me last night there is a "sense of excitement" about my opus at the ABA convention, winding up here now. I went out there and smiled on cue and signed books and laughed at jokes I had heard a hunnert times and my Greek wife found out the Book Lady for Woodward & Lothrops here is Greek too, and they fashioned such a friendship I am afraid they will elope, but the result looks like a big window display and helpful salespersons, and Big Advance Orders. All of which can help, as I understand the rules.

My eight-year-old son is lying on his pallet (we are Poor Folks) bugging me about the Civil War. His Grandad, his Teacher and his History Book in Texas all teach him that the South Really Won, and I am having a terrible time explaining that they are Mistaken. I of course believed this same thing until I was twenty-six, when a lady of a certain vintage told me better on a barstool in, I think, Perth Amboy, New Jersey. I hit her in the mouth. . . .

June 10, 1966

The Reagan Leggs,
Midland, Texas

Dear Reagan & Jean:

Bless you for your telegram. Perfect topper to a great night.

Everythang coming up roses, except my kids who are here may tell their Mama I am worth a Million when the announcement is premature. I currently am worth $1.98 if you count my body chemicals.

Cheryl Ann [now Alix] attended book party, greeting guests at the door, getting publicily introduced by one Jim Wright and feeling 100% Grand and Loved and a Celebrity. *That* made me cry, too. (Reminded me of when we called on then Vice-President LBJ, Judge Legg, and he cried over how his Mama loved him *and* he loved his Mama and your Mama loved *him* and *his* Mama, and *you* loved ever-goddahm-body and *he* did too.) Raff-the-Mad* popped in, stayed 10 minutes, pled other engagements and left. I've been trying to corral him since our last telephone talk without success. Told him I wanted to see him re "a mutual friend in Midland" (in the presence of by-standers) and he flashed a ghostly smile and mumbled something I didn't understand and shortly disappeared. Later, I heard tell from J. T. Slick Rutherford that Ralph has of late been checking around to see if there's any "demand" for you—in other words, if he's hurting with Liberals if he doesn't go with you. I'd therefore increase pressures if I were you. (This is 100% true, but don't let Slick or Ralph know I told you that Slick told me that. Slick swore me to secrecy on it: carrying tales, etc. But it *is* true.)**

Let's get together and praise ourselves, the Democratic Party and God during July 5th-9th. . . .

*Senator Ralph Yarborough.
**Legg, a long-time Yarborough loyalist, hoped to be appointed to a Federal Judgeship, but Senator Yarborough repeatedly chose someone else.

June 10, 1966

Dear Lanvil:

John Kenneth Galbraith's letter, addressed to me, finally got here after going through NAL and my agent, and I thought you'd like to have the full text for the record. Hence:

"Dear Mr. King:

You are probably waiting with some interest for the first returns. For what it may be worth, I think you are in. If it will recruit any customers, which is doubtful, you can let your publisher say that I said: 'It is the best political novel since *The Last Hurrah*.'

Congratulations and for God's sake, remember that it is the *second* novel that separates the men from the Drurys.

> Yours faithfully,
> John Kenneth Galbraith

P. S. The breaking of Stanley Dutton is a small masterpiece.

> J.K.G."

The Lord Giveth, and The Lord taketh away: he wrote a green ink postscript: "The love interest is *terrible*—how wise you were to keep it brief!"

He Giveth, however, more than He Taketh.

Rushed. Sent Billy Graham book review off to *Book Week* today. Will mail copy when in print. *NY Times* Ad due re: quotes from Galbraith and others on either June 19th or 26th or had I said that?

June 10, 1966

Dear Sterling:

Your bookkeeper has done you a signal service, and me a dirty deal, in finding that your generosity toward me extended $180.00 past our pact. We are both surprised, though yours was the most pleasant.

The point is, I don't have $180.00 right now. In fact, I have begged of Willie and Bob advances on future work (Willie on a piece he has in house or some future work) and Bob on the second novel, because I am so desperate for money what with my kids here, quarterly taxes due, and so forth. Could you find it in your heart and pocketbook to carefully extract the $180.00 a few bucks at a time until we get some meaningful money from some source lurking off out there in The Future? I will be grateful if you can. . . .

Abilene, Texas
(On-the-road)
July 10, 1966

Mr. David Halberstam
The New York Times
37. Rue Caumartin
Paris, France

Dear Mister Hoot:

There you are in Paris, France, threshing out your passions with your lovely moom-pitcher star wife and drinking white wine and speaking, no doubt, in foreign tongues. And here I am in Abilene, Texas, where the Baptists, Methodists, and Cambellites play, and it is Sunday night—a circumstance by which The Law deems it improper to sell beer or liquor or wine even to thirsty wayfarers with beards. And Holiday Inn has the sheer gall to bill itself as "America's Innkeeper."

Why I am in Abilene has to do with Book Promotion. Book Promotion is the nearest thang we got left in this Wunnerful Country of Ours to debtors' prison. Or maybe to The Rack. Anyway, I am out here with my pretty Greek wife (you may not know about that: happened February 20th, 19-and-65—which goes to show you that if you can marry a Pole I can marry a Greek, and serves to prove Joos can't get too far ahead of us White Trash) On the Road just like Jack Kerouac (except I don't have any pot). Book promoting all over Hell and Texas and Mississippi this swing. NAL's publicity people are Geniuses. They send me to John Birch Country to promote a book that calls for Brotherhood of Man in its special wacky way. We will not sell enough to pay for the gas.

You say if I see Bill Brammer tell him hello. There are millions wanting to tell him much more than that, only nobody can find him. He has disappeared into Texas Limbo again, after having conned NAL (with my help) into buying him out from Hootin'-Mifflin' and, of course, without writing a single one of the many lines he pledged to write if they would buy him. He has got his parents trained so that they will not admit knowing his whereabouts, nor even admit blood kin with him. One of these days when the Sheriff is gaining on him fast he'll pop out of the toolie bushes all goggley-eyed and abstracted and wanting to borrow $5 and to be hid-out. And of course I will loan him the $5, even if I have to borrow it, and will hide him out. . . .

Austin, Texas
Saturday night
July 16, 1966

Mr. Bob Gutwillig
NAL

Dear Northern Friend:
Thomas Wolfe was right.
Well, we have been out in the hot sun a lot and under the TV lights and have spoken well of ourselves and our product, and I personally shall whoop with joy when we cross the Potomac going North. The first person who showed up at an autograph party in Odessa, Texas, was a bank official come to seek satisfaction on an ancient $300 note I had conveniently forgotten. He got a lot of vague promises and the bum's rush. Then one day on TV I shared a 15-minute show with a doctor who specializes in female sex organs, and he talked a whole lot about bleeding uteruses, which made him a hard act to follow. And in Midland-Odessa where the last celebrity in town was Will Rogers' mother who visited in the 1920s, Dean Martin was playing in the Pro-Am Golf Tournament and attracting 4,000 folks per day and getting all the TV, radio and newspaper space. Then here in Austin, two hours after I checked in, the switchboard said a man name of Cal Thornton was trying to get in touch with me, and I got him back, at which point he said: "Mr. King, I'm sorry but that girl can't go. She said she's too busy all this week and she just can't date you." Whereupon I said, "Well, that is a blessing in disguise, for my wife is here by my side and wondering what the hell is going on, and I would like to go on record as saying I love her very much." Turned out he was calling *John* King. (Gasp! Choke! Shudder!)

. . . The Holiday Inn sign ("Have You Read *The One-Eyed Man?*") has been put up at all stops and has caused considerable commotion and word-of-mouth comment. My own good wife thought of the gimmick the day we checked into the Holiday Inn in Midland, promising the Midland manager that we'd stay at Holiday Inns all along the tour if he would guarantee the signs. The pact was signed, and so thousands of weary travelers have seen it and have wondered, no doubt, what the hell is going on. Reckon Publicity could get one a few paragraphs in *Publishers Weekly* or some place? I myself am gonna do a little blurb and send pix to the Holiday Inn magazine, which is left in all the rooms all over this wunnerful country of ours. . . .*

*The Holiday Inn magazine did run a short piece with photographs.

July 24, 1966

Mr. Jay Milner,
7140 Richland Road,
Fort Worth, Texas

Dear Jay:

Your welcome and funny and interesting letter reached me by round-about route in Austin, Texas—two days after I had left Fort Worth. I had made inquiries about your whereabouts, but nobody would admit knowing it.

Made a "swang" through Texas for more than two weeks, bragging on myself in such Eden-spots as Midland, Odessa, Abilene, Ft. Worth, Dallas, Austin, and Houston. Got a right smart ink, TV, and radio time. Even spent a delightful 24-hours in your old stomping grounds of Greenville, Miss., getting drunk with old friends of yours including Hodding Carter III. Sold about 50 books in Greenville, which astonished and pleased me. The attached ad carries an old quote from your two-year old *Star-Telegram* story, which I had filched for promotional purposes.

Reviews of the book have been good—everywhere but in Texas and in *Book Week*. Running something like 27 to 3 in our favor at last

count (counting the *Observer*'s Dave Hickey and A. C. Greene of
Dallas Times-Herald as two of the three chicken shits) though the *N.Y.
Times* dismissed me today in about 20 lines that didn't say much other
than to fault me for writing of an incident that is "too old" to be inter-
esting—which seems strange, considering that M. Mitchell did *Gone
With The Wind* a few months after the Civil War in, I think, 1936.
Fuck The Critics! . . . .

I really do 'preciate all your kind thangs said re my work during the
past year. I have been right fortunate in placing pieces everywhere.
Example: I was in Austin, forlorn and all hung up about Money, when
out of the clear blue comes a telegram from my agent saying that
Playboy had just bought a piece I did a year ago called "Life Among
The Super Americans"—and at a handsome fee—which had been
kicking around magazine offices for months and months without anybody offering even to publish it free. (It was so old and hopeless a case
that I had even forgotten about the damn piece!). Then *Harper's* just
bought two more from me. Then I have another assignment from
them to do a piece on William A. Buckley, and tomorrow I leave to
go to Carlisle, Pa., and do a piece for *Sat. Eve. Post* on Ollie Matson of
the Philadelphia Eagles. Also, *SEP* has asked me to write one of those
"Speaking Out" dissenter-type thangs in the front of their book, and
a fairly new mag called *The Washingtonian* is bugging me to do work,
and so maybe we will not starve plumb to death during the current
calendar year. . . .

Let's talk about that great and good man Jay Milner for awhile.
After you disappeared into the night with my pennies, where did you
go?* I hit Texas a few weeks later, telephoned the *Star-Telegram* and
asked for you. After a long silence I was advised that you had mysteriously not shown to take the job you had when you left here. Later
on, somebody (I forgot who) defamed you by saying you met a sweet
girl on the Greyhound and she taken you to Tulsa, Oklahoma, and
was keeping you for a house pet. Though I could not check on the
story, it made such a good one that I told it as Pure Truth to every solitary SOB since encountered. . . .

Heard tell one Edwin (Bud) Schmuck** was to be in Houston

about mid-week as I was leaving for Greenville. Tried to find him, but to no avail. Just as well, perhaps. Might not have got to Greenville at all, if I had. He is a very bad influence on young, Christian, American boys.

I got a hunnert damn letters to write after the road show I just came offn, and before I hit the trail again tomorrow. Do drop other missives this way. And *don't* disappear into Limbo again without letting your old friends, protectors, and benefactors know your whereabouts: I listed you as a dependent on my last tax return, and if they challenge it I'll need your affidavit. (You can claim me next year.) . . . .

*King's wife, as a joke, had given Milner a milk bottle full of pennies as "mad money" when Milner left Washington allegedly to take a job at the *Fort Worth Star-Telegram.*
**Bud Shrake.

August 15, 1966

Mr. Dan Blocker,
c/o Herb Gold,
9034 Sunset Blvd.,
Los Angeles, California

Dear Dan:

I have been intending to write you since I was recently in Odessa and saw Lev Davis at a party Warren Burnett gave me in connection with my promotional tour. Late in the evening, with drink in the air and tongues thicker than milkshakes alone can make them, Lev began to bug me about some ancient conversation we had in 1960. He seemed to be saying that I had once told him that I "didn't gave a damn" whether Nixon or Kennedy won the election and he volunteered that he had told you and you commented that "you could hardly believe" I had said such a thing. You are right. By prodding both Lev and my memory, I finally recalled the conversation and the point I tried to make: that from the working [Democrat] politician's *practical* standpoint, it would be "better" for Nixon to win than Kennedy looked at in purely selfish terms. Because as "outs" we could damn the

Republican "ins" and blame all things that went wrong on them. But that as "ins" (should Kennedy win) we'd be responsible to a conservative West Texas constituency for everything from a Liberal Administration to getting jobs for the homefolks. But—I added—But, we can't play the game that way and we're out here hustling for Kennedy to win, etc. Apparently some of the finer points evaded Lev (not surprising, since it occurred in a bar at a late hour) and I've been vaguely uncomfortable ever since he mentioned it. Ok, the record's clear—and I still have enough political instincts to fret over the record. . . .

Drop a line when you aren't shitkicking in front of the cameras, riding in parades, or opening supermarkets. Let's start us a union and lobby against Promotions unless we get a cut of the action for ourselves. . . .

August 15, 1966

Dear Sterling:

The thing did not go extremely well with Gutwillig. As I surmised (and you verified) he wasn't really receptive to spending much more money on *The One-Eyed Man*. He did agree to buy another ad in October *Harper's*, but that's about it. (Showed me figures that they've spent over $8,000 in ads already, though they were not itemized too much and I accepted them more or less on faith.) According to his figures (and he let me see the reports) the book has sold 7,510 copies— good enough for 4th on list of 20 NAL Spring and Summer books. Topped by *Octopussy, White House Nannie, The Door Fell Shut.* I'll probably pass the latter, Bob says, at the current rate. He anticipates sale of around 13,500—said they'd had a second printing (small, I think 1,500 copies.)

He mentioned doing my book of articles but volunteered that he "wasn't extremely enthusiastic about it," adding that "books like that won't sell much—it just might be something we'd like to do between novels." I said I wasn't too enthusiastic about it either, adding casually: "A couple of other houses seem a bit more enthusiastic than either of us about it, though." He looked right shocked and said, "You can't go changing *publishers* on me." I said, "Well, nothing's really set. I haven't talked about it much." He said, "Well, don't. It's a horseshit idea." I said, "The other two houses don't think so." We sparred awhile and I finally said, "We don't have a contractural obligation with anybody for such a book," and that I'd prefer to wait "and see what happens." He grunted and changed the subject, and we left it right there. As I said to you, I'm inclined to do a book like that at a more conventional (read "old-line") hardback house, and it may be that I'll talk with Willie (who approached me for Harper & Row) about it before long. . . .

<hr />

August 25, 1966

Dear Sterling:

Thanks for your report from Gutwillig. Turns out they've spent about $1500 less than he had indicated to me from what he called "educated estimates," but at this juncture I don't feel capable of too much emotion either way. I do think if the LBJ piece stirs 'em up we should push for some new promotional effort, but will adopt a wait-and-see attitude.

A letter from Willie Morris recently said, "Evan Thomas, one of the big men at Harper & Row, read the piece and is most enthusiastic about it. He wants to have lunch with you next time you're here, and is interested in doing the book." He means, of course, the LBJ piece, and he means a book of my essays and articles. Then yesterday I talked with Willie by phone. He said Thomas is "most enthusiastic" again, and has inquired if I'll be in N.Y. any time soon. It turns out that I will. Next week I'll be in Philadelphia, and am thinking of driving to N.Y. one day. If I do, I think I'll have lunch with him and at least listen to what he has to say. Frankly, I figure that if we try to take the book to H&R our friend Gutwillig will be testy to deal with, and I'd want to talk the whole thing over with you very carefully before making any final decision. . . .

About three days ago Willie Morris called and asked me to write the Guest column for "The Editor's Easy Chair," November issue of *Harper's*, on the subject of Texas Congressman Joe Pool. (Who came to prominence because of recent stormy HUAC hearings.) Said keep it to 3,000 to 3,500 words. Pay $500. (Willie claims that $200 over normal for that column when guested.) I agreed. Deadline is Monday. I've turned to and have been working on it. In our talk yesterday, I told him [Willie] that in keeping with my usual operation the damn piece is running much longer. He said go ahead and try for the deadline (I can make it, just barely) and don't worry about the length. If it's too long, he said, he'll use it in November as an article—at, of course, a higher rate than the $500. So when he lets me know where they intend to use it, you can bug him for money. . . .

I also must get that lobby piece out for *N.Y. Times Magazine* within the next month. I think I told you they'll pay $400. Will advise when it is in. And, oh yes: after all that's done, I want to do the "Speaking Out" thing for *Sat. Eve. Post.* You'll recall they mentioned, I think, $1,500 (or you said that's the minimum they pay, I believe). Anyway, they want a suggested item (in the nature of "dissent") or topic we can agree on. Any suggestions from your department as to something I might "dissent" about? Been so busy I haven't thought of it much. . . .*

*The *Saturday Evening Post* article appeared as "Congress Is Hypocritical," pointing out that it's members exempt themselves from many laws applied to other citizens.

September 28, 1966

Dear Lanvil & Glenda:

A story. . . . I was sitting in the Congressional Hotel bar this afternoon with Willie Morris and one James Dickey, who is Poet-in-Residence at the Library of Congress and who also won the National Book Award for Poetry this year. We had talked at some length of writers and writing: Styron, Larry McMurtry, Warren, Welty, William Humphrey, Ralph Ellison (whom Dickey had left just before joining us) Twain, Baldwin, you name it. We had talked about the Academic

Life (or *they* had—I wisely kept my Cotton Patch University mouth shut), Jewish Intellectuals, all manner of Uplifting Things. Soon Rosemarie joined us, and then Ed Martin, a young man who directs the Subcommittee where RM works. I offered the intelligence that Ed Martin had taught at the University of Alabama (Poet Dickey having taught Almost Everywhere), at which point the following conversation ensued:

Dickey: "Do you know Howard Such-and-So at Alabama?"

Martin: "Oh, yes. I know him very well. Quite a dapper old gentleman."

"He," said the Poet-of-the-Year, "is an asshole."

End of story. . . .*

*Four or five years later, King and Dickey had a fistfight while drinking at a Chicago hotel bar during *Playboy's* writers convocation. Two hours later, King came upon Dickey choking novelist Michael Crichton in a *Playboy* hospitality suite. King pulled Dickey off Crichton amidst profane shouts, later referring to these skirmishes as "intellectual discussions complicated by fermented grapes."

October 5, 1966

The Reagan Leggs
902 Country Club Drive
Midland, Texas

Dear Friends:

In case you have not been to Walgreen's, you should know that October's *Harper's* with my latest slander on the President of the United States is now offered for public sale. Jack Fischer of the magazine was talking to Harry McPhearson of the White House a couple of days ago, and McPhearson made some grumbling reference to the piece. Fischer asked if the President had read my article. "Yes," McPhearson responded, "I saw him reading it." Fischer asked what the President had said. McPhearson: "Nothing, yet. But he smiled in a grim sort of way."*

We've reached accord on my collection of pieces to be put in book form. Be out in the Spring. I am writing some new material to go with it. Don't have a title yet. I wanted "Something Old, Something New" but the publishers, saying that collections generally don't sell too well, want to hide from the public the fact that it is a collection. I then suggested "Not A Collection" as a title, but they got mad and went home to New York City. . . .

* Later King would learn that LBJ branded his article a "damned dirty story."

November 25 (I think), 1966
Friday midnight

Dear Lanvil & Glenda:

I have not forgotten my benefactors of long standing, but have simply been swamped with work. Thus my long and uncharacteristically silent period.

To recap: have recently done two reviews for *The New Republic*. Turned in 177 pages toward my new book, the non-fiction, within the last two weeks. It has been going very well and Gutwillig thinks its very funny stuff. Have just finished almost two weeks in New York (actually, four days once and five days once in that period) on the Buckley article for February *Harper's*. Deadline five days away and I am fighting to make it. No doubt I will. By December 12th must complete a book review for *Book Week*. Coming to Arkansas and Texas around December 5th on one story for *Saturday Evening Post* and two more for *Harper's*. Stalling *True* on an assignment right now because I am busy and want a better topic (lobbying) than they offer. Other than guesting for 50 minutes on one Washington radio show recently, an hour fifteen on another, appearing three times on a Canadian Broadcasting Company hour-long special on Washington, and having consented to be interviewed by *The Times* of London about Texas, LBJ, and oil tycoons I have simply frittered away my free time. Yes, it is action and you can't hardly get it in children's ready to wear, as Bruce Jay Friedman wrote, and I love it.

I got a big thrill in New York when I was introduced to Jules Feiffer and Alfred Kazin, and they knew of my work. Also met, talked, or drank with Norman Mailer, George Plimpton (went to a party at his house), Michael Harrington, Murray Kempton, and Irving Howe. And, oh yes, Terry Southern, and not knowing who he was I told him he was full of shit with respect to a political announcement he had made and he went off in the corner and sulked the balance of the evening. Went to one posh party at which Rose Styron appeared but Bill did not. Also worked in a fair amount of juicing with such old friends as Willie Morris, Gutwillig, Bud Shrake, and Dick Schaap. Met a lot of actors and actresses but forget their names. . . .

Maintaining my reputation as World's Leading Critic of Non-Book Books, I have just reviewed for *Book Week The Wallace Story*, as written by George Wallace's former press secretary. I haven't any idea when it will run. I am proud of the lead: "Alabama's George Wallace, who has been a Southern Governor and soon is to be the husband of one. . . ."

November 30, 1966

Mr. Willie Morris
Harper's Magazine

Willie:

Thanks for offering more time on the Buckley piece in your letter arriving today; however, I "relinquish the balance of my time," as Congressmen say when trying to gain points with The Speaker. The article is finished, I am very well satisfied with it, and it will go out in the mail under separate cover about one hour behind this. It is as long as a death-bed scene where Bette Davis is the die-ee, but like her melancholy oration I think it blurts some awful truths. I hope you like it as much as I think you will.

Am hopeful, too, that Jack Fischer will believe it worth the coin I now have on my due books to *Harper's*. Incidentally, when I saw him he said he'd get a $100 check down toward expenses on my Texas stories. Would you see that it gets on the way, by checking with him as a reminder?

I'm leaving here Saturday for Texas and Arkansas in connection with the two stories for *Harper's* (oil worker, minor league football) and for *SEP* re: the Brazilian dope cats. . . .

December 27, 1966

Mr. Bob Gutwillig
New American Library

Dear Sweetie Pie:

Now that the tinsel glitter of Christmas is gone with all its vulgarities (John Wayne as a Roman Soldier crying in the shadow of The Cross, Broderick Crawford as Santa Claus, Truman Capote as the Yuletide Fairy) let me wish you a heart-felt Bah Humbug and the same throughout the coming New Year.

I arrived back from my Texas sojourn just in time to spoil the holiday season for everybody in the nation's capitol, kicking newsboys around like so many Tiny Tims and merrily shouting seasonal threats to my immediate wife. My mother gave me the usual socks for Christmas and the IRS presented me with a gift certificate in their favor for yet another batch of back taxes. Which leads me to the point that I have messaged one S. Lord to fire over our contract for the *Dirty Book* to you and extract as quickly as possible the pittance you are to pay in return for all that raw talent. Please do hurry. . . .

December 27, 1966

Mr. Robert A. Gutwillig
New American Library

Sir:

Having read the December 6th issue of the *New Leader* I am reminded of the old saw about the swain who, visiting a house of ill repute, attempted to give a personal cheque to the lady of his yearnings in exchange for her favors. "Hunny," she said, "I got me an agreement with the First National Bank—if I won't cash no checks, they won't sell no pussy." If you won't write no more articles I won't edit no books, fair enough?

It was real delightful, and enjoyable, and you done good and even had the courage to admit you didn't buy two best sellers offered cheap. I thank you for not foot-noting that you *did,* conversely buy, *The One-Eyed Man.*

I feel cheated, however, in that I paid forty cents for the magazine and you finished the yarn in a foreign language. I have polled the neighborhood to find out what "Plus ca change, plus c'est la meme chose" means, and report the following results:

All The Way With LBJ	3%
I Shall Fight It Out On This Line If It Takes All Summer	1%
The Third Reich Will Endure A Thousand Years	16%
Let 'Em Eat Cake	12%
Remember Pearl Harbor	22%
In Your Heart You Know He's Right	4%
Opposed	38%
Undecided or Don't Know	5%
Rather Not Say	1%
Lucky Strike Green Has Gone to War	1%

Yours in Christ,

———————————

December 29, 1966

Dear Sterling:

Willie Morris called last night and we discussed the money and expense situation. It was determined that we could best handle the Buckley expenses through a letter to Jack Fischer, a copy of which is

enclosed. For what might be termed political reasons, you will make
no mention in that letter of my having talked to Willie. I think this
best.

There is little I can say and nothing I can write re the situation
over there [at *Harper's*]. Suffice to say that these past expenses shall
be held in abeyance for a few months, and it is better not to mention
them until that time. At that point I think we can pretty much call
our own shots.*

In the meantime, however, I have reached the private decision to
accept no more work from *Harper's* after I finish the two stories I am
doing for them now. They have a backlog of two of my articles
(Popcorn Bay and a piece on why Dallas is such a terrible place).
Since I've got to depend for the next several months on finding work
outside the *Harper's* pages I therefore ask, beg, and implore that you
give special thought to selling me to *SEP, True, Life,* or some of the
better-paying publications. . . .

It was necessary for me to bring my teenage daughter back from
Texas with me, and put her in a private school. That lick ran $1,000
for tuition, and as I mentioned a few days ago the IRS folks are clamoring for several hundred in taxes resulting from an audit of tax year
1963. In short, we must fight the wolf away from the door with night-
sticks and .45's for the next few months, and I shall appreciate any
aggressive selling job on me that you can do.

*This was a guarded reference to Willie Morris soon taking over from Jack
Fischer as editor-in-chief, which did occur in the spring of 1967.

4

Riding High at *Harper's*

The exuberant success of *Harper's* magazine under the editorship of Willie Morris was the high point of an unusually rich period in American journalism and essay writing. During the 1960s, many of the political and cultural issues that held America in a gripping tension were played out in the pages of its monthly magazines and quarterly journals. Long essays on Vietnam and civil rights and violence American-style could be found alongside reviews of New Wave cinema, profiles of Muhammad Ali, and learned analyses of the lyrics of Bob Dylan and the compositional strategies at play in *Sergeant Pepper*. *Esquire* led the "New Journalism" with the writers Gay Talese and Tom Wolfe and gave American magazines a new look—a Christmas cover that featured a glowering Sonny Liston dressed as Santa Claus typified their eagerness to shock.

In his 1993 memoir *New York Days*, Willie Morris delineates the transformation of *Harper's* from a somewhat stodgy, family-owned magazine to the journal of ideas that everyone read. The writers he brought to the magazine included Elizabeth Hardwick, Truman Capote, George Plimpton, Irving Howe, Alfred Kazin, Robert Penn Warren, Ralph Ellison, Philip Roth, and Walker Percy. Most memorable, perhaps, were the special issues of the magazine: one that featured Norman Mailer's 90,000-word essay titled "On the Steps of the Pentagon" (which won a Pulitzer Prize for Mailer when it was published in book form as *The Armies of the Night*); the other featuring a lengthy excerpt from William Styron's 1968 sensation, *The Confessions of Nat Turner*.

Willie Morris's vivid descriptions of the tumult of talent present in 1960s New York make it clear that while the high profile names attracted attention to *Harper's,* what held the magazine together were its four young contributing editors: John Corry, Marshall Frady, David Halberstam, and Larry L. King—described by Morris as "a burly, bearded Texan, with a hardy and questing eye, the only dropout I ever knew from Texas Technological University" *(New York Days)*. During Morris's tenure as editor-in-chief, from 1967 to 1971, all four rose to national prominence. It was natural that Larry King began his years with Willie writing about politics.

When King's first *Harper's* piece appeared in January, 1965, Morris had influence on the magazine but the helm was still firmly in the hands of Jack Fischer, who had guided the venerable publication for many years. In "Washington's Second Banana Politicians," King described his life and those of his fellow administrative assistants in congress, attracting an immediate unsolicited fan letter from none other than Harvard's John Kenneth Galbraith, whose note to the magazine said: "I haven't enjoyed anything by anybody so much in years." King's first cover story was the memorable "My Hero LBJ" that told the tale of his foolhardy bravery in standing up to Johnson on the campaign trail.

"My Hero LBJ" combined politics and autobiography, and after it appeared King had a nationwide following in the pages of *Harper's.* By the beginning of 1967 there was already talk about NAL and Bob Gutwillig publishing a collection of King's magazine pieces. It was published in 1968 under the title *. . . And Other Dirty Stories,* but the editors, without consulting King, omitted the first part of the title, *My Hero LBJ,* feeling that would be "piling on" after President Johnson had just announced that he would not run for re-election. The collection brought together the cream of his *Harper's* pieces to date, "Requiem for a West Texas Town," the LBJ piece, and his memorable profiles of Texas Congressman Joe Pool, *National Review* editor William F. Buckley, and the inimitable Louis Armstrong. Added for the book were his profile of Sugar Ray Robinson done for *Sports Illustrated,* his report on literary New York for the *Texas Observer* titled "Making the Scene at Mailer's," and a couple of bookend autobiographical pieces, "Confessions of an Obscure Famous Arthur" and "The Obscure Famous Arthur Grows Older." Across from the title page was a list, customary in new books by established writers, of previous works produced—OTHER BOOKS by Larry L. King: *Crime and Punishment, Huckleberry Finn, A Tale of Two Cities, The Deerslayer, An American Tragedy, The One-Eyed Man*, Winesburg, Ohio, Hamlet, For Whom the Bell Tolls, You Can't Go Home Again, The Great Gatsby, The Book of Job, Dr. Zhivago* *Especially recommended.

The ebullient spirit reflected in the book continued in King's remaining work for *Harper's,* four year's worth. Wille Morris was a gifted talent scout, and his gamble on King as a teller of stories on paper had paid off in spades. He had assembled a superb staff at the magazine who knew they were doing important work for a great editor. As editor-in-chief Morris not only formally added Halberstam, Frady, Corry and King to the staff at salaried positions, he also brought in Robert Kotlowitz as managing editor and Texas A&M graduate Herman Gollob to head a new book publishing wing, Harper's Magazine Press. Only *Esquire* rivaled *Harper's* in stylish content, and only the serious journals such as Norman Podhoretz' *Commentary* and the young *New York Review of Books* rivaled Morris's range and intellectual commitment in treating important topics.

Although still based in Washington, King made his mark as a

major-league New York City carousel. Often accompanied by fellow Texas expatriates Dan Jenkins and Bud Shrake, who wrote for *Sports Illustrated*, King held down a regular table at Elaine's, an East Side literary watering hole presided over by the gruff owner, Elaine Kaufman. Among other regulars that might include Norman Mailer, William Styron, David Halberstam, Jack Richardson, Gay Talese and George Plimpton, King led the way in the revels, a six-foot-one West Texas wild man, half profane and half speaking the language of Jeremiah. Although ten years later he had become—in his own words—"about two-thirds rich" from the proceeds of *The Best Little Whorehouse in Texas*, nothing matched the professional satisfaction and camaraderie of the heyday of Willie Morris's *Harper's*.

Although his status as a *Harper's* contributing editor ("not one of us edited so much as an expense account") guaranteed a stable income, King had a family in West Texas to support as well as a seriously ill wife. Recognizing the exigencies of the freelance life, King still scrabbled for magazine assignments. Although he was now attending parties with the elite of literary New York, he welcomed his anonymous $300 book review gigs with *Time* as well as the $100 rate paid him by Irving Howe's *Dissent*.

By the beginning of 1969, King was exhausted with the freelance life, and when Willie mentioned to him applying for a prestigious Nieman Fellowship to attend Harvard for a year, he was interested. More aware than anyone of his educational shortcomings as a double dropout from both Midland High School and Texas Tech, King nonetheless applied to Harvard based on his sterling publishing record and his splendid references. His letter to *Harper's* publisher John Cowles early in 1969 confronts head-on the primary structural roadblock to the fellowship: the fact that he had just turned forty, the Nieman committee's cutoff year.

After he won one of the Nieman spots, Larry and Rosemarie moved to Cambridge in August 1969 just in time for the most combustable year in the twentieth-century history of the university. King was a forty-year-old grandfather and a natural leader among Harvard's 1969/1970 Nieman fellows. Perhaps because of the times

this particular class of Nieman fellows were a little wilder and wooli-
er than most, and perhaps it was because of King, who led something
of a revolt from a spot at a Cambridge institution called the King's
Men's Bar. Ironically, it was Dwight Sargent, a good friend and former
colleague of King's Fort Worth friend Jay Milner, who incurred the
brunt of King's criticism of the program. Sargent was the Nieman
curator, and as such planned all of the activities for the group, particularly social events on campus and outside speakers. Soon restive with
Sargent's safe programs and dull gatherings, King began to plan campus appearances by his New York writer friends, memorably Willie
Morris, William Styron and Norman Mailer. Among the bright students that King got to know were Jim Fallows and Frank Rich, both
of whom were big men in campus journalism.

In the fall 1970 *Harper's* published his account of his year on the
Harvard campus. This was a cover story and the inside contributor's
page featured a photograph of King arrayed in full academic cap and
gown, studiously examining a copy of *The National Informer* whose
cover story read, "I Grooved In Bed With My Sex Dummy."

— Richard Holland

January 10, 1967

Mr. Willie Morris
Executive Editor
Harper's

Dear Willie:

Went to a $25 per person "Appreciation Dinner" for—hold on to
your hat—Joe Pool last night. Seriously. (No dinner: it was just a
drinking match at the Demo Club where my book party was held.) A
few nights ago, I was sitting in the Rotunda with Bob Gutwillig, when
out of the haze this fat hand grabs my arm and a voice sez, "Larry, Yew
old liberal thang, yew. I read that piece you done about me."*

"Joe!" I said. (Clasping him to my breast.) "Well, did you like it?"

"Only one thang I didn't like about it," he said. "That was when you said how quick and easy I am with mah money when it comes to pickin' up bar checks. Hail, I got too many Baptists to get that kinda story goin' around. Let me buy you boys a drank!"

Gutwillig is dying laughing. Joe doesn't know why.

So Joe buys a drink and then gives me a free ticket to his $25. "thang" last night; exits, beaming. Gutwillig whoops and hollars "Fantastic! Can you believe that son-of-a-bitch?"

Last night I entered the room after Joe's "thang" was in full sway (had been to an earlier, staider one that Raff Yarborough gave for Bob Eckhardt) and several people looked at me as if they cannot believe I'd have the guts to show at a party of Joe's "Appreciators." (One fella, in fact, asked me how I had the guts to show, and I said I had come to pay my respects because Congressman Pool had just appointed my Daddy as Postmaster and he left with his jaw hanging). Joe spotted me as we came in, grabbed my hand, yelled "Ah, my favorite arthur!" and went into spasms of mirth. I was damn near the last to leave. Drank $25 worth of Scotch, I know.

Life's funny, sometimes. . . .

    *"Congressman Joe Pool: McCarthy in the Round" had just been published in *Harper's*, expressing "minimal high regard" (House Speaker John McCormick's phrase) for Pool.

February 10, 1967

Dear Warren, Emma, and Precious Children:

. . . . Have been getting so much work I have trouble doing it all. Got final agreement with *Harper's* last week in meeting with John Cowles (*Look*, Minneapolis Tribune family) and Executive Editor Willie Morris to do five pieces, plus liberal travel expenses, annually at the most money they've ever paid anybody.* Also agreed to do book reviews for *Time*. First one out next week on Elia Kazan's *The Arrangement*. Following week I'm doing a first novel, *Applesauce*, for them. They want me to do at least 20 a year. Guess I will. The money's good and I don't have to sign my name to them, thus doing the necessary gut-shooting from ambush. Shot Kazan dead, if not in the back. Didn't want to: combination of bad book and my high personal integrity. . . .

*King later learned that John Corry and David Halberstam had both joined the *Harper's* staff at a higher rate, despite earlier representations.

[April, 1967]

Dear Warren and Emma:

A few quick lines before I am off for Yazoo City, Mississippi, for a week. Now, this is well known neither as a vacation resort nor as a Free Thinking Community; nonetheless I am going there in the company of Willie Morris, editor of *Harper's*, Norman Podhoretz, editor of *Commentary* and Ralph Hutto, A.A. to Senator James O. Eastland, whom we are taking along to insure our safe passage. The deal is similar to yours at Austinville [Va.] a year or so ago: Willie, as a Local Boy Made Good, is being invited back to address his old school's student body. He wanted company, touted me and Podhoretz (a Jew from New York who has never been South at all) to go with him, and I, in turn, was smart enough to enroll Eastland's man for the trip. Hodding Carter III is coming up from Greenville to meet us and throw us a big-do party, and we are going to loll around Mississippi for several days and eye it with our writers' eyes. Eastland's man is a nice fellow but an Innocent of sorts: he will have much explaining to do to Senator Jim and the constituency, no doubt, ere our conduct evaluations and our writings are o'er.

Miss Rosemarie and I returned yesterday from a week on the beach at Ocean View, Delaware, where the temperature was just below freezing all week. Upon my return from Mississippi we are going there for another two or three weeks. We've had the loan of a beautiful beach house up there, owned by the columnist Robert Novak. Novak is currently on a European swing of six weeks and we are living like rich folks at his expense. It's 80-odd here today, but all last week it was very cold and the Atlantic Ocean, which roars up the back door (the beach house sits up on pilings so high one feels like one is working the midnight tower on an Ector County rig) was boisterous and loud and sounded very threatening to a desert-type who has never lived in a house stuck out in the Ocean (at high tide, anyway).

I am in receipt of a clipping from the [weekly] *Midland Flare* showing Miss Joy Billington of the *London Times and Telegraph* (London, England, the Midland paper stressed, as if fearing the readers might think it was London, Ireland or London, Japan, or New London, Texas) interviewing on the front porch of 1010 North Whitaker one Clyde King, said Clyde King in khaki clothes and with his collar buttoned tight against the weather or some other menace unknown, and his eyes, it looks to me like, right on Miss Billington's hem-line, which had somehow wormed its way up to a startling (for Clyde King, anyway) patch of flesh. They (my parents) fed her fried chicken and were as nice as they knew how to be and, of course, fretted that they would not tell her the right things. I shall endeavor to see that she sends us copies of all she wrote about Texas and Texans. . . .

April 26, 1967

Mr. Robert Gutwillig
New American Library

Dear Sister George:

I am safely returned from Mississippi, though not without incident, and ask the musical question "Have you ever seen Norman Podhoretz in a Delta cotton patch?"

Tomorrow we are going back up to the Novak cottage in not-so-sunny Delaware, there to finish up the non-fiction book for you. The whole shooting match will be done and in your hands within two weeks. Unless you have sneaked in some fine print, I read the contract that you will owe me a paltry $2,000 upon completion. My entire fortune right now is considerably less paltry than that amount, and a summer in Texas awaits demanding cash-in-hand. The purpose of this letter is to inspire you to begin, without delay, the complicated process of getting my check run through its various machines and computers in the hope that it will be ready to send to me when you have received the final copy. Do not run off to Oshkosh without taking care of this if you value my life.

One Dick Schaap was a guest in my Christian home last evening. I taught him the Lord's Prayer. He will make a fine minister of the Gospel, and is now waiting to hear whether his application will be accepted at Bob Jones University. He promises not to wear lipstick or listen to jazz on the radio, as BJU's leaders oppose. One day we will be mighty proud to say we knew that boy.

We had three small riots in Mississippi. If it ever gets to the point where NAL editors associate with their hard-working writers, I may tell you about it.

Last night I dreamed I was a Famous Arthur in my Maidenform Bra. . .

May 10, 1967

Dear Warren:

I returned last night from a couple of weeks at the Delaware shore to find one letter and numerous poems from Abner Burnett.* At the hazard of betraying some vague confidence, and feeling sneaky about it, I am enclosing his letter for your perusal—possibly out of some misguided sense of brotherhood in the Union of Parents. (I don't care what the hippies say, there *is* a generation gap: it is Us vs. Them. Hooray for Us.)

Abner has asked me to criticize his poetry. This is a delicate thing: I hate to confess to the boy that I do not know Poet A from Poet B, that I write no poetry and, really, have read damn little of it in my time. Personally, my taste in poetry runs toward limerick land: "There once was a lady in France," and so forth. We were large on such "poems" in the public schools of Putnam and Midland, Texas and even Jal, New Mexico but we did not put as much stock in The

Masters. I am being asked to critique a painting without knowing its colors and damn little English.

I do note that Abner is a "ness" man: blindness, gladness, oneness, starkness, likeness, stillness, nothingness, even birdness. He is also fond of the words vomit or vomited. He speaks of nonsense around him. (This shows he is smart.) He cannot spell cat, though perhaps this is a strange complaint coming from me. He writes lovingly of nature and objects, and rather disparaging of himself and other human clay. He is just about the right amount of Dramatic for a fourteen year old boy with literate reflexes.

Willie Morris tells me the big announcement of my association with *Harper's* as a Contributing Editor, his own elevation to Editor-in-Chief, and other internal shifts at the publication, will be made public early next week in the *New York Times* and possibly in *Newsweek*.

Finished my non-fiction book at the Delaware shore. January publication. It's pretty funny. Tomorrow I start on two stories on Capitol Hill: profile of Rep. Mendell Rivers of South Carolina for *True*; one of Senator George Murphy for *West* (of Los Angeles) and probably, on the same publication date, the same story will appear in Sunday magazine supplements in Detroit and Washington and possibly Chicago. . . .

*Burnett's teenaged son, who when grown became an attorney and took over his father's law practice.

Editor's Note: Larry King's good attorney friend Reagan Legg successfully argued before the U.S. Supreme Court on behalf of his indigent client, Mr. Marvin Clewis, gaining him a new trial in a murder case conviction upheld by lower courts. King wrote an article about the case for *The Texas Observer*.

May 10, 1967

The Reagan Leggs
902 Country Club Drive
Midland, Texas

Dear Reagan & Jean:

I cannot think of adequate congratulations in the case of Marvin Clewis v. State of Texas. The happy—but not surprising—news reached me on the shores of Delaware last week, where I was holed up finishing my non-fiction book. Talked with Warren Burnett, on the occasion of his 40th birthday, and he flashed word. Delighted, and so much appreciate your being thoughtful enough to send along the Fortas opinion.

I thought you would appreciate *not* being invited to Mississippi. This may be among the nicest things I have ever done for you. How Burnett got invited was not exactly planned. He telephoned me in Washington, found that I was in Mississippi, and telephoned to urge that I not let any natives try to teach me to swim with chains. After a few moments he spooked me enough that I demanded legal counsel, and he [and Malcolm McGregor] flew in. He was damned small help. I don't know if he told you the straight of it, but he was the Benedict Arnold of the "Morris Marauders." Each time the host or hostess wanted to fight (normally, this occurred about 3 A.M., though one short-tempered fellow began the preliminaries at his home as early as 1:25 A.M.) Burnett by actions, deep-dish Virginia honeyed fake accent, and words of flattery, disassociated himself with our group. I have little use for such summer soldiers. . . .

I'll be in Midland around June 1st, taking up the responsibilities of fatherhood for thirty days that two over-zealous West Texas lawyers and one willful West Texas judge contrived on my behalf, with possibly no more than two of the three conspirators influenced by malice. Keep the beer cold. Catch up on your rest so that you will not tell me in grumpy tones that I must leave your house at 9:15 P.M., no later. . . .

May 23, 1967
Tuesday noon

Dear Lanvil & Glenda:

Several things will never happen in this life. I will never be wholly satisfied with nature's order, Hubert Humphrey will never be President of the United States, the lamb will never lie down with the lion, and you will never fulfill your many promises to write me a letter. I know and accept each of these Absolutes in the order of reluctance corresponding to their respective listings.

Thursday we are going to New York, driving up in the A.M., the object being to attend a swank party some rich Central Park West lady is giving in honor of Willie Morris' promotion as Editor-in-Chief of *Harper's*. Friday I will dick around the city and then Friday afternoon we shall drive to Willie's country place outside Paterson to begin the Second Annual Old Country Boy's Weekend. Styron and C. Vann Woodward will repeat with me as guests; Robert Penn Warren isn't scheduled to return, I understand, and Ralph Ellison will probably substitute in his place. We shall probably return here Monday by car. I shall fly to Texas probably on Wednesday, May 31st, holing up at Warren Burnett's that afternoon and evening for a drink-n-talk session, then appearing in Midland* on Thursday, June 1st, as if I had only reached West Texas moments before.

I surmise that you saw Willie Morris' pix in both *Time* and *Newsweek* last week, in connection with the Big Elevation, and noted that yours truly was given a line of type in each article. I liked *Newsweek* calling me "a Texan with a touch of Mencken." This is a vast improvement over what William F. Buckley, Jr. called me.

Spent all last week and yesterday on Capitol Hill, readying stories on Senator George Murphy of California (as Show Biz-to-politics Original) and Rep. L. Mendell Rivers of South Carolina as war hawk, Dixie Pol, Character. The former will appear in *West* magazine in L.A., and also in Sunday supplements of papers—to date—in Washington, Chicago, Detroit, and two cities I have forgotten. I am writing it now. Rep. Rivers is for *True*. I must somehow find time to write that in Texas. I must get back to George Murphy. I left him on page five with his mouth open and in mid-sentence. Gutwillig just called. We talked forty minutes. He laughs easily.

God is love. He has got to be or he would hit Lyndon with a bolt. Evidence: yesterday's *Washington Evening Star.* Banner Headline: "Hanoi Blasted in Big U.S. Raid. City Reported Without Water and Electricity." SAIGON (AP)—"U.S. planes ignored a Communist cease-fire for Buddha's birthday today and raided Hanoi," etc. Number Two Story Headline, right by the banner story: "Johnson Appeals to Hanoi; Asks May 30 *Peace Prayers.*"

*At his parents' home.

May 24, 1967

Mr. Robert Novak
Washington, D.C.

Dear Bob:

Enclosed find $50 toward the damage we did to your nice beach cottage. I am very sorry about the fire, water damage, gas explosion, broken windows, soiled draperies, dented stove pipe, burnt formica, and plugged commodes. I feel especially bad about the second floor balcony. When you let us have the place again next year we will try not to have such rotten luck.

Really, thanks for the use of the place. It was absolutely delightful. My wife is insisting on a place like yours in the same vicinity. I cannot explain that I am a poor, struggling Artist and you are a successful, rich, powerful, all-knowing columnist, author, and adviser to kings and Presidents. Want to trade jobs?

The cheque is to cover utilities while we were up there. We made two trips, and stayed a total of 10 days. If you should find that this is not enough, let me know what the actual expense was and I'll reimburse you for the additional charges. Again our thanks, and welcome home. Doubt if I shall see you for awhile. I'm off to New York tomorrow, then to Texas for a month, and then on the road for *Harper's.* . . .

Editor's Note: King's 1967 profile of Louis Armstrong in *Harper's*, titled "Everybody's Louie," captured the life-embracing humanity of the great jazz artist. The piece threw King together with "Pops" on the road for several weeks and was the one article on Armstrong included in the program at Armstrong's memorial service.

July 12, 1967

Mr. Willie Morris
Editor-in-Chief
Harper's

Dear Willie:

I have marked this "very personal" out of a sense of protecting the sweet young things who secretary faithfully in your care, but just had to tell the story. Last night, after Louis Armstrong's show, I juiced with him in his suite until 4 A.M. and got some tremendous stories. One cannot be trimmed nor altered to make the *Harper's* scene, but I don't want it to go completely to waste:

"Man"—Louie says—"if there is one thing I try to be it is tolerant! But I can't stand *squares*—especially square chicks. Now, you get all turned on to some chick, see, and you think she's grooving with you and the next thing you know you in bed with her and all her clothes come off and you think, 'Yeah, Pops, crazy Man, everything gonna be okay.' Then you drop down and kiss a couple of inches below the navel, Man, and she sit up and cross her legs and look all bug-eyed and say in this *hysterical* voice, 'You ain't a *cocksucker* is you?' And all you can do with a square chick like that is either get up and put your britches on, or else say 'Yeah, baby, that's my bag' and get on with it. But she's already spoiled the fun."

"Pops" and I have, as you see, gotten down to the basics. . . .

July 15, 1967

Mr. Maury Maverick
114 Bellview
San Antonio, Texas

Dear Maury:

Joe Pool made the front pages here today for getting drunk, ramming into a car stopped at a stop sign, knocking it 100 feet, and spending five hours in jail. ("He told me he was a Congressman and couldn't be arrested," the arresting officer was quoted, "but he didn't sound or act like a Congressman." (Somebody should tell him that Texas Congressmen rarely do.)

I am damn discouraged over Viet Nam. Especially after the latest escalation songs coming from McNamara's Band. . . .

September 25, 1967
Annapolis, Md.

Dear Lanvil & Glenda:

The paperback of *One-Eyed Man* was pushed back from this summer to this coming January. I have seen the cover and am ashamed: two nekkid folks in hot embrace. I had, however, earlier consented to "sexing up" the cover by phone, when Gutwillig explained how competitive is the paperback field and how sexy covers will sell books better than famous names or seals announcing awards. I was not, however, prepared for all those buttocks and tits in the pictorial flesh. *My Hero LBJ and Other Dirty Stories* due in hardback come February. Literary Guild Book Club is looking at it to see if they want it, but no decision yet. I am not counting on it. I am now into another non-fiction book called *Letters Never Mailed* in which I write to various public figures. I think it will be both funny and informative and overall pretty wild. Gutwillig likes the idea; Sterling is hopeful of selling some excerpts to magazines around publication time—whenever that is. I will probably finish that book in about six months. That means its publication is a year away at best.*

Incidental information: I have finally discovered that *One-Eyed* sold 22,000 in book club copies; around 11,000 in publisher's edition. Thus the publisher has taken in almost $66,000; the book club about the same amount since they almost halved the price. I find it hard to believe that I can write a book that actually causes the great American public to spend $130,000 plus—and get such a small dab of it myself. I do not believe that royalties are high enough for the creative person. Pray on this.

We live in a new development of town houses in a semi-rural area of Annapolis, about two miles from downtown.** We are temporarily in this one, while our "permanent" one is being readied. (These are all new and everyone has moved in only recently.) Living room, dining-kitchen, half-bath downstairs; three bedrooms (one I use for an office) and a bath upstairs. It is spacious and all that, but I am not sure I like it. We are camping out in this place, with most of our worldly goods still crated in the "permanent" place. We must buy much furniture.

Rosemarie is working two days per week in Washington for her old boss, Congressman Collier of Illinois. We are trying to put her earnings—which are not bad for a part-time position—into our kitty for a housing fund toward the eventual purchase of a home. Going in one recent morning our goddam car caught fire. It is also shot, having been driven long and hard, and would cost so much to repair that we are now in the market for another car, and that of course means more money expended. Our life is something like Morton's salt: when it rains it pours. . . .

*King quit the *Letters Never Mailed* book early and never went back to it.
**King and Rosemarie had moved to Annapolis on assuming custody of his fifteen-year-old daughter, Cheryl, but after she opted to return to Texas they gladly rushed back to live in Washington.

December 2, 1967

Dear Judge Legg:

Thank you very much for your recent letter informing me of certain developments within the Ector County, Texas legal community.
In that connection you may be interested in a short note I have today
dispatched to Warren Burnett, a copy of which is attached. *

I realize that you reported on the incident out of a sincere deep
devotion to the Truth because you are, after all, a Sunday School
teacher and I know that your sunny personality is such that you suffer personal pain at the thought of any humiliating experience
befalling one of your personal friends; further, it has been my observation that you are the last man in the world to pass on degrading
tales of the human experience. I am deep in your debt for the sacrifice to which you have forced yourself.

In order to protect you from vengeful counter-attacks by Mr.
Burnett (though, apparently, there is little reason to fear that such
attacks might assume frightening physical form), who might not be as
understanding as I am and who, in fact, might consider you something
of a rat-fink stoolie, I am prepared to swear—if asked—that you did
not hint to me of his most recent joust with *Life*. It is my intention, if
asked, to say that his opponent, [the fighting] Judge called me personally to give a rather one-sided report of the fracas on or about the
evening of November 15, 1967, and that on or about the 15th day of
November, same year, I received a telegram from one Emma Burnett
reading "JUDGE F. WHIPPED WARREN'S ASS TODAY ON THE
NORTHMOST PORTION OF THE COUNTY'S COURTHOUSE
LAWN."

I regret, of course, that one of the two outstanding lawyers in West
Texas has seen fit to reduce himself to a public brawl although I will
admit, from your report, that he tried to extract himself as gracefully
as possible once in the soup. Nor can one blame the Judge for asking
physical satisfaction when called a son-of-a-bitch. As I understand
the laws of libel and slander, Judge F. has no real legal recourse open
to him, any law suit running the risk of his being labeled by the jury
exactly what Burnett called him. I do wish that while Burnett was in

the cursing business he had seen fit to call his adversary a Campbellite
son-of-a-bitch, at once showing himself a man of more imagination
and at the same time stabbing his adversary a bit more deeply because
the insult then would have assumed more personal connotations. I
surmise, however, that Burnett was being consistent in leaving God
out of the matter as he does in all things. . . .

Spent most of November tracking around with Nelson Rockefeller
and then returned here to write the piece under deadline pressures.
Did not finish until 3:30 A.M. on the last day of the deadline—two
days ago—and still feel wrung out from the experience. It was the
toughest piece I have done. I suppose this is because I wanted Rocky
to come off another Stevenson or John F. Kennedy, and kept waiting
for him to do it, and he fell far short; additionally, I had one set of
impressions when I left him, but as they ripened in my second
thoughts and as they came out on the typewriter, they changed—and
not very much in his favor in some cases. I still think he is better than
what we have got in the White House at the moment, and better than
anything else the Republicans can offer, though in saying so I am
merely revealing that we are, at present, pretty short of Presidential
timber—with the possible exception of the undersigned, you, and
Norman Mailer. The fact is that Rockefeller is a very cool man in the
soul—the type of man who moves around shaking hands and proclaiming "I'm excited" without showing any excitement at all—so
that one wonders what *really* is going on inside that head or heart
(assuming, of course, that he has a heart) and I guess I wound up writing a great deal about that. He ain't no Louie Armstrong. . . .

Write and be careful who you call dirty names. Your partner in
mischief . . . .

*See following letter.

Editor's Note: Burnett and a local judge had engaged in
fisticuffs that included biting and gouging. King remarks,
"Legend has it that the judge ultimately went to Jesus bearing
Burnett's teeth-marks on the leftmost cheek of his ass. "

December 2, 1967

Dear Judge Burnett:

Sports Illustrated, True, and *Ring* magazine have indicated an interest in my doing a feature article on you as "The Fighting Lawyer from Texas." In doing my basic research I find that your ring history is not completely clear in my mind. I realize that you won a decision from Lawyer Zeisenheim in the middle of Old Highway 80 some years ago, that you won a shoving match with Judge Harold Young in the Midland, Texas courtroom, that you have decisioned Miss Emma 26 of 33 fights, with two draws, but the record is incomplete. It occurred to me to inquire whether there are other old excursions into fisticuffs in which you may have participated that now escape my memory or whether, indeed, you may have recently been engaged in a battle you would care to tell me about. The sole purpose of this letter is to make that inquiry, so I shall not bother you with idle chit-chat on additional subjects at this time. . . .

Jan 15, 1968
Midnightish

Dear Lanvil & Glenda:

Well, this has been a good day. It started with the morning mail. Sterling Lord messaged that Arnold Ehlrich, once editor of *Venture* and for whom I did a piece you may recall, has moved over as executive editor for *Holiday* and "would really like to get some pieces going with you" at good money. Also, Helen Gurley Brown, editor of *Cosmopolitan*, is hot for you. Same price range. Anxious to chat with you next time you are in town." Then: "Also, Herman Kogan, editor of *Book Week* is mad to use you. What upcoming books do you want to review, he asks. Check off some from the list of future biggies in the current *Time*."

So then Willie Morris calls. We have been going back and forth on my book, *My Hero LBJ & Other Dirty Stories,* since he read galleys some time ago in order to write a Foreword. Willie thought the book was (1) badly edited (2) somewhat overwritten and (3) somehow deficient in "tone." The first I could see and agree on; likewise the second; the third, however, eluded me. Willie was vague. "What do you mean by it needs to have a change of tone?" I would ask in all anxiety and only slightly threateningly, and he would mumble that Well, Hell, the *tone* needed changing, and for six weeks I have sulked and cursed and poured over it, and reedited, and took out two whole chapters, and spot re-wrote here and there and remained Confused and Unknowing Re: Tone. Today Willie called just to see really how I am doing and I said just about what I said above about Tone and Confusion; and he said come on up and do it at *Harper's* expense and attend the Wednesday editorial board meeting and make a show of being in the office a couple of hours each day, and we will work at nights and this weekend galley-by-galley on that book and get it done; so I am going Wednesday and return here all Straightened Out come next Monday morning.

Then on top of all that, Rosemarie today bought me and had delivered a desk, all dark and mahoganyish, and with a curved left end, and wider and longer than anything I have had before and I am crazy for it; and then she bought me some new shirts of several kinds and underwear and a turtle-neck job and socks and well, friends, it has been a very good day. . . .

Jan 21, 1968

Mrs. Willie Morris
250 West 94th St.
New York, N.Y.

Dear Celia:

I want to apologize for leaving you a dirty chili pan and explain about how It Came To Pass and All My Good Intentions: I was up reading Mailer, see, and myself in the latest *Harper's,* and found both of our works inspiring, and so real late got real hungry and heated up some of your excellent chili. And resolved on eating it to wash the pan. And on eating it fell asleep almost in place. And intended to get up early to wash it before you found it. And when I woke it was late and you had washed the dirty chili pan and gone, probably cursing your Unthinking house guest, and I don't blame you.

So I am sorry and beg forgiveness.

Thanks for the hospitality. I enjoyed you. Next time I will try not to burden you with my old friends who attack me in your home for becoming a Crazy Bohemian Writer and for deserting my kids and for Making It (with apologies to Podhoretz) and for every Sin or Omission since I helped Pontius Pilate lynch Christ.*

*King's good friend Craig Raupe was present for a dinner party at the Morris's with his wife Joyce, who lectured King sternly about leaving his Texas family and embracing a bohemian lifestyle.

February 18, 1968

Dear Lanvil & Glenda:

Arrived back here from Nashville and my "Grand Ole Opry" story Thursday evening; almost immediately tumbled into bed with a head-chest cold. It still has me feeling wretched. Nashville's music scene is quite comprehensive and exciting. I also went "on the road" with Marty Robbins and his band, and that was the making of the story I think. We left Nashville by bus on a Thursday night and drove directly to Trenton, NJ for a Friday night club date; Saturday night in Wheeling, West Virginia for the WWVA Jamboree and then Sunday in Indianapolis at the State Fair Grounds for afternoon and evening performances. Arrived back in Nashville at 5 A.M. on Monday. I do not think I have ever been so weary.

When I last wrote, *Holiday*, *Cosmopolitan*, and *Book Week* were offering work; I have accepted all. Will go to Oxford, Mississippi about March 6th to do a *Holiday* piece on "Faulkner's Oxford"; agreed to do a piece about what young Southerners think of the North for *Cosmopolitan* (it will largely be humorously faked; who the hell knows?), and am to do a *Book Week* review of Roy Cohn's book. . . .

Yesterday, head cold and all, I was filmed here in our happy home by British TV as part of a one-hour documentary on LBJ. I was told that my comments were "the most candid" filmed; this no doubt marks me down for Special Attention by the FBI, CIA, and IRS, to name a few.* Also, as if that isn't enough, I just wrote for *Harper's* April issue the "Easy Chair" guest column on the topic, "The Death of Lyndon Johnson." (I did, however turn down a *Cosmopolitan* offer to write a piece about friends of LBJ's daughters who have landed cush government jobs, on the theory that while I do not mind battling The Man himself I do not want to snipe at his women-folk.) British made quite a production of it: had all kind of cameras, lights, and seven folks running in and out of here; Rosemarie was very hopeful the neighbors would notice. . . .

Have you read Justin Kaplan's "Mr. Clemens and Mark Twain"? I am about half-way through it and find it delightful. Willie Morris has been touting it to me for months and months, and I regret having postponed getting to it for so long.

Was notified some days ago that I (along with Willie Morris and Bud Shrake) have been elected to Texas Institute of Letters. Same letter dunned me for $5 dues. That took a little of the glamour out of it. TIL having its annual banquet in Dallas on March 23rd; Willie will make main speech and Shrake and I presumably are expected to show for walk-on roles.

* Editor's Note: King has said that he confidently assured the British of LBJ's running again in 1968—only a matter of weeks before the President withdrew.

April 27, 1968

The Jay Milners
2615 Greene St.
Fort Worth, Texas

Dear Jay and Beth:

Come September 24th you can watch me on a semi-regular basis on the magic tube. The CBS news show I told you about, "Sixty

Minutes," is definitely on. I met with Don Hewitt, the producer, last week and he fell in love with me 'til I thought we would have to get married in the interest of decency. He pledged that I will be on that maiden show, September 24th, and as regular as possible thereafter. He said that Mike Wallace, who along with Harry Reasoner will be the main on-camera wheels, has been bugging him about how great I am for weeks, so I appear fairly well set there—provided I don't fall on my face. I will do two minute essays, writ and spake by my very own self, on most shows; occasionally, I will work on a longer, in-depth subject. The "shortie" pieces will bring $500 each and the longer ones are subject to negotiation. And of course the exposure will be absolutely wonderful. . . .*

My heart is broke plumb slap-dab in two, sorta. First Les Slote (Nelson Rockefeller's press secretary), and then Emmitt Hughes (his chief speech writer) and next the Governor hisself made overtures to get me to take on some speech writing work and an advisory capacity to Rocky. I was flattered but not interested, though decided if I could do it part time it might not be bad, and Rocky having so much money and all I had Sterling say I would do it for $300 per day [Sundays included] plus expenses. Well, they accepted in a minute! Whereupon I began to really want the gig. And then, goddamn it, Willie Morris and his *Harper's* executives decided I couldn't do it unless I take a leave of absence from the magazine, and then it looked like it might screw up the TV deal, so I had to make a decision against it. I did so because, possibly wrong and possibly foolishly, I felt my future writing depended upon a continuation of what I am doing, more or less, and I didn't want to sacrifice the potential for a short-range goal—but you see why my heart is sorta smashed, don't you? (Miss Rosemarie had already spent the first ten days' pay, though only mentally Thank The Lord). . . .

*King filmed three "Sixty Minutes" pieces in early 1969. Hewitt and CBS used none of them, although he was paid for all three. King felt that they were pulled because all of them attacked the Nixon-Agnew adminstration at a time the Republican candidates were attacking the media and sowing seeds of fear.

May 26, 1968
Sunday night

Dear Lanvil and Glenda:

First things first: Rosemarie is having surgery at the National Institute of Health this coming Friday, May 31st. As you will recall, she has been getting periodic checkups at NIH since shortly after her surgery of November, 1965. A few weeks ago NIH called to say that they had detected abnormalities in her latest x-rays, and to please come in to the hospital for extended tests. She entered the hospital approximately 15 days ago. At the conclusion of tests the doctors recommended that her ovaries be removed, they having discovered difficulties by their tests which would not have appeared on x-rays for possibly six months or one year. They think that removal of the ovaries will likely suffice and that she will be in the hospital for about three weeks, or until roughly June 20th.

Rm is in much better spirits than I could be facing surgery on Friday next. We are gratified beyond measure, of course, that she has access to the facilities and physicians at NIH and we much look forward to her being restored to her old zip after surgery and recuperation. She has not felt very well, off and on, since last October. The last two weekends she has received passes home, but will report back to the hospital Tuesday and remain there until discharged. . . .

Editor's Note: During the late 1960s, King was an infrequent contributor to Helen Gurley Brown's *Cosmopolitan*. This letter responds to a request from the magazine's public relations staff asking for contributor's information and a photograph, "playing tennis or driving a car."

May 29, 1968

Miss Bobbie Kaplan
Cosmopolitan
1775 Broadway
New York, New York 10049

Dear Miss Kaplan:

It is going to be terribly difficult to find a picture of myself winning a tennis trophy or climbing into my car. The last time I played tennis I was defeated in straight sets by an elderly lady with at least one gimp leg, and it is well known that my wife, Rosemarie, chauffeurs me everywhere I go. (I am, I confess, one of the world's all-time great drunk drivers, but fortunately no photos exist to prove it.)

Pictures of me are almost extinct. Three of the four enclosed show me gazing soulfully into the Potomac River, which is about as far as I go in the way of exercise. The other one, a more typical pose, catches me thumping my antique typewriter. About all I do other than write is read, and I don't have much time for that. Since going into the word business four years ago (following 10 years on Capitol Hill) I have written more than 100 articles, essays, and book reviews for more than twenty-five periodicals and have finished two books and am finishing a third. When would I have time to play tennis or drive a car? Besides on May 17th I became, at the tender age of 39, a grandfather and this has done me in both psychologically and physiologically. . . .

I am now writing another non-fiction book, zippingly titled "Book No. 3," and neither I nor my editors have been able to figure out what it is about. However, you must remember that I am only half way through it. Four publishing houses think I am writing a second novel for them. They have been lied to. . . .

July 23, 1968

Hon. William Brammer
Famous Arthur
4701 Avenue F
Austin, Texas

Dear Billie Lee:

I was glad you are not lost summers on a Injun reservation as certain people have told on you. . . .

This is to attest and reaffirm that when I get to NYC in about one week, I will make contacts re the Pete Hammill and Clay Felker gigs.* My approach to Felker is probably best handled through Dick Schaap. I'll also scout around another place or two if I can and let your immediate availability be known. I don't know if you and *Time* parted thinking highly of one another, but if you did and all else is closed right now I hear-tell they are all-time having staff turnovers. They offered me a job maybe two years ago and I turned it down, then they said would I review books on consignment? I said yes, and did about two books per month at excellent money for a year, and then the chickenshits dismissed me on the grounds that they would ship no more books outside the Luce chambers unless to "a potential staffer" and we both agreed I did not qualify. Anyway, I will report to you once I have run some swabs.

FLASH! BULLETIN! "KING BECOMES GRANDFATHER!" Yes, Sports Fans, on May 17 last my daughter Cheryl, whom you will remember as the tiny tyke who once woke Bill Brammer up of a-morning with phone calls for money,** presented me with a grandson name of Thomas James Trulock, Jr.. . . . I personally inspected Thomas James Trulock, Jr., just a couple of weeks ago, and found him a remarkable child possessed of ten fingers and a like number of toes. He also does nasty in his paper pants when being held by his grandfather. The day he was born I said, "A United States Senator was born today," so that I am on record when Booth Mooney writes "The Thomas James Trulock Jr. Story." [Ed.: King's note says, "Mooney wrote "The Lyndon Johnson Story" while employed by LBJ. It found no fault."]. . . .

The editor of *Status Magazine* called today wanting me to profile
Sam Houston Johnson; I told him that Sam had all the load he could
carry in the Brother Department, and was a cripple besides, and a
good enough fellow generally that he ought to be left alone and not
set upon by scamps and scalawags and others masquerading as journalists; the fellow meekly apologized and agreed.

Do you see or hear-tell of Shrake and Cartwright? I thought the
article Gary did for *Harper's* on his sports writing days was tremendous.

Wal, I see by the old clock on the wall I am nearly out of paper . . . .
Do write gossipy letter whether gossip is true or not. . . .

> *King, at Brammer's request, was trying to help him find work assignments.
> **Brammer had "hired" nine-year-old Cheryl King to wake him every
> morning and talk until he felt alert enough to report to LBJ's Senate office. He
> promised to pay Cheryl $1.00 per call. Three months later, despite three dun-
> nings, Brammer had not paid. So "Daddy" King paid her, and let her believe
> the money came from Brammer. .

July 29, 1968

Dear Lanvil and Glenda:

The only really exciting thing that's happened is that somebody
stole our car. Took it out of its assigned spot in our apartment garage
anywhere from three days ago (when the theft was discovered) to
eight days ago (last time we saw the car) and so the thief rides hours
ahead of the Metropolitan Police Department posses which, thus far,
have not seemed as enthusiastic about the loss, the crime, or Justice
as one might ideally hope. Insurance will surely fall several hundred
short of what we still owe on it, and then on top of that we'll probably require a new car. I am sure ours will be either sold outright,
wrecked, or stripped and sold. I know lots of reasons why Heaven
should have it in for me, and know that God is a grim jester if one may
trust to History, but this is getting out of hand. I prayed today as follows: "No need for further tests: I withdraw from contention as Job's
successor. Simply haven't the patience."

Some weeks ago I wrote Mother that if run-of-the-mill relatives (those old names I can no longer put their current faces with, and sometimes have trouble putting their old faces with) want to buy my book I can get it for them at a $2 discount. Guess who was the first (and thus far the only) to say yes, rush me fast a cut-rate copy of that dirty book? Aunt, naturally, Ida. Someway she will make a nickle off the mortician on the way to the grave. I only wish I had inherited a streak of her *saving* grace. . . .

Remember the Buckley-Levant review? A card came from Buckley: "Dear Larry: You should have *told* me you wanted to see my good pieces a year ago, and I'd have shown them to you! How are you? Best, Bill." All at once real buddy-buddy. I dropped him a short note tonight saying that I prefer to make discoveries for myself, and how's that for philosophy for a Liberal? Then closed with this line: "I think your Pope has blown his Holy cool." Buckley is so Conservative a Catholic that he probably thinks the Pope is wrong for permitting sexual congress at all.

Enclosed *New Republic* for your collection of King letters; take it you saw the last two *Harper's* with Grand Ole Opry and Lindsay articles. Oh, *Reader's Digest* sent me a copy of their condensed version of Grand Ole Opry they are considering publishing. They gutted the piece to death and thus shamed my prose, but if they take it I'll get $2,500 for nothing more than selling myself out. So I signed the release. Faulkner, forgive me, for I know not what I do. . . .

August 8, 1968

Dear Norman Mailer:

Holiday magazine has asked me to do a long and though I blush to use the words "in depth" piece on one Norman Mailer: Mailer the Writer, Mailer the Movie Star and Producer, Mailer the Whiskey Drinker, Mailer the Pentagon-on-Marcher, Mailer the Man; the whole schmere. Now, quite naturally, I would love to do the article. It would give us a grand excuse to get together for a postponed whiskey drink. I would like to get with you sometime in September, or, that failing, October, if you are agreeable. If you are not, then to hell with the piece, we will simply do our whiskey drinking unencumbered by either Duty or Art. Of course, I do hope you'll agree. My only condition is that you do not chew off my ear or break my jaw, and I will make you the same deal. . . .

I asked NAL to send you a copy of my new book, . . . *And Other Dirty Stories,* containing a chapter on a party at your pad and I hope you enjoy it. You should have your copy any day if it's not there.

Hope you survived the elephants in Miami Beach. . . .*

*A reference to Mailer's coverage of the 1968 GOP convention for *Harper's.*

Editor's Note: When King and Mailer got together, Mailer argued that friendships between writers were difficult and complicated at best without writing about each other. King abandoned the project.

August 10, 1968

Dear Hon. Gutwillig:

Your outer-office personnel may have told you that during my most recent visit to New York I telephoned you no less than six times, stopped by your office once for ten minutes and another time for forty-five, and yet somehow managed to get out of town without (1) seeing you in the flesh (2) hearing the sound of your voice or (3) even having my telephone calls returned. This was, of course, excellent for my morale, and quite naturally I have notified my Solicitors so that their records will be complete in the matter of King vs. Gutwillig, NAL, Et Al. . . .

With a minimal amount of rummaging in your bags while visiting your Washington hotel room some weeks ago, I found your ad budget and discovered that Miss Judith Viorst and Mr. Larry L. King are each figured for a total budget of $1,500 only, while other Famous Arthurs were listed for sums like $3,500 and $7,500 and $13,500 and $15,000 and one even for $20,000, I think, though maybe I went into shock

somewhere about the middle of the list. You will recall that my
attempts to talk to you on this subject then were more pronounced
than yours to discuss the same subject, but you had this convenient
shuttle flight to catch, and I have not bugged you about it until now
but do so now. Please remit. My solicitors are beside themselves. They
think we got the thing won.

August 28, 1967

The Jay Milners
2615 Greene St.
Fort Worth, Texas

Dear Jay & Miss Beth:

In celebration of the first—and good—review of my new book (see
enclosed from *The New York Times*) yesterday I took Mike Adams* to
a nine-hour lunch. We began at 1 P.M. at The Place Where Louie
Dwells, et steaks and drank on Scotch and Bloody Marys. They got us
out of the place around 4 P.M. Whereupon we repaired to the round-
table at the Plaza Bar, ultimately being joined by one Ralph Hutto and
several of his Senate comrades, where we occupied ourselves with joy
and singing until maybe six, seven P.M., for by this time we were not
keeping real close tabs on the hour. Thence to the Democratic Club
for a couple of drinks. (We had switched to beer at the Plaza.) Then
to the Rotunda for more beer. Shortly before 10 P.M. Mike got real
silent. He tottered off to the rest room. Fifteen minutes later I sent
Hutto to see after him (I don't think I could have climbed the stairs
myself) and he found him scraping the upchuck off his shoes. I took
Mike out for a three or four block stroll to get some air; he was pale
but lucid, and convinced me he could drive home. (Rosemarie missed
all the hi-jinks, she being in New York shopping for clothes.) Mike
called around noon today, said that he guessed he was gonna live, and
that despite upchucking on his shoes he had "the best time I just
about ever had in my life."

After he got a few drinks under his belt, over at the Plaza, I very carefully got him into a Vietnam War argument with an old, sour, 76-year-old Senate employee from South Carolina, and enjoyed the debate very much—cheering in the right places, booing now and again, finally drawing several other spectators in as cheerers and booers. Mike's face was flushed, his arguments sound, his speech near the end perhaps a little blurred; he acquitted himself well, and I sat between him and the old man so as to be a buffer against the generation gap. He is off to New York on his way home. He is a bright young man, and I'm glad to have helped get him his job. He'll be a good drinker when he's been on the varsity a little longer. Nine hours before caving in ain't bad for a literary sophomore.

Yessir, how 'bout that little ole *N.Y. Times* review? Quite different than the opening reception I got last time, when *Book Week* reviewed *The One-Eyed Man* two or three weeks before pub date by saying it was about the worst disaster since the Chicago Fire. On Monday I had a letter from the editor of *Book Week* (now published by the *Chicago Sun-Times*) saying he is crazy about . . . .*And Other Dirty Stories* and that he is personally reviewing it as the lead review in his publication on Sept. 22nd. . . .

*Mike Adams was a recent journalism graduate of S.M.U. and a former student of Milner's.

September 7, 1968

Mistah Bill' Lee Brahamer,
Boy Bull,
4701 Avenue F
Austin, Texas

Dear Billie Lee:

In the very first place I been meaning to tell you I wrote you up full of praise a month ago or such in *New Republic* and I doubt whether anybody in my Vast Reading Public has ever called it to your attention and so enclose good thangs about yourself.

In the second place I cannot imagine why you have not heard from

Frank Zachary at *Status Magazine*, on account he seemed all thrilled at the prospect of corralling the Famous Arthur who Arthured *The Gay Place*. Short of the explanation that some other editor whom you screwed for Advance Money in your Foolish Youth might have warned him against that old tactic, I can only offer as a possible explanation that both Frank Zachary and *Status* are very screwed up right now and might be running two, three weeks behind in all departments including mailing advance airplane money. Zachary, see, has been Art or Photography or some such Director for *Holiday* all these years; new shake-ups within Curtis Brothers Publications snatched him off that roost and made him editor of *Status,* and he is going through very cunfoosed period. Would you like that I should ask him What Happened In The Brammer Affair? Please transmit wishes.

I had a letter from Budrow Shrake several days ago telling me he thought the best part of my new Dirty Book is the part with his name in it, and yours, and indicating that had I put more Shrake and Brammer in it I would have (1) come closer to Real Art and (2) have more easily convinced the world that I hang out with gentry. One of these days Don Meredith is going to go into a football game with his head so mellow he will throw interceptions to the other side on purpose, and then stand goofing and grinning while they run them back for touchdowns, and will feel Pure in his heart and full of Brotherhood, and the Dallas Cowboys will lose the World Champeenship because one time Bud Shrake offered Don Meredith a funny Cigarette.

I really do truly appreciate all them nice thangs you say about my Dirty Book. It got a good review in *New York Times* (daily) last week, and as good a one as Leonard Sanders is capable of writing in *Fort Worth Star-Telegram* last Sunday, and today one came out in the *Washington Post* by Geoffrey Wolff which I was terribly pleased with considering who wrote it. He said seven good things and two bad ones, but seeing as how I consider him the toughest of Eastern Seaboard Critics and he has got a Smart-Ass Harvard Education and is as humorless as McGeorge Bundy and represents everything that my countryman's instinct fears, I feel like doing a rain dance. *

I have saved this story for last, figuring by now that you have read the enclosed *New Republic* since I said it said good things about you; now that you've read the review you will understand this story better. Anyhow, Alfred Steinberg (Famous Arthur of "Sam Johnson's Boy") wrote me a letter thanking me for my "effeminate" review, saying I am obviously "very young and lacking in knowledge of history," and otherwise abusing me for several paragraphs before closing: "My image of you from your review is that you are a pile of maggoty garbage." I should not have responded, of course, but did, briefly and with the following observation: "On the basis of your book and your letter, my opinion is that you are a dry-balled, humorless, spoiled old shit. Very truly yours, etc." Then came a second letter to me from Alfred Steinberg, saying he thought my letter was "so representative of your character that I xeroxed several copies and sent them to the editors of *The New Republic*, *Harper's*, to some newsmen in town, to a few Senators and to your special hero in the White House." Then two days later I get a postcard in the mail from *Mrs.* Steinberg saying she is displaying "your letter to Al" on the mantlepiece next to an ad for "Sam Johnson's Boy" and concluding with a diatribe that "I believe both you and your hero should be consigned to spending the rest of your lives in Walter Reed Hospital looking at some of the boys who have sacrificed for your ideals." Me, who has demonstrated against the Vietnam War, now, and cussed LBJ in print and got the IRS after me as a result. Some Famous Arthurs is terribly sensitive; also their wives. . . .

*I was wrong about Wolff being "humorless"; we became friends and he has kept me laughing for years. Also, he graduated Princeton, not Harvard.
—LLK

September 8, 1968

Mr. Wm. Brammer
4701 Avenue F
Austin, Texas

Dear Billie Lee:

Sitting around here juicing and otherwise pleasured, I just read over your letter again and find I want to comment on something I forgot yesterday. And that is to your reference to the hang-ups you been through and especially the following: "Writing is just so murderously hard for me in recent years—unaccountably so—though my skull feels livelier than ever," and again: "Really pains me to recollect how much I once enjoyed—and gushed nearly to a fault—writing down words on paper. Delicious as a really well-prepped for scarf job."

I have reached that point in time where I can say you didn't invent it, it ain't unique, what makes you feel different and so on. What I mean is that I feel increasingly those very emotions: that the word struggle isn't as much fun as it once was, that it has become puredee ole goddamn shitty work, that the keen anticipation and boyish pride and the look-Maw-I'm-writing phase is gone forever in its best and largest sense; oh, a given article or passage or idea may hum ones bones and ego now and again, but briefly, quickly and shallowly, like cat's breath. But I'm not *alarmed* by it—it doesn't mean that the juices are drying up, that the well is dry, that I was or am a one-book man. It just means that I am getting more professional. And while I don't want to over-simplify either your condition or my own, I think in a large measure that perhaps when this phase came on you—after *The Gay Place,* and you bogged down—that you let it scare you and that you have been running in some nameless terror from the Brammer-written word ever since. You had some rough breaks that I did not have, of course: *Esquire* screwed you on "Fanny & Gooey"* and Ladybird took away your $5000 *Ladies Home Journal* piece [on LBJ] and gave it to India Edwards, and probably some editors and writers and publishers were too quick to spread the story of your problems and so they fed on themselves and magnified and scared you more.

And you had one burden that did not face me—your novel was so good, was so *goddam* good, that it excited the critics to laurels and led everybody to expect *War and Peace* and Scott Fitzgerald and Edgar Lee Masters and Shakespeare combined when your next book appeared—and that would discourage any man, of even normal sensibilities, from finishing that book. It would make him want to run.

But you have run far enough. You know and I know and every bone in you knows that you were by talent and design meant to be a writer, and you became one—a good one, very good—and then you unbecame one on the market place but—and I do not want to begin to sound as preachy as I am or as Buckle Down Winsocki as I fear—you did not cease to be a writer in that jumping head of yours, and so misery and hang-ups and thangs.

There is something in your recent letters and our phone chats (some sense of not quite Repentance but dangerously close to it; at least some hint of Resolve not there before) that convinces me you've whipped most of those old problems. I think the one holding you up now is that writing isn't "fun." Well, fuck it being fun—it's more than that, it's *important* and in your case it is more basically important than with most of us because—and I say this not to massage a shriveled ego or to calm an old fear but simply because it is true—you got more talent than most of us. Than *all* of us from what folks call "The Texas School" or the "*Observer*" school. You can write circles around Ronnie Dugger and Willie Morris and William Humphrey and the Bode Boys and Larry L. King and the only Texan I rank in your class is Larry McMurtry. You simply use the language better than the rest of us; you are better at form and technique (if there is such a thing as technique) and you got greater sensitivity and better things in your guts when you will spill them out. So I have never given up on Billie Lee Brammer (though I have cussed you for a wastrel and a fool and have thought your crime great, because I hate to see Talent dissipated there not being enough of it anyway) and I have envied [your having] more talent than I have and so sometimes have judged you harshly and for that do here apologize. But as basic as it seems to say it, I must say it: all that is so much shit unless you *work*, Billie Lee. Forget it being "fun" and face work for a while. Do you think it is any particular joy to pound out crap as I do for *True, Cosmopolitan, Sat. Eve. Post* and so forth, on subjects I do not give a shat about? No, but it is necessary to support myself so that I can keep my name in the game and learn my craft and maybe live to do better writing than I am capable of doing now and *that* goddammit *is* important to the writer. It's the most important thing of all. I give not a shit for the rest of it—give me that and I'll get by. You, now, should feel even stronger about it because as the larger talent it should mean more to you because it should mean more to the cause of good writing.

So let me suggest this way of starting to come back: begin by writing a few *Texas Observer* pieces: forget the money at first; you might coax them out of a few token dollars (I do) but more importantly you would start coming back in print, learning the work habits again, maybe even to discover a flash of fun in it again but if you do not, then fuck it, for what I most want you to discover again is your pride again and yourself again. Do them articles on anything: a piece on your hang-ups of the last few years, if that be therapy; or a political piece, or one on the dope movement, or whatever. You needn't confine it to *The Observer*, of course, because you can publish anywhere. But if you need that to get started, do it there. The point is (being too much belabored, I know, because my thoughts are racing and jumbling and I am full of the Sincerities and Wanting-To-Help) *do* an article or two or three or better four, and mail them off somewhere, and they will sell, and you will be Back and everyone will see you as Reformed and you can take up again with—by your own admission—a livelier skull.

I write this in all confidence, not to be made sport of or taken lightly, and do pray to whatever gentle or profane Gods that it will help you straighten out in your skull those things you already know in the secret places. . . .

*A funny piece Brammer wrote parodying J.D. Salinger's writing style. *Esquire's* editors reportedly feared angering Salinger, from whom they hoped to receive stories.

September 20, 1968

Hon. Herman Kogan
Friend-To-Man
Editor, *Book Week*
Chicago Sun Times
400 N. Wabash
Chicago, Illinois

Dear Herman:

Mama was so crazy about your issue to be published Sunday* that she inquired whether you could mail me about five more copies? Mama and I promote the hell out of her Baby Son. We do a more consistent, if not better, job of it than either my publisher or my agent. The only one who holds a candle to us is my wife. She has gone to Nome, Alaska with a dogsled full of *Dirty Stories* on account of she was not happy with the Antarctic sales figures on my other book. We expect her back in the spring. . . .

You must think I am goofy or else you would not even tentatively invite me to Chicago in February. The only invitation I have had to top that is one in Presidio, Texas for next July. If you watch weathercasts you will recognize Presidio, Texas as uniformly and almost without question the hottest spot in the nation from May forward through August or September. However, if you feel at a later date there is any place in Chicago for me in May I might be happy to consider such a fine offer. I am probably disqualified in that I do not have another book coming out then. I am yards and yards of copy away from another novel being published, and probably two or three years away from it in time. I expect to do another non-fiction book but it won't be published for a year or more. . . .

*That issue contained both a review written by King and a good one of *his* book, . . .*And Other Dirty Stories,* written by Kogan.

Editor's Note: Ralph Ginzburg, founding editor of *Avant Garde* and *Eros* was on his way to prison for publishing "obscene" materials, but his trial was perceived as political because of his outspoken opposition to the Vietnam War and his contempt for authority. He obviously thought he had found a soul-mate in Larry L. King.

October 4, 1968

Mr. Ralph Ginzburg
Editor, *Avant-Garde*
110 West 40th St.
New York, N.Y. 10018

Dear Ralph Ginzburg:

I am highly flattered, and was for a while tempted, over the prospect of being editor of *Avant-Garde*. But hell, whom am I fooling? I am not certain that I can edit and even if I can, there are better men for you and what I really want to do above all else is write. And so I decide to say thanks for the offer but decline because there are all these books in me and stories wanting to be told. You know the feeling. . . .

October 15, 1968

Dear Onkle Jay & Auntie Beth:

Last night a dentist pulled two of my cherished teeth, and I bled all night and hurt and stayed groggy on the novocaine and codeine and certain other thangs I applied my ownself, and am just now getting — at late the following afternoon — to where I can stand to swaller or hear a cat stomp. It was only the first (though we hope the last extractions) of more than $600 worth of dental miseries I have got to put up with in the coming months, my old mouth somehow a-playing out before my liver did. Hopefully I will be recovered in time to dash out of here Thursday night for Austin, Texas and very hopefully my jaw and gums and all will tolerate cold liquids in the upcoming weekend. If not, I had just as soon not go.

Rosemarie is down town trying to buy me enough clothes to get me to Austin and back, I now owning little more than a pair of six-year-old khakis and absolutely refusing to go into clothing stores. I wish it was like it was in the old days, when you could write to Sears Roebuck or Monkey Ward and they would rush you $9 worth of clothes by return mail and you could wear 'em five years.

The only reason Herman Kogan called me "clear-eyed" in the *Chicago Sun-Times* was that he has never saw me in the red-eyed, blood-shot flesh. And I wrote Willie a note when the *KC Star* called me "Editor-in-Chief" of *Harper's* and instructed him to clean out his desk and move on. I was up there last week, however, and he had not done it. Today's mail brought about a dozen new reviews and I'm a sum-bitch if they wasn't all good 'uns: *Chicago Tribune, Denver Post, Miami Herald, Salt Lake City Tribune, Library Journal, Seattle Something-or-Other, Sacramento Bee, Roanoke Times, Amarillo Globe-News, Lansing What-Ever-Tis, North Hollywood Citizen-News, Cleveland Press.* And a note come from Cliff Olofson at the *Texas Observer* saying that—don't faint—Billie Lee Brammer is reviewing me for the *Observer's* upcoming issue. I have had a private letter from Billie Lee claiming to be plumb fool about said book and only hope he has guts enough to make the same claim in public. If Brammer finishes the article, that alone will make me feel like progress has been made and old wounds healed. From recent exchanges with him, I do think he seriously is on the verge of a comeback.

It does seem like you got your PhD faultlessly planned, and the only thing I worry about is whether when you become so highly educated you will not appreciate George Jones to the extent that you formerly did. I have never thought as much of Roy Acuff as I should have following my six weeks of learning at Texas Tech. . . .

Well, I got to hush this and go do glamorous Writer Thangs: take the laundry, grocery shop, and doctor my tooth . . . .

October 16, 1968

Dear Jay:*

That whut you said about how Cullie Blanton**represents that region down there and its rather painful, slow but aggressive, etc. transition pitted against that part of it that resists change, and all, is mighty impressive and from now on when folks ask me what Cullie represents I will tell 'em that, where once I just reddened and sat dumb in awkward pauses and wished they would go off somewhurs and leave me alone. Because I never have been much good at thinking about my own writing in terms of symbols and representings and fourth and fifth layers of meaning and all like that. As a matter of fact such talk usually embarrasses me much more than profanity—it is too much like talking over some pretty dead girl's cold body about how much Puss has went to waste with her death. (You may read this to the class if you and TCU are ready for it, but if you do, spell Puss out P-U-S-S like that so the younger children will not be affronted nor shocked because I hear TCU is a Christian School.) Now as to who Cullie was in terms of men: more in his heart ole Earl Long than anybody, I guess, with a dash of Lyndon (though not nearly as much as has been popularly and critically credited) and a dab of Hummin' Talmage the First and a speck of Alfalfa Bill Murray and crazy little touches of Cyclone Davis and Huey Long on the shinbone and Don Kennard on the anklebone and in his very best moments a little of myself. I don't know really who the old bastard was, but I wound up knowing him pretty well and like him and one day may visit him briefly in another book in his old and desperate age. . . .

*Milner.
**In *The One-Eyed Man*

November 1, 1968

Dear Lanvil and Glenda:

I received today an advance copy of upcoming review of *Dirty Stories* in this Sunday's *New York Times*; review is by Saul Maloff; he's a tough bastard, but I got at least a B- out of it and he says I've got a good heart (hah!) and am funny, and that "King is a knight among magazine writers, and his book can stand comparison with any such collection in recent years." The only thing is he doesn't think collections ought to be published in book form, apparently. My first "knock" review was a short notice received in Bill Buckley's *National Review* (which came as no surprise) and even then some grudging admiration for some talent was expressed. . . .

Editor's Note: The novelist Dan Wakefield had written King that a friend had told him that he was mentioned in King's new book but that he found to his chagrin that he had been used as an example of a good writer who made small money.

November 12, 1968

Dear Dan Wakefield:

One of the problems in writing books . . . is that your red-hot information is stone cold by the time the book is published. Your own sorry financial circumstances, for instance, improved very greatly only shortly after you poured out your poverty woes in "Between the Lines" and then in the two years between the time you were published and I was published you made more money than H.L. Hunt. Unhappily, in my own case, the financial report remains timelessly accurate. I imagine that even NAL could get a book out saying that I am desperately poor and no matter how they botched editing, production, distribution, advertising and publicity they would be right on target no matter how exotic or prolonged the delays.

I am delighted that Mary Moore Moloney conned you into buying *Dirty Stories*. I, myself, bought twenty for cheap Christmas gifts and loyal old friends have bought almost two dozen, so that we have placed at least fifty books counting the book store and mail-order trade. Too sad a tale to tell, Dan Wakefield, and I cannot help it if you are on the listening end: I have got to date maybe fifty-six or so reviews, none doing me major damage, all saying good and kind things rating on the curve from B-minus to A-plus about me or the book or both (Buckley's *National Review* alone failing me with an F for the book and maybe a grudging C-plus personally, save for knocking me as a "political propagandist," though come to think of it wasn't Tom Paine?) and the first modest little printing of 5,000 was snapped up before publication date. And do you think the second printing was ready on time? Of course not! I had to delay an autograph party in Austin, and to this date NAL has not filled back orders in stores I personally know of in Washington and Dallas and two or three other places and has not been able even to furnish me my 10 freebies. Go out and buy 10 and send us the bill, Gutwillig said, and I finally found and bought them and of course have not been reimbursed by them and in all likelihood never will be. And one other thing: I have wrote them bastards two books, one of which made a Book Club, sorry as it was, and a paperback, and according to NAL's royalty statements even though my novel sold some 7,000 in hardback (not counting the 22,000 in book club) and the paper sold 76,000 to date and my new book has gone out, all 7,500 of 'em to the stores, my royalty statement from NAL shows that I owe them $6,000 more *than they have paid me!* Maybe they are using the new math, though Sterling Lord and my solicitors are calling on them to make more exact explanations. Yes, you are right: if NAL gets in the parachute business we will be fair game for the invading armies of Mexico. Fuck NAL, I say, and The Queen for that matter, should she cast her lot with them.

I am a jealous man and so—despite the fact that I dwelled on your poverty—it took the breaking of many old habits to praise your work in my book. Said praise was Sincere (though no doubt you should consider the Source): I long followed you before I was myself a Famous Arthur and somehow your old *Playboy* piece "The Prodigal Powers of Pot" stuck with me in my old head and rang it for a long, long time. Besides that, I hear you are a good fellow: most persistent advocate of this point of view is Midge Decter, whom I am going to marry when the current Mrs. King has fell out of favor and Norman Podhoretz is safe in the grave, she being so good at flattering Famous Arthurs and Mothering us and able even to praise Other Writers in

146

our presence without getting her block knocked off. I would very much like to get together with you and Willie and the four or five jugs of Jack Daniel, but I must decline on the company of the four or five aspiring young poetesses on account I am of the highest moral character, besides which the current Mrs. King does not allow me no outside nookie and has threatened me with dire consequences should it ever cross my mind. She is a sweet woman, but mean, and I honor her beliefs. . . .

November 14, 1968

Mr. A.C. Greene
Route 6
Box 145-E
Austin, Texas 78746

Dear A.C.:

That was a mighty nice and touching letter that you wrote. As a writer you know that little else is as rewarding as to know that something you put on paper in the quiet solitude of the trade has *reached* somebody; has caused them honest emotions, whether of rage or joy or nostalgia. Yesterday I had a letter from an old aunt of mine, getting along in years now (she is the "Aunt Ethel" of my book, mother of constant-companion Cousin Kenneth, wife of the late Uncle George of grocery store fame) and living with her third or maybe fourth out-lived husband on a ranch in Oklahoma and she said something like, "I did not notice the things you wrote about at the time—only later do we look back and see them, and only you managed to bring the corn out of those days in a way that made us proud that we were there and a part of it." I don't think I'll ever get a book review that I will appreciate more.

Damn you for beating me to the march on a real West Texas book! No danger that I will be out before you (and no danger, for that matter, if I should be) as I am at least one book away from my West Texas book; I don't even know now if it will be fiction or straight autobiographical, though I expect the truth lies somewhere in between—"a fictional memoir," I think Frederick Exely calls it in his new book, A *Fan's Notes*. (Which I think is by-God superb.) So I shall eagerly await April and A *Personal Country* from Knopf. I may even ask my friend Mike Magzis for an advance copy if such low-lifes as the undersigned qualifies, though usually such are reserved for the likes of Podhoretz and Styron and Galbraith and Mailer. . . .*

*King wrote a foreword to A *Personal Country* when it was republished by Texas A & M University Press in 1979.

19 December 1968

Dear Warren:

When last we talked I thought I was going to Random House for about $25,000; however, I was publicly auctioned off last Friday in New York, like a Negroid slave, and the bids were—in ascending order of importance: Houghton-Mifflin, $15,000; Simon & Schuster, $17,000; Harcourt-Brace, $20,000; W.W. Norton, $21,000; Viking, $30,000. So I am signing up with the Vikings. If they are good enough for John Steinbeck, Bill Buckley, and Frank Conroy, among others, they are good enough for me. I am accepting $5100 on signing next month, then $1,700 per month for the next 15 months. . . .*

*This ultimately was for King's non-fiction book *Confessions of a White Racist*, nominated for a National Book Award when it was published.

January 3, 1969

Mr. John Cowles, Jr.
President and Editor
The Minneapolis Tribune
Minneapolis, Minnesota 55415

Dear John:

Willie Morris has passed on your note to him on the Nieman

Fellows selection processes, and the Harvard press release covering same.

You raise the question of whether I am under forty. As of three days ago I am not under forty. John Corry, himself an ex-Nieman Fellow and a man of elastic morals, simply counsels me to lie about my age by putting my birthdate back a year on my application. Willie Morris, as ever pious to a fault, doubts the wisdom of such a lie. I have little enough against lying as a general practice, and in the instant case would sleep untroubled having authored such a helpful lie, a lie free of malice and wishing to do no harm to others. However, the lie might not be the thing to do as a matter of strategy. Perhaps the Nieman Fellows judges are men easily offended by lies, and who knows but what they assess one a penalty of ten points, fifteen yards, or perhaps burn his application on the spot? On the other hand, if they are going to bar the gates to all us old codgers of 40 out of hand, then I am inclined to lie to them with a smile on my face. My problem, Dr. Cowles, is to lie or not to lie and I would appreciate your best advice. Perhaps you know some way we might judiciously determine how serious Harvard is about its 40-year-old rule before we settle for good and all the question of lying. . . .

Editor's Note: In February 1969 King applied for a Nieman Fellowship at Harvard for the 1969/1970 academic year. The Nieman Fellowship was aimed at mid-career working journalists who would benefit from a year away from deadlines and the freedom to sit in on any Harvard courses or activities. In his application to the Nieman Fellowship Committee, King confronted a technical problem with his application—the fact that on January 1 he had turned 40, the cutoff year for the fellowships. A letter from King's immediate superior was required for his Nieman file—in this instance Willie Morris.

February 10, 1969

Mr. Willie Morris
Editor-in-Chief
Harper's Magazine

Dear Willie:

I have now filled out my Nieman application, along with statements of purpose, course of instruction (American History), and so forth. I note from the application that you, as my "Immediate Superior" should write directly and confidentially to the Nieman Fellowship Committee, 77 Dunster Street, Cambridge, Mass. about my qualifications and potential. In my own letter, I plead my old age: don't turn away this ignorant, if brilliant, Old Shit, and so forth. You might hit the same subject a lick. Do not be afraid to praise me. You, or John Cowles, must write a *second* letter directly to the Committee supporting the application and granting leave of absence in the event I am selected. . . .

I am asking John Corry to be one of three people (others: Styron, Galbraith) to write commenting on my "journalistic abilities and potential" as is required. I would appreciate everybody getting letters in as quickly as possible, so my pitiful little application will be made more impressive by my famous sponsors.

Larry L. King
(Putnam Grammar School, '37)

February 11, 1969

Mr. Elroy Bode
818 Baltimore
El Paso, Texas

Dear Bode:

Our evening together in El Paso didn't turn out as I had planned, thanks to an over-abundance of whiskey, Judge Woodrow Bean, and a lot of drunken Revolutionary talk. I guess the only way to visit is to get off by ourselves, limit the whiskey, and possibly the matters under discussion. . . .

Poor Steinbeck. I confess to having knocked him myself, over his Viet Nam views, and then about two months before his death I was in New York and his sister-in-law (Jean Boone, from Austin) took me to his 34th floor pad, all glass walls almost, at least all outer ones, looking over the City with the river on one side and Central Park on another, and got to telling a great number of stories about him—Old Man stories, his laments in his last days, he then lying near death at Sag Harbor—and I became ashamed, for *Red Pony* and *Grapes of Wrath* and *Cannery Row* and *In Dubious Battle* started coming back loud and clear. And he was entitled to be wrong on Viet Nam, of course, and to much more. One of my favorite things written by anybody was the dedication in *East of Eden*. It begins about how someone named Pat* came upon him carving in wood and asked him to carve a box to put things in, and he wrote: "Well, here's your box. Nearly everything I have is in it, and it is not full. Pain and excitement are in it, and feeling good or bad and evil thoughts and good thoughts—the pleasure of design and some despair and the indescribable joy of creation. And on top of these are all the gratitude and love I have for you. And still the box is not full."

I very much enjoyed your piece from *Southwest Review*, and appreciate your sending it along. He [Steinbeck] was so much better, in my view, than the Updikes and Malamuds and some others who are raved over now, and you are right when you say he tied "the bloodstream of his books to the bloodstream of your own experiences." (Incidentally, I noted in *Saturday Review* today, only glancing at it on the newsstand, that he was ranked second of all "living" American writers in some poll that publication took. I don't remember who was first, and can't imagine who it might have been. . . .)

*Pat Covici, Steinbeck's long-time editor.

Editor's Note: In 1969 King's West Texas lawyer friend
Warren Burnett placed his son Abner at an alternative sec-
ondary school in Washington, D.C.—the Washington Free
School. In this letter King reports that the school may have been
a little freer than both Abner and his father anticipated.

April 12, 1969
Sattidy

Mr. Warren Burnett
House of Music
900 North Whitaker
Odessa, Texas

Dear Judge Burnett:

The chances are, of course, that this will lie in your House of Music
mailbox unnoticed for weeks, since you generally do not leap to the
box in keen anticipation of anything other than Occupant mail.
However, I send it to said H of M on account of the message, concerning your son Abner, is somewhat private in nature.

Ab survives, let me hasten to explain. Ab is not, however, getting
any school in at the Washington Free School. He tells me (through
long conversation last night and today up until he left a half-hour ago,
he having over-nighted here with us on the couch) that both students
and teachers at the Free School have lost interest in classes and
that—save for one class in adolescent psychology, in which all students were asked to state what they thought on that subject, whereupon classes dismissed without the instructor imparting either information or his own personal viewpoint—no classes have been held for
two months; nor, he says, does it look as if any more will be held.
Everybody just sits around sorta on the nod, and Abner says he is
spending his time playing the guitar, sleeping, and wishing to God he
had something to eat.

I do not write all this to bug you, but merely to state a new attitude,
I think, in Ab. Said attitude stemming from one week at the Free

School. Which attitude is, that Ab has decided he is in need of education that the Free School cannot, or will not provide, and suddenly Ab finds himself worrying about that formerly contemptuous thing called The Future. (He even said this morning that lately he has been thinking of taking up the law as a career.) Also, he is already speaking with something like nostalgia of The Good Ole Days at St. Stephens. To the extent that Ab is seeing a side of life less paved with gold and roses than he had heretofore possibly imagined, he is having The Great Adventure you left him here to have. However, in the academic sense he is learning nothing. He is coming back over to the neighborhood on Monday to see if he may be interested in (next year, if not this) attending the next-door school here, Hawthorne, if they will accept him and assure him some classes. They are rather well structured (compared with the Free School, anyhow) and might be good for him.

I have done more Daddying this week than is normal for me, having talked by phone with Ab several times. Then last night myself and RM took to dinner Ab, Melissa Dooley, the Morris Udalls, Mrs. Udall's 18-year-old son and his date, and a hippie boy friend of the Udall stepson. Ab, who had come upon little or no food during the past week, ate the biggest Mexican plate he could find, ate all the side dishes, and picked off the plates nearest to him. Upon leaving, Rm and I took Ab and Melissa only to a Hot Shoppe to get them some dessert: whereupon Ab falls in, eats a whole chicken, a mound of french fries, a second salad, a root beer float, and a chocolate sundae. (Ab's story is that of the $211 you left him, he bought $8 worth of groceries and returned them to the Free School, whereupon his classmates et it all up and he's subsisted on soup and ice-cream bars when the Good Humor Man comes around twice daily. Ab apparently waits for the Good Humor Man's two trips to the ghetto daily as eagerly as Wee Willie Shoopman ever awaited the pouring of the next whiskey.) Ab still had, incidentally, $200 of his money but of course it was in two big bills and was of no use to him. Also, a house thief at the Free School has robbed nearly everybody but Ab and he has been afraid to sleep for fear his money will disappear in slumber. I have just dispatched him to the American Express office here, with instructions to put his money into $10 Traveler's Cheques save for perhaps $20 for incidental purposes.

Additionally, the health inspectors are threatening to close the Free School for obvious reasons; a second arm of the D.C. government is threatening to padlock 'em on account of they are authorized to sleep no more than six persons and are sleeping 13 there. (I think Ab feels much a fifth-wheel: all the boys have a girl to sleep with on a regular basis except your son, and apparently there is much honor among thieves about their pussy in that the Free School girls are not giving out any side meat but are staying true to their regulars. Two of the girls, incidentally, have lately discovered their pregnancies and are working on trips to Tijuana for obvious reasons.) Also, Ab cannot bathe because the bathroom is too filthy and there are no locks on the door and he proclaims modesty, and says that boys and girls together wander around pretty nude and he finds it kinda embarrassing.

Certainly he can no longer claim that he hasn't material for books, stories, or even poems.

The headmaster of the school has not been seen or heard from in some weeks, and the school rent is behind. Eviction for that reason is threatened by the landlord. Additionally, Blacks in the area do not cotton to the Whitey Free Schoolers, and have turned them in for various violations. And, except for Ab, almost everyone at the Free School has at one time or another been rolled for his money upon stepping outdoors. Ab has not yet got an apartment, and I think he is intimidated by thoughts of getting out where somebody might scob his knob and take his money.

In short, I think Ab would give several thousand dollars of your money to be somewhere other than the Free School. It could be that we did not check it out as carefully as possible. . . .

Editor's Note: This fan letter from King to the humorist H. Allen Smith was occasioned by the publication of Smith's book on the Terlingua chili competition, *The Great Chili Confrontation,* and by the fact that Smith and his wife had inexplicably moved from Mt. Kisco, New York, to Alpine, Texas.

July 12, 1969

Mr. H. Allen Smith
Side-of-a-Mountain
Alpine, Texas

Dear Mr. Smith:

One morning last week, even before my cocaine, I dropped into my neighborhood bookstore and there shattered our local Blue Laws by paying the going price for your new book, *The Great Chili Confrontation.* As one of your most loyal fans, I was never more disgusted in my life. This was a judgment not made until I had read your book.

Why in the name of God and the Trident Press, other than for money, would you heap glory on such as Wick Fowler, John Henry Faulk, Xerox Tolbert,* Rex Ivey, and M. Maverick, Jr.? Save for the citizen Tolbert, these are all people whom I know personally. Though, I say with pride, none happens to be my friend. You are new to Texas and might have saved some grief had you thought to check out your associates in front. Much the same might be said for Robert Finch and Dr. John Knowles.**

The citizen Fowler is an old woman in the swearing department, and when he troubles to drink beer he drinks it warm. Until such time as he grew to such girth as to inspire the question of what Blimp squadron he served with, the citizen Fowler claimed to have been a war correspondent. I understand he was best known for his love of the individual G.I., and to the best of my knowledge he never had the luck to be assigned to the WAC Corps. The citizen Fowler not only knows nothing of making chili, he is equally learned in other fields. He cheats at dominoes, and owes me six weeks wages from 1951 when I served him as goat-keep. Goat-keeping was not my original vocation, but one of the conditions of being hired as a reporter on the *Midland*

Reporter-Telegram when he mismanaged the managing editor's job, was to keep his goats, children, and books. None were well-balanced.

The citizen Faulk comes from good people, though some are understandably ashamed of their kin. His main claim to fame was that during the McCarthy era many whispered of him as a Communist. This is almost as unique a distinction as being cheated by a publishing house. The best I can say for the citizen Faulk is that he holds his liquor as well as can be expected. Much the same was said of my Uncle Rip by his doctors as recently as Wednesday-a-Week. Thursday-a-week we buried him of a complicated liver.

Rex Ivey is a goddamned Republican, and was one before it became fashionable.

Comes now before the bar the citizen Maverick. It is not his first such appearance. He tends to cry when drunk, motivated by things like the latest Middle-East War, mal-treatment from ex-wives, and other common occurrences. Once he cried into my own tortillas. . . .

In a weak moment I once made contact with your friend Xerox Tolbert, only to be saved from major contamination because it thankfully was by telephone rather than in person. My purpose was to pick his bxxxxx(!xxxxxbxxixxx69xx brain (I had to credit him with one four times before my typewriter would accept the word) on some subject in which he qualified as expert, and which I found myself doing a magazine article on. The subject of the article escapes me, though possibly it was on how bad a thing is a preposition to end a sentence with. On the other hand, it may have been on women who put out for pay. At any rate, the citizen Tolbert was inspired to say that (1) he was writing a book on the particular subject at hand and (2) would not meet me out of fear that I would steal his thunder in tandem with his prose. Well, of course, I would have! I say anybody who doesn't recognize the right, to say nothing of the frequent necessity, of literary theft is a rank amateur and, further, knows precious little of chili. I will give you an affidavit to this effect should Xerox Tolbert additionally defame you into a law suit. . . .

In a certain summer, which may have belonged to the year 1967, I found myself stranded in Alpine, and there chanced on a certain private citizen in a cafe. I had been amusing myself with the *San Angelo Standard-Times* and there, complete with pix, was a story heralding your move from the Mt. Kisco goat farm to the side of an Alpine hill. Other than making the judgment that you had been writing too long to be held responsible for this decision, I worried little over it. Until this prominent Alpine-ite arrived and announced that according to the paper "Some Big-Time Writer Is Moving Down Hyar Purty Soon." "Big-Time Writer's Ass," I said (by which I meant nothing personal), "Did you not never hear of H. Allen Smith, you ignerent bastard? Are you not read *Life in a Putty Knife Factory*, or *Rhubarb*, or *To Hell in a Handbasket?*" and I went on to list thirty-eight other or so of your works, they having been handily listed in the *Standard-Times* down three columns, and all I got was a not of "Shat Naws" strained through bites of very sorry-looking eggs and sausage. . . . If it is any comfort, however, he didn't do any better when I quizzed him on who may have authored *Hamlet, A Christmas Carol,* or the *Autobiography of Mark Twain*. Though he did suspect Barry Scobee of the latter.

I have wrote two books my own self, one on grammar and one on modesty, and am thus only thirty-odd titles behind you. Counting the chili book. Which was, of course, marvelous and I am yours in $4.95 worth of admiration. . . .

* "Xerox" Tolbert was Frank X. Tolbert, *Dallas Morning News* columnist and chili expert.
** "Liberal" Republicans who joined the Nixon administration but then were isolated from the President and quit in disgust.

July, 1969

Mr. H. Allen Smith
Alpine, Texas

Dear Mr. Smith:

Last I heard from you, you were threatening to divorce your wife. Let me give you a piece of advice, and trust that it arrives in timely fashion: never marry a young woman. My own woman is now boppirouetting around our quarters, insisting that I listen to the words of "Hair," a hippy-type musical comedy as I understand it, and insisting that I got no appreciation for peculiar art forms. Very well, Dr. Smith, I plead guilty. I do not like Julie Andrews in "Music Man" (or was that Preston Foster?) any more than I appreciate all these ex-waitresses and truck drivers hoo-hawing their way through "Hair." The way I hear it, doctor, the English language is misappropriated any time it is hitched up with music, especially if the players wear costumes and bound around the stage. I would not give thirty-five cents to see King Kong fuck Arlene Francis at center stage, with the Philadelphia Philharmonica blowing its respective asses off, and Maria Callas lurking in the wings attended by Snookie Lanson. Never marry, as I said, Mr. Smith, a young woman.

I was late in New York and told one Willie Morris how fortunate would be *Harper's* should you consent to grace their pages. He stared at me goggle-eyed and said "H. Allen Who?" and then fell deep into his dinner plate, which is par for the N.Y. literary scene. I saw him the next morning and asked if he remembered the conversation, and he expressed amazement that we had been together on the previous evening. I predict he will go far and people will write books about him after his death and credit him with a major renaissance in Amurican letters. Much the same as was did for Harold Ross.

That fellow Burnett, the Odessa lawyer, about whom you wrote me kind thangs, for which thanks are expressed, in connection with my most recent *Harper's* outing,* is hell on whiskey and sees all the absurdities. You and him ought to get together once or twice before you hi off to Hawaii. Last winter, when I was trailing him about for the purposes of my Art, Lawyer Burnett asked whether I was acquainted with you personally. I blushed, and denied it, and said only through your great works. He said we ought to call you and invite you to drink and [share] soulful considerations of all the problems we as civilized men mutually faced, being careful, of course, to eat great amounts of chili cooked from your recipes and keep politics out of it, and I agreed, and a funny thing happened to us on the way to the phone, which I forgot exactly what was but generally had to do with whiskey. I do not expect to be back down there before you get off to Hawaii, with or without the current Miz Smith, on account of I am going up to Harvard soon to get very well educated and you and Sul Ross [College] can go to hell. And take Burnett with you. But I recommend you each to the other.

Why I am going to Harvard is I got a Nieman Fellowship, and never been to school before. Except for Texas Tech, and not long enough there that I collected all my laundry. *Harper's* has some notion this will improve me. There is an implied insult in their attitude, but I have decided to be real big and ignore it.

Smith, one of these days when you are between books and depositions, you got to tell me whatever absessed you to move to Alpine, Texas? (The use of the word "absessed" as employed above has to do with honoring the memory of the late M. Newman, late a Justice of the Peace in Odessa, Texas, who drank cheap whiskey and loaned money to the poor blacks at exhorbitant rates, and who had a practice of saying sorrowfully to the poor folk who came before him for Justice, "Whatever absessed you to break the law that-a-way?")

Otherwise, I sayeth not. . . .

*Smith had written King praising his *Harper's* profile of Warren Burnett, "A Country Lawyer and How He Grew."

August 5, 1969

Dear Dr. Shrake:

Current lamentations: weight, Cambridge rents, pressing deadlines. To take in their order: puffed up to a squishy 215, I did, and Miz Kline got me eating little but lettuce and pears, and I have come down to 208 within a few days and got 18 more pounds to go. Cambridge rents: Terrible. Had to pay $390 per month for one-bedroom place. However, it is handy to Harvard Square and Harvard Yard and in a nice new building. Cambridge has very few nice new buildings, except two-three high rises where rent starts at $1,000 the month. We spent three to four days looking at houses, and kept getting took to old squalid ratty filthy places where folks wanted $250 upwards and finally decided we'd druther pay right at $400 and have bright, clean digs. . . .

Pressing deadlines: Trying to bootleg all possible thangs to the writing money market before September (I'll be ineligible to write thangs to publish while at Harvard). I have took on quick notice a piece for *Holiday Mag* styled "Why Dallas Is Despised" or some such, and got to have it in by September 1st. I got many old memories of Big D, and lots of old files to steal from, but could use help on what transpires there currently. I'd be obliged if you'd sit at typewriter when in jolly mood—within next week, pray—and write me two-three pages about Dallas, you being an old Dallas type in the best sense. Also, tell me a little about what's *right* with Dallas. If any. Indicate what part I can quote by name, and what I can merely use for background or put in the mouth of nameless Sources, and so forth. This will be heap big favor and keep me from having to borrow money to move to Cambridge, provided *Holiday* pays on time. (Incidentally, current *Holiday* advertises that I will be featured in September issue with piece styled "Don Meredith and his Cowboy Gang"—but ain't true. They kilt the piece on account of Meredith's retirement. Damn shame. I had quoted from you three-four times, and stole lots more from you without crediting it, and had several good quotes from Dandy Don, several of which he had actually said. Down the drain. Oh, well, I had already been paid. . . .)

Too bad you missed New Yawk party honoring the undersigned. I understand I had a good time, but admit this is second-hand information on account of Willie and I started drinking our lunch on the dot of noon and the party wasn't until five, and all I remember much of happened before five-thirty, and the party went on, I am told until tennish. At some time I made not one but two lengthy orations purporting to thank everybody for the nice party while bitching because there was no Going Away Gift, if reports are correct and I suspect they are. . . .

Editor's Note: Soon after King arrived in Cambridge, he and most of the other 1969/1970 Niemans began to chafe under the programs planned for them by Nieman curator Dwight Sargent. In reaction, they began to invite their own speakers to visit Harvard. King arranged for appearances by Willie Morris in the fall of 1969 and William Styron and Norman Mailer early in 1970.

October 6, 1969

Hon. Willie Morris
Chief Honcho
Harper's Mag
2 Park
N.Y., N.Y.

Dear Willie:

Unless you got objections, I shall within a few days circulate invitations to select Niemans and their ladies, plus two-three other Harvard heads, saying as follows:

Upon Conclusion of the Nieman Address by Hon. Willie Morris, Editor-in-Chief, *Harper's Magazine,* on the evening of October 21, 1969, at approximately 10 P.M., you are invited to 14 Concord Avenue, Apt. 218, where Mr. Morris, Contributing Editor John Corry, and the undersigned will give demonstrations in the Art of Drink. Beat Yale!

Naturally, I will find some way to charge the mag for the whiskey but will bear breakage costs myself. . . .

Editor's Note: Written on the same day as King's invitation to Morris, this "student progress report" shows his high spirits when first on the campus.

Office of Student Reports
Harvard University
Cambridge, Mass.

October 6, 1969

Mr. Willie Morris
Editor-in-Chief
Harper's Magazine
2 Park Avenue
New York, N.Y.

Dear Parent and/or Guardian:

This Preliminary Progress Report is submitted with respect to your charge, Mr. Larry L. King, a Nieman Fellow. Be assured we do not wish to alarm you unduly, ever-mindful that young people in their initial academic experiences sometimes require a period of adjustment. We do agree, however, that perhaps your charge would benefit from your early counsel.

All new Harvard students are rated by faculty members who have the opportunity to observe them in classrooms or in social circumstances. Our IBM cards show that while Mr. King has been variously described, the consensus word in reports on him is "peculiar." Not wanting you to think he has been hastily judged or judged without evidence, we submit the following behavioral information on your charge.

First, Mr. King insists that he came to Harvard to study "Astrology and Christian Science." Though multipally advised that John Harvard University does not offer those courses in this particular academic year, Mr. King has refused alternative courses. In point of fact, he has sent word directly to President Pusey that until such time as those courses are offered he shall "wait it out in the King's Men's Bar," a place of low repute among Harvard Gentlemen. This is perhaps a good time to relate that Mr. King exhibits certain hostilities, not always repressed, in insisting on giving a pronunciation to President Pusey's name that is neither appreciated by the President nor out of the realm of the vulgar. On those rare occasions when Mr. King does pronounce the President's name correctly, he uses it in sentences such as "You been getting any good Pusey lately?" We find this unsatisfactory.

One of Harvard's most learned and nationally acclaimed professors of economics, known to be a man of considerable wit, does not object when students laugh during his lectures. Normally, that is. Our professor finds Mr. King's predisposed laughter patterns objectionable, however—i.e., Mr. King does not laugh at the flashes of wit, but laughs loud and long when the professor states his academic and/or economic maxims. In one class your charge laughed for seventeen consecutive minutes out of a possible fifty-two. Our valued professor is rumored to be flirting with Yale.

In a sincere effort to achieve maximum communication with our students, Harvard professors traditionally end their lectures with the words, "Any questions?" Mr. King invariably asks one or more. His sample questions include "Who promoted Peress?" "Which came first, the chicken or the egg?" "If you're so smart why ain't you rich?" and (most regrettably, we feel) "You been getting any good Pusey lately?" The latter question, incidentally, has been painted overnight on the Cambridge Water Tower, underneath a companion slogan "Midland High School Seniors, 1946." Confronted with questions as to whether he had a hand in the water tower incident, Mr. King says only that he did not graduate from high school. Though we believe him, we find this an inadequate defense.

In other anti-social behavior, Mr. King has referred to distinguished members of the faculty as "Junior" or "you young whippersnapper," and questioned whether President Pusey has ever met a payroll. . . . At a reception for Nieman Fellows attended by local representatives of the mass media he repeatedly shouted "Fuck the *Atlantic Monthly.*" We are progressive, perhaps even permissive, but we do feel cause for these minor complaints.*

Very sincerely yours,
J. Saltonstall Lodge Cabot IV,
Director of Student Reports

October 19, 1969

Dear Lanvil & Glenda:

I had presumed that by now I would be conducting my correspondence in Latin; unhappily, Harvard has let me down: I must continue
with what we in Putnam called "Anglish."

What to say of the experience to date, some five weeks after the
Nieman program began? Disappointing, I guess. Sometimes I am certain of this, and sometimes less certain. Perhaps I expected too much:
waking after a few weeks walking 'round The Yard to discover my I.Q.
increased five-fold, perhaps, or a midnight visit from the ghost of old
John Harvard bearing a certificate attesting that I had become A Man
of Knowledge Pure. I don't feel much smarter, except in a negative
sense, and by that I mean that perhaps I was not as dumb to begin
with as I had hoped. And by that I mean that several of the under-
grad courses I visited, mainly in American History and American
Literature, seemed terribly basic: I already knew something of
Jefferson's attitude toward the Church, and I had read the
Leatherstocking Tales. So I have pretty much revised my thinking on
how I will use my year—not digging in pursuit of refinement of my
knowledge about the American Past in general, but concentrating in
the main on the novel.

I am taking several approaches to this, having found three good
courses (two of which deal with the novel almost exclusively, and a
third including it) on writing and all taking different approaches. One
course is a creative writing offering on the novel and the short-story,
taught by an aged New England gentleman of excellent reputation,
Theodore Morrison, whose main claim to fame in a public sense is
that he taught an ex-Nieman named A.B. Guthrie (*The Big Sky,* as

you will recall, and others) how to write fiction. Morrison is teaching me something, too: sometimes I find that I knew, or in some corner of my soul suspected, some of his favorite maxims; it helps, however, to hear them articulated; other of his ideas are entirely new and helpful. He is, in short, putting the abstract "rules" of the novel into words I can grab with my brain, organizing my thinking a bit.

A second course is one called "The Novel since World War II" (though it began with Celine's *Death on the Installment Plan*). There is a hellaciously long reading list. The prof, a young man named R. J. Kiely, who appears to be so bright he could probably read in the dark, lectures on the author, the author's ideas of writing and life, as much as on the work itself. I find it fascinating and, discovered suddenly a few days ago, that the lectures have helped me read at, I suppose a deeper level than I normally have: to pick up some of the nuances I have heretofore missed. . . .

My favorite course is "American Writers and Radicalism"; we are dealing, currently, with the period shortly after WWII. Dr. "Kip" Pells, the instructor, began the first class by saying he was "born during the time of Pearl Harbor," making it sound as if it were only six weeks after the time of Christ, and aging me immensely. The kids in that class— Christ are they bright! Of the 90-odd seniors who applied for the course, he admitted only fifteen. He also turned down two Niemans who applied to audit the course, but—flatteringly—when I presented myself for interview, I found he was a regular *Harper's* reader and something of a fan. So I was admitted, even swung it so that Rosemarie could attend, and she agrees with me that it's the best course I've found. The kids are fantastic, and I am taking as many notes on them as I am the course. I am, incidentally, the Devil's Advocate in that course, since I am the only one (including Dr. Pells, who was a mere child) to have lived through the '40s or who existed during the '30s. Most of them, in fact, were born in '48 or '49, and I am called upon to defend why "you"—meaning America, or the American Government—did thus and so in the dim distant past. (I came in touch with my age in the first class, rudely in touch with it, when Pells referred off-handedly to the execution of the Rosenbergs,

and one super-bright kid said, "Who were the Rosenbergs?") Great
reading list in that course too, and I am really digging to be prepared
for that class since I seem to be the unofficial but lone spokesman for
America from the FDR period on through Eisenhower's years.

With some regularity I am attending John Kenneth Galbraith's
course in economics; I felt obligated to, since he was one of my
Nieman sponsors and gave good quotes for both my books. Frankly,
however, and confidentially (because I perhaps uncharacteristically
do not wish to bite that particular hand that fed me) he puts me to
sleep: drones on in a monotone, stutters, stammers, and is altogether
disappointing. I can't understand that: I've had a couple of private
conversations with him, and he informally bull-shitted with the
Niemans for two hours at lunch one day, in very entertaining fashion.
From the lectern, however, he is a dud. (Invited to the Galbraiths for
dinner on Wednesday evening upcoming, and perhaps I will be able to
unlock more of the mystery of the Great Man after that experience.)*

I am concentrating on reading foreign novels on my own (mainly
the Russkies) from a list supplied by Norman Podhoretz. We've had a
variety of speakers talk to the Niemans at luncheon, afternoon, and
dinner seminars, ranging from Red Smith to Nathan Glazer, most of
whom have been disappointing. This is because Dwight Sargent, the
old-maidish man who is Curator of the Nieman Program, tries to supply speakers for his own academic-political advancement; they generally feed us Establishment or Administration pablum, and Sargent is
upset when several of us—yours in the forefront—twist their nuts a
bit in cross-examination. (Which should be the purpose of these seminars; that is, they should promote give-and-take exchanges of information, and excite intellectual passions. I have helped lead a revolt
against Sargent in this [and a few other] respects; last week we met
with him as a group and took away his getting seminar speakers for
the spring term: hereafter, we will invite our own speakers for greater
variety and stimulation. The fall speakers, unfortunately, are all
already locked in.)

One of whom, day-after-tomorrow (or Tuesday evening) will be
Willie Morris. Rosemarie and I have rented a spacious room in the

Harvard Faculty Club (Niemans have access to the Club on a level with the faculty) to give a 9:30 P.M. to midnight party for Willie, David Halberstam, Herman Gollob and John Corry, all of *Harper's*. We're having a number of faculty people (including the Galbraiths, Adam Yarmolinskys, Pells, Kielys, Morrisons; some newspaper and magazine people I know up here; all the Niemans and their wives.) *Harper's* will foot the bill.

Looking back over this, it sounds better, somehow, than it is. I find myself often despondent, really dragging my chin, feeling that I am not getting all out of this that I should, asking myself what a 41-year-old fool is doing interrupting his budding career for a year. The answer, on my good days, comes back: "'Cause you ain't had no schoolin' Fool, and 'cause you so fucking iggernent." On bad days, I have no answer. I feel a bit insecure, a bit out of the main stream, and I'm not as well-recognized here as in New York precincts in the matter of Personal Fame, and all this chomps on my Big E Ego. (Though I have helped by giving a speech at Tufts, and am to be interviewed by a Cambridge paper next week.) I feel lost and guilty not writing, and don't have any goddamn *time* to write. With classes, necessary reading, and damn near mandatory social activities far beyond our usual schedule, I feel all this press for time and often a waste of time, and there are days when I wish I had not come here.

I marched five heel-blistering miles in the Vietnam War Protest last Wednesday, from Cambridge Commons (across the street from our apartment, or one block up, really) to Boston Commons. That evening I went into a church for the first time in 13 years, save to bury the dead, to attend a pray-in (where I could think of no prayers, so spent the time spying on the crowd), after which we—and a couple of thousand from other churches—marched into Cambridge Commons, all carrying candles, for hymn-singing, more prayers, and speeches directed to Heaven about what a shit Nixon is.

This place is full of history. Walking across Cambridge Commons to class one morning, I saw an old, gray, stone marker and paused to read that there — on that very spot, under a certain huge tree, had gathered one evening in the long ago a force to march down to

Lexington and fight the Redcoats, the church I went into the other evening dates from 1775; there are markers in its cemetery dating from 16-hundred odd. I can't get all that fixed in my mind. It wasn't so long ago, of course, as the history of the earth goes, or even man's recorded history, but it is a damn sight longer ago than they built the Scharbauer Hotel in Midland, and I have always related historical dates to that year.

There are some few good fellows among my colleagues, though some few duds to match them. My favorite is Wallace Terry of *Time-Life,* a black man, 31, ex-Brown University with roots in Indiana, and for the past two years a war correspondent in Saigon. Cliff Terry, movie critic of the *Chicago Tribune,* is a good little fellow, and so is Barlow Herget III, a young kid who is managing editor of the *Paragould* (Ark.) *Daily Press.* Bill Montalbano, Latin-American correspondent for the *Miami Herald,* is also fine. Rick Smith, diplomatic correspondent for the *N.Y. Times,* is bright, but cannot forget that he is a Timesman and a diplomat to boot, and is a bit much of a straight arrow for me. Lou Banks, 52, (only man in the group to whom I am junior, and he has a special "research" fellowship rather than a regular Nieman one) is managing editor of *Fortune,* and smart and pleasant, but is also a bit stuffy for one from the Wild West. The rest are mainly Blahs, except one, who is not only a Blah but also our Problem Drunk. This ain't the pot and the kettle: he makes me out a tee-total. . . .

In the writing department, I am doing nothing now. However, *Harper's* will publish in December or January a long, 18,000 worder called "Reflections of a White Racist."** *Holiday* has recently accepted my piece on how Dallas got to be such a terrible place, and also has for some future publication my piece on Cajun Country. And I am soon to write (on the sly, since we really aren't supposed to write here) a piece for Willie.

There is little else to relate, save that Harvard has no Spelling course— evidence of which you have found, I am sure, on every page. . . .

*One-on-one, King found Professor Galbraith to be interesting and amusing at that and subsequent dinners.

**Later expanded to the 1971 book, *Confessions of a White Racist.*

Editor's Note: The Nieman Fellows traditionally played a football match against the staff of *The Harvard Crimson*. King, as the oldest Nieman, served as the player-coach and thus responded to the challenge issued by Jim Fallows, the *Crimson's* president that term. Fallows went on to become a noted journalist, editor, and author.

King remarks: "Niemans lost 12-0, but I wrote it up for the *Crimson* claiming a 14-12 win due to two 98 yard punt returns by my ownself in last 90 seconds."

October 27, 1969

Mr. Jim Fallows
President
The Harvard Crimson
14 Plympton Street
Cambridge, Mass 02138

My dear Mr. Fallows:

The Nieman Class of 1969-70 is happy to accept the touch football challenge of an effete corps of impudent snobs who characterize themselves as intellectuals.

If one did not fully appreciate the generous ignorance of Youth, one might be required to demand a forty-point handicap in payment of your foolish letter. We ask no quarter, however, and give none. You are in for the most one-sided contest since Spiro Agnew last matched himself against Reason. To make an affirmation of the obvious, your role shall be that of the Greek.

We choose Saturday, November 8th, as the Day of Truth, so that you may live in proper dread for the maximum period.

You should be warned that the current Nieman class includes several of the greatest athletes of all time. I know this to be true, because my associates have many times related their unusual football talents at our strategy sessions in the King's Men's Bar. These are mature men, dedicated as are the majority of journalists to pure Truth, and therefore may not be suspected of even the smallest exaggeration. Therefore, I have found it unnecessary to call the Niemans together to practice for such callow, amateur teams as your own.

Spirit is high among the Nieman Fellow Blowhards. We have a rousing fight song ("Pusey Forever"); our team motto is "Hit 'Em In Their Dangling Participles." True, one malcontent on our squad made the motion that we forfeit the football game and meet you only for purposes of drink. High morale caused this motion to be soundly defeated, 6-5, our representative from the *Christian Science Monitor* abstaining. It was his position that your team has probably gone to pot.

Our acceptance of your silly challenge is conditional only to the degree that we insist on equal space in *The Crimson* to match whatever inaccurate story you propose to publish after your upcoming humiliation. Our best writer shall be chosen for this task (though modesty prohibits my naming him), and we suggest you assign your best writer—in the event that you have one. . . .

November 11, 1969

Mr. Elroy Bode
818 Baltimore
El Paso, Texas

Dear Bode:

I don't know the proper way to address a Fellow. I will settle for something like Your Majesty, Learned Fellow of the Universe, Sir Your Holiness. That should take care of any contingency.

The Harvard experience is perhaps best described as confusing to one who had but a slight acquaintance with Texas Tech. Much of the literature we have covered thus far reflects the 1940's and 1950's: because of my obvious years, I find myself being the reluctant explainer—if not, indeed defender—of the Eisenhower Years. . . . I have also heard very much academic jargon and bullshit spoken, most of which creeps in one ear and out the other. I haven't written much here. (We agree, in fact, not to write anything to be published while we are here.) John Kenneth Galbraith says I'm crazy and should get to work: that the writer's primary function is to write, that Harvard can't teach me all that much by my sitting in classrooms for a year, that I'll waste a year unless I write. I am more and more convinced he may be correct.

Yes, Frederick Exeley was very little (shamefully little) reviewed. Word-of-mouth caught on a bit last year just before they nominated him for the National Book Award . . . but dropped from sight again when [his book] failed to win. I haven't found ten people who have heard of the book, outside certain New York circles, and find that distressing because it was so very fine. His is one of the books I want to read again. *

I have lately become a fan of Aleksandr Solzhenitsyn, catching up to him a bit late. But what courage the man has to write as boldly as he does considering the limitations placed upon the Soviet artist not willing to serve the state by silence. Only the other day I read that he is under great pressures and attack in his homeland now, and found out for the first time that except for *One Day in the Life of Ivan Denisovich* (which was, you recall, published in Russia in the post-Stalin era) his other books (*Cancer Ward, The First Circle*) are unknown except in the West. As with many Russian writers, I find the going a bit spongy at times and have hell keeping up with the cast of characters, and it is too goddamn wordy. But he has that something alive, writing from the gut as he does, and he can fair put a country boy into a stark gray Russian Winter mood. . . .**

---

    *Frederick Exeley's *A Fan's Notes* became, in time, a "cult classic" and then a popular success still in print these years later and now used in many college and university classes.

    **King later became disenchanted with the exiled Russian writer's pedagogical scoldings and dismissed him in public print with a cutting reference to "Solzhenitsyn's bullshit."

January 24, 1970

Hon. W. Burnett
Attorney at Law
310 N. Lincoln
Odessa, Texas

Dear Edsel:

Let me tell you a story about a Virginia boy. Name of William Styron. I invited him here to speak to the Niemans; he accepted. Some few days later he called to express the thought that perhaps we could arrange for black folks not to ask him questions, or to ask him gentle ones, on account of he has about had enough attacks to suit him as a result of alleged racisms liberally sprinkled through *Nat Turner*. I promised to try to find tame 'uns. He came up, appeared somewhat nervous, and indeed, had some cause to be so, as all the blacks were not real tame (and some I thought might be got wilder than I would have suspected), and all the questions were not easy. Whereupon we repaired to my quarters with 16 or so guests from among the 60-odd at the larger Nieman function. This crowd was considerably tamer and Brother Styron relaxed himself with numerous drinks over a period of some hours, at the conclusion of which he somehow got a-holt of a bit of Mexican boo smoke. Shortly (maybe 3 in the A.M.) he describes himself as feeling peculiar. He flops on the couch and bespeaks of death. He commences quoting poetry. He falls on the floor and his wife cradles his head in her arms, and they speak passages to one another of what I think was Shakespeare.

Whereupon Styron bolts upright, proclaims with a wild gleam that he can "see the other shore" and rushes off towards the outdoors, where the temperature is then around zero degrees, without no coat on—possibly to shake the hand of Jesus, who knows? I trail him into the night with his coat, he proclaiming he's got to go since he's "crossing to the other side." We are trailed by the Mesdames Styron and King, and the three of us thrust him into his coat, though he is jerking around in a little dance and still bespeaking visions of "the other side." I attempt to calm the crazy bastard, do get him, indeed, fairly easy so that he walks well without a rope. Right near the American Trial Lawyers Building, you may recall it, he frees his elbow from my gentling grasp to ask me please to hold his hand. Well, now, it is on a public street and our wives are with us, and I feel nearly as peculiar holding his hand as I would your own or V. L. DeBolt's* or maybe even my ex-wife's, but I am amidst the gentling processes, and it is, after all, cold and late out and no one about except the girls, so I lead him along by the hand. He jabbering now, about crossing over and such matters, every step. As we near the Sheraton-Commander Hotel, he loosens his grip upon my digits and tumbles half-assed to the icy sidewalk; I catch him, curse him under my breath so Rose Styron won't hear me, and—much in the manner of a Faith Healer— instruct him to walk. He does very well for about a dozen steps and then with no warning droppeth like a ton of pig-iron to the sidewalk, making much noise, and it being right obvious he was out stone cold before he hit the ground. I wrestle to upright him; he, being out, and weighing in the 190s or so, will not budge. Rose and Rosemarie grapple to help me, no dice; the ice and snow are commencing to seep through his nice new suit and, hopefully will revive him, but does not. One of the ladies dashes into the Sheraton-Commander Hotel and returns with a bellboy who may weigh 127 pounds tops, and who, upon seeing the scene, is quick to proclaim that he is 62 years old and not of a mind to lift heavy objects. Styron finally comes around enough that I curse in his ear threats to abandon him should he not, like Jesus on the third day, rise and walk. Threats, myself, and the two women carry-drag him into the hotel and thrust him perhaps rudely upon the nearest couch or divan, the bellboy helping through instructions that we should not drop him in the interest of his health.

Styron is flat on the couch or divan, proclaiming it his place of death, telling Rose where the key to the lock box with all the secret money is hidden, and perhaps confessing to an old infidelity or two, and begging her to remind the children that their daddy had been a good man and loved them to the last. Even at 3 A.M. this attracted a considerable scene, elevator boys and other bellhops (where were *they* when I needed them?) gathering around, and Rose again cradling his head and answering him in Shakespeare, and between her best passages instructing me to get the rescue squad, the best doctor in Cambridge, etc. I am not of a mind to move quickly on any of these, on account of Styron is now talking audibly of his "trip" and hinting he has had more than Dr. Pepper, but, blood perhaps on my hands if I don't, I do. The rescue folks cometh and cops till Hell won't have it, and Styron faints again a time or two while they strap him in a stretcher gadget, and I am relieved at this because except in suspicious circumstances in the Southern Courts it is not possible for an unconscious man to blurt his confessions and/or involve others as material witnesses. The cops put me in a cruiser and take me to the hospital hot on the heels of the rescue squad, and I am too drunk to sit silently, so jabber like an idiot in the hope of making friends, coming out for the Vietnam War, police salary increases, and stronger dope laws to the extent that they—noting my beard and long hair— begin to look so suspicious I finally fall on a stricken silence.

At the hospital they take Styron to Emergency, attempt to strip him and do medical things, and he—arousing now—begins to say let him die with his clothes on, let him tell his wife goodbye, let him join the others on the yonder shore, let him take no more trips. Meanwhile, I have telephoned the Justin Kaplans (the Mr. Clements and Mark Twain [book] man you recall) who had been the only ones here other than ourselves and Styron when the boo-smoke was blowing, in order to discover the name of Cambridge's most efficient doctor, and had done the same thing at Rose Styron's behest with Adam Yarmolinski, and soon they all fall upon the hospital, and while we wait Rose makes it known that if it hadn't a-been for the boo-smoke, etc. I, of course, poo-poo this and talk of how many whiskeys have been drunk by the ill Mr. Styron, and how his nerves was on edge, and maybe the cold got to him, and what not. Police, of course, are running around filling out the required forms, and hospital personnel are doing the same, so I am speaking in hushed (if passionate) tones, and hoping both Mr. and Mrs. Styron will do the same.

After many tests and long past the time my own nerves are hanging and I am about ready to ask have they an extra emergency bed, the doctors say that contrary to his own expectations the Famous Arthur will live, though they have discovered heart palpitations, nerve twitchings, and high-blood pressure, plus some liquor in the blood. Their attitude began to be a bit more cavalier, and I was personally for taking him back to the hotel on the theory he might die in his sleep not fully confessed, but Rose insists on his staying in the hospital a few more hours. We claim him around 8 A.M.; he still saying things like "I have seen the other side" and "I been in a terrible world and a place I don't ever want to go again" and carrying on, generally, like a Baptist fanatic. I talk over this, loudly congratulating the doctors and their interns and nurses on their special skills, nice hospital, modern equipment. Finally got him out of town in the afternoon, though he again insisted on saying what a "trip" he had and blaming it on the wrong thing as far as I am concerned, and I have heard no more from him and [currently] hope that I never shall. Thanks to the Kaplans and the Styrons' own big mouths, however, the word is too generally abroad in the Harvard community about his collapse and about what he suspects brought it on. And where it happened, of course.

And Mailer, God help us, is still to be faced. . . .

Contracts signed on *White Racist* book and I am at work. Also, a book just published by the Free Press (subsidiary of Macmillan Company) entitled *Representative Men*, a study of pop-culture heroes, reprints my Buckley article; also, a fellow name of James Mc-Something Dabbs, an old literature critic of some repute, I am told, is publishing a book on novels dealing with Civil Rights and devoted a generous chapter to *The One-Eyed Man*; also, a feller is flying to tape-record me for a book on Southern Writers to be published by LSU Press soon. Also I just done a book review for *Chicago Sun-Times*, a little essay for *Harper's*, and am at work on two reviews for *N.Y. Times* and one for the *Boston Herald-Traveler*. All this, Harvard, and Styron too. . . .

---

*Resident publisher of the *Odessa American*, who complained to his editors that he did not "understand" King's humor or "aggressive attitudes" against many of the newspaper's policies.

May 4, 1970

Senator Ralph Yaborough
The Methodist Building
Capitol Hill
Washington, D.C.

Dear Ralph:

You're still my Senator. I never had one from Texas except you. I do not exclude "the mighty" LBJ.

I remember the day you arrived in the Senate, thirteen years ago, and did the Burro Club the favor of speaking to us before you'd had time to remove your coat. I remember long before that, going back to the 1952 race against the Shivers Gang. Yours is an unbroken record of service to the people, and talking sense to the people, and the last man I could really say that about was Adlai Stevenson.

My regrets are many when I think of your loss to the Senate, but my main regret is that such a good man could become a victim of the times and the temper thereof. Sure, I know it was the same old Big Money Shivers-Connally-Daniel-LBJ crowd, but you had tamed them with victories in 1957, 1958, and 1964. And you would have defeated those same enemies of the people again, I am confident, save that during the Nixon-Mitchell hysteria you had enough man in you to stick to your guns. I wrote a novel about a Governor, a good man like you, and like you he was finally defeated in terrible times. "I just got in the way of goddamn History," he said. So did you. . . .

July 16, 1970

The Wallace Terrys
46-A Dana
Cambridge, Mass 02138

Dear Wally, Janice, and Precious Children:*

I have had my ass glued to the chair and my fingers in place on the typewriter almost since returning home from Harvard. *Confessions* has been finished and in Viking's hands for a couple of weeks now, about 8,000 words on Brother Dave Gardner have been completed and will be in the September *Harper's* and I expect to finish my Harvard experience within 10 days for the October issue. The latter is, if you will pardon the expression, going to be longer than Joe Louis's dick (an expression of my childhood, where, of course, everyone was an expert on the subject.) I think Willie intends to use it for his lead piece. I've already written approximately 11,000 words and expect to add another 5000 or so. You and I are the only persons I have not creamed. Dwight Emerson Sargent, a number of former Niemans, and half the faculty will have trouble controlling their bodily functions. Jesus, writing about those cold dispirited days, as I have been doing now for a couple of weeks, is damn near as depressing as having lived them. . . .

Willie was down here July 4th weekend and we drank up a fair share of Washington's whiskey. He told me (in strict confidence, and I pass it on to you under the same circumstances) that the *Harper's* ownership got on his butt for running $90,000 over the editorial budget in the last quarter, and told him that (due to Nixon's recession) he must cut back. I mention this to you because, from what he said, I take it he is not going to be hiring any more contributing editors until the situation is improved.

We had planned to leave here for Texas in about 10 days, or as soon as I had finished the Harvard piece, but yesterday Rosemarie's doctor said he would require her presence here for extensive tests during the next month, so there goes our plans to vacation with *our* Precious Children at Padre Island, on the Gulf of Mexico. Now, I just don't know what will happen—whether I'll have the kids here, or go down there briefly, or just what the hell. . . .

*Wally Terry, who came to Harvard as a Nieman Fellow after covering the Vietnam War for *Time*, was King's closest friend there.

August 27th (I think), 1970
Thursday, 4 a.m.

Dear Lanvil & Glenda:

I arrived back here Sunday night, extracting Rosemarie from the clutches of NIH, to learn that my adrenal glands must soon be removed if I am to keep pace with her. I have not seen such a whirling dervish since my youth. If she felt any better, I could neither stand her nor life. However, it is a comfort to say that last evening, after 72 hours of absolutely maniacal activity by my spouse (including marching on crutches in a Fem Lib rally!) she suddenly felt tired and sore and collapsed into early slumber. May she continue to regress. It is my only hope.

Clyde King cannot forget his trip to Austin and environs short of the grave. I took him and Cora and Estelle and the Precious Children to Seminole last week to visit sister Libby, whereupon he spent the afternoon relating everything from old maps to witnessing the Alamo to his hot pepper adventures. Cora, of course, gave him something of the evil eye, not approving his having enjoyed himself and, possibly, considering it something of a personal betrayal. She attempted to get even by calling up her 1955 trip to Washington, a thing which eventually silenced him but even she knew that he had the latest if not the greater Adventure. I think I told you that, once Cora and Estelle debarked in Cisco, Clyde didn't shut up again until [after] we reached and stayed in Austin and, indeed, returned to Cisco. There he momentarily went into eclipse, only to revive his tongue when we reached Seminole. On return to Midland from that point, however, he again became the Silent One, permitting Cora to dominate the conversation and, as always, pretending to be deaf as well as speechless. There is a glint of amusement in his eye that was not there before, however, and he has revealed a side of himself that we neither suspected nor had heretofore discovered. . . .

On arrival in Putnam, it was revealed that Aunt _____ was not present. She had collapsed with mysterious fevers and chills at 11 P.M. the previous evening, and had been rushed to the hospital in Baird. We were a good two hours quitting Putnam, Aunt Ethel requiring that much time to explain exactly how she had won $37.00 some years or months ago playing the two-bit slot machines in Las Vegas, and being unwilling to brook the slightest interruption. The best I could figure, she had waited a long time to tell it. She asked how was "Jean's" can-cer?* I said as well as could be expected. Meanwhile, my mother sat and stared and brooded over Aunt _____ collapse and the suspicion that Clyde had enjoyed himself in Austin. Your mother locked her sightless Orphan Annie eyes on a given spot on the floor and obvi-ously was not a large part of the proceedings. Dad in his whispery old voice tried to tell Uncle _____ of the miracles of Austin and San Antonio but Uncle _____, being deaf, sat in wonderment second only to Aunt Clara's.

In Baird, Aunt _____ looked like death warmed over. Cousin _____ informed Uncle _____ that he feared for her life, and Uncle _____, not understanding that _____ had said "Dad, I'm afraid Mother is really bad off this time," looked around uncertainly and then laughed heartily, ending it in *EEEEEEE*, which shocked by-standers and nurses having no clue that he is stone deaf. . . .

Came the hour, finally, when we would depart the Baird hospital. I went to the car to get the air conditioner working ahead of the old folks' arrival. As mother was being loaded in the car, she of the most uncertain balance these days, there was a great crash and a loud cry from her and Clyde shouting, "Weldon,**come help me with your Mammy." Mother had contrived to fall half-way in the car and half-way out, and to become hopelessly entangled with one knee jammed under the gadget on the door that rolls up the window and one leg sprawled outside the car, and she flat on her dear old ass in the back floorboards. Clyde just flapped around ineffectively in the way, unable to lift Cora, which I had hell's own time doing, dead weight being what it is. After a near heart attack and broken back I straightened up to see my healthy, if underworked, cousin regarding all this with a grin from six paces and Uncle___—who may be deaf but surely is not blind—greeting the scene with his patented *EEEEEEE*.

From Midland to Alpine, where I called on the writer H. Allan Smith, we being old pen pals who had never met. I phoned him from

Midland on a Sunday to say I would arrive at noon the next day and
call on him, with his permission, he saying—in the tones of excess
Scotch—"Son, I may be drunk on my ass," and my response being,
"Sir, I guarantee you I shall be." At noon the following day I called to
find him two months drunk out of his mind. We had, however, a
pleasantly wet visit for some two hours, he praising me as the bright
young writer of this generation between telling me stories of his own
glory days in the presence of H.L. Mencken, Gene Fowler, et al. Until,
in a given moment, his eyes glazed more than normally and he said
stridently: "You long-haired bearded communist cock sucker, what
makes you think you can write books?" To which I responded, "Only
the endorsement of such great men as you," whereupon his wife leapt
in horror to apologize and send him off to bed and beg that I return
when he is "feeling better." In a pig's eye, I mumbled. . . .

There was more, including Burnett filing for divorce while I had
one of his sons on the road with me, but I have gone past the point of
relating it.

Peace. Oh *God,* peace!

Yours in Christ and some confusion,

Weldon Raymond Floyd King

*Jean was King's ex-wife.
**In their later years, LLK's parents—when in stress—often called him by
his brother's name or Raymond or Floyd after old uncles.

Sept. No. 21, 1970

Mr. William Brammer
Dept. of Journalism
Southern Methodist University
Dallas, Texas

Dear Billie Lee:

I been seeing Larry McMurtry some. We drive down to rural
Virginia and eat at a place where you can get hot-biscuits and red-eye

gravy and listen to Ernest Tubb on the juke box and play like you back home again, though I don't know why we bother. I think we got cultural shock. He is one of the most enjoyable persons I ever been around not to drink much whiskey or smoke no dope.

I am writing this letter to keep from having to write for real. You know the feeling. I've got to re-write the last six pages of my manuscript for a book called *Confessions of a White Racist* which Viking is so foolish as to publish come Sprang Time, and a piece for Willie, and a book review for the *L.A. Times,* and work on my plagued novel (which Viking was also foolish enough to buy) all about three generations of Texans who bear a strange likeness to the King family, they having lots of clod-hoppers and Baptist fanatics and abortions and divorcements and rednecks in their midst. I have thought on this novel a whole lot and have claimed in weak moments to have wrote much of it, but I ain't really writ much. Not hardly any. I set out to describe West Texas and how it got that way, and carried it plumb back to Creation and wound up with 88 pages on how the world got made and where man come from, and while it may be very instructive it has not got a damn thang to do with my novel and I guess I will have to throw it out and start again at the opening scene where my protagonist is drunk and puking on the statue of the Texas Ranger lawman at Love Field.*

Speaking of Love Field, I was there on a Sunday about a month ago and spent a dollar's worth of dimes calling all the Brammers, and none of 'em admitted knowing you and I even got a Bill Brammer and we talked for five minutes before it was discovered he don't teach at SMU or read or write books but is a man who flit-sprays insects for hire. . . . I don't know who he thought I was. So I called A. C. Greene and he came to the airport and got me in new clothes and a big new Lincoln, and lo! I learned he had become rich in some mysterious way I do not understand, having to do with being gifted with a huge hunk of *Times-Herald* stock by, as I understood, some formerly demented old lady now gone to Jesus. I wish I had made good friends with some formerly demented old lady now gone to Jesus, leaving riches behind. It would be even better than the Oil Bisiness.

I was in Austin and seen briefly Budrow Shrake, Fletch-the-Boone and Japanese (Ah-So) Cartwright, none of whom made real good sense. Shrake has bought two fierce police dogs, and they kept sniffing my crotch and looking hostile, and so I did not have much fun. There came a time when I half-wished they would bite me, to end the suspense. Ah-So Cartwright had some scheme where I am supposed to sell his and Shrake's novel drawn from an original screen play, claiming to my agent and editors I had discovered a live-wire writer named M.D. Shafter who had wrote the great novel, and when it came time to produce M.D. Shafter in the flesh, Fletch-the-Boone[**] was the one to be produced. All this on account of Ah-So and Budrow discovered tardily their contract on their screen play says a novel from it cannot be sold until after it has been released as a movie, or something, and so they wanted to use me to set up this felonious deal where their novel is sold under M.D. Shafter's name, who is, remember, supposed to be Fletch-the-Boone, and then after or on or about publication they (Ah-So and Budrow) would sue Fletch-the-Boone for stealing their idea, or he would sue them, or maybe they would sue one another jointly; I forget just how it worked. Anyhow, I hoo-hawed and smiled and acted friendly and never gave them the satisfaction of an answer about doing their dirty work for them, and escaped town before they could press me a second time. . . .

[*]Another project abandoned, in due time. — LLK
[**]Austin friend Fletcher Boone.

5

"Rough and Rocky Travelin'..."

In a span of less than two years—from October 1970 to June 1972—King lost his father, the working companionship of his cherished *Harper's* colleagues, and his wife Rosemarie, who finally succumbed to cancer. At the same time he was at the peak of his career as an essayist and commentator, with the publication of his most popular *Harper's* piece, "The Old Man," and the nomination of his expanded *Harper's* story, *Confessions of a White Racist*, for the 1972 National Book Award.*

Clyde King had suddenly died in October 1970, the same month that *Harper's* published "Blowing My Mind At Harvard." Willie Morris loved King's tales about his father and had been after him for years to write a story about his "old man." After his funeral, King called Morris and said, "Willie, I can write it now." He did, finishing the piece before Christmas.

There had been portents of internal unease at *Harper's* before the breakup in March 1971. The dissolution of the country's premiere magazine staff was important news that spring. King's letters to Frank Rich and to Lanvil and Glenda express both the shock and the heat of battle—his published accounts include his essay "Looking Back On The Crime or Rememberin' Willie and Them" published in his 1974 collection *The Old Man and Lesser Mortals*, and perhaps the most complete rendition of the magazine's demise ever published in an interview included in John Carr's *Kite Flying and Other Irrational Acts: Interviews With Southern Writers*, published in 1972 by the LSU Press.

Exacerbating the *Harper's* disaster was King's temporary estrangement from Willie Morris. A Washington argument ended badly with a midnight fistfight in the streets of staid Georgetown, bringing, as witness Warren Burnett commented, "the cultures of Odessa, Texas, and Yazoo City, Mississippi, to the heart of the high-rent district." The old pals were distant for several months. Even after they made peace, the two saw very little of each other for the remainder of the decade. Morris had fled Manhattan for the outer reaches of Long Island and started writing a novel, *The Last of the Southern Girls*. His new chums on Long Island included the writer James Jones and Jones' wife Gloria, and the writer Truman Capote, who was then beginning a long personal and professional decline. King made one week-long trip to visit Morris, in the summer of 1974, hanging out with Willie, Jones and the actor Peter Boyle at Bobby Vann's piano bar. Otherwise, the two met only when they happened to run into each other at Elaine's, during the infrequent trips Morris made to Manhattan. "Willie pretty much exiled himself from our old *Harper's* gang," King says, "and I stayed in close touch only with David Halberstam."

King made new connections and friends in the magazine and newspaper worlds: editors Steve Gelman and Berry Stainbeck at *Life*, Arthur Kretchmer and Geoffrey Norman at *Playboy*, Ben Bradlee at the *Washington Post*, Jim Bellows at the *Washington Evening Star*; all would hire him to write. Down in Austin, an ambitious new magazine,

Texas Monthly, provided a good outlet for Texas oriented material. After *Confessions of a White Racist* was nominated for a National Book Award, an extraordinary number of publications bid for King's work, and he signed a fat book contract with a $100,000 advance to write the "definitive" biography of Lyndon Johnson.

Through February of 1972 King wrote playful or mock serious letters to Tom Guinzburg at the Viking Press, the playwright George Axelrod, Frank Rich, and Bud Shrake among others. Shrake thought at the time that "King handled personal adversities as well as anyone I'd ever known. Later, I realized he had been putting up a front because he truly couldn't come to grips with what was happening."

"What was happening" was that King's dying wife was in the cancer ward of the National Institute of Health for most of the last six months of her life. He spent long hours at her bedside, almost daily, "tongue-tied and wretched, and departed each day almost indescribably depressed and desperate." He would go home and drink himself into a stupor. When Rosemarie visited home, it was necessary for King to give her increasingly strong shots of morphine, every four hours, to ease her pain. King has written that this experience "was painful and melancholy and sleepless for both of us." Rosemarie died, at age 43, on June 8th, 1972. Two days later Congressman Mo Udall delivered her eulogy at a well-attended memorial service in Washington, after which King went on "a wasteful and destructive but what seemed to be necessarey spree all across the country. I was like a man escaped from jail."

King later said, "Willie Nelson's old line, 'rough and rocky travelin,' pretty much describes those years. I blew professional opportunities. Had no more discipline than a two-year-old. Couldn't sustain any work project for long or find that concentration necessary to my craft. I recall it all as almost surrealistically helter-skelter, and now realize that I was carrying around a lot of anger and fear. My 'solution' was to hide from reality by drinking and much aimless wandering about."

As might be expected, King wrote relatively few letters just after Rosemarie's death, or much of anything else compared with his tremendous output earlier. He abandoned numerous magazine pieces without cause and made only occasional false starts on his LBJ biography. During this period he only produced one book, the very well-received collection *The Old Man and Lesser Mortals*, published early in 1974. "It got great reviews," King says, "and sold like shit sandwiches."

King had by then accepted a teaching job at Princeton, hired on the recommendation of David Halberstam. He was appointed to a two-year chair, but hated the academic life—he left with six months left on his contract and was replaced by *New Yorker* writer John McPhee. By now he was under the gun from his agent and editors to make some rapid progress with the highly touted LBJ book. He sporadically turned in only enough to "temporarily pacify the disenchanted," though one chapter about Vietnam titled "LBJ and the Alamo Mind Set" was published in *American Heritage* and has been many time anthologized. "In my heart," he now says, "I knew I would never finish that book. For a long time I blamed people who were afraid to talk to me while LBJ was alive, and then felt the same fear with respect to Lady Bird. And there was a great deal of that. But, in retrospect, alcohol and fear kept me from doing that book. As Bill Brammer feared he could never match *The Gay Place* with a second novel, I became paralyzed by publicity bursts and high expectations about my LBJ book. And I didn't help matters by pretending, in interviews, to be making great strides when, in fact, I was making little or no progress."

By 1976, King was into a deep funk about his career and feared it might be over. Letters near the end of this chapter give us glimpses of that bleak period.

*Confessions of a White Racist lost to an early '70s favorite, *The Whole Earth Catalog*, a glorified list. King later referred to the winner as "faddist solutions for would-be tree-huggers, whale-savers and dirt-patters, most of whom would have died from exposure if outdoors for twenty-four hours."

—Richard Holland

Editor's Note: During his Nieman year, King formed a lasting friendship with Frank Rich, a senior at Harvard and a member of *The Harvard Crimson* staff. During his year on the campus,
King recognized Rich's writing talent and in 1974 helped place
Rich on the staff of *New Times* magazine as film critic. Rich went
on to become chief drama critic and columnist for *The New York
Times*. This is one of several letters King wrote about the firing
of Willie Morris from *Harper's* and the subsequent resignations
of most of the writing staff. Rich had editorialized about the
Harper's debacle in the pages of the *Crimson*.

March 15, 1971

Mr. Frank Rich
19 Hovey Avenue, #2
Cambridge, Mass 02138

Dear Frank:

Well, what can I say about the *Harper's* fiasco except "It's all over."
The dread finality of it is hitting home now that the excitement is gone,
and I guess it will all be forgotten in a twinkling once this week's news
mags pass. I cannot help but feel some irreparable split, some unrecov-
erable loss. The fact that I can make more money writing for other magazines is of small consolation: that's been true for some time, but I chose
to stay on at *Harper's* because I believed we were truly giving America
a national journal free of the sneering provincialisms of New York,
one that spoke in several strong voices, one that allowed the writer to
extend the language and himself as no other journal has done in our
time. This was not to say we always published perfect pieces or near-
perfect issues: no, we had a few clinkers, some gray pages, but for each
of those, I think, we had several that were bright and free and seeking. Willie Morris—given all his giant warts and personality quirks—
was simply the best at getting the best from the writer, and we worked

with him—and each other—in a partnership of hot excitement over the potential to be reached. There were friendships there, and understandings for all the egomania in each of us; and among the eight of us who quit I do not think anyone disliked anyone else save for a moment or two of drunkenness and jealousy here and there. For writing folk who live by their wits and talents and egos that is a rare thing indeed.

We tried to give that fucking John Cowles a chance to save his magazine—for we had every reason to believe that as a property owner he would want to save it—and to preserve its content as was, for he had told us five years ago in our initial meetings of his own desire to own a national journal of excellence, one that would probe and inspect the country and its time, and said, too, that he wanted to be an intimate part of it. I did not significantly hear from the son-of-a-bitch again until he met with us on the night of the big walkout. He was a curious study that night: refusing to back an inch, yet begging us for more time and when I charged him with my intent to quit and loomed over him on that silk couch (which *Newsweek* called "plastic" although, to the best of my knowledge, I was the only person to describe it to them) there was in his eyes—what?—some sheepish amazement, a little fear, disbelief. I do not understand the man, nor he me. Ah, shit. There is too much of this to write down, and my brain is tired of it, and yet I can think of little else. I'll fill you in when I see you. No word today from Sterling re my writing it for *Esquire.* I am going to push that tomorrow, for I want to write it to purge myself of it, and I want it told because it was at once high drama and good comedy and foolish as is the human race, impetuous and suicidal, and I want to try to leave the reader some sense of what it was we all killed.

Willie Morris just called, and though I am mad enough to kill the son of a bitch over his mis-handling of the politics involved in the fiasco, there was a plaintive note that touched me and set me remembering the good in the sorry bastard. I read him your 2nd paragraph, which both pleased and touched him as it did me. The other day I took Willie about 3,000 letters and telegrams that have come in supporting him, many of which said cancel their subscriptions if we all left, and I must admit that in our beery rancor they were pleasant to read.

Thanks for your comments on "The Old Man." My mother wrote that she had read it three times in two days, "laughing some and crying some" and adding, "I could almost hear him." There is some satisfaction in knowing that I can bring The Old Man back for her each time she reads it, though I suspect Blair and Cowles* would not understand what I mean by that. The June *Harper's* will carry my Udall piece—about 24,000 words, my longest—as its leader. And then no more L. King in *Harper's*. Fuck shit pussy hockey.

Oh, I had dinner and drinks with Kurt Vonnegut last Friday. I much liked him. He was a quiet man, shyer than I expected, but when he talked he made sense. I'd like to know him better. I met him through a photographer, Jill Krementz,** who took my pix for *Life* (they're to run a review of *White Racist*) . . . . Incidentally, I ate on his ass—mildly and as a gentleman—because you didn't make his writing class. He asked did you turn in a short story about a truck driver (I think) who killed a dog. It does not sound like you, but I inquire. Anyway, the problem was that Vonnegut lost the goddamned story and although he thought it the best of all he could not further identify the writer and so excluded him from the course. If it was your story, naturally you going to puke and put a hit price on Vonnegut with the Mafia. And I will pay half the cost.

I must black my boots and get ready for N.Y. Enough. Brain and muscles drained. . . .

T. Texas Tyler,
folk singer and geetarist

PS—Today's *Newsweek* had it wrong: I said Fuck it, not Screw it, and I didn't drawl. And until now, I had not thought of myself as a "rusty-bearded Texan." They fuckin' up mah image, son! I've much to say, later, on the shitty reporting done on this story. Every time I am a part of a story and know the true facts and situations as opposed to how they are reported, I think less well of journalists and more highly of whores.

* "Business side" *Harper's* moguls.
** Then Vonnegut's fiance, and later his wife.

March 15, 1971

Dear Lanvil and Glenda:

You have the basics of the *Harper's* fiasco, I suppose, from the Texas papers. I do not know how they played it there. The *N.Y. Times* was generally accurate, *Time* and *Newsweek* a bit less so. They were all propagandized a bit by Willie (and by an innocent Norman Mailer, who had been led to believe that his "Prisoner of Sex" piece had much more to do with the blow up than was true) and did not do much digging beyond what rumors or quick quotes they could round up by phone. Truly a shoddy performance by the press. . . . There is much that should be told, and I think John Corry is to do a piece on it for *Saturday Review,* and I want to do one for *Esquire* if the money's right and they'll give adequate space.

I do not know yet whether I will try for a contract with another magazine, or free lance again. I have agreed to do two pieces for *Life* (though we've not yet discussed subject matter) at better money than I have received per-article before, the idea being that if I'm happy and they are happy then we'll get together on a contract. *Playboy* sent word to get in touch re a possible contract or some writing assignments, and I today wrote a note saying I'll listen if they want to talk. *Atlantic Monthly* asked me even before this broke in the papers to give them a call should I leave. *Cosmopolitan* says it will use all I'll do at top prices. The *Washington Post* has asked me to write a job description and see if they can meet it. There are some other nibbles. So, I've no problem. Actually, I can make more money free-lancing or at another magazine or two than I was getting at *Harper's*—but still, it cannot for me be the same.

I have never seen such bad amateur politicians: Willie was a clod the way he handled his end of it, and Blair a fool and Cowles—well Cowles was stupid and remote and somehow unreal. Once we got into the two-week convolutions, it became apparent to me that neither Willie, Blair, nor Cowles have been understanding what the others said in their many months of quarterly meetings, and I am rather vaguely surprised that it didn't blow before now—or, perhaps not:

perhaps it did not blow only because they were involved in verbal shadow boxing, could not close with the foe, and erupted only when Willie threw the first real punch. They might have waltzed on another two or three years without that first punch by Willie, and for a long time I am going to wake in the night wishing he hadn't thrown it.

The details of the last two weeks are much too complex to attempt here: read 'em someplace, or I'll tell you in person when next we meet. High-lights: the night I kicked an antique chair across a posh New York living room and threatened to kill Norman Mailer, standing over him and shouting the vilest abuse, because he was oversimplifying the issues, and, as an outsider with a million bucks at his command, was trying to tell those of us in less commanding positions that resigning was the only honorable course . . . . the night he apologized to me, after learning more of the facts, and took me to dinner. . . . Halberstam, crying in the halls of the St. Regis Hotel after the near three-hour debacle with Cowles. . . . Bill Blair. . . . of the money men . . . . pulling strings and running into offices should he meet us in the hall out of a well-placed fear that one of us might kick the shit out of him. . . . the hours we spent lying to the *N.Y. Times*—or at least not telling them the truth—about where and when the Cowles meeting would be and then, after slipping up dark allies to enter the St. Regis under dark of night, encountering on the lobby bulletin board in letters a foot high: Harper's Editors Meeting In Suite 203. . . .

Mother continues to write of her loneliness, sad and repetitious little letters of the kind I am sure you were receiving a decade ago, and seems almost to yearn to fill the empty grave out there in that dry and windy-land cemetery. We are coming to that stage in our lives, I guess, that Blanche speaks of in "Streetcar Named Desire"—I have forgotten the exact line, but there is something of "that long and tireless parade to the grave yard" and how it seems endless once it has begun. That's my cheerful thought for the day. . . .

March 29, 1971

Mr. Bill Moyers
76 Fourth St.
Garden City, N.Y.

Dear Bill:

There are honest and touching letters as well as articles, and yours certainly qualifies. Thanks much. The reward of "The Old Man" has been that a number of people, including rank strangers, have written to say they are sending copies to their fathers with the hope that their fathers will receive a message of love. I think that Clyde C. King would have greeted all this with his wry country smile—but I also think he would have received some satisfaction from it. . . .

March 29, 1971

The Edwin Shrakes
5 Cheyne Place
London SW 3,
England

Dear Onkle Bud and Aunt Doatsy:

My, we do wish Willie [Morris] had not popped the cork until after we could have come inspected the Queen's herb gardens with you. The sad fact is that nobody in the whole Newnited States publishing world seems destined to send this Innocent abroad, so you may leave the pictures crooked and the pee puddles unmopped.

J. D. Milner was in town over the weekend, bringing whispers that one B. Brammer was busted in the company of exotic plants and spices, syringes, et al. He has not yet gone before a grand jury, so the tale is not yet public knowledge. Billie Lee hired him a young radical lawyer with flowing locks, the better to impress the Dallas Grand Jurors, of course, and W. Edsel Burnett is prevailing on him to get one of the big Dallas straight downtown Rotary Club type lawyers (and I think is furnishing him one.) Edsel Burnett hit town to offer his legal assistance to Brammer, who told him on the phone he was sorry but he had not been given enough notice and had big plans that night and could not see him. Edsel was alternately wryly amused and properly horrified. Brammer will never be a true revolutionary: he does not value personal freedom highly enough.

I do not know yet what I am gonna do in the way of the writing binness. Got some offers from other mags, but am gonna hold what I got for a while and think on it. Meantime, I got two assignments promised from *Life* and *Playboy*, plus all the work I want from *Cosmopolitan*, and the *Washington Post* wants to work it out where I do some long pieces for them on occasion. Nothing much appeals to me. I can make more money, surely, but then had that been the prime motive I would not have kept renewing my *Harper's* contract anyway. It are sad and I feel a loss. Willie-the-Morris was down here the last two-three days, laying around drinking and lamenting and getting up the nerve to go to L. I. to attack the novel.* He's had all kinds of editing jobs offered in publishing houses, opportunities with TV, foundations, and the like. Willie is a funny fellow, however, and has not even responded to the first letter or phone call. I think he's still in shock that they accepted his letter of resignation, and cannot bring himself to make a definitive move.

Home front jottings: N. Mailer and Carol Stevens the parents of a new baby girl, born about a week ago, which Mailer claimed to me all one drunken night at P. J. Clark's they had named Lady Bird Johnson Mailer, but investigation proved the name was something less exotic, I forgot. . . Buzz Farber hit me a hard punch in the gut one night at Elaine's, by way of friendly greeting, and I was so zonked I didn't know it until somebody told me. . . I [later] boxed an English journalist's ears there. Now fearing law suit. . . Notes from Bill Moyers and Ronnie Dugger saying my piece on my old Daddy, in April issue, done made 'em both cry. I may write soap operas if I can touch such hardened souls. . .

You sumbitch! You don't know how to brag on yourself proper. If I had wrote and sold an original screenplay, I would be able to fill up six pages boasting of the details. More on "Dime Box," please.** Have anything to do with Texas town of the same name? Why don't you and T. Dan Jenkins get me a big-paying job vaguely servicing your various movie and TV projects? I swan, yawl get rich and I still write for $40 for *The Nation*. Gonna send you my Old Man article. You want I should mail you the Mailer sex thang?

Miz Rosemarie joins in sending love, bear hugs, hoo-haws, Scriptural citations, merry songs, good things on you. . . .

* Morris's *The Last of the Southern Girls* was published in 1973.
**Filmed as "Kid Blue," starring Dennis Hopper.

March 29, 1971

Mr. Frank Rich
19 Hovey Ave, #2
Cambridge, Mass. 02138

Dear Frank:

I guess by now you have got the dismal word from Iowa. A letter awaited when I returned from my Peggy Lee sojourn, [for *Cosmopolitan*] from Wm. Price Fox, to the effect that his and Vance Bourjaily's lobbying failed. They liked your journalism out there, but did not feel proper affection for your fiction. Fox says of your fiction, "I thought he assumed a very dumb reader and that he ought to write more for himself and let reader do more work." He also said, "Tell him to try again next year and send in more fiction and no journalism."* So, are you gonna take Harvard's $3200 Shaw money and roam Urrip?** There are worse ways to spend time, including resigning from magazines. . . .

I wish I *could* take credit for Vonnegut's line re Styron's throwing *Love Story* out [from a best book list] because it wasn't enough like *Uncle Tom's Cabin*, but I do not recall Styron's name being mentioned when we reveled together.

Tell Scott [Jacobs] I got no quarrel with his definition of the "real" radicals as opposed to the establishment ones. In fact, I like the theory so much that only modesty prevents me from writing a long article about it for somebody. I think he may soon place Halberstam in the "real" group, the meeting with John Cowles, Jr. perhaps radicalizing Halberstam more than anything has before.

Reports on "The Old Man" are good to hear and, I boast with pardonable pride, fit the pattern. Scott's act of sending it to his father was duplicated by a number of people who wrote me. Moyers wrote and said it made him cry and to decide to spend Easter with his own daddy. I guess I have not gotten finer mail or better comments on a piece at any time. . . .

Ashley T. Goodfellow

*Rich had applied to attend the University of Iowa's Writer's Workshop and King had enlisted Fox and Bourjaily to help him.
** That is, Europe.

April 16, 1971

Mr. Steve Gelman
Senior Editor, *Life*
Time-Life Building
Rockefeller Center
New York, New York

Dear Steve:

Sterling Lord tells me you want to know a bit more on my proposal for a piece on Loving County, Texas.

I guess my big purpose is a study of isolation, and what it does to people, of space and distance and how they contend with it. Loving County is large, 647 square miles in area, bordered by thinly-populated sections of Mexico, New Mexico, and West Texas. The 1960 census counted only 226 people there, and while I have not checked the 1970 figure, the Texas Almanac for 1970-'71 estimated population at a mere 124. The only town, Mentone, in 1960 had 44 people; now I understand it's about a dozen. The entire town consists of a courthouse, a school going through the first six grades, and a combination store-cafe-gas station. Almost everyone lives on widely scattered ranches or on isolated oil leases; it is 53 miles to Pecos, a town of 10,000, and unless cable TV has come in—and I doubt the economics make it worthwhile—it may be one of the few places in America without TV reception. There are no blacks in the county, a few Mexican ranch hands, no Jews that I know of. There is no crime to speak of, and likewise nothing to entertain or titillate. What the hell do these people do? Why do they stay?

I am reminded of the early pioneers on the Western frontier. True, Loving County knows no Indian raids, but it does know severe temperatures (up to 106 or above in summer; 10 below has been registered in winter), dust storms, hard scrabble land (principal industry is oil, followed by cattle raising) and an isolation that is staggering once you've been out there in the eerie desert silence.

Politically, it isn't a very partisan place and there are few issues locally: generally people vote on the personalities involved and it can get quite heated. I recall a very bitter election for some minor office there three or four years ago, resulting in law suits and charges of fraud, and elections in the past led to fights and a gun or two flashed. On most elections, the county is split almost right down the middle—not over five or six votes difference. This means, of course, that the "swing vote" politicians must court is small, indeed, but more importantly it means that they cannot afford to offend more than that over the course of their terms without courting defeat. Of course, the big time pols never go there—of their last four Congressmen, I know of only one who has even bothered to come into the county.* Their local or county races, however, are hotly contested and campaigned.

I'd like to roam that vast wasteland by car, talking to about everybody in the county, seeing how they deal with isolation and space and that endless, unengageable West Texas wind, and with each other. It may be the most atypical place in America in these days of urban rot and exploding population and TV beamed in from around the world. Then again, it may not: the petty feuds and law suits and small personal wars in the county may make it more typical than we like to realize. I guess I want to do a pop sociological study, in a sense, though really I just want to talk to those old nesters and their young and other survivors of Cowboy and Indian territory.

If you're interested—and I plead my case by saying this story has popped in and out of my mind for the past two or three years, I generally find that a pretty good sign—I'd like to go there in the hot days of July and knock about for a couple of weeks. . . .**

*J.T. Rutherford.
**King's Loving County article appeared in *Life Magazine* as "The Lost Frontier" and won the Stanley Walker Journalism Award given by the Texas Institute of Letters.

April 26, 1971

Dear Alan Williams & Rich Barber:*

(I tossed a coin to see who'd get the original. Years in Congress makes one aware of the smallest divisions, and touches one's soul with cowardice. That's the thought for the day.)

Have you birds seen the Dan Wakefield review in the *L.A. Times* Book Review? If we are readying an ad campaign for pub date time, which I of course assume in my fantasies, then can we not suggest all or part of the following for inclusion:

". . .Where we well-meaning white writers have failed to root out racism and expose it, and attempt to eliminate it, is in ourselves. . . . Have you ever seen a racist in your own living room? Or in your own mirror? If you really are interested in giving an honest answer, I recommend that you first read Larry L. King's new book, *Confessions of a White Racist*. . . . For a long time we liberal whites felt that we could help expunge racism by "studying" and "understanding" the plight of the Negro in America, and all that time we were being told by the subjects of our sympathy to study ourselves instead, and finally one of us has done it. . . ."

Or something like that, with maybe consideration to a line or so from Wakefield's concluding paragraph.

While I am in the ad business, I note a line from *Publisher's Weekly:* ". . .

an honest and thoughtful book worth putting on the bedtable with Willie Morris's *Yazoo*" (I do not mind the comparison, nor plugging Willie; maybe we'll get some of his fans). To show I am an artist, I can even find hope in *Kirkus*, if one is right selective: "Sorrowful and full of forebodings, he is haunted by a sense of historical retribution that promises 'a racial Armageddon' on red-neck and liberal alike. . . . Free of breast-beating, this is a muted *mea culpa* which offers no promises of a new day. Everything about King's coming of age in America seems very familiar. . . .But then, that's exactly his lugubrious point." (Christ, I have no shame!) I wonder could we get away with inserting what *Saturday Review* said about the *magazine* version. Well, hell, I seem to have lost it, but something about it revealing all sorts of mysteries usually reserved for the interior of introspective novels, and what not and like that there. As you know me for a modest man, shy and retiring beyond any singing of it, self-effacing and salt of the earth, you understand that these suggestions are equal to personal sacrifices for the good of the Company. Don't you?

I anxiously await word for my promotional sked. Rich, you gonna go with me and hold my hand, right? I need sponge baths and powdering and prayer captains and whiskey aides when I go onna television. My wife is going with us to Boston to the Book Seller's deal, and I am sure that a grateful Corporation will insist on picking up her tab.

That feller from the *National Observer* is to interview me inna week or so.

Alan, where please are my ten freebies? Also, consider this an official order for 30 more copies at Author's Discount. (Modest man has a lot of cheap relatives and friends.) Bill me soonest.

May the light of Heaven smite you blind. . . .

*Editor and Public Relations Director of the Viking Press, respectively.

May 7, 1971
Friday night

Mr. Frank Rich
19 Hovey St., Apt. #2
Cambridge, Mass. 02138

Dear Frank:

Well, I got my tentative sked for book promotion today, by phone, and Jesus H. Keerist there is no time for idleness or succor. To wit: Atlanta, May 25th-26th; Washington, May 27th; Boston, May 30th-31st; New York, June 1-2; Chicago, June 3-4-5; Detroit (!), June 6th; Boston (again), June 7th and 8th; Texas—varied points not yet set—June 9th, 10th, 11th, 12th; Los Angeles, June 15, 16, 17; San Francisco, June 18th & 19th. (I struck Philadelphia and Cincinnati, screw it.) Then I return here and motor back to Texas to assume month-long custody of the Precious Children.

Actually, the ABA thing in Boston only requires me on Monday, May 31st; probably, however, we will come up Sunday the 30th. Will let you know. Monday I will be flapping around shaking the hands of mean little old ladies who own bookstores in the most dark and distant American provinces, smiling at critics, etc., and Monday night there's a Viking Press whiskey drank for me, George Axelrod, and Garson Kanin. In addition to the book sked, I have agreed to do for *Life* a short (1500 words) piece re the social functions attending the Kennedy Performing Arts Center preview here May 27th; as I understand my function, I'm supposed to be funny or cutting (or hopefully, both) about it. It must be wrote good within 48 hours of the event or less; and put on a Teletype and all kinds of Corporate Life shit. Then I agreed to do another piece for *Life* on the least populated county in the continental U.S. (Loving County, Texas). Was my idea, and I got a call from the editor who'd solicited me saying he liked it, but could I give him "a peg"—something he could show his editorial superiors and sell them. So I spun abuncha shat about how it will be a study of what Space and Isolation does to The Human Spirit, and the silly bastards bit. And all I want to do is write about some poor old West Texas nesters, and how they grew. . . .

Oh, dig: Avery Roan sent me a memo Jack Fischer wrote the staff the other day. Among its highlights: *"Harper's must not be identified in the minds of potential readers as a 'literary' magazine. No literary magazine has existed during my lifetime, either in this country or in England, without a continuing subsidy . . . With all due respect to Willie, I think it is unfortunate that, at least during the last year, he seemed to be trying to change Harper's more and more in the direction of being a literary magazine. No such magazine has ever sustained a circulation greater than about 50,000 copies. . . . We shall have to devote less space to books, writers, fiction, and literary criticism. We need to devote a higher proportion of our editorial space to science, medicine, business, the changing cultural scene, and other aspects of American life . . . Harper's could become a magazine that large numbers of people feel they need to read because it will help them to make intelligent decisions in the planning of their own lives. . . . The implications of the foregoing are apparent"*—Fucking-A, Jack—*"We need articles about the future, not the past."* And here, Frank, I take it personal: *"We don't need pieces about dead people. We don't need articles about defeated politicians. We don't need nostalgic reminiscences of childhood. We need material about people on the way up—not on the way down."* Wow! Horseshit. Fuck 'em. . . .

*Fischer, who had been replaced as Editor-in-Chief by Willie Morris, briefly returned to run *Harper's* following the resignations of Morris and his fellow editors and writers.

June 25, 1971

Mr. Ben Peeler
1605 N. Colpitts
Fort Stockton, Texas

Dear H. Ben:
Rosemarie broke her leg virtually on the eve of our departure for Texas, and rather than shoot her they operated last Monday. Assuming her recovery in time, we'll now be going to the Padre Island

beach place on July 10th and stay there three weeks with the Precious Children. Will briefly visit the Old Folks in Midland about August 1, then return home. Then I'll fly almost immediately back to do the Loving County piece for *Life* and will get in touch.

Warren Burnett was in Austin—briefly. He was to stay all weekend, as I was, and yet only four hours after I met him at the airport he slipped off from revelers at Scholz Garden and left word, indirectly, he was going back to Odessa. I know that going back involved more than Odessa tugging him emotionally or sentimentally, but I do not yet know of the offensive causations—unless it was that the party was for me and maybe enough folks did not clap hands and sing over Mr. Burnett to fill his ego up properly. . . .

June 25, 1971

Mr. Frank Rich
19 Hovey Street, Apt. #2
Cambridge, Mass. 02138

Dear Frank:

As I told you by telephone a night or so ago, the book tour was a bone-grinding bitch. I am just now getting the fatigue off my spirit, after one week, and can begin to see some of its comic aspects.

One of which was a P. R. lady of indefinite years in San Francisco, whom Viking had hired to handle my promo in her city. Very early did it become apparent that the lady loved her liquor. I arrived at the SF airport strung out and tired to the marrow, and en route to my hotel the lady inquired whether I would not like to stop by a certain bar and have a drink. I demurred, saying I wanted a hot shower and bed. Soon the lady decided that she had left an object there the night before—a purse or some such—and if I didn't mind we'd stop just long enough to pick it up. Once inside she mentioned nothing save straight vodka—her favorite, I would soon learn—and I was four hours getting her out of the place by which time I, myself, was quite drunk and no longer gave much of a shit about being tired. Which attitude, of course, only makes you all the more weary the next day. Miss J., who resembles Marjorie Main in the face and Jackie Gleason in the body—and has Durante's nose—had carefully scheduled my public appearances in San Francisco so that she could drink vodka at least one hour—preferably two—between appointments. By noon each day she was skunk drunk. By midafternoon she was literally out of it, drunk driving and hitting curbs and threatening pedestrians. Also, about this time, she would decide she was cute and begin to flirt. It was no trouble to keep my virtue intact. One afternoon we entered the largest bookstore in S.F., whereupon Miss J. determinedly introduced me thirty-six times as "Larry Green." In what was probably San Francisco's second largest bookstore, my escort inquired of management whether it had my book in stock. Yes, indeedy, they did. "And I bet you haven't sold a goddamned one," said my P. R. lady, slurring her words. After having heard my Brotherhood spiel no less than 10 times, she announced—as we lurched down the street, marginally avoiding cyclists and cable cars—"You can take some of these Goddamned Orientals home with you. One thing about 'em, though, they have more ambition than the Colored. Or the Goddamned Hippies. You can take several pounds of 'em back. Good riddance," etc. She turned three nights and two days into six weeks. Jesus with the loaves and fishes never did a better job of elongation. . . .

In Chicago, George Axelrod and I shared a one-hour live TV show late at night. George carries a vodka bottle in his briefcase, and occasionally belts it. We were drunk at air time, and the M.C. made the mistake of telling us before hand that we could freely use the language and boasted of how liberal his policy was on "The Marty Faye Show," etc. So right off we threw in some goddamns and hells and sons-of-bitches, and finally, at the climax, I had baited Axelrod about his need for white racist guilt until he shouted—pounding the table—"I don't have any fucking white guilt. Not one fucking bit!" Marty Faye nearly shat. You can hardly bleep live TV. Axelrod, incidentally, I grew to like, despite the fact that the first line I heard him utter was "When 'Itch' made me 1.3 mil . . ."* We had a funny scene on one show where

George contrasted our backgrounds—he born to Governesses and silver spoons—whereupon, I cracked, "George, we had quite a bit in common. I picked the cotton your governesses used to clean your ears." When I got to L.A., staying at the Beverly Wilshire, George was already at the Beverly Hills and had a bottle of champagne sent to me with a note saying, "Welcome to Show Biz." On a radio show in Chicago—the M.C. boasting it was being heard in 32 states—there was a strange little man with a 1930s face and a bow tie that neither George nor I could stand. We shouted at him for 30 minutes on the subject of Government Censorship before learning it was the Lt. Governor of Illinois. George had cussed a time or two, and finally the M.C. asked him to cool it in deference to the public official, and George said to the Lt. Governor, "What is your favorite charity?" And the Lt. Governor named some Museum of African History in East St. Louis, whereupon George wrote him a $1,000 check to that purpose—the Lt. Governor looking uncomprehending throughout—and then George said—presumably to be heard in 32 states—"Now, Goddamnit, I can say anything I want. And I say you, Lt. Governor, are full of crap like most politicians." Yes, George is weird.

Dallas and Houston loved me not. A woman in the *Houston Chronicle*—ironically, as hillbilly a shit as I ever met—interviewed me at what I thought was a friendly lunch and then shafted me with a headline calling me "A West Texas Hick." (I wrote "Fuck you" across it and mailed it to her. Not very original, but certainly an accurate reflection of my feelings.) On call shows in Dallas I was told, "Don't ride in any bubbletops, remember JFK." And in Houston, a purported Klansman called to threaten my bones. Others called in such messages as "State whether or not you are a Communist," and "You goddamned traitor, I hope you turn black" and "Is your dress"—I had on a white cord suit—"an imitation of Castro?" and "You are too negative about everything and are a disgrace to Texas" and other such love notes—the point being, I take it, that the good folks out there in TV-land were *not* racist as I had claimed. Oh yes, in Los Angeles I had a live-on-the-air fight with Regis Philbin (former sidekick to Joey

203

Bishop) on account of he said something that made me call him a white racist. Other than that, and save for cursing in the Boston Ritz, it was a pretty gentle trip. . . .

Zigfield Folly

*Axelrod's hit Broadway play, later a big movie, "The Seven Year Itch."

Editor's Note: *Confessions of a White Racist* met with a warm response from a wide array of American writers, including those emerging in the African-American literary scene. During his book tour in June, 1971, Maya Angelou wrote King a fan letter from Stokholm in care of Viking. It reads, in part, "I had read *And Other Dirty Stories* and sensed your perception, but had no idea of your startling courage. I applaud you man. And pray you stay alive. I want to shake your hand." King responded a month later after he had Angelou's letter in hand.

July 6, 1971

Dear Maya Angelou:

Bless your heart. I was in San Francisco some time ago when someone from Viking read your letter to me on the phone. I asked that it be forwarded to me here and—finally—it was. So I say thanks. I so much enjoyed—admired is a better word; was moved by—*I Know Why the Caged Bird Sings* that your approval is especially welcome.

Do you think people in this country ever will get their heads together?

LLK

P.S. I saw you once in Elaine's—months ago—and wanted to say hello. Sorry I didn't.*

*King later met and got to know Ms. Angelou after she asked Bill Moyers to include King at a small dinner party in her honor, held at Moyers' Long Island home.

July 6, 1971

Dear Willie:

This may never reach you. Your whereabouts is a pluperfect mystery. Thought you might like to see this *Washington Post* review from today's (Tuesday's) paper on your sorry old book.* Did you see that Hodding 3rd treated us right well Sunday last in *Book World*? (*Wash. Post & Chicago Trib*).

Everywhere I went bragging on my book, people wanted to talk about *Harper's*. And you. I got damn tired of answering the question, "What is Willie Morris going to do?" So I varied my answers, so as not to bore myself. Among the more popular reponses I used are these: "He has just been named assistant football coach at Tatum, New Mexico . . . . He is in Osteopath's School in Joplin, Missouri . . . . He has gone blind and is in the County Home for the Blind and Deaf at Post, Texas . . . . He is living in sin on a Greek isle with Ethel Kennedy, except on weekends, and then he is the pastor of the First Baptist Church of Homa, Mississippi . . . . He went to pee and the hogs ate him."

Rosemarie fractured her hip a bit over two weeks ago, while I was in San Francisco, and required surgery. She gets out today. We are leaving Thursday for Padre Island, Texas for a month. Gonna drink a little beer and stare out the window at the water. May even write some. How Rosemarie cracked her leg was, she moved quickly to avoid the assault of a goddamned German shepherd and—crack! I told you dogs won't do!**

I've a long summer upcoming: trips for magazines immediately after the Padre Island sojourn, so don't guess I'll see you until the frost is on the punkin or some such.

*Yazoo.
**Rosemarie King never truly recovered from this accident.

———————————————

Editor's note: Larry King has no memory of a letter from Mr. Woods, who must have lodged a complaint with *Harper's* regarding King's less than perfect punctuation.

November 15 comma 1971

Dear Mr period Woods colon

New paragraph Your letter reminds me of the fellow who described the Grand Canyon as a big hole period Punctuation should not be held as inviolate as a nunnery period The purpose of punctuation should be to assist the writer in the orderly flow of language comma much as a traffic light regulates the flow of vehicles comma though no writer seeking his own rhythms should be bound to honor the red lights of his nit hyphen pick predecessors period Faulkner comma himself comma knew the joys of free punctuation period This hardly handicapped his art period I am enclosing a varied assortment of punctuation marks which you may employ as needed in rhyme with your individual taste period Hope this sees you through the night period How is your old dangling participle hanging question mark

Sincerely comma
Larry L period King
' , / ? , , ? . . " ! ! ! , , , . : , ? !

December 21, 1971

Mr. Frank Rich
Flat 7
42 Queens Gate Gardens
London SW 7
England

Dear Son-of-the-Shoe-King:

(Figure that one out, J. Edgar!)*

You were considerate to write by postcard, so the FBI lads won't have to steam their fingers in opening your mail. Your contributions, I take it, to Good Government.

Incredible story about your tribulations with the Authorities there. Don't tell the bastards nothing! This goddamned intimidation and spying and bugging and Gestapoing has got to by-God be stopped, or the Nixon-Agnew-Mitchell-Hoover boys will be marching us in lock-step to the ovens and gas showers and concentration camps. I mean it, the bastards have not one idea of what civil liberty means—and what little of it they understand scares them—and the Supreme Court will soon have a 5-4 bulge for the views of Mussolini to last until the first years of the 21st Century. Ole Bill Shakespeare, he had it right about the evil men do living after them and I cannot improve on his sentiment or prose.**

The LBJ book is official; I go to work March 1st after clearing my magazine decks. I'm taking $7,500 on signing in early January; $10,000 on March 1st and the rest at $2,500 per month for 30 months with a $10,000 final payment on completion: total, $100,000. I like the way that looks! My first book went to McGraw-Hill for $1,500 advance—upped to $6,000 when I jumped house with it to NAL; then NAL paid $6,000 for *Dirty Stories;* Viking $15,000 for *Confessions,* then $37,000 for my (much unwritten novel) *Growing Old,* and now this for LBJ. So I am going in the right direction, though maybe not so spectacularly as such great writers as Gay Talese and Jackie Susann. . . .

Rosemarie and I went out the other day and bought a stereo set, and I then popped the eyes of the record salesman by buying $130 worth of country western, and Rosemarie—culturally deprived in the shit-kicking music department—must be a little tired of constant gut-thumping guitars and whining fiddles and sad laments of how life and wimmen and whiskey has screwed up many a good man. But I have been having a ball, going back to my roots. Willie Nelson. Buck Owens. Hank Lochlin. Ernest Tubb. Jerry Lee Lewis. Ray Price. Charley Pride. Hank Williams. You name it. . . .

Seems you have much to relate about the Paris trip and other meanderings. I hope you are keeping some half-assed journal. I know it is difficult, but do try to jot down at least notes and impressions and places and dates. It will be invaluable later, said the old man. (And speaking of that, USIA is publishing *The Old Man* in Russian and Polish editions, which means all of $25 to me, but somehow I like the idea of Clyde King being read about in Moscow.)

Willie Morris has, since I wrote you, run off from Muriel Murphy three times to the arms of Barbara Howar, and off from Barbara Howar four times to the arms of Muriel Murphy. Which makes it 4-3, game-point, with Mrs. Murphy currently having custody. I got drunk at a Sally Quinn (*Washington Post*) party recently with, dig it, Barry Goldwater, who begged to be interviewed for my LBJ book: "I'm not gonna say anything now, because I'm drunk, but I want to be interviewed. I like ole Lyndon but there's some shit ought to be told on that son-of-a-bitch." I found Barry terribly foul-mouthed, good fun, and were it not that he would throw around bombs and cut off welfare, would think him a fine fella. David Brinkley was there, swearing that if Nixon wins again he will retire: "He takes all the fun out of my work, and I'm too goddamned old to give him four more years." Larry McMurtry was there, rightfully basking in the praise of his sensational new movie, *The Last Picture Show*—which you must see at the earliest time—and Doug Kiker and Bill McPhearson and Nick Van Hoffman and Barbara Howar and Fred Harris and enough egos, generally, to light the city for a thousand years. Rosemarie and Miss Howar hang out now. They had a drunk lunch today with Ella Udall. I stayed home and opened a can of chili and listened to my tear-jerkin' shit-kickin' music. . . .

*Rich had some reason to believe his mail was being examined because of his campus political activity at Harvard.
**Note these brilliant and accurate comments were made much *before* Watergate. —LLK

Editor's Note: In 1952 King was a 23-year-old newspaperman in Odessa when he met Harold Young and his wife Mary Louise. The couple had moved back to West Texas from Washington, where Harold Young had played an important role as chief aide to Henry A. Wallace, who from 1940 to 1944 served as FDR's Vice-President, and later was Roosevelt's Secretary of Agriculture and Truman's Secretary of Commerce. Young left Wallace's office during his chaotic campaign for

President in 1948. Mary Louise Young worked in Lyndon Johnson's Dallas and Washington offices both when he was Congressman and Senator. King has remarked that Harold Young had the best library in Ector County and extended full borrowing privileges to him.

January 5, 1972

Hon. Harold Young
Attorney-at-Law
100 Block of East 4th St.
Odessa, Texas

Dear Judge Young:

The people over at Viking Press have lost their minds, and have signed to pay me $100,000 advance royalties to write "the" definitive biography of one Lyndon Baines Johnson. I mention the sum only because it looks so good on paper, and reminds me that never again shall I have to suffer at the mercy of the Hoiles chain.*

Anyway, this is supposed to be a careful and unbiased study of LBJ—I am supposed to forget how often I have found him a cutthroat son-of-a-bitch—and so I am, and shall be, for the next three years, interviewing hundreds, reading and re-reading history, private documents, letters, and so on. Many of the latter-day Johnson staffers—Moyers most prominent among them—have promised me all sorts of cooperation, and ex-Cabinet members, Senators, Congressmen, and what not. Naturally, I want to interview you and Mary Louise when I am next in Texas. That may be some months from now, however, and in the meantime I'd appreciate a letter from you addressed to one item re: LBJ. To wit and as follows:

The more I read, the more it seems to me that perhaps as time has gone on, LBJ has stressed his closeness to FDR a bit much. True, he endorsed him cleverly in winning that minority [special election] race for Congress in 1937, FDR took him aboard his train shortly thereafter, LBJ announced from the White House steps for U.S. Senator in 1941 against Pappy O'Daniel, etc. But few of the New Deal or Fair

Deal histories or memoirs Ickes Diaries, FDR's intimate's books, Truman's biography, and so on—mention him, or do so only in passing. It would be helpful, therefore, if you'd write me a page or two—whatever it takes—to give me your recollections of the FDR-LBJ relationship from the old days when you were the power behind Henry Agard Wallace. I should consider this a personal favor, and did it not sound presumptuous I might even call it a small favor to History. . . .

*A reference to King's employment at the *Odessa American* from late 1952 to late 1954.

Jan. 25, 1972

Dear Jay Bird & Miz Beth:*

I, too, heard Billy Lee's voice recently. He called up and required $900 to stay out of jail—his probation would be revoked, or some such, if he didn't pay that much on his fine within 3 days of our conversation and Lord, I don't know what all. Anyhow, I went in partners with Edsel Burnett and Malcolm McGregor, and we all sent him two bills toward the total, and I thank he somehow arranged the rest. (Probably the fine was $300 and he had enough left to buy him lots of good dope: I would have worked it that way.) Burnett and McGregor have since called me—to thank me, I'm sure, for cutting them in on the deal—but I have always been "in conference" and have not returned their calls. I did not contact them direct, you see, but authorized Billie Lee to call them and say that I suggested we all go $200 each in defense of his Freedom. I personally thank Bud Shrake for asking Brammer to call me, and passed the honor on to share with Burnett and Malcolm. Frens got to stick together, eh wot?. . .

I read that Cartwheel** piece where you are named Bambi, cheating by reading it at the newsstand and not buying it, and unless you are prepared to swear otherwise I think it smacks of the Shrake and Jenkins technique involving one Fletcher Boone: they been quoting him, identifying him as "an Austin artist," when we all know if he ever painted a picture he won't show it to nobody and that he was quoted on subjects that never crossed his mind until he read what he had said about it. Personally, I think such shoddy journalism is dangerous. As well as unethical and UnAmerican and other unsatisfactory things, and only under the greatest pressures do I use Warren Burnett in the same way. When he reads my upcoming *Life* piece on Loving County, he will be astounded—at all the learned things he said about Life in Desert Isolation, Mankind, and So Forth. I tell him he drinks a whole lot and cannot be expected to remember all he puts out.

It is late. I tire and grow red-eyed and grumpy. . . .

*Jay Milner and his wife Beth.
**That is, Gary Cartwright.

Editor's Note: This letter was inspired by the scandal surrounding the writer Clifford Irving when it was revealed that his best-selling "as-told-to" biography of Howard Hughes was a hoax. Irving had claimed that he had secretly met with the reclusive billionaire for a period of years, and these meetings resulted in his authoritative biography. Tom Guinzburg was so taken with King's letter that it soon made the rounds in New York and was eventually published in the March 12, 1972, *New York Times* Book Review. Irving, incidentally, went to jail for his hoax.

February 1, 1972

Mr. Tom Guinzburg
President
The Viking Press, Inc.
625 Madison Avenue
New York, New York

Dear Tom:

By this letter I offer you a unique opportunity to obtain the publication rights to a manuscript nearing completion. I am asking $500,000 advance royalties for myself as the author, and an additional $1 million for my source.

Over the past 15 months, in various places throughout the Free World, I have met with— and have transcribed the life story of—Jesus Christ. Once we walked alone in a garden. Another time I joined my source and a dozen of his friends for supper. Still another time, we went to this big picnic where all they served was bread and fish, though there was plenty to go around. We have met at various times in shepherd's fields, in chariots, on mountain tops, and so forth. Because my source insists on complete and total secrecy, I cannot at this point provide additional details. When the time comes, however, I will see to it that you get yours.

My source insists that we accept his story on blind faith. Of course, he is accustomed to dealing under those terms and points out that millions of others have so accepted his story. You, as a publisher, know how difficult writers can be and I sincerely doubt whether my source will compromise his rule in this respect. He appears adamant and even agitated when one suggests alternatives.

The manuscript itself must be closely held. I cannot provide you the stone tablets on which the story was set down by my source: it was necessary to copy from the stone tablets which were then—as I understand it—put in the care of a certain Mr. Moses. I am confident that my source is no imposter. He has turned water into wine for me, parted seas, healed the lame and the halt, etc. to the extent that I am convinced we have the real McCoy. Also, he wears a beard, a robe, and has scarred hands.

True, other books have been written on this subject. None, however, were officially authorized. Also, this will be the original first-person treatment. My source informs me, incidentally, that numerous errors of fact exist in the most popular work treating his life. Stories involving his immediate family he finds particularly embarrassing: the fact is, he was adopted. He has on reflection come to believe that a single author may have done a better and more cohesive job than did the numerous authors contributing to the other work—though he does volunteer that, as anthologies go, it sold very well. As to why I was chosen for this work, I suspect it is because of my Texas origins: we have long known that Texas is God's Country. Or perhaps my source is intrigued that my agent is a Mr. Lord.

No more than these bare facts may be shared with those bidding for magazine, movie, foreign, book club, and paperback rights. I cannot too strongly warn against *any* leak or premature publicity. This is so as to preserve through publication date the time and place of The Second Coming. My source originally planned that event for his 2000th birthday, but I believe with persuasion might push the date forward to coincide with promotional activities. Probably it would be better to bring this book out on the spring list. The fall list would conflict with the football season, making it difficult to obtain a stadium large enough to accommodate maximum Second Coming crowds. These details are, of course, subject to review and/or accommodation as we move forward. (My source naturally wants to stage the Second Coming in Texas, but is dubious about the Astrodome because he fears the impropriety of returning to artificial turf.) By the way, when the Second Coming date and site firms up, *please* be certain that adequate hotel accommodations are available. As the manuscript will reveal, my source was severely marked by a childhood experience in this regard.

It is futile to request my source to show himself to you or others involved in this project. No other person on earth has been privy to our meetings or possesses knowledge of them: not Billy Graham, not the Pope, not Oral Roberts. When we make the official announcement, these and others of the spiritual trade may be depended upon to denounce the authenticity of our claim on the theory that my source rarely moves without consulting them, and on the further grounds that they speak with him or to him with great frequency. (Incidentally, I once heard Rev. Graham say on the radio, "I talked with the Lord the other night in Cincinnati," and my source tells me he has never been there.) Atheists will scoff at our revelations for their own obvious reasons. We simply must be prepared to ride the storm out, to have—as my source put it—"The faith of a mustard seed." I only wish that circumstances did not preclude my submitting a recent photograph, to convince skeptics, but I am simply locked in. I remain confident, however, that once you discover the rich details in the manuscript—things like the real inside dope on Lot's wife, what really happened with Eve and the apple, what a terrible temper my source's father has, etc.—you will have no doubts of its authenticity. The information simply could come from no other source.

My source, saying he knows no Viking editors, is indifferent as to who edits the book. I personally prefer Alan D. Williams, though should we ever entice my source to come into the office for final cuttings, I do hope you will ask Mr. Williams to limit his outrageous puns to the lowest possible number. As to payment, you may consult my agent, Sterling Lord, concerning workable details for my own remuneration. On the matter of checks for my source, it is his wish that you make them out to "J. H. Christ" and entrust them to me for personal delivery—minus, of course, Sterling Lord's 10% off the top. I realize this is a deviation from the norm but you know that my source has a history of dealing with as few middle men as possible. His endorsement of the check will constitute your receipt.

I am enclosing a longhand note from my source authorizing me to write the work and to offer it for sale under terms disclosed in this letter—subject, of course, to negotiated escalation clauses. Do not worry about the archaic language therein—"thou" and "hath" and "payeth" and so forth. I am cleaning up such usages in the manuscript. As example, in telling one story, my source quotes himself as saying, "Peter, lovest thou me?" I have made this more acceptable to the times and to the reading public by changing it to, "Hey, Pete, don't you dig me no more, man?"

Do let me hear quickly. And remember: mum's the word. Best wishes from,

Larry L. King

PS: We offer an option on a work-in-progress by my source's father: "My Son the Martyr."

Editor's Note: In a follow-up letter to Guinzburg, King says: "Oh yes, for the title I have decided on *Naked Came the Saviour.*" After the piece appeared in The *New York Times* Book Review, King received a letter from Harvey Aronson, editor of the collaboratively written *Naked Came the Stranger,* a sendup of a Jacqueline Suzanne/Harold Robbins-style novel. Aronson jokingly threatens King with a lawsuit and suggests a better title might be *From Here to Eternity* or *Leave Him to Heaven*.

Feb. 25, 1972

Mr. Frank Rich
Flat 7,
42 Queens Gate Gardens
London SW 7
England

Dear Mr. Hoot:

By the enclosed copy you will find the [playwright George] Axelrod address. . .

That whiskey drank we started on your last day here went on into the wee hours. Phil Carter helped me close the Rotunda, on Capitol Hill, at 2 A.M. and I drove home in a sleet storm and the next day it looked as if I had dipped my clothes in a vegetable stew, and then rolled around in the snow and dirt, and I felt defeated and flushed and constipated and like my soul had fled. And had to rise early, driving in snow gales, to Bethesda to fetch Miss Rosemarie home. She ain't feeling real good. I've been trained to pop her with .45 ccs of morph every four hours, and insist that she call me "Doctor King" at all times, and may go out and take me some brain surgery lessons and already I know the AMA is freedom's last bastion and we should cut out some of the wasteful foreign aid and lower taxes for the rich and impeach Earl Burger. RM claims she don't get no euphoria from her poppings and, indeed, that it hasn't been real effective about the pain. However, she's a shade perkier this afternoon than in the last week.

Well, I introduced around on Larry McMurtry for 10 minutes at the Women's Dem thang, [a luncheon]and had the pleasure of chatting with Mrs. Joel Fischer,* now known to me as Pauline, and bought her a drink and lied shamelessly to her about your good character, great potential, and so forth. It was a real "snow Mother" speech, and

I reckon you owe me about $50 for it. Both Km and I liked her. Ella Ward Udall sat at the table with your dear old mama while McMurtry and yours truly bragged on ourselves and each other and, it later developed, she determinedly called her "Mrs. Rich" throughout the day. I do not know to what degree, if any, Ms. Pauline Fischer was offended.

I so impressed everybody by explaining McMurtry's work in my intro—including him—that it was bandied about that perhaps I should be invited back to speak to the group on my own. I'll do it, of course, for the money. In the receiving line, after about 10 ladies had gushed over my *Harper's* work, McMurtry had yet to receive any compliments and he said in my ear, "I think we'd better switch places and let me do the introducing and you the speaking." He did really well: it was all about the troubles writers have with Hollywood, and translating books into film, and you would have really enjoyed it.

Guess I'll wind this down. Will send you my upcoming pieces in about 10 days. Hang loose, do good work, and live a moral, upright life. Yours in Christ,

Rex Whoopee,
The Singing Cowboy

*Rich's mother.

Feb. 25, 1972

The George Axelrods
84 Eaton Square
London, S.W. 1
England

Dear George & Joan:

Greetings from the colonies. We are struggling along without our President this week, and of course that makes it extremely difficult on the average citizen. Unless we are on guard against it, Nixon will include a domestic Great Wall in his platform this year. I have never trusted the examples from history that man prefers.*

You will be hearing by postcard or phone from one Frank Rich. Mr. Rich is a whiskey-drinking, funny-smoking young friend of mine, graduate last year of Fair Haavaad, now boondoggling it in Europe on some sort of floating grant. Mr. Rich presumes to write articles and novels. He sold his first to *Esquire* awhile back in the former category, and is now plotzing through a first novel. He is good folks and all right and gonna be a fine writer sometime, and I want you to meet him and greet him and inspire him to great heights in the tradition that I, as his original teacher, mentor, and advisor established as the pluperfect example. . . .

Did you receive from *VIP* mag that double-truck color photo of the 70 writing geniuses at the *Playboy* goatroping, mixed doubles, and literary whiskey drank? Almost all of us are in costume though you, George, stand out in your Brooks Brothers Undertaker's Outfit. George, you've simply got to do something about your clothes. I am tired of having to defend your mode of dress in bars, and besides you are shaming your old friend Robert L. Green.** Do not be reluctant to preen a bit.

The Goddamned Press, without help from me, spread it around recently that Tom Guinzburg has lost his mind and advanced me $100,000 against a big fat LBJ book, and I am getting all sorts of warm letters from ancient creditors, certified enemies, forgotten relatives, and one or two actual friends, all of whom have sad stories about how life has treated them of late; they tell such pitiful tales as to qualify them for Queen for a Day, and request anywhere from $900 to $76,000 each. I am marking all letters "Deceased, Return To Sender."

George, I know I am a poor boy who never went to school—and when I did it was nine miles in the snow, and uphill both ways, and I was barefooted—and hardly had enough to eat besides, and you were raised in Old Dame Luxury's lap and she swabbed your pinky baby ears out with the cotton I picked, and it is a class thing, but risk a little democracy by dropping me a note now and again. You will find those of us among the great unwashed masses to be truly fun, and occasionally educational, and besides you can brag at your club about having moved among the common folk for purposes of amusement and studies of sociology. . . .

*President Nixon was on his history-making trip to "Red China."
**Robert L. Green was *Playboy's* Fashion Editor and Axelrod somehow felt a great antipathy for him. —LLK

March 12, 1972

Mr. Bill Brammer
1737 Napolean
New Orleans, La.

Dear Wullum:

You rat fink bastard. What about your pledge to send me all that Lyndon material you compiled, assembled, wrote up, and what not? I hustled my ass and got you your bail and dope money and you drop me like Texas politicians do when one does a favor for them. Get your ass in gear.*

I lately ate on spare ribs and drank beer with McMurtry, and we talked Texas and literachure and Brammer and so forth. Have not seen Uncle Bud Shrake as I have not sallied forth to New York in some time. I've been sticking close to home, because Rosemarie's been having it pretty rough. She's been hospitalized for a couple of weeks as the good doctors try varied drugs and methods to attempt to lessen her pain but they have not been astonishingly successful to date.

Did you see the March 10th *Life*, in which I got a pretty fair foot-stomping Texas-style piece on Loving County?

Ain't no news much. It is late and I tire, and hanker for you to keep your promise about the LBJ material. Hang loose and don't tell the bastards nothing.

Yours in Christ. . . .

*Brammer, who had worked for LBJ and claimed to have valuable documents and "research" of his own, proposed that King pay him $500 for it to assist King in his own LBJ book. King did pay Brammer and eventually received a huge box of old news magazines and newspaper stories available at any decent public library.

May 8, 1972

Hon. Herman Gollob
Editor-in-Chief
Atheneum Publishers
122 East 42nd St.
New York, N.Y.

Dear Glob:

It is nothing personal, and I hope you will understand, but me being a recent graduate of Harvard College and a nominee for the National Book Award besides, it don't seem seemly that I be seen publicly with Texas Aggies. I mean, Herman, I got this image to maintain and it is well-knew that you are the kind of Aggie who will take the gourmet Sterling Lord to eat beans and barbequed goat at The Dallas Cowboy,* and I'm sorry, Herman, but I have got lots more Klass than that.

To show I am still Democratic, however, I send the following quote on D. Jenkins' book:

"If *Semi-Tough* isn't the funniest novel of the year, please tape my ribs before leading me to the winner. Until I read Dan Jenkins' book, I thought Mark Harris' *Bang the Drum Slowly* to be the funniest and most perceptive novel I had read about pro athletes. Sorry Mark, make room for Dan.". . .**

*An ersatz Texas cafe in Manhattan that somehow charmed Gollob, belying its culinary accomplishments.
**Gollob edited Jenkins' best-selling football novel.

Editor's Note: This report to Frank Rich on Kurt Vonnegut's birthday party is one of a number of letters that comment on the New York literary scene, during King's "whiskey sabbatical."

Nov 1, 1972

Dear Frank:

The lucky ones were those who did not go to Kurt Vonnegut's 50th celebration. I do not say this to make you feel better. I say it because it was true. I was the only one there wearing bluejeans.

It was crowded and smoky and hot and noisy and I don't think K.V. had any more fun than I did, though he was game and danced and tried to grin a lot. But now and again you'd catch him looking off into distant mysteries, sweating and drinking rapidly and looking a little more than agonized, and then he'd snap back and grin, gamely, and dance another 'un. I do not do me much dancing, being expert only in the box step—usually employed to regain balance when walking real drunk—and the Texas stomp, which largely consists of jumping around and yelling like you're trying to stampede a cattle herd. Miss Kristi Witker, obviously culturally impaired, did not know either of these dances. I didn't know hers, either, so we sat and tried to yell at each other over the loudest fucking Dixieland Jazz band I have ever heard. Everyone sitting at tables had their faces inches apart, or actually touching, and shouting into each other's mouths, ears, and nostrils. It looked like a roomful of domestic quarrels—maybe the National Finals—or ballplayers bitching to umpires. I ain't heard shit anybody said till yet, which is just as well. It wasn't exactly the most interesting crowd you ever saw. It *should* have been, for certainly there was an incredible mix—Vonnegut's relatives, and Jill's nutty (meaning neurotic, probably) friends, and lots of folks who looked like loan sharks and several of whom you'd see at Cosa Nostra gatherings, maybe, and some who seemed to be cast for Bar Mitzvahs, and a few shaggy media types and a sprinkling of writers and unemployed actors and some who defied description and a few fags. It might have been fun had they let us talk. But we did the stand-up cocktail party bit—

60 folks crowded into a space more suited to a third that—and then the band drownded us out and there were little tiny tables holding four-to-six, with *nameplates*, now. I do not know how good the food was, because it was too hot and loud to eat. There was just one bartender, and he would disappear right frequently and stay for the longest time. Confusion. Chaos. Somebody got shoved over a table holding about 200 or more plates, cups and saucers, and about half of 'em broke and sounded like the pop-pop-pop of machine gun fire, and in this spooked society half the folks there thought we'd been attacked and jumped and spilled their drinks on each other. I shouted, in the shocked silence, "So it Goes" and only Vonnegut laughed.

Jill . . . did not have a place setting for Kristi, and made a big thing of saying how she didn't expect uninvited guests.* She kept saying she didn't know what to do about it. Kristi was embarrassed; I was mad. So I said, "Hell, here's your solution." So I reached over and got a place card at random—it turned out to say "Amanda Burden"—and wrote "Kristi Witker" on it and put it back. Jill smiled like a rattlesnake had bit her, and moved on. I do not know if Ms. Burden ever found a place to sit. I caught Vonnegut grinning at that action. It was, in my mind—and possibly in his—the night's highpoint. Jill wasn't through: when we sneaked out, or tried to, she caught us and made a big thing of saying all sorts of flowery and syrupy things about how delighted she was that Kristi could make it. Kristi gave it back to her, just as sweet and deadly, about how it had been the grandest party ever and how she was delighted to have been included. Vonnegut missed that. He was pretty drunk by that time and sort of had quit pretending and was doing a lot of glum staring and smoking and hootching.

So it goes.

The only writers there that I knew, except me and Kurt, were these: Frank Conroy, George Plimpton, Jane Howard, Nikki Giovanni, and the rest of the "literary crowd" seemed to consist of Dave Scherman, *Life's* book editor. My conversation with Conroy consisted of an exchange of howdys and his question did I have a match? Plimpton yelled in my ear for about 12 minutes and I grinned and watched his face and tried to react as his expression seemed to indicate, but what with the band all I know is that it was something about the Baltimore Colts. Jane Howard and I said "How are you? Fine, how are you?" Vonnegut and I had three minutes together, during which we mainly looked at each other and drank. I gave him his birthday gift—a night for two on the house at Elaine's—and it seemed to embarrass him, and he mumbled thanks and we drank some more and studied our shoes.

So it goes.

I met a purty girl who works for CBS-TV and asked her name three or four different times in about thirty minutes, and it pissed her off. So I said, "If I didn't really want to know, I wouldn't keep asking." And she said, "If you *really* wanted to know, you'd remember."

So it goes.

Another girl, attractive and looking demented, took my wine out of hand and tasted it and handed it back and said it wasn't very good and I never saw her again. Another asked if I might by any chance be [actor] Rip Torn. I told her I might by chance be, but it was very doubtful and never saw her again. Another told me as openers that she thought it was funny what Lyndon Johnson had said about how panty hose had set finger-fucking back several decades or maybe it was centuries or eons. I asked who was Lyndon Johnson? and never saw *her* again.

So it goes. . . .

*Vonnegut had told King he *could* bring a date, but added: "If it upsets Jill, I know nothing!"

January 25, 1973

Mr. Barlow Herget*
Apdo. 567
San Miguel de Allende, GTO
Mexico

Dear Barlow:

One month ago today, in Odessa, Texas, while drinking to the birth of Our Lord and Saviour with Warren Burnett, he solicited your

Mexico address on the theory that he goes there reasonably often and would look you up. I just telephoned it to him 10 minutes ago. Turns out his teenage son Paul (second son) is in your city this date; Edsel said he would wire you asking you to contact young Paul and be hospitable. Small world.

Edsel and I laughed Xmas Day about how three years ago you tried to alert us to the Mafia menace, and we laughed at you, and then came *The Godfather* and Joe Colombo and all to follow and we wondered how you knowed about it down in Paragould, Arkansas when we did not know it in Texas and Washington.

Reckon the Meskins have told you Lyndon died. The credibility gap being what it is, I refused to believe it until he failed to rise on the Third Day. Reckon its for real. I feel an amazing loss for the old bugger, more than the usual pious hypocritical beargrease brought forward by death. Not surprising, I guess, when you realize that for most of my life he has loomed in it—for good or ill—like the Pyramids. . . .

*Herget, an Arkansas journalist, was one of King's Nieman colleagues at Harvard.

February 13, 1973

To Lanvil & Glenda, Greetings:

When in the Course of Human Events it becomes Necessary, then do whatever it is.

Full of very self-centered news. Will commence in September being a professor at Princeton University for one year. Five minute pause honors your fit of mirth, gaspings, choking, incredulous exclamations, et al.

(Time passes).

It remains true. I will be called Visiting Ferris Professor of Journalism. Teach one course one semester in political science; one 'tother semester in creative writing. $20,000 plus $6,000 expenses. Nine months. Works out good. Required on campus only two days per week (though they require I take up residence there). Will split time between school teachin' and writin' on LBJ book (or, more accurately,

interviewing in Washington: for that purpose, shall keep place here).
Bird nest on the ground. Shameful. Sinful. Ought not to be allowed.
Burnett opines that "King, not only have you not never taught no
school, you ain't even seen much taught." Possibility of renewing for
one more year if mutual satisfaction twixt King-Princeton. Cross that
bridge later.

Edsel also of a mind it's my duty to Mankind and Irony and a lot of
vaporous elements to seek out Yale in some capacity: he can't get over
the possibility of a high school dropout being honored in sundry ways
by all of the Ivy League's Big Three.

Got word (unofficial, so don't broadcast it until you see the whites
of their Press Release) that I won the $500 prize given by the Texas
Institute of Letters for best piece of journalism on Texas. (*Life* mag
piece, re Loving County). Probably come to Texas in the spring for
presentation ceremonies and pure ego trip. Intend to give the money
back to the Institute's Paisano Project in Rosemarie's name; it will be
the first of an annual donation I intend to make in her name for that
purpose for an indefinite period. Think she'd like it. Also, mailed in a
new collection: *The Old Man & Lesser Stories.* [Wisely published
under the title *The Old Man and Lesser Mortals*. Ed.] Don't know
when the pub date will be.

Kathy Lowry and I went to Norman Mailer's celebrated 50th birthday party in Gotham. She met lots of Famous Arthurs: Mailer, Breslin,
Plimpton, Frank Conroy, Jules Feiffer, Gene McCarthy, et al. She
didn't get real overly impressed: the next day, when Mailer invited a
half-dozen of us to his private quarters, she declined for herself on the
excuse she had to go buy some lipstick. At Big Party itself, she talked
for 15 minutes to Feiffer. As she turns away briefly, or blinks her eyes,
Feiffer vacates his immediate turf and another celeb, Paul Desmond,
the Famous Musician, steps in. Without missing a beat, Kathy greets
Desmond with the puzzling question, "And what did you think of what
the movies did to your *Little Murders?*" Took a while to straighten that
out. . . .

April 14, 1973

Dear Buck:*

From my Home Entertainment Center, Buck Owens is singing how they should "Close All the Honky Tonks," and I take time off from musing over my West Texas novel on account of such music is Perfect-to-Write-Buck-Ramsey-by.

Approximately the 26th of April, which is to say less than two weeks, I will be in Odessa, Texas for about 10-15 days, and it would not surprise me should I there encounter Edsel Burnett. Given history, it should surprise me even less if said Edsel Burnett and the undersigned "availabled" themselves of several whiskey-drankin' opportunities. Now, it would seem to me that after a hard winter, an old Panhandle Boy would find it altogether fitting and proper to come down to Odessa, Texas during that period and hold up his end of the whiskey drankin'. And bring his gee-tar. What say?

Never did write that *Leaving Cheyenne* piece, starring Tony Perkins, on account of *Life* had the bad taste to fold whilst I was on location.** I didn't come away with much faith in Mr. Perkins as a wrangler. He sure had a pretty girl, though. I tried to cut her out of the herd a time or two, with thoughts of putting a temporary brand on her, but she was too wiley. Guess I'll have to get me a new cutting horse. . . .

I ain't sure the folks got a movie out of it. The producer keeps putting me and Larry McMurtry off when we ask to see a rough cut, saying they want it scored and polished for us, on account of it's such Fine Art, and what not. They're seriously overdue, and I'm betting on the side of no movie or next-to-none. Their research was the shoddiest I ever saw. Examples I called to their attention (and which they ignored): rural route mail carriers in the Texas of the early 1940s did not wear uniforms; crimped manes were unknown to working cow ponies in the 1920s; cowboys do not sit on their horses *outside* the corral while cattle are being loaded on a train and, if they should, they wouldn't sit by the goddamned loading chute; there were no pastel painted buildings in the small Texas towns of the 1940s; and you *do not* string fence by driving the fence posts into the ground with a sledge hammer, rather than using post-hole diggers. I ain't no rancher, but come on! Then they wanted to dub in some Hank Williams music as background to 1920s scenes; *did* talk them out of that. Tony Perkins don't know how to drive a buggy—there was a real-life cowboy/wrangler in charge of Perkins' horse-and-buggy. Between takes, he walked just outside camera range in case Tony got run away with. All flim-flam and tinsel and mock shows. . . .

I just done a *Playboy* piece, called "Getting Off" which is all about doing dirty with your clothes off. Whoever sends a copy to my 80-year-old Midland Mama when it comes out will have revealed themselves as my worst enemy. I am coming to Texas to do a piece for them [*Playboy*] on small town newspapers; come on to Odessa and tell me some Amarillo paper yarns. Also, being from the Panhandle, you must thirst to have somebody to cuss Nixon with and we'll provide that, free of charge. . .

*Buck Ramsey, of Amarillo, a writer later to gain fame as a cowboy poet and singer before his death in 1998. King used Ramsey's name as an unseen drinking and poker-playing cowboy in his 1980s play, *The Golden Shadows Old West Museum*.
**This article was later picked up by *Texas Monthly* as "Leavin' McMurtry."

April 14, 1973

Dear Willie:

I appreciated your call a while back.

Maybe the less said the better about our little scene last summer; it was a dark time for all hands, and we were not "at ourselves." Two old boys, one who is "good as grass" and the other "better'n rain" ought not to be mad very long.*

I have finally got back to work after a long terrible time of just staring at the walls, getting drunk, and gazing on the dark side of my spirit. Lost about a year, I guess: those last awful months of the death watch I was incapable of putting words on paper (or even matching them coherently in my head) and only recently have I started back. . . .

*King and Morris had fallen to fisticuffs a few months earlier in presence of

Washington socialite Barbara Howar over which of them owned title to her affections. Neither of them did for long.

———————

May 21, 1973

Dear Lanvil & Glenda:

I have waited all too long to send you a report of the surrealistic trip to Midland-Odessa, and do so now, in the wee hours—almost two hours later than Monday night by the clock—in hope of recording more of humanity's foibles, tricks, and madness. . . .

Scene: Cora King's living room. Characters: Herself; Estelle;* Myownself; My Three Children. Mother speaks:

Mother: Lawrence, will you git any time off from teaching school up yonder?**

Lawrence: Yes, there are holidays and so on. And I'll only work a couple of days each week.

Mother: Can you take trips?

Lawrence: Well, yes.

Mother: Could you come home in case of any emergency?

Lawrence: Well, sure.

(Tense silence, as everyone thinks Mother is thinking of her Mortal Demise. Her sudden tears seem to suggest it.)

Mother: (Choked, crying, inaudible.)

Lawrence: What? Come on, now, Cora.

Mother (Wailing): Estelle's getting *married!*

(Looks of astonishment all around, including Estelle)

Mother: Yes, she is. She hasn't told me, but I know! They're afraid I'll stand in their way. (Renews crying)

Lawrence: Well, sumbitch mumble mumble. Ah, well, Estelle, who's the lucky man?

Estelle: (Laughing now, almost beyond speech, signifying innocence and denials)

Mother: Now, young lady, don't think I don't know who you've been a-setting by at Church.

Estelle. What are you talkin' about!

Mother: *You* know. Who you been a-settin' with?

Estelle: Why . . . Mrs. This and Mrs. That, and Ole Lady Such-and-so.

Mother: A man! A man! A *man!*, Estelle! (Shaking finger: the D.A. intimidating recalcitrant witness.)

Estelle: Oh, Mr. Whatzis?

Mother: *No!* Try again! (Crying.)

Estelle: (Serious now, fearful, embarrassed): Why—oh, Mr. Somebody, you mean?

Mother: Well, *him too!* But he's not the main one!

Estelle: (Helpless shrug.)

Mother: How about Mr. *Whoozit?*

Estelle: (Laughing, relieved): Mr. *Whoozit?* Lord, if he's set by me more'n once I don't remember it. He don't even have any *teeth.* . . .

Mother: I know, Estelle. I won't stand in your way. You all won't have to worry about me. (Crying, huge sobs now.)

Estelle: (Laughing; obviously much amused.)

Lawrence (Looking on stricken faces of children): Well, come on now. Dammit. One cries and one laughs. Who do I believe?

(Mother and Estelle cry and laugh in concert; Cheryl looks as if she's visiting a loony bin; Brad smiles secretly; Kerri goes unregistered: blank stare.)

Lawrence: Well, Estelle, have you dated this fellow? Do I say congratulations, or what?

Estelle: No, I haven't never dated. I don't know where in the world you got this idea, Mother.

Mother: Well, a certain woman told me and never mind who.

Lawrence: Well, Estelle, I'll damn sure come home for the wedding. Name a date.

Cheryl: Me too, Aunt Stell. I think it's groovy if you have a boyfriend.

Estelle: But I *don't.* (Laughing) *Honest!*

Mother: And that same woman told me people is talking at the Church because Mr. So-and-So drives Estelle to Church regular, and *he's* married and his wife don't go to Church much.

Estelle: Listen now, you tell me who is *saying* all that! (Angry, now.)
Mother: That's all right.
Lawrence: Well, Mama, she sounds to me like one of those Sinners I told you about, whoever she is. Damn such gossips. (Long silence. Mother blows nose, changes subject.) End of scene.

Brad and, especially, Cheryl could not get over that Tennessee Williams script from above. Kerri only said "gol-lee" in support of their private astonished musings. Cheryl: "You know, this is the first time I've ever seen Nannie as anything but the saintly Grandmother. The first time I've seen her as an *adult*, a *person* . . . and I'm sorry Daddy, but as a crazy old woman." Well, yes, child: be assured Daddy has seen it before.

After mother's performance, I listened to her talk for the first time in a while: her tedious, repetitious old pointless stories have long put me in a cataleptic state, near to comatose, so that I turned my mind off and said "hummm" and "yes" and "what about that" by instinct, but didn't hear. That day, thereafter, I listened. It dawned on me, after 10 long recitals near too dull to be remembered, that she was the undisputed heroine of each: the most compassionate, the prettiest, the calmest: whatever, she claimed all the virtue in all the stories. And it dawned on me, then, that it has been so *for years* and I had not noticed the obvious pattern! So I shared this information with my children and then with my brother who was amazed that I hadn't known it since about 1939: he went into a tirade, almost a frenzy, about how she near drives him crazy and has for years, and told me how they have to chew her ass out—and have, long before Dad died—for melodramatics and fantasy and trouble-making. I tell you, for the prodigal son long gone from the daily warp-and-woof, it was most instructional. (Now, in retrospect, I wonder how much truth was in the story she told me of Dad's philanderings the night we buried him; recall, afresh, his consternation and tears and fright when he told me, several years before his death, that she was accusing him of "not keeping my pecker in my pants," did so without cause and persistently till it was half-driving him batty. All fantasy, perhaps! Well, then, why did Estelle corroborate that night-of-burial story?)

One man's family. . . .

*King's then 59-year old never-married sister.
**A reference to King's impending appointment at Princeton.

August 24, 1973

Dear Dr. Herget:

Glad to know your whereabouts.* Have cancelled the Mexico search party, which was to leave in 10 days. Some of the boys are sore that the trip is off and may go anyway. If they find another Herget down there, probably they'll rope him and bring him back anyhow.

I am off on September 1st to be visiting Ferris Professor of Journalism at Princeton. Some say I am turning into an Ivy League bum. . . .I teach one hour each week, which means 24 total hours over a nine month period for $20,000 plus expenses. Sure beats pickin' cotton.

Was in Texas recently with Warren Edsel Burnett, who got drunk and paid $3,300 for a motorized sailboat which we took out on Lake Brownwood. We got right smart drunk on the water and, coming in, scooted in too fast with the little motor turned on and snagged the bottom on stumps, rocks, shoals, etc; ripped the gears out and the ass out and all them sails of duckin and the wood poles the duckin was on crashed about our faces and ears. Miz Burnett and others on shore began variously shaking their fists at us, a-laughin' and a-hootin' and so on, and speaking ill of our sailorship. Edsel drew himself up as dignified as he could and said, "We done sailed our asses off for six hours [sans motor] and you summer soldiers judge us on the last two minutes."

I did a piece recently for *Playboy*, which will be published in January, called "Getting Off," which is all about how to screw; and I am doing two more for them right now, one about my old Texas newspaper days and another about the recent closing of the world's best whorehouse in LaGrange, Texas.** Also, I have did a piece for *Sport* mag, about how I coached and quarterbacked a luckless football team in the Army during my youth (November pub) and I am to do within the next month a piece called "The Day the World Stopped Working," for our new venture, *New Times,* due out October 8th, for which me, Breslin, Pete Hammill, Joe McGinnis, Brock Brower, Dick Schaap, Sara Davidson, and others will be contributing eds. . . .

Professor Kang

*Herget had returned to the U.S.
**Transformed later into the hit musical comedy *The Best Little Whorehouse in Texas.*

November 16, 1973

Dear Senor Deeck Wes':*

Bill Broyles probably told you that he over-nighted some weeks ago and reveled up a jolly old time of it. Halberstam, who has come and gone in his role as my guest lecturer, sings the praises of Richard West most highly. Claims you served him well professionally and socially, and he gave you the highest possible recommendations. I told him wait till he knows you better. Then, because he's so serious and literal minded, I had to spend 20 minutes convincing him you are a truly good fellow like he thought all along, and that I was only joking. . . . When he seemed convinced I said, "Of course, the damn fellow has one problem: he's a chicken thief. Been arrested for stealing chickens 10, mebbe 15 times or more. Can't keep his hands off the the other fellow's chickens. I dunno, it must be a disease, sort of a sickness." And no more than six questions later about why you steal chickens, he figgered out I was joking again. Halberstam thinks I am not serious enough. He may be right. . . .

This school teachin' is the easiest thing I ever seen. Had I but known it was so easy, I would have went to school to learn it. Apparently it don't take much practice. All you do is have a captive audience to bullshit three hours on a Monday afternoon, and make them call you Professor and Sir and all, and write papers on which you mark red marks, saying things like "This ain't done good enuff" and "horseshit to such statements" and "what are you doing after class Little Girl, and would you like a A plus?" To think I spent all them years carrying letter routes and pissanting pipe and digging sump-pits when I could have been professin' for money! Incidentally, they offered me a second year on the job last week with a raise. . . . I taken it quick as a wink. I don't know anywhur else to make that good money on Monday afternoons, beside which I take to this bossin' young 'uns real natural. I make them rise and sing a little song when I enter. It goes:

> Howdy-doo and welcome 'Fesser King,
> Are you gonna learn us Anything?
> Oh we know you'll do real good,
> Wouldn't cuss you if we could,
> For we love and worship on you 'Fesser King.

They only have to sing it three times at the beginning of each class.**

There are a few good people in the Princeton comunity: writers like Geoffrey Wolff, Fletcher Knebel, John McPhee; my department chairman, an old boy from Little Rock with much Ivy League and Rhodes Scholar furbishing (though not enough to spoil him: he gets drunk, sometimes, and sangs country songs and gets his accent back); and one or two others. But mainly a dismal lot. But we are only an hour by train from Gotham, and [writer] Joe McGinnis lives over in the countryside near the Delaware Water Gap, about an hour fifteen away, so we ain't entirely out of it with our kind. . . .

'Fesser King

Texas Monthly writer Richard West.
**This is King's parody of the song he swears Lyndon Johnson had his Cotulla, Texas elementary school students sing to him every day.

Editor's Note: Dallas Cowboy tight end and novelist Pete Gent became friends with King in the late 1960s when King met him while writing an article for *Holiday* magazine on quarter-back Don Meredith. After the success of *North Dallas Forty*, Gent moved back to his native Michigan, building a house for himself and his wife Jody. Late in the fall of 1973, Gent wrote King an apologetic letter rescinding an invitation for King and his girlfriend to come to Michigan at Christmas. This letter is King's reply.

December 9, 1973

Mr. Peter Gent
Rural Route 2
Grand Junction, Michigan

Dear Pete:

Okay, I consider myself disinvited for Christmas. It's all right. I understand. I bear no grudge nor ill-will. I'll get along. Of course, it may be more difficult in the future, when folks tell me how your getting rich and famous turned you into a chickenshit human turd, to defend you in light of this new evidence. But I shall try. I really shall. When people say those things about you, I've always been quick to say, "Listen, Pete Gent does the best he can with what he's got." And I'll try to keep on doing that.

Probably we'll spend Christmas alone in a motel. I had promised friends visiting the East they could have our apartment here, since I expected to be in Michigan. And now I can't disappoint them. But don't worry about it.

We had planned to be there on December 22nd, staying only until January 9th because my two children who are coming for the holidays have to be back in school by then. Kathy's mother wasn't expected to join us in Michigan until Christmas Eve and would have lingered no longer than January 2nd, anyhow. All this sure is causing an inconvenience. On second thought, fuck you. The rest of this letter is to Jody.

Hello Jody baby-darlin': how you? How can you stand to be married to that Indian-giving turd? Thank you for your nice fan letter. It must be a pleasure to get to read something that's written well, and I'm happy for you because I know you can't do that at home. Hoot

Shrake was here recently and I let Hoot and Jerry Jeff Walker go off drunk to New York in a car rented in my credit card's name and number. Sure was foolish of me. They lost it, of course, and it couldn't be found for days. Finally it turned up impounded with about $200 worth of charges on it. Merry Xmas, Larry, from your old frens Hoot and Jerry Jeff. Don't tell your Old Man, but he hadn't invited us for Christmas in the first place: he said come in the spring. Too bad the kids and Kathy's mother won't be able to make it then. Kiss kiss on you. Reasonably good sentiments to Peter Gent. . . .

April 23, 1974

Dear Edsel:

Thanks for cluing me to Mr. (Stanley) Elkins' *Searches and Seizures;* I had read *The Dick Gibson Show* by the same author. The new book is worth the price merely for the passage on page 124: "We die dropouts. All of us. Disadvantaged and underachievers. I have questions. I'm up to here in questions. I never needed to be happy, I only needed to know," and so forth. Edsel, that sumbitch is getting real close to the bone there: he's asking his version of "What are the purpose?"

I thought he went a little far when the English Lord fucked the bear. . . .

August 12, 1974

Dear Brer Broyles:*

I've been working this morning on using the four banned words— fuck, cunt, balls, and dick**—in one sentence, in a way they would have to be published. But I am having a little trouble with it. The first part is easy: "Four balls," cried Dick, "take your base." But the others, now, they're giving me a lot of trouble. . . .

It do seem to me that the morality of Texas might be more effectively improved if we spent our time catching thieves in public office than in censoring writer's words but, then, it is well-knew that I am a Godless Communist Eastern Ivy Leaguer, so what do I know? But to apply the New Rule to my sentence of the first paren, I guess it would read, "Four male genitals," cried Penis, "take your base."

Ah well: you win some and lose some and some are rained out. . . .

I've a few direct letters from ole frens about my Redneck article, and am glad angry Texans apparently are not going to bomb the *Texas Monthly* building because of it. . . .

Gotta run. Doing "Goodbye Penis Nixon" piece for *New Times*, with deadline 48 hours away. . . .

     Texas Monthly Editor Bill Broyles.
     **Declared out-of-bounds for use in *Texas Monthly* by publisher Mike Levy.

---

251 E. 32nd St.
Apt. 4-F
New York, N.Y. 10016
September 12, 1974

Mr. H. Allen Smith
Alpine, Texas

Dear H.A.S.:

Since last May I have had addresses in Princeton, Washington, Austin, and now Manhattan Island; which explains why it took the P.O.D. nearly all that time to track me down to deliver a copy of your *Return of the Virginian*. By the time it arrived it had more stickers and scratchings on it than a carney barker's valise. It arrived in good shape, however, and has been read and appropriately appreciated. I broke up every time I read of the *Chinga tu Madre* Mountains, half the fun being—as I'm sure was the case with you—in knowing that a high percentage of the readers, and possibly 100% of the Doubleday folk, didn't know what that meant. A good job, and thanks for the generous inscription. You speared and gored Alpine and several of its citizens, whom I think I recognize. I truly would like to see you do a nonfiction book on your Alpine experiences, but not limiting it to that:

turn your ole Illi-*noise* and Mt. Kisco eye on Texas, the whole dern kit-and-kaboodle, and far both barrels. I believe you could write a funny, instructive, popular and profitable book on that outrageous place—one that no native could accomplish. How about it? Seriously. Git in your car, if need be, and roam about the country and talk to the idjits and put 'em down in writin'. I would pay good money for such a book by you, might even sell it from pushcarts everywhere from the corner of 2nd Avenue and 32nd St. to Wink, Texas.

I moved here because I am going to teach at Princeton again this year and couldn't stand one more week living in that precious inbred place. Believe me, it ain't no better—and may be worse—than Alpine. Pretty yes, but pretty don't last. I hated it: all those pipe-sucking academicians strutting about with frowns to show they were Serious and thinking Big Thoughts; a Princeton dinner party is equal to three weeks in Hell and a weekend in Kermit. I think it was Kingsley Amis who said "The problem with Princeton is that it is more English than England is." I can't afford, as an old cotton-picker, to turn down the $25,000 they pay for one day per week; but that's all they git: I'll train and/or bus down each Wednesday morn and be back on the island by dark or before. . . .

September 16, 1974

Dear A.C. and Bettye:*

My experience with *TM* mag** has been good, by and large; had a little problem with the Redneck article because the publisher, Mike Levy, was upset about his Mama reading the dirty words; the only compromise they got out of me was they could write the vulgar word for the act of copulation as F- - - ; I didn't mind that, though I thought it was silly on account of not a man, woman or child in Texas will fail to supply the pertinent three letters. . . .

Bob Manning*** is getting together a special issue on Texas; I'm doing a piece as is McMurtry, Molly Ivins, and—out of state—David Broder, Charlotte Curtis (*NY Times*) and somebody I don't know named James Conway. It's scheduled for the spring, with copy due about Thanksgiving. I've talked to Bob about it, and a week ago he still had not assigned pieces on Texas fiction, Texas poetry, Texas education, and Texas sports; if interested, why don't you message him about one of these subjects or suggest your own? McMurtry is doing the "big" overview piece; Broder is doing Texas clout in national affairs; I'm doing the rural to urban transition; Curtis is doing Texas lifestyle and tycoonery; Conway is doing oil. Bill Broyles and the *Texas Monthly* staffers are doing sidebars: best-and-worst, a gallery of big Texans, Texas cuisine, Texas jokes and folklore and tall tales, etc. Bill Wittliff is doing a portfolio of pix. . . .

    *A.C. and Bettye Greene
    **Texas Monthly* magazine.
    ****Atlantic Monthly* editor-in-chief.

Oct.10, 1974

Dear Willie:

I handed Princeton College my resignation yesterday, effective at the end of the current semester: in other words, I decline to come back for the spring term. Fuck professoring. It ain't much fun. It breaks my writing rhythm and I hate those clenchjawed Ivy League academicians and the commuting down there and the whole bit. In short, as I said in my resignation letter, "I had to make the decision whether my own writing career is more important to me than the possible future writing careers of others, and I have resolved the question in my own favor." . . .

Talked to Uncle Drunk Shrake on the phone today; he's got him a mail-order commission as a parson and on Saturday will perform his first wedding—uniting Fletcher Boone and a gal named Libby Davis. Strange world, ain't it?. . .

Editor's Note: King had introduced Ella Udall to Congressman Morris Udall when she was Ella Ward. She called

King asking for advice about how to handle the press after her husband announced he would run for President in 1976.

December 18, 1974

Miz Ella Mae Udall
C/o Redondo Towers
8 Paseo Rodendo
Tucson, Arizona

Dear Potential First Lady:

Some thoughts on your tortures as you quiver at the thought of media interviews:

First, and though it may sound like an affirmation of the obvious, be yourself. I think you'd make a mistake to rare back and try to talk of the problems of Western Civilization or quote from the Great Books. From what you told me on the phone, I think you're handling it right in saying that your parents wanted to send you to college but you married young, had a baby, and after your divorce went to work first for Kaiser Industries and then came to Capitol Hill. If it should ever arise about Buster being raised by his father, I think your answer should be to the effect that "Well, I knew the boy would have a better life if he lived with his father, since in those days men had economic opportunities where women did not, but we always lived in the same town and he [Buster] spent weekends and summer vacations with me. We've maintained very close contact, and I'm proud of that. I'm proud of my son, too." Then a word or two, perhaps, about how well Mo and Buz have gotten along over the years. As for the Richard Ward* thing, I do not believe I would volunteer it: if asked, however—and eventually you probably will be—I'd say something like, "That was a painful experience, one of those human mistakes lonely people fall prey to. It was short, and it ended I hope, without anyone being hurt too badly and without it being anybody's fault." And the less said after that, the better. I don't think anybody much will push it if you present it in those terms.

When it gets to the "hobby" area—what do you do with your time,

Mrs. Udall? etc.—I'd stress a devotion to jazz music, which you can talk about on your own better than I can instruct you. As to reading, I wouldn't pretend a lot: say you enjoy "light" reading—such novels as Jimmy Breslin's *The Gang That Couldn't Shoot Straight*, or something along those lines that you've read. (Incidentally, you might like Erica Jong's *Fear of Flying* if you haven't read it; also Gore Vidal's *Burr*, and Barry Hannah's *Geronimo Rex*, in the novel field.) It's always safe to cite Mark Twain as a favorite; I'd recommend *The Autobiography of Mark Twain*, and *Huckleberry Finn*—both Hemingway and Mailer say it is the Great American Novel from which all other American novels are derived. If asked "What are you reading now?" I'd put myself in a position to answer "William Manchester's *The Glory and the Dream—a Narrative History of America, 1932-1972*." It's really quite a remarkable work, and puts into perspective most of what's happened in this country during the past 40 years. It's a big, fat $20 book and worth every penny, and it's pretty new. You should get it.

I feel disadvantaged in attempting to suggest your answers with respect to your interests in the public affairs field, because I don't know your inclinations. I guess a general safe answer would be that after working so many years as a congressional secretary you've been content of late to run your home and assist Mo in the way wives can; but I think it would be good to say something like, "There are natural areas of interest I'd like to know more about—women's rights, for example, because only in recent years have people come to realize that women haven't had the opportunity to become complete persons. I think women are on the way to living fuller lives now, and I believe that's good." (You'd be surprised how vague generalities will be accepted by most interviewers, whether the reporter is male or female.) If they get down to asking what you think about the Middle East or Economics, I'd simply beg a lack of expertise—nobody expects you to know all that—and perhaps say with a fetching grin, "Right *now* I'd be content to know President Ford's position on these matters" or some such. (Provided, of course, Mo isn't reserving all the funnies for himself.)

Now, if I were a mean reporter and had done some research on you, Miz Ella, I might be inclined to ask if you drink to excess, if it isn't true you have a flash temper, and that through a combination of these you've made some enemies you haven't spoken to in years. I'm not sure anybody will do that, but if they do I would consider responding something like this: "There may have been a time, when I was unhappy, that I drank a bit much but I'm glad that's over. I am strong-willed, I guess, and perhaps I've offended a few people by excessive candor or by standing up for myself. But I don't keep any 'enemies list' and I'd rather talk about my friends. I believe I have a few." Then be prepared to name some.

I don't know, this is rambling and may not be worth anything; you (and Mo) of course reserve the right to ignore any or all of it. If you think I can contribute anything in the specifics that you think of, I'll always have a ready ear and I'll try. Again, I say, just relax and answer out of your heart; remember that they can't make you say anything you don't want to say and recall that old rule so many of us forget: "Engage Brain Before Putting Mouth in Motion." I've seen you charm even Martha Mitchell, so I don't worry a lot about your performance. Cool it on the juice before or during public appearances. Afterwards, call me up and we'll get dronk and talk dirty. Love on you, Miz Ella, and on Mr. Mo. . . .

*Another ex-husband.

Editor's Note: Ella Udall, dispirited by the declining health of her husband—afflicted with Parkinson's Disease—committed suicide in September 1988.

December 18, 1974

Hon. Morris Udall
8 Paseo Rodendo
Tucson, Arizona

Dear Mo:
Season's greetings, old scout.

I had occasion recently, at a *Playboy* Magazine awards luncheon, to talk with a number of writers including Tom Wicker, Gary Wills, Nat Hentoff, Margo Hentoff, Jules Feiffer, and a half-dozen or so others, all of whom—knowing that we think reasonably highly of each other—asked many questions about you and said they'd like to know you better. Margo Hentoff made what I think is an excellent suggestion: that I arrange, fairly soon, a series of perhaps three evenings, here in New York, so that you can meet about 25 or 30 writers at a time and they can really get to know you better. We wouldn't want one big mob scene, but about three, small intimate affairs so that you can informally talk with these people—Eastern Seaboard Liberals in the Communications World. These are the people who can call you to the attention of the country at large through their columns, magazine articles, TV appearances, and so forth. They also can usually raise some money from their rich friends if inspired enough. Their main function, however, would be to spread the Udall name and deeds in print. Naturally, we ain't gonna score 100% and many won't be making endorsements but that's not what we want: we want, simply, to impress them with your good qualities, give them some hope (they have no candidate now, and need one), and then let nature take its course.

This will cost a little money, which I don't have. But if your campaign chest could afford it, I think it's well worthwhile. I'll be happy to act as host and front man: we might have one at the home of David Halberstam (much larger than mine) and then rent hotel suites for the other two with booze and grazing foods. I could attract people from just about every mag, newspaper, TV, and radio station around and would be happy to consult with you or your representatives, as well as provide you a little sketch of each person before each meeting. What say?*

*Three such meetings were held: at King's Manhattan apartment, at the home of Arthur Schlesinger, Jr., and in a hotel rented for the occasion.

April 7, 1976
4:10 A.M.

Congressman Morris Udall
Longworth House Office Bldg.
House of Representatives
Washington 25, D.C.

Dear Mo:

The day after Ike beat the much-superior Adlai Stevenson, in 1952, my old hero Murray Kempton wrote: "The sun was shining and it was the same old 42nd Street; the taxi drivers growled the old fraternal obscenities at one another. Nothing had changed; nothing ever will, I suppose. There was no surface sign that this was the end of the world. But for my money, it was the end of the world, and neither sun or the amenities is going to trap me into saying something pleasant about it. The knuckle-heads have beaten the egg-heads. You're not going to catch this baby jumping over the net and extending his hand to the winner. . . ."

Me neither.

I associate myself with all that Kempton said, except that part about it being "the end of the world." It was a cruel reversal, yes, that Wisconsin thing,* and I hurt with you and for you. But no matter what happens, your world has not ended. You are good and strong, the same fine person as before, and you will go forward. You have something few have: a healthy sense of the absurd, and the knowledge of who you are. These are precious gifts. I would not have you trade them for even the headiest of victories. They will see you through.

You may yet win the nomination, or you may not. In the event of the latter, the loss will be the country's more than yours or mine. Do not, please, forget that. Stay as you are. If I ever have known what is called "a great man" then you are that man. I love you, and I love Ella, and you are much in my thoughts. If the fates do not have it in mind for you in 1976—and they yet still may—you are none the worse for it among those who honor and respect decency, truth, honesty, and all the things you are. Walk in the sunshine, Mo. Keep it all in balance.

Fire your best guns, celebrate when you hit the target, and grin when the ammunition's gone. Seize the day. In the words of the Mickey Newbury song: "You only live once in a while/between the last breath and the very first smile."

Fight the bastards, yes. And should the knuckleheads win, there's always tomorrow. Nothing's permanent if we won't let it be. My old friend: you have achieved a state of grace which passeth all understanding. We shall yet laugh whatever happens; we will not "sit upon the ground and tell sad stories of the death of kings."

I am with you. I am for you. I am here. We have buried the dead together. We have, and will again, share resurrections. Again, good man, I love you. Peace. . . .

*Television reported that Udall had defeated Jimmy Carter in the Wisconsin Democratic primary and Udall publicly claimed victory. By the following day, late-reporting rural votes gave Carter a razor-thin win.

---

251 East 32nd Street
Apartment 4 F
New York, New York 10016
January 8, 1976

Mr. William Broyles
Editor, *Texas Monthly*
Austin, Texas

Dear Bill:

As I said to you on the phone, I'd like to keep our plans as confidential as possible. I know you'll have to talk to Mike Levy, and perhaps others, but I would ask that you urge them to dummy up until we are right on the actual date on which I would join you. Several of the more personal matters I hope you will reserve strictly to yourself: I shall reveal them because (1) I am talking to a friend and (2) you have every right to know my entire situation and my mind-set. The latter definitely is not good.

I'd like to come by March 1st if possible. I think the quicker I shuck this place and its burdens—financial in the main, though more and more my soul is involved—the quicker I'll be on the road to rehabilitation in my own mind. I do not intend (and I don't say this unkindly, but as one aware of what can happen to people) to turn into another Bill Brammer. When, in 1964, my personal life had gone up in painful smoke and my writing life was just beginning, I found it worked to return "home" to Austin, and I feel it will again. There is something primitive in that need to return home when all has gone sour elsewhere, and my need is great.

The pressures of having to earn a *minimum* of $40,000 per year to get along here is something I cannot much longer tolerate. That money is terribly difficult to earn without having profitable books going, and my books aren't getting done because I'm on the treadmill hustling from one magazine assignment to another. I'd like to do enough work for you, and be adequately compensated, so that I can devote all other work time (save the *New Times* column) to my books. My life simply does not and will not amount to much until they are accomplished. It's difficult for me (and probably for you) to say just how much work would be required at the *Monthly* in terms of time. Perhaps we can work out a formula for X pieces per year for X dollars with an understanding that I'd do promo work for the magazine— some radio or TV and speeches to various groups—though, of course, I would defeat my purpose if that latter consideration kept me on the road for great gobs of time. I have in mind, in that regard, select appearances rather than on-going responsibilities for same. The *writing* for you would be the vital factor; the rest would be icing on the cake.

Whatever the pay formula we set, it would bring order to my life if I could be paid regularly on a monthly basis. I would know, for example, that my *New Times* column would be bringing in $900 per month (after the agent's cut) and then whatever I would be earning from you; this would permit one to plan, budget, know what to expect. I realize your money problems until the new fiscal year, beginning July 1st. Do you think you could afford to pay me $1,000 per month from March 1st to July 1st, and then $1,500 per month for one year thereafter? Or is that unrealistic? I just don't know. Please be candid about it and tell me, in turn, the best you can do. I would include in my duties certain in-put as to suggestions for stories and writers, provided you want such a service, and think I can make a contribution there. (Example: the *Monthly's* one shortcoming, I think, has been a lack of covering "the other Texas"—the poor, the blacks, the chicanos, etc. I do not mean to say that you should become a bleeding heart magazine, but it does appear to me that a vital part of what constitutes Texas is being missed there.) I think too that by rattling and banging around Texas by car I'll be able to discover other stories and ideas for other writers as well as for myself. You in your own right may have some suggestions as how I otherwise can contribute. . . .

What am I bid? . . .

October 27, 1976

Jon Larsen, Editor
New Times Magazine
2 Park Avenue
New York, NY

Jon:

Amazing. You fire me out-of-the-blue and by letter and then "hope this will not end either your relationship with the magazine or myself." I am afraid it does. I will never write another line for *New Times* so long as you are associated with it.

The only thing I agree with in your letter is that you proceeded in a cowardly fashion. For the record I'd like to point out that I was the only one of the original contributing editors who stayed with the magazine and that I helped George Hirsch raise the seed money that founded it. I also recommended its first two top editors and Frank Rich, the best writer and editor ever to work there. I would have thought this would entitle me to be fired eyeball-to-eyeball rather than by special delivery letter.

I refuse to go along with your suggestion that the upcoming issue "quietly and gracefully" bury me with the notice that I am taking a "sabbatical" to write a book. If you say anything at all, tell the truth: that you fired me. It might be good for a magazine editor to tell the truth at least once. I insist on that.

Kiss my ass, Jon.

Editor's Note: Later that night King—"lacking a little in timing and balance"—called Western Union to send Jon Larsen the following telegram: "If you write that I quit to write a book, knowing it is a lie, I will whip your ass. Believe me." The Western Union lady refused to send it because of "bad language."

King redialed Western Union, got another person, and dictated the same telegram except for changing "whip your ass," to "flog your tochis." After a pause, the young woman said "Sir how do you spell 'tochis'?" The telegram was sent. King says he was never given a reason Larsen fired him as a *New Times* columnist at a time when he was drawing more fan mail than any other of the magazine's writers, but suspects "it was so he could bring in one of his good buddies to take my place." *New Times* folded in 1979.

Top: Clyde C. King, "The Old Man," in King's famous piece published in *Harper's* shortly after his father's death in 1970. Courtesy King Private Collection.

    Above: King *(right)* in the Austin home of his cousin and "lifelong best friend," Lanvil Gilbert, in November of 1959. This book is dedicated to Gilbert. Courtesy King Private Collection.

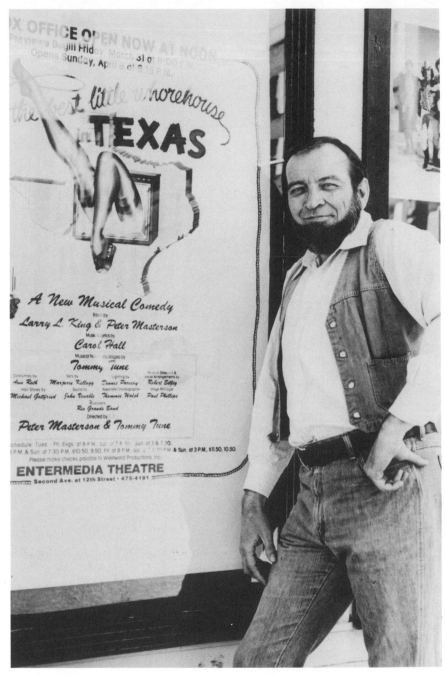

The playwright looks confident enough on the afternoon of the Off-Broadway opening of his first stage work. In his heart, however, King was sure the musical comedy "would close quicker than a switchblade." Twenty years later, *Whorehouse* gets worldwide productions. Photo by Diane Smook, courtesy Southwestern Writers Collection.

Top: Twenty-six-year-old Larry L. King, a rookie of less than a year in Washington, chats with Truman's secretary of state, Dean Acheson, on the grounds of the Supreme Court in 1955. King introduced Acheson at a noon luncheon of the Democratic "Burro Club." Photo by Craig Raupe, courtesy Southwestern Writers Collection.

Above: Willie Morris and Larry L. King, looking a bit the worse for wear, when King spoke at the University of Mississippi in 1982. Morris then was writer-in-residence at Ol' Miss. Photo by *Oxford Eagle,* courtesy Southwestern Writers Collection.

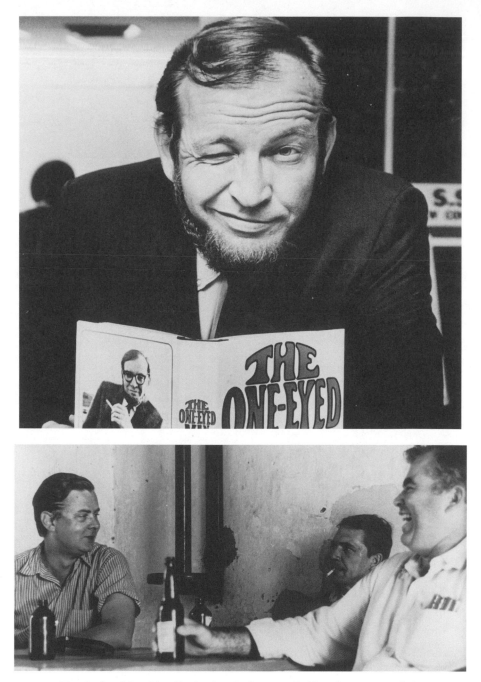

Top: Author "flogs" his first book at Dallas Love Field in the summer of 1966, cutting hi-jinks for the photographer. It was King's first interview as a "Real-life Famous Arthur" of books. Photo by *Dallas Morning News,* courtesy Southwestern Writers Collection.

Above: Three "old pals" of King in border-town Mexico in the 1970s. Left to right: Willie Morris, Warren Burnett, Malcolm McGregor. Photo by Neil Caldwell, courtesy Southwestern Writers Collection.

In the summer of 1972, King visited his friend, fellow-writer and historian David Halberstam at the latter's summer home on Nantucket Island. The two writers have been close friends since 1961 and were *Harper's* magazine colleagues. Photo by Joan Bingham, courtesy Southwestern Writers Collection.

The author behind a stack of his second book " . . . *And Other Dirty Stories*" at Scholz Beer Garden, Austin, in October of 1968. Behind King, left to right: artist Fletcher Boone, writer William A. Brammer. Photo by William Wittliff, courtesy Southwestern Writers Collection.

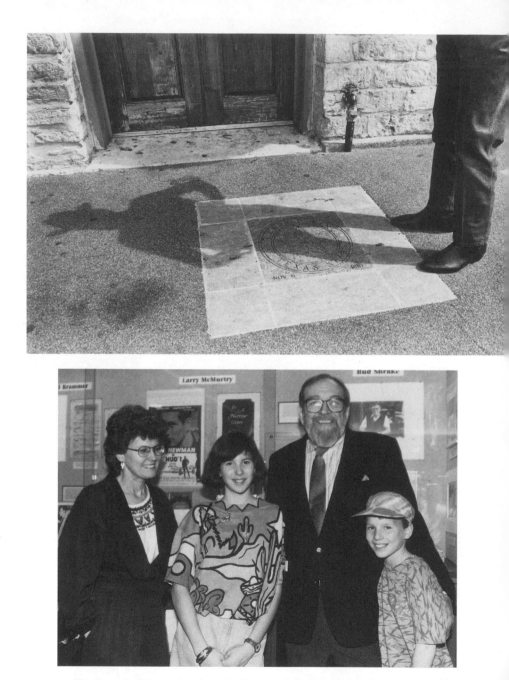

Top: Larry L. King casts a long shadow over his sidewalk "star" on Austin's 6th Street. Photo by Alix King.

Above: Barbara Blaine, Larry L. King, their daughter Lindsay and son Blaine at the Southwestern Writers Collection, San Marcos, Texas, 1991. Photo courtesy Southwestern Writers Collection.

Above: King at his mother's family burial plot at the Putnam, Texas, cemetery, 1994. Photo by Dr. Stanley Gilbert.

Left: Larry L. King, son Blaine and daughter Lindsay as the youngsters take their first train ride, from Washington, D. C., to Baltimore. Photo by Barbara Blaine.

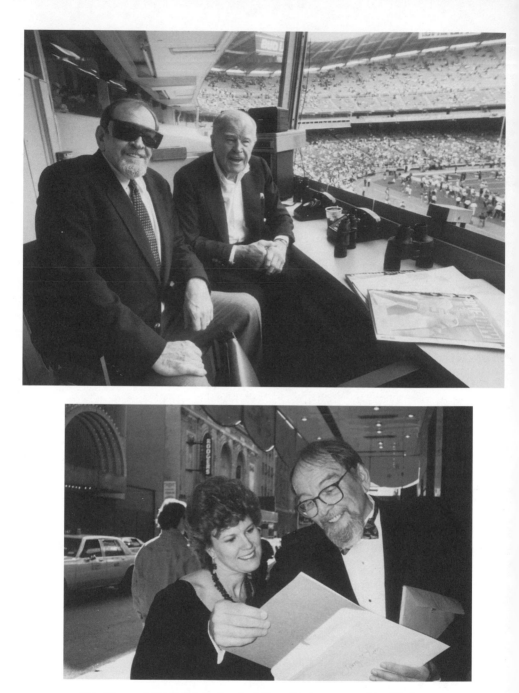

Top: King and his friend the late Jack Kent Cooke, owner of the Washington Redskins football team for 20 years, in Cooke's box at RFK Stadium in 1996. King was a regular guest in the owner's box from 1982 until Mr. Cooke's death in 1997. (Photo by Alix King)

Above: King and his wife, Barbara Blaine, dressed in formal finery, on the sidewalk in front of the Lunt-Fontaine Theatre in New York on opening night of "Ho-House II." Courtesy King Personal Collection.

6

"The Missing Years"

The answers to many old mysteries are present in Larry L. King's ample archive in the library at Southwest Texas State. One of the advantages of placing personal papers in an archive is that you have a trained staff to help you bring order into the inexplicable past, or check dates, or establish a sequence of ancient promises either kept or betrayed. For all its richness, however, King's archive actually creates one mystery, and that is: what happened to the letters of the late 1970s?

There is a shocking lack of content from late in 1976, when King was in a very bad place professionally, to May 1979, after he has struck gold with *The Best Little Whorehouse in Texas*. This period stretches from King being so down in January 1976 that he is begging *Texas Monthly* Editor Bill Broyles for a job (and actually contemplating moving to Austin, seemingly in defeat) to, much to his surprise, striking it rich with a Broadway hit and falling in love with and marrying a feisty young Texan and Ivy-League-educated attorney, Barbara Blaine.

About this period, King says, "It seems remarkable—as well as disconcerting—that one who seems to have saved his smallest jottings over much of a lifetime can provide literally no personal correspondence for the 1977/1978 year—nor can my friends and associates." The plausible explanation is that there weren't many letters from these busy days and what few there were could have been lost during a move or by a book publisher. This flies in the face of every other period in King's busy life during the last forty years. King "clearly recalls" using copies of some letters from that period—as well as a journal he kept during the writing of the *Whorehouse* musical—when he wrote *The Whorehouse Papers,* his uproarious account of his collaboration on the show. Although the current staff of Viking/Penguin looked in their files and came up empty-handed, King insists "they must be reposing in some dank and distant warehouse." Unless of course, King himself misplaced them (unlikely, giving the care given all of his other records) during this hectic period. Our solution to what we came to call "the missing years" was for Larry to write a long letter recapping those years, which are also treated in *The Whorehouse Papers* and in *None But A Blockhead.*

After perhaps the nadir of King's professional career, with his desperate letter to Broyles and his threatening response to *New Times* Editor Jon Larsen after Larsen fired him, things soon began to perk up. After a dozen years of isolated work as a novelist and freelance non-fiction writing, suddenly King was involved in two collaborative projects. In mid-1976, Peter Masterson and Carol Hall persuaded him to join them in making a musical comedy from his 1974 magazine story for *Playboy,* "The Best Little Whorehouse in Texas." Meeting with fellow Texans to talk about a musical comedy was purely speculative work at this point and to make ends meet, King entered into a contract to ghost Bobby Baker's story for W. W. Norton. Baker was a legendary Washington operative and was facing a prison term for his activities as secretary to the Senate Majority while Lyndon Johnson was Majority Leader. The picture of King enforcing a drinking regimen on Baker so that they could be drunk, sober and hungover at the same time speaks volumes both about King's lifestyle in the mid-'70s and the understandings between the two collaborators that resulted in the best seller *Wheeling and Dealing*.

At precisely the same time, the summer of 1976, King entered more seriously into what would become the most lucrative professional partnership of his life, that with fellow Texans Carol Hall and Peter Masterson. Masterson had found in a theater dressing room a 1974 *Playboy* that contained King's story about the closing of the "chicken ranch" in La Grange titled "The Best Little Whorehouse in Texas." King had known Carol Hall as a cabaret singer in Washington and New York and she had arranged a meeting for the three of them. Having absolutely no stage credentials at all, King entered into meetings with Masterson and Hall as a bemused outsider, thinking that his working on a crackpot idea for a musical comedy was the longest of shots. Much to his surprise, less than a year after their initial meetings, the early version of "Whorehouse" had a "workshop" production at the famed Actor's Studio in New York and then a fuller "showcase" production. It would go on to become a staple of American Theatre. Lightning had struck, King's money scuffling days were over. His other 1976 collaboration, that with Bobby Baker, had also paid major dividends. *Wheeling and Dealing* became a bestseller.

As a capper on the 1970s, King in 1980 produced his third collection titled *Of Outlaws, Con Men, Whores, Politicians, & Other Artsists*. As a grouping of his magazine pieces post-*Harper's*, it presents the range of work that he produced for *New Times*, *Playboy* and *Texas Monthly* among other publications. More Texas oriented than his other collections, this volume contains several classic pieces including "The Best Little Whorehouse in Texas," "The American Redneck," and his accounts of playing dominoes with Amarillo Slim and attending John Connally's Milk Fund trial.

King's attraction to Texas during this period was strong. As his letter to Bill Broyles indicates, he seriously considered moving to Austin, where there were companionable friends and a constant party. Austin

In the middle seventies actually was the "groover's paradise" of legend, with cheap rents, easily available marijuana, and music everywhere. King's friends included the founders of Mad Dog, Inc. Bud Shrake, Gary Cartwright and Jerry Jeff Walker, who instigated many good and wild times and acted on their slogan "performing indefinable services for mankind."

In his introduction to *Of Outlaws . . .* , King announces his new life style, because he fears "damage from my old liver and my new lady. Hereafter, as part of my ongoing rehabilitation, I plan to hang out with fewer outlaws, ward heels, and whores. I expect, instead to consort with solemn bank clerks, saintly parsons and proper iron maidens. I'll write you about it when I do." A symbolic end to this period had occurred in 1978 with the death of King's dear friend Bill Brammer, who never missed a party. Brammer, who in the opinion of his peers possessed the brightest talent of his generation of Texas writers, died penniless at the age of 49 having published only *The Gay Place.*

—Richard Holland

April 29, 1998

Dear Dr. Holland:

It is damn-nigh impossible, from my present position of comfort, to recapture the helter-skelter life I led from the mid-1970s to near the end of that decade, though I must try because of the missing letters. I fear the recall, however, will cause ancient aches, pains, angers, and disappointments to revisit my bones.

Simply put, I had not scuffled so hard to stay afloat since my cotton-patch, oilfield and low-paying newspaper reporter days. In moments of despair I actually questioned whether I had done the right thing in leaving a good Capitol Hill paycheck for the rigors and salts of the literary adventure. New York City rents and grog prices kept my nose to many grindstones, to say nothing of three levels of taxes—city, state, federal—and I was putting my son Brad through an expensive boarding school (Selwyn, in Denton, Texas) and paying for travel to visit him or for him to visit me. And, of course, I had the obligation to wine and dine various consorts. A prudent man might have cut down on his boozy socializing and have spent many more productive hours at his typewriter. History shows, however, that I rarely have been brought up on Public Charges of Prudence.

Seeds were planted beginning in 1976 and 1977 that would eventually bear sweet fruits, but I then had no way of knowing that. The most fortuitous of these would prove to be when Peter Masterson and Carol Hall persuaded me in the summer of 1976 to join them in writing a musical comedy from my two-year-old *Playboy* article, "The Best Little Whorehouse in Texas." At the time, I thought they were crazy and finally agreed to participate only because it occured to me that I might sell a funny article about shooting for Broadway and missing it by several zillion Light Years. My collaborators had never written a play, nor had I—should one exclude a stage work I tried in my early 20s that amounted to nothing other than a public display of my abysmal ignorance of the theater. A few of us, most loosely connected with the Permian Playhouse Community Theatre in Odessa, performed a staged reading of that so-called work in, I think, 1953 and it was so bad I would have left mid-way in the first act had I not carelessly cast myself in a leading role. So I had no confidence in myself as librettist when we started the *Whorehouse* experiment.

Since *Whorehouse* was being written purely on speculation, I could work on it only when not writing for guaranteed pay. Which meant the usual grinding out of magazine articles, book reviews, and other hasty piecework. In late 1976 I signed a contract to write Bobby Baker's as-told-to biography—with W. W. Norton Publishing Company—and this required my bouncing between New York and Washington so as to tape Baker, read documents of record, trial transcripts, speak often with one of his former attorneys—Mike Tigar—about Baker's trial and appeals; I also interviewed a couple of ex-cons who had done time with Baker in Lewisburg Federal Prison. All this meant I had to pay rent in two cities and foot my own expenses while the book was being shaped. Although I received 45% of the $155,000 advance paid by W. W. Norton, money arrived only as each chapter of the book was completed to the satisfaction of the publishing house. So I had to continue a certain amount of magazine grind-work.

Additionally, I perhaps unwisely took on another job: writing three columns weekly for the *Washington Evening* and *Sunday Star* for a period of four months as part of that publication's "writer-in-residence" program. Jimmy Breslin, Willie Morris, Jane Howard and Jane O'Leary were among the writers who had preceded me in that role. Bobby Baker fumed and pouted because I did not exclusively work on his project because (1) he got paid only as I performed and (2) he felt he had made a great personal sacrifice in agreeing with my dictate that he could drink only when I did so that we would be drunk at the same time, hung-over at the same time and capable of working at the same time.

Looking back, that hectic time in Washington—and hurried returns to New York for on-going business—plays out almost as a farce. On a typical day I would arise with the dawn in my postage-stamp sized apartment near Dupont Circle, step across the sleeping form of my visiting teenaged son, Brad—who slept on a couch-bed we shared—and wedge myself into a small chair in front of a tiny table to write my column for the *Star;* our bags and Brad's guitars took up considerable space in our one-room-and-tiny-bath quarters and until he got up and folded the bed into its couch form I literally had not an inch of wiggle room. I had approximately three hours in which to hammer out 1,500 words before rushing downstairs to hail a cab, inspect the driver's face for signs of honesty, and then trust my copy to his care for prompt delivery to the *Star* offices in a distant part of Washington. Meanwhile, Bobby Baker, impatiently patting his foot in his apartment a few blocks from my own, would have called two or three times to curse and fuss because I had not shown up to tape more of his tale. I would then grab my over-sized tape recorder, grunt it to Baker's apartment, and wheeze and gasp for breath during the first half-hour of my questioning of him. Every week or ten days I sneaked off from Baker to catch a shuttle flight to New York the better to work on *Whorehouse* scenes or view scenes being done under Pete

Masterson's direction at a workshop production at Actors Studio. Then I would repeat the cycle until all signs of life were gone.

Fortunately, most of the *Star* columns were about politics—a subject that came easily to me—and a new President, Jimmy Carter, and a spirited race for the House Majority Leadership, provided ample fodder. At least one such column proved to have rather long-range political consequences. The tale was revealed by Marshall Lynam, long-time aide to Congressman Jim Wright of Fort Worth, in his 1998 book *Stories I Never Told the Speaker* (Three Forks Press: Dallas) and with Lynam's kind permission I include excerpts here:

> On Sunday, December 5 [1976], the day before the Majority Leader election, the Jim Wright brigade struck two telling blows. The first Jim Wright never knew about. It was carefully orchestrated by Craig Raupe and his longtime friend, Larry L. King. They both had arrived in Washington in 1955 as impecunious, fresh-faced political novices—Craig as Administrative Aide to Jim Wright, Larry as AA to Congressman J. T. Rutherford of Odessa.
>
> Later, Larry himself served a stint as Jim Wright's AA and then went on to become a highly successful writer. In the future he would win renown as the author of *The Best Little Whorehouse in Texas*. But in December, 1976, he was far more interested in another House, even though the charms of its occupants were admittedly less obvious. And now. . . . Craig and Larry, both seasoned and resourceful in the ways of Washington, saw an opportunity to strike an unusual tactical blow in behalf of their longtime pal.
>
> By a fortuitous coincidence, Larry had just signed up as a writer-in-residence for the old *Washington Evening Star.* Now defunct, this venerable and respected daily was required reading by the denizens of Capitol Hill. What then could be more appropriate, Craig and Larry wondered, than for Larry to speculate in the *Star,* which of the four Majority Leader candidates would the new

President, Jimmy Carter, prefer to work with! Such a story could hardly be more timely, especially since the article would be published on the Sunday before Monday's Majority Leader election.

Of course Jimmy Carter knew full well the danger of a President's dabbling in the internal affairs of the House. In a candid moment he had admitted that yes, he had a favorite, but he wisely kept his mouth shut about which of the four it was. To any conscientious journalist, this would offer an irresistible professional challenge. After all, isn't it the solemn obligation of a sagacious newspaper writer, brimming with truths and insights hidden to lesser mortals, to shine the bright light of truth on the innermost thoughts of a President, up to and including things he would be crazy to say out loud? In the face of such a compelling journalistic responsibility, Larry wrote a long piece examining the pros and cons of each candidate and concluded that Jim Wright had more of the former and fewer of the latter than any of his competitors.

"Jimmy Carter has a favorite. He has said so," Larry wrote. "Mindful of the jealous prerogatives of the Congress, and respecting tradition requiring non-intervention, he carefully has failed to name him. The suspicion here is that Jimmy Carter's favorite is Texan Jim Wright" and went on to tell why he thought so. In the meantime, from a commercial printer, Craig ordered several hundred bright blue gummed labels reading "See Inside: Larry L. King on the Critical House Majority Leader Race."

At 5 A.M. Sunday, Craig Raupe climbed out of bed and met a truck bringing enough copies of the *Star* for each Democrat in the House.

Above the fold on page one of each paper, Craig methodically began sticking his gummed labels. As he worked on this chore at the mail delivery entrance of the Longworth House Office Building, another early-riser unexpectedly arrived. Congressman Phil Burton, Jim Wright's fiercest rival in the race, strode briskly past, entering the building completely oblivious to

Craig Raupe and his ongoing handiwork. As Democratic members of the House received these papers, some may have mistaken Craig's gummed labels as a promotional notice put on by
the Sunday *Star* at its printing plant. Regrettably, such a mistake
could not be helped. . . .

Well, Dick, you may recall that Wright won that race by a single
vote—147 to 146—and served as Majority Leader for a decade before
succeeding Tip O'Neill in January of 1987 as Speaker of the House. I
don't know how many votes my column gathered for Jim—if any—
though at least six Democrats later told Wright's staffers that Jimmy
Carter's "preference" (as stated by me in what really was no more
than a wild guess and a fond hope) influenced them to vote for
Wright. I like to *believe* that's true, though there's no way to measure
for accuracy.

At any rate, I had little time to revel in Jim Wright's victory or stick
around to take bows. Things were humming and popping with
Whorehouse up in New York. On the basis of the workshop production
of the first three scenes of the musical, Carl Fischer—a lawyer and
working associate of Actors Studio's top gun Lee Strasberg—granted
the King-Masterson-Hall trio an $11,000 budget to do a full "show-
case" production there. This did not sit well with some at Actors
Studio, they being serious "method acting" types and uncharmed by
the notion of a rowdy Texas musical comedy about whores being presented on famed and sacred boards. Strasberg himself, in fact, stayed
away from any association with us —until huzzahs from trade papers,
gossip columnists and word-of-mouth among New York's showbiz and
literary cliques caused him to suddenly appear at the last few performances with well-heeled and well-connected personal friends in tow;
most theatrical types have good instincts when it comes time to take
bows.

The Actors Studio showcase was done from late October to mid-
November of 1977. Near the end of our run, a second "happy accident" occurred—one almost matching Pete Masterson's having found
a two-year-old copy of my *Playboy* article, without knowing who had

placed it in his dressing room while he was acting on Broadway in *That Championship Season* and his knowing composer Carol Hall, who, in turn, knew me, and put us together.

The second happy accident was set in motion when Stephanie (Stevie) Phillips, freshly hired by Universal Pictures to buy potential movie material in its behalf, was persuaded by the screenwriter William Goldman to attend one of the last few *Whorehouse* performances, Goldman being a friend of all three of its creators. Ms. Phillips later said she was tired, needed to wash her hair and had seen so many showcase productions of dubious quality that she almost did not attend. Praise Jesus, however, she *did* attend and almost immediately began negotiations to acquire both the stage and movie rights of *Whorehouse*.

It would be months, however, before I saw any significant money and so, in the meantime, I continued to bounce down to Washington for final Baker book interviews so as to conclude the final chapters. I also scuffled more magazine assignments and made trips to Texas with Stevie Phillips to line up the real-life Chicken Ranch Madam—"Miss Edna"—and the real-life sheriff, T. J. Flournoy, upon whom we had based our cussing stage sheriff Ed Earl Dodd. Universal offered $40,000 each to them to sign waivers; Stevie Phillips blinked when Sheriff Flounoy said "I don't want no personal money, give it to her" and nodded toward Miss Edna. The money had been offered because we had contrived—we thought—a stage romance between the Madam and the Sheriff and did not wish to be sued. Flournoy's gift of $40,000 to Miss Edna was our first clue that the two actually *had* enjoyed a real-life romance, truth being—as they say—stranger than fiction.

Though I had enjoyed the making of the show at Actors Studio, working with Pete and Carol, I was less enthused about changes that began once Univeral's big-wigs got involved. First, they wanted to change the title because it might be found "offensive" by, I guess, Nuns and Baptist Preachers. I battled them fiercely, ultimately resorting to a big bluff by saying to each of my tormentors in turn: "Okay, fine. Go see Lew Wasserman"—head of the parent company, Music

Corporation of America—"and tell him *you* are the goddamned genius who wants to change a million-dollar title into something pallid. Then come back and tell me what Lew said—if Lew doesn't fire your ass." This implied, perhaps, that I was a close friend of "Lew's" never mind I had not yet met him or communicated with "Lew" in any way. But nobody took the challenge, and so we kept the title. Not for nothing did I study politics and power at the feet of LBJ!

I knew *nothing* of musicals, having only seen two or three, and not liking any though the ones I saw were certified hits, and so it pained me when I began to lose "book" dialogue replaced by singing and, especially, dancing. Made me mad as hell, in fact. I pissed and moaned that my play was being turned into "a goddamned cartoon" and that it was being "danced on, stomped on, sung on and generally pissed on." Tommy Tune fretted to Peter Masterson that he feared I might "strike him" and at Masterson's suggestion I sought Tune out to assure him that I would not; still, anytime I criticized *anything*, Tune pouted or teared up or flounced out of the room—as he did about 24 hours before we opened off-Broadway, at the Intermedia Theatre, in mid-April of 1978 when I predicted to my collaborators that *Whorehouse* was likely "to close quicker than a switchblade."

Looking back, I realize I was a pluperfect horse's ass to everyone, including my long-suffering co-writer and our co-director Peter Masterson, who somehow held everything together despite my snits, cursing and general insanities. I think this was because (1) I was damnably ignorant of musical comedy practices and techniques; (2) I was still working on too many projects and lived uptight and weary to the bone and (3) I superimposed far too much liquor on top of ignorance and fatigue; it is no surprise that the booze proved not helpful to my natural churlishness or my instinct to try to be in charge of everything, everywhere, at all times. And of course I was as wrong as can be about the "cartooning" I objected to. Carol Hall's funny songs, and Tommy Tune's inventive choreography contributed *greatly* to the success of the show and it is embarrassing that I did not recognize it at the time.

We perhaps made a mistake in signing "Miss Edna" to a bit part in the show; our original notion was that the real-life Chicken Ranch madam would assist publicity. And she would have had her comments to the press been as raw and natural as they were away from interviews. But everytime we put her in front of a microphone, she prattled of growing up in a Christian home, having gone to Sunday School, and made other sleep-inducing comments not helpful to ticket sales. Contrarily, backstage and behind the scenes, she was as churlish as I was —if not more so. One old actor hoping to bum a little romance off Miss Edna persuaded her that *she* should be playing herself in the show rather than Carlin Glynn, who was simply wonderful and won a Tony. So Miss Edna ran around referring to Carlin as "that bitch" and saying "she wouldn't know how to run a whorehouse if her life depended on it" and otherwise stirring up a hornet's nest. It was a relief when Miss Edna quit the show about a month ahead of her six-month contractual obligation. Nobody tried to hold her to it!

(All this blood-letting—and, I make the brag, a goodly amount of funny stuff—is detailed in my 1982 book, *The Whorehouse Papers,* written from a journal I kept and a few letters. These were submitted to Viking Press along with my book manuscript, however, and were never returned and have not been found. Unfortunately, the book is out of print and may be found only in libraries and occasionally in used-book stores—even though it has been used in numerous drama classes in colleges and universities to acquaint students with the salts and sours of showbiz.)

Anyhow, I am still bouncing like a yo-yo to varied jobs and as if I ain't got enough troubles, here comes goddamned Cupid to shoot me through with an arrow, an instrument I had long thought myself impervious to. At the hazard of quoting from my own works, it was told thusly in my 1986 book *None But a Blockhead* about as accurately as I could again relate it so here it is again:

> While covering the milk-fund trial of John Connally for *Atlantic Monthly* in the winter of 1974 I had met, and quickly become friends with, a fellow Texan and lawyer named Lynn

Coleman. Coleman then headed the Washington offices of the huge Texas-based Vinson, Elkins law firm—in which John Connally was a senior partner—and after the trial I began to drop by those offices to visit Coleman when down from New York. In the summer of 1976 he invited me to a weekend at his country place (which he shared with California Congressman Peter Stark) on the Maryland Easter Shore. There I was introduced to another Vinson, Elkins lawyer—a young lady from Texas, one Barbara S. Blaine; she was a close friend of Coleman's fiancée (now his wife) Sylvia de Leon.

"We met at Yale," Miss Blaine said during the introductions.

"I beg your pardon," I said, "but I have been to Yale only once in my life and I can hardly remember it."

"I am not surprised," she countered.

That got my attention. I began searching my mind for old Yale details. I had been invited from Harvard to appear in connection with a symposium on Texas politics at Yale's Silliman College. On the train ride from Cambridge to New Haven I had fully enjoyed club car hospitalities. Arriving, I was greeted by Willie Morris, Bill Styron and a group of Texans that included State Senator Don Kennard, State Representative Malcolm McGregor and lawyer Warren Burnett. We feverishly celebrated in New Haven bars and hotel rooms throughout the afternoon. I was not, therefore, overly alert when our group repaired to a Silliman College reception and dinner in our honor.

Barbara Blaine, newly transferred from Mount Holyoke College as one of Yale's "pioneer women" in the first year it had accepted female undergraduates, had been assigned to Silliman College there; she was one of a handful of Texans the headmaster had dragooned into appearing to "honor" us. By luck of the draw, she claims to have been seated next to me; I am in no position to argue the point.

Those several years later, at the Maryland shore, I required Miss Blaine to refresh my memory: what had we talked about at

Yale? "On learning I was from Texas," she said, "you immediately offered a long lecture about how it was my duty to return home after Yale because "Texas always exports its best brains and that is what is wrong down there." I then asked how long since you had lived in Texas. I believe you confessed to something like twenty years. I suppose it now would be about twenty-seven years you have deprived Texas of your brains, wouldn't it?"

I tugged my forelock, mumbled that it was good to have seen her again and sidled away from Miss Blaine's lovely claws. On subsequent trips to Washington, when visiting Lynn Coleman in his law offices, I sought out Miss Blaine to exchange pleasantries. She showered on me the full attentions she might have visited on a doorknob. Nonetheless, being a good fellow, I telephoned to ask her to dinner, in early 1977, shortly after renting a tiny apartment in Washington to work on the Baker book. Miss Blaine reported herself earlier booked for that evening.

How about tomorrow night?

Sorry. Busy again.

The night after?

Still busy, I'm afraid.

Uh. The night following the night after that?

So *very* sorry. Same story.

I don't suppose there's a chance in the world the next night is—

She feared that was correct.

Thank you very much, I said, the perfect gentleman; I replaced the phone and shouted, "Miss Blaine, you can go suck a goddam lemon! I have been humiliated at your hands for the last time!"

Miss Blaine, too, apparently sensed that she had humiliated me for the last time unless she amended her position; soon she called back to say that perhaps she could cancel one of her engagements three or four nights hence, it not amounting to as much as her others, if I still insisted on buying her dinner.

Barbara and I were married on May 6, 1978, at the home of Lynn

Coleman and Sylvia de Leon in Washington and moved into her Capitol Hill apartment. Barbara thought when I first courted her that I must have a seat on the New York Stock Exchange, judging by the money I spent in restaurants and night clubs, but that was before she understood my financial theory: that it would be far better to die deeply in debt and full of fine memories than to die with an accumulation of saved money never to be pleasurably spent. She began to get her first glimmer of the realities when I borrowed $500 from her to get us back from our honeymoon in Ireland, England and France; her second lesson came quickly, post-honeymoon, when I had to call to confess to her that well, er-ah, the I.R.S. boys had swooped down on Broadway's 46th Street Theater, see, to ur-uh, garnishee all my *Whorehouse* royalties save $50 per week until, er-ah-uhm, see, they-hadcollectedalittleover-thirteenthousanddollarsinbacktaxesowed. Much to my relief, my bride laughed and said that she wanted to be as good to me as Uncle Sam was being so she, too, would give me $50 weekly until the I.R.S. had gorged its legal fill. (Thus encouraged, I don't think I ever mentioned paying Barbara Blaine back for that honeymoon loan. . . .)

Whorehouse, of course, became an international as well as a Broadway hit, spawned three National Touring Companies and became a Summer Stock staple and still is done in dinner theaters, community theaters and college theaters both here and abroad these twenty years later, and has went a long way in keeping me off the streets and off welfare rolls.* Want a dash of irony? The Baker book became a best seller but *Whorehouse* was by then making so much money I hardly noticed the book royalties!

And it seems to me that's a good high point on which to end my recollections of my dazed, if eventually dazzling, 1970s.

Yours in Christ,
Larry L.

*King's 1982 book, published by Viking Press, *The Whorehouse Papers*, treats details of the musical saga from concept through "the joys, sorrows, confusions, and small murders" attendant to the making of a smash Broadway musical.

May 7, 1979

Dear Precious Children:

I write this collective letter to announce two things, the first of which Brad probably knows from his close proximity to N.Y. and the show: *Whorehouse* today was nominated for seven Tonys. Best Musical, Best Book (Masterson & Myself), Best Choreography (Tommy Tune) and Best Direction (Masterson & Tune). Additionally, Joan Ellis, Carlin Glynn and Henderson Forsythe got nominated for acting.

The other is that according to medical science, you and each of you shall have either a half-brother or half-sister about November 13th. If a boy we shall name it Kong. If a girl, Konga. Here's to Kong King or Konga King, whichever. All good wishes and much love to the Original Three, from,

Ol' Dad*

*Lindsay Allison King was born on November 16, 1979.

December 18, 1979

Ms. Constance B. Sayre
Director of Marketing
Viking Press
625 Madison Avenue
New York, N.Y. 10022

Dear Ms. Sayre:

You have wrote me a awful nice letter, as we say in the Ivy League, and I imagine you mean most of it. And I am flattered as well as grateful that you good Viking folk think my third non-fiction collection might do well.* But out of the cynicism of experience, I question whether it will. And I don't think it really makes a damn what we try to do about it. I think it will sell within 1,000 copies of a median figure whether (1) I tout it all over America for two years or (2) claim that I didn't write it and refuse all interviews.

This is because I have been over this ground before. My first non-fiction collection was published by NAL-World in 1968. It got reviews that would have caused envy to accrue to Shakespeare, to say nothing of Faulkner, and I tooled around the country crying my wares for two weeks. And it sold 6,000 copies. In 1971 I wrote a book for Viking called *Confessions of a White Racist.* It was nominated for a National Book Award. Again, the reviews were such as to shame Scott Fitzgerald and Hemingway. Alan Williams sent me all around the country for 28 days, in the friendly custody of Rich Barber, and they got me on all the TV "biggies"—Kup in Chicago, *Today,* Dick Cavett, et al. And it sold 7,000 copies. And in 1974 I done another non-fiction for Viking: *The Old Man and Lesser Mortals.* That time I refused to go anywhere except to Philadelphia for one book-author luncheon, because I was living in Princeton and Princeton even makes Philadelphia look good. And again the reviews were such as to shame Styron on his best day. And it sold 6,000 copies too.

So I just don't believe the kind of book we are talking about, with respect to *Con Man* as well as others, is the kind of book that can be promoted or hawked past a certain barrier. I am glad that you people love Ort—as we say in Texas—well enough to publish Ort and even want to push Ort. But I do not think you are gonna sell much Ort in vast quantities. . . .

Of Outlaws, Con Men, Whores, Politicians and Other Artists (Viking Press, 1980; Penguin Paperback, 1981).

7

"The Play's the Thing"

lthough during the decade of the 1980s six Larry L. King books were published,* after his Broadway hit *The Best Little Whorehouse in Texas,* he became more and more drawn to the theatre both as playwright and actor. King wrote and had produced three stage plays in that decade: *The Night Hank Williams Died, The Golden Shadows Old West Museum* and a one-act play, *Christmas: 1933,* adapted from his earlier book *That Terrible Night Santa Got Lost in the Woods.* All were set in Texas, all were influenced by King's early experiences as a boy or young man. Each met with some measure of success: *Hank Williams* won the Helen Hayes Award and Theatre Lobby's Mary Goldwater Award as Best New Play of the 1988 Washington season, beating out David Henry Hwang's *M. Butterfly,* Ford Theatre's musical *Elmer Gantry* and Arena Stage's commissioned *The Rivers and Ravines.*

Because of difficulties in casting an authentic-sounding West Texas barkeep, *Hank Williams* Director Peter Frisch "drafted" King for that role; King later repeated the part of Gus Gilbert at the Off-Broadway Orpheum Theatre in New York, where his show moved for a commercial run after debuting to good reviews at the WPA Theatre there. *Hank* also enjoyed runs at Austin's Live Oak Theatre, at the Circle Theatre in Fort Worth, the Houston Repertory Theatre, and productions in Ohio, Virginia and Florida. The Samuel French Company bought licensing rights and the play continues to receive productions in Texas and elsewhere, the most recent being at the Permian Playhouse, Odessa, in early 1999. **

In the mid-1980s King was invited to a production of *The Best Little Whorehouse in Texas* at Memphis State University. While there he made a fortuitous connection with another West Texan, Dr. Keith Kennedy*** of Lamesa, then Chairman of the Memphis State Drama Department. "We became soul mates in about thirty minutes," King says. He told his new friend of having just begun writing *The Night Hank Williams Died;* Kennedy immediately asked King to send him each scene, as he wrote it, suggesting that he and his drama students stage the scenes and then give the playwright their reactions and suggestions. This was done, and in 1986, Kennedy directed a show-case production of *Hank* at Memphis State.

Keith Kennedy and his students provided a similar sounding board for King's next effort, *The Golden Shadows Old West Museum,* based on a short story by Mike Blackman, then executive editor of the *Fort Worth Star Telegram.* Memphis State staged a showcase run in the spring of 1987. *Golden Shadows* received its first professional production at Arkansas Repertory, Little Rock, in January of 1989. This was followed by *Golden Shadows* productions at the New Playwrights Theatre in Washington, the Live Oak Theatre in Austin, Fort Worth's Circle Theatre and the Abilene Community Theatre. ****

Christmas: 1933, a one-act dramatization of events from King's Eastland County childhood, was first produced from November 4 through December 21, 1986 at Circuit Playhouse in Memphis, Tennessee. The Samuel French Company bought licensing rights; the one-acter is still staged, seasonally, though—King says—"mostly in churches, basements, or by high school kids in interscholastic competition. It does not bring in the type of royalties one can retire on."

Still, King maintains that he loves playwrighting above all. This is because, "Dialogue comes easily: it's almost as if I see the play in my head and hear the actors talking among themselves." He has rejoiced that playwrighting also eliminates the need "for all that descriptive work so necessary to novels or even most non-fiction. Once the playwright has written his set descriptions and defined the costumes, he can pretty well occupy himself with the nutting-cut basics: dialogue and movement." He has admitted that the "instant gratification" of seeing audiences react to his plays is a thrill. "I have never yet caught a stranger in the act of reading one of my books, short stories or magazine essays," King says. "You write the things, they're thrown on the market, you get a few fan letters, some reviews and then your works disappear into the literary black hole. It is like a small death. Only in a play that lives awhile may most writers see the worlds they have created come alive and hear one's 'precious words' repeated and repeated. Good actors and directors help immensely in the necessary interpretations: blocking, pacing, gestures, facial expressions, body language. If they do it right, and if I have properly done my job, then the audience is captivated and reacts as one might hope. And when the magic works, there's no satisfaction quite like it."

King derives little satisfaction from acting in his own plays: "I feel divorced from the material. It's as if I didn't write it. If I'm sitting in a theater, or pacing at the back of the house, I derive pleasure. But on stage, each laugh line is merely a technical pause. One must listen for musical cues or other sound cues. What it amounts to is hard goddamned sweat work. One doesn't have the time or opportunity to mentally preen or strut. And, frankly, I don't know how actors stay interested in doing the same role night-after-night for weeks or months or even years while trying to make each performance 'fresh.' It would bore me to tears or suicide."

While waiting backstage for a cue in 1989, during the Orpheum Theatre run of *Hank Williams*, King, "out of boredom," hit upon the idea for a new play. His notion was a work involving characters representing Lyndon B. Johnson and Richard M. Nixon. "I knew, right off, they would pretend to be friends while secretly trying to slit each other's throats. And that at some point, they would gang up to cheat somebody out of something so as to surmount some huge obstacle. I just didn't know where they'd be —the venue —or what the obstacles might be."

King the playwright mulled these problems as he began reading books by or about LBJ and Nixon, Watergate transcripts, and recalling his own personal observations of the ex-presidents as Washington politico and journalist. Eventually he would hit upon the play being set in "The Afterlife." LBJ and Nixon—along with former presidents Harry Truman and Calvin Coolidge—would be in a "holding pen" while attempting to persuade Heaven's "Evaluation Committee" (which the stage LBJ complains "is made up of a buncha narrow-minded goddamned Saints") that they are ready to see God and receive their final judgements. In due course, LBJ and Nixon cheat God's staff assistant ("H.B." for Heavenly Bureaucrat) in a card game, and do indeed avoid the Evaluation Committee. When they see God, She turns out to be black, and quick mental adjustments must be made. King would not begin writing *The Dead President's Club* in earnest, however, until the early 1990s.

At the outset of the 1980s, King was working on books "owed" to Viking Press in repayment of the $100,000 advance for the never-completed biography of LBJ. Viking had accepted *The Whorehouse Papers* and *None But a Blockhead* toward King's debt, with a stipulation that he also owed them a "free" novel, that, when published would fully satisfy his contractual obligation. King worked for more than two years on a "wordy and disjointed" novel set in West Texas during World War II, his protaganist being a teenager as he had himself been during those years. Viking's ultimate rejection of *War Movies* sent King into a funk. Hungry to accomplish fiction, he began plotting to write more stage plays.

By 1980 King had developed what he understatedly calls "a thirst for spirits." In a letter to Frank Rich written that year he writes of having been committed to "the drunk looney bin" and later refers to having attended "Whiskey School." In truth, he was in a conventional twelve-step alcoholic rehab program. King entered treatment in early July 1980, and was not always a Whiskey School model student; he resented being there and was only "half-convinced" he needed rehabilitation. Upon "graduation" he mixed periods of sobriety with many lapses off the straight and narrow. King says he attended Alcoholics Anonymous meetings "sometimes sober, sometimes drinking, sometimes drunk and sometimes not at all." During a sober period in 1981, King wrote and narrated a one-hour television documentary on state politics for *CBS Reports,* to which the network gave the cutesy title "The Best Little Statehouse in Texas" (despite the work being less than admiring of the Texas Legislature). The documentary took King to Austin where he wandered the floor of both the Texas House and Senate chambers. It won King an "Emmy" and good to great reviews. King did not really get a handle on his drinking until the summer of 1983, after which he became active in A.A. and otherwise claims to have "done the Lord's good works."

King originally feared, however, that he could not write "if deprived of my long-time dependency on various mood modifiers." This ultimately proved untrue, but King did work erratically "for about fifteen months before getting back into a good working groove." From late 1984 forward, he began a burst of playwriting, producing books and magazine essays, making this his most productive period since the breakup of *Harper's* in 1971.

On the downside, King lost to death in October of 1988 his longtime dear friend Craig Raupe. Raupe had attended the opening night performance of *Hank Williams* at the Live Oak Theatre in Austin; the last King saw of him, his old friend was laughing and talking with fellow playgoers in the Live Oak lobby. Exactly one month later, King delivered an emotional eulogy at Raupe's funeral in Washington. Raupe had suffered a stroke and died during surgery.

In November of 1988 King and Texas lawyer Warren Burnett had a falling out that has not yet been repaired. Their friendship traced back thirty-six years, to 1952, when King became active in Burnett's successful campaign for District Attorney of Midland and Ector counties. The two lived across the hall from each other in an Odessa apartment house when King worked at the *Odessa American*; for years, when King visited West Texas, he "officed" at Burnett's law firm; he often was a guest in Burnett's home and himself hosted Burnett in Washington, at Harvard, at Princeton and in Manhattan. The 1988 contretemps occurred in Austin at a performance of *Hank Williams*, and that is all King is willing to say, for the record at any rate. The two formerly close friends have not seen each other or spoken in more than a decade.

Blessed with a successful marriage to Washington attorney Barbara Blaine and two children born during the decade, King's personal life was more stable than it had been in a very long time. He would enter the 1990s "feeling as good about my life and my work as is possible for a soul born to be alternately manic and melancholy."

Of Outlaws, Con Men, Whores, Politicians and Other Artists (Viking Press: New York, 1980); *That Terrible Night Santa Got Lost in the Woods* (Encino Press: Austin, 1981); *The Whorehouse Papers* (Viking Press: New York, 1982); *Warning: Writer at Work* (TCU Press: Fort Worth, 1985); *None But a Blockhead* (Viking Press: New York, 1986); *Because of Lozo Brown* (Viking Krestel Books: New York, 1988).

**SMU Press in 1989 published a handsome edition of *The Night Hank Williams Died*.

***Upon learning that Kennedy was a "real doctor," King began calling him "Doctor Doctor Kennedy."

****TCU Press would publish *Golden Shadows* in 1993.

—Richard Holland

Feb.28, 1980

Dear Glanvil & Linda:

Barbara and I hosted a cast party here on Saturday night, the 16th, for Alexis Smith and the [touring] *Whorehouse* crew at a restaurant on Capitol Hill. We had a smattering of newspeople, politicians, writers and personal friends—to some extent I guess most of them qualified in the latter category. Had about 170 all told. Went from 11 P.M. (after the show) and was still going when Barbara and I left a bit after 2 A.M. I think it ran well past three. Larry Hovis (Melvin P. Thorpe) and Brad [King] took turns singing country-western and the show band—plus the fiddler from the Broadway company [Ernie Reed] who took a night off to play here at my request—did it up brown. Guests included Bobby Baker, Cong. Bob Eckhardt and Celia, Cong. Charlie Wilson, the Donley Chalmers Kennards, Dr. Mike Halberstam and wife, Pat Oliphant, Cong. Mickey Leland, Sen. Gene McCarthy, J. T. Rutherford, Lynn Coleman and Sylvia DeLeon, Taddy McAllister, Sarah Weddington, and Norman Mailer and Norris Church Mailer. Mailer and Norris were our house guests for the weekend. I'm liking old Nawmin more and more: he's mellowing some with age and in a strange way his economic reversals in recent years—the final costly divorce, a couple of his homes being sold for taxes—seem to have made a better and less egotistical fellow of him. And he continues to be about the most exciting or interesting conversationalist I know—when I understand what he's talking about. He has a theory for everything, some of which are full of bullshit, but always fun to hear. He and Barbara get along well and Barbara and Norris really like each other.

There was a poor little country girl there, covering the party for the Huntsville paper and several other small Texas papers, who asked Mailer (1) if he was a member of the *Whorehouse* cast and (2) if not, how was he connected with the show and so on, and he just grinned and said he was a personal friend of Larry L. King's. Finally she asked his name and when he said Norman Mailer she looked blank, then brightened and said, "Oh, I think I heard of you!" I missed that scene, dammit, but Barbara Blaine saw it and reported it with much glee. Mailer was a gentleman and took it well. Norman got drunk and told me and everybody that I am America's Brecht, which is more of his bullshit but naturally I found it enjoyable. . . .

LARRY L. KING

May 17, 1980

The Editors
The Texas Observer
600 West 7th Street
Austin, Texas 78701

Dear Sirs and Madams:

Flowers and huzzahs to Laura Richardson for her delightful spear-
ings of one Norman Podhoretz with respect to the silly comments he
makes in his book, *Breaking Ranks.* (*Observer,* April 25) The only trouble with criticizing Podhoretz, who has won such reputation as he has
largely by looking down on prose other than his own, is that he
employs a Catch-22 clause against the guilty. "Oh," he says to all criticism, "you are just proving what I have many times said: everybody
despises me because of my courage." Mr. Podhoretz is, I admit, fairly
easy to despise, but courage plays a much smaller role in the despising
than he suspects.

I happen to have run socially with Mr. Podhoretz on numerous
occasions some years ago, in the *Harper's* days of Willie Morris, and
while he was not as much fun as one might have hoped, I recall him
being reasonably affable. He was, it is true, given to periodic long-
winded harangues on what he thought to be Large Subjects, but we
handled it by saying "Aw, shuddup, Pod, and have another one of
them dranks." Which he always did. If you could have measured our
bladders at the end of such evenings I have little doubt that Mr.
Podhoretz would have measured up to any bladder in the crowd. And
now I read in *Breaking Ranks* that Mr. Podhoretz thought us a terrible
bunch of boozers who might have become Presidents if we'd stayed a
shade more sober and had a few more brains. Maybe Ol' Nawmin ain't
President for the same reasons me and Willie ain't.

I will say this for Podhoretz: he is one of the funniest writers in the
United States. He will resent this accolade, I am certain, because fun
is not his purpose. Indeed, he could serve as Secretary of Solemnity in
any administration grim enough to appoint him. And I guarantee you
the Godless Communists cannot beat, or probably even match him,

with their very best Puckerbrow. One cannot help but be amused, however, on reading at Tolstoyian length of how Norman Podhoretz, Boy Radical, converted to Limousine Liberal and then, seeing the light, courageously became a Responsible Intellectual Neo-Conservative or whatever he thinks he is. He was in his so-called Radical Days about as peppery as baby powder—I mean, Okay, so he voted for Adlai Stevenson and Jack Kennedy; but 'Ol Pod never was of a type to rush barricades or even walk picket lines to my knowledge. Frankly, until he went to blathering about his conversion recently, I always thought he probably was a Republican.

Anyhow, some years ago Podhoretz wrote what I thought was a pretty good book called *Making It*. True, the *New York Review of Books* crowd beat him with sticks and perhaps a few other critics did. I mean, hell, what did the man expect? He, himself, had broken the fingers and hearts of many a writer under the critic's dirty flag, and so might have presumed that a certain number of people would be ready to jump him from ambush. Frankly, I thought the critics unfair to that book in sneering that Pod hadn't "made it" to the extent he thought. After all, a fellow who has come a way probably knows better than others how he got there, how tough the trip was, the odds against getting there and where he wanted to go in the first place. So I wrote Pod a friendly letter saying, in effect, "Don't pay 'em no mind, just go ahead and do your work."

But, sad to say, Pod has brooded upon being criticized for so many years he now has determined it was because he so courageously rehabilitated himself politically. I wish he knew it isn't unusual for people to become more conservative as they age, or see their former theories fail to work to perfection, or maybe drink and fret a shade too much before the fire at night. If he knew that, I don't think he'd insist his ideological conversion has covered acres so much as inches. Nawmin just got his itsy-bitsy feelings hurt, that's all, and now he has become a public scold almost as sour and boring as me and Solzhenitsyn. So I say again, "Aw, shuddup, Pod, and have another one of them dranks."

Anyway, Laura Richardson did a wonderful job of popping Ol Pod's balloon. . . .

LARRY L. KING

August 18, 1980

Mr. Frank Rich
30 Beekman Place
Apt 6-A
New York, N.Y. 10022

Dear Frank:

I've been away—in more ways than one—and take typewriter in hand to catch up on what's been happening.

I was released four days ago after 40 days in the drunk looney bin. Turned myself in for treatment to kick alcohol and light drugs right after the July 4th weekend, which I barely remember.* Detoxed at Washington Hospital Center and then spent a month at a plush drunk tank for rich folks, Melwood Farm, near Olney, Md. Feel better than I have in a long time and have experienced no strange cravings. Believe I'm gonna be O.K.

Looks as if Hollywood is gonna really do a number on the *Whorehouse* movie. Word is that Stevie Phillips isn't going to be allowed to produce it, Pete and Tommy are out as directors, and they're bringing in some guy to re-write it so that it will fail to resemble anything of the stage show. The director, I hear, is to be one Colin Higgins; he is advertised as an English fag. Ned Tannen is alleged to have said—and this comes to me third-hand through Stevie as filtered through Pete—that all he wanted of *Whorehouse* was the title so he could make a film in which "Bert and Dolly screw their brains out." I had always thought we had a little more in mind.

While I was away at the nut farm I got a call from Tannen's office ordering me to report to Hollywood next day to write some new sex scenes for Bert and Dolly. "You don't understand," I said. "I'm not allowed to go past the mailbox here." It was arranged that I would write the scenes and call them in, which I did, late at night. And, of course, I'm receiving all these crazy calls and comments from those Hollywood types—me standing at a pay phone at the nut farm, now—and it occurs to me, "I'm the one supposed to be sick and *they* are out there running free."

Don't guess there's anything I can do about them screwing up the movie. You know, when you write a book you have the final and ultimate voice if there's a conflict with the editor over copy, and pretty much the same situation exists on stage. But if you write a movie, you don't have any more power than a stage grip. Since Universal is bringing in another writer, Pete and I will be screwed out of a bonus we were to have gotten had we been the only screenwriters. That's my only real regret; I'm just so sick of scuffling with those Left Coast bastards I'm kinda relieved not to have anything else to do with the film. If they do a real turkey, I intend to insist that my name be stricken from screen credits and I may go into a campaign to advertise what a shit job they've turned out. **

One more word on the Hollywood intellect: Burt Reynolds told Stevie and Pete he wants the movie to be "Smokey and the Bandit visit the Whorehouse." 'Nuff sed. . . .

We haven't been to The Big Apple in some time, so we'll be coming up soon and hope to see you. I'm harmless now that they've taken my hatchet away from me. . . .

*King had been in Austin then, attending the world premier of Willie Nelson's movie *Honeysuckle Rose.*
**King hated the movie, and said so in the media at every opportunity, but did not remove his name from the screen credits once his wife-lawyer-agent explained that such an act would cost him many thousands of dollars in residual monies.

September 24, 1980

The Editors*
Esquire Magazine
NYC, NY

Dear Sirs:

The most punishing review I have received as a reward for putting words together came from one R.Z. Sheppard, then doing mischief for the old *New York Herald-Tribune's Book World.* . . . Re my novel *The*

One-Eyed Man he generally advised me to take up plumbing or the civil service and maybe to inquire into the possibilities of a frontal lobotomy. It was the first review I had received and I damn near took him at his word. Mr. Sheppard now criticizes literature for *Time. Time* has never reviewed one of my books. Thank God for small favors.

As to theatre, John (Ratfink) Simon greeted *The Best Little Whorehouse in Texas* as he might hail someone stealing his purse. But, then, as my pal Dan (*Semi-Tough*) Jenkins says, "Simon ain't never liked nothing that don't have a lot of rain in it and wadn't in the original Czechoslovakian."

I would enjoy seeing Mr. Sheppard and Mr. Simon have a head-on automobile crash, and have the thrill of being the only person available to summon aid. . . .

*Written in response to an inquiry.

March 21, 1981

Dear Brother Broyles:

Damn if I don't believe you *Texas Monthly* dudes are the most defensively sensitive dudes in America. The two or three times I have been even mildly critical of the publication, somebody writes me a propaganda stream-of-consciousness attempting to convince me that Levy ain't in it for the money and that no mistakes are ever made. Why don't y'all relax? My God, you'd have strokes if you had to be subjected to critical judgements by every jackass who owns a typewriter like us purveyors of books and plays! Stand on your record and tell everybody to go fuck themselves! Or don't tell 'em anything, which is even better. Well, I don't want to get as riled as you apparently did so I'll say no more other than I *still* believe the political reporting there could be more hardball, more detailed and more immediate. Of course, I said many good things about the *Monthly,* including how it has performed a vital function in providing Texas writers a Texas place to write, how it has given readers a better overall and more cohesive view of the state than they've had before, on and on, but naturally that didn't make the quotes. So fuck it, I'm through with the subject for all time.

We're just back from 15 days in England. *Whorehouse* opened there Feb. 26th with all-English cast save for Broadway originals Henderson Forsythe and Carlin Glynn. Good production, though a little drama was present in not knowing what moment flat Texas accents might without warning convert to Cockney. We won the reviews 14 to 6— getting the good papers, such as *Times of London, Sunday Times, The Observer, Guardian, Financial Times*—and the audiences reacted well. We should have a good run if we can overcome the troubles of the British economy, the luxury tax Maw Thatcher has put on theater tickets so as to double their price, and consequently the worse over-all theatrical year at the Box Office in London since the Great Depression. . . .

June 8, 1981

Dr. John Kenneth Galbraith
207 Littauer Center
Harvard University
Cambridge, Mass.

Dear Ken:

Just returned from three weeks in Texas to find your good note of May 28th. . . .

I *am* intrigued by the notion of passing your way in the Vermont hills later in the summer. Right now, I'm tied up for about a month editing the *CBS Reports* documentary I just finished shooting on the Texas Legislature; add to that the complication that Wednesday I shall close the deal on buying the fine old home of the late Senator Tom Connally, and then must stand by to goad, poke, and generally agitate a battery of contractors, decorators, and architects we've engaged to make such changes as my bride desires. That will no doubt consume us long *past* the summer, but surely by August we will need a break. I'd like to get back in touch later to see if you are in place and the invitation still holds.

I'd like you to meet Barbara Blaine, my young lawyer wife, a Texan by way of Mt. Holyoke, Yale, and the University of Virginia Law School. I stole her from the John Connally law firm, where she was bored with the Alaska Pipeline case, and she now has her own shop doing literary agenting, entertainment law and— while that builds— some corporate stuff. (Connally told Lynn Coleman of that firm, "I always knew Larry King would screw me out of something but I didn't dream it would be one of my young lawyers"). Barbara knew on the evidence, and on my word, that you were a Great Man, but I'm not sure she was a 100% convert until she read in "The Girl I Left Behind" what you said to [its author] Jane O'Reilly: "I think we should have talked more about women's liberation. This will have a more permanent, a more lasting effect than any of the things we have talked about." So now you qualify as a Hero. . . .

June 8, 1981

Mr. Willie Morris
University, Mississippi

Dear Willie:

I don't believe God wants us to see one another. I don't claim to know His reason, but preventing me from coming to Mississippi and then spending days in Austin and still not getting to lay eyes on you— well, that is a potent brew, stirred somewhere amongst the stars and firmament, any good old Bible-raised boy just *knows* that. Perhaps 'tis wise we did not push our luck.

Saw Ronnie Dugger the morning after the posh party in honor of myself*—he said you guys came by around 10:30 P.M. I, exhausted and still fighting to retain my voice, had slipped away from said gathering shortly before that time and went meekly to bed. I never had been so tired, Willie, as after two weeks [on the road] and then three more working 12-16 hours per day for the TV boys. Face it, I've lost a step. Come home, hugged the wife, kissed the baby, and slept for three days. . . .

I believe without doubt the dumbest S.O.B. in the Legislature is an old boy from Fort Worth. One morning he ran up to me in the House Chamber and said—with reference to a Black legislator from Dallas—"Larry, you know what that sumbitch Ragsdale called me? He called me a racist!" I mummered and clucked. "You know what?" he said, slicing his hand across his Adam's Apple—"White folks is up to here with smart-mouthed niggers!" I began to laugh and laugh. He said, "I mean it!" "I'm sure you do," I said, and kept cackling, much to his puzzlement.

There is a fellow in the House nick-named "Ding Dong" for obvious reasons. It was of much concern to him that each day we "wired" a different House member to get a flavor of what went on between the guys during horse-tradings. He came to me each day to learn who was "wired." I could not tell if he wanted to avoid the man who was, or wanted to seek him out the better to get on TV maybe. Anyway, about the eighth time he asked me "Who's wired today?" I looked around conspiratorially and said, "Why, Charlie, you are!" He looked astonished, ran backwards, and began to tear at his shirt until it dawned on him that he might not be. . . .

*A party in King's honor thrown by then Lt. Governor Bill Hobby.

July 27, 1981

Dear Lanvil & Glenda:

Got back from Midland Friday night, ready to associate with the healthy, wealthy and wise. We spent a couple of days going through all of Mother's effects, throwing out useless stuff she had pack-ratted, and making a few assignments of family items.* The only thing I wanted (and got) was a number of old pictures and a 1940 Watterson battery radio. Dad bought it a week after Pearl Harbor, at Mom's insistence, so we could keep up with the War News. It was the first radio I knew us to have, and I got a great deal of pleasure out of it in my youth. Looks as if it came fresh from the crate—beautiful wood with a high sheen. I am going to have modern fixtures put in, and use it in my office in the new home. . . . We found—under rugs, in shoe boxes, in the tops of closets, and in other improbably places—a dozen or more caches of cash Mom had hidden away and then forgotten. Totaled $1,696.00.

Found a letter awaiting me here saying that London [Whorehouse] company will close August 23rd, after six-month run. Economy there does not look as if it is on the way up, and Stevie Phillips is tired of struggling with it. Glad we got a trip out of it, anyway. I'll get about $24,000 or more out of it in deferred payments, under my agreement with Universal, and that beats a sharp stick in the eye. . . . Barbara is a good predictor: she predicted three months ago that Stevie would fold it when Carlin and Henderson had done their six-month contractual obligations. She was right on the money. . . .

*King's mother had died just short of her 88th birthday.

January 30, 1982

Dear "Foo":*

Ah, a voice out of the distant past! I can't recall if I first met you in the latter half of 1949 when I was fresh home from three years in the Army, or in the first half of 1950, but in any case I was 20 or 21 years old, depending, and now I am 53 and counting. Back in those old days God was about the age I am now; I suppose by now He has become rather elderly. . . .

I haven't spent much time in West Texas in the past 15 years, and when I have—except for traumatic events such as my father's death (1970) and my mother's (last July)—it usually has been a hit-and-run visit. A couple of times—the last of those being in 1974—quaffed a few beers with Keith Ward, but mostly I've made "duty" visits to relatives and that's about it.

I do expect to be in West Texas this April or May, depending on when Viking Press sends me out to promote my new book, *The Whorehouse Papers*. The promotion tour probably will come no closer than Dallas-Fort Worth to Midland-Odessa, but I intend to come out there mainly to tape record some old-time baseball players—our age, those "old-timers"—for a novel I am doing which is set in Midland-Odessa in 1950 and which treats, among other things, the beginning of the post-war oil boom and the start of the Korean War. So, yes, I'd be happy to see you and Imogene and to break cheese or cocktail glasses with your colleagues at Odessa College. . . .

I wish you could have seen me strut my stuff a couple of years ago as the leading man (Sheriff Ed Earl Dodd) in my own show for a month on Broadway—especially since you and I and Bill Holm knocked them dead on the stage for Art Cole at Midland Community Theatre in *Streetcar Named Desire.* When, 1953? At any rate, as I stood in the Broadway wings—mouth dry, heart a-flutter and having last-minute second thoughts about trying to sing to 1,500 people who'd paid an average of $35 to hear it—I thought of those days and wished you guys were there to help me. . . .

I remember, Foo, there in early 1950 when we both were single, our going to Odessa several times on Saturday night in your car—I didn't have one—to try to find girls to chase. As I recall all we did was wind up eating chicken-fried steaks in a truck stop and driving back to Midland. Right out of *Marty* it was. Yet somehow fun, too. A lot of it was fun—broadcasting the football games, joking around the studio, going to Lubbock to watch Ike campaign [as radio newsmen], just farting around in general. I guess you have more fun with less effort and resources when you are young and energetic and your life is one long, existential moment because you do not know how it will turn out. There is mystery to it, and juice that eventually disappears—or, when we are older and jaded and tired, do we merely romanticize it? Well, enough of the philosophical . . . I never was too good at that shit. In my youth when I would haltingly attempt to articulate something abstract, or muse on the concept of infinity, my old daddy would say, "Lawrence, if you think about stuff like that too much it'll drive you crazy!". . .

*Wally Jackson, who worked with King at the Midland radio station KCRS in the early 1950s.

March 23, 1982

Mrs. V.
Bonham, Texas 75418

Dear Mrs. V.:

I appreciate your recent letter, the clippings, and your interest in my writing a book about your late husband. I am grateful, too, that my good friend Tommy Thompson referred you to me. Tommy is a real pal, and I shall not forget his actions—I assure you.

Unfortunately—and this must be confidential—I will be unable to work with you on this project due to health problems. It is not generally known that I am suffering from a rare, incurable disease and I shall appreciate your keeping that confidence. I am sure you will understand that I must husband my flagging energies.

However, I do want to sincerely recommend to you as the potential author of the book about your husband my good friend Dr. Edwin Shrake. Dr. Shrake not only is a fine writer, but a great American and a wonderful Christian friend. His doctorate, you know, is in the field of religion. But he is a real He-Man and natural athlete, whom I feel confident, is *exactly* the type of person you need. You may reach Dr. Shrake at the enclosed address.

I very much hope my suggestion proves helpful to you. Very best wishes and yours in Christ. . . .

Editor's Note: Mrs. V. persisted with her request to King's "wonderful Christian friend" Bud Shrake, who passed her on to other writer friends. King's imaginary incurable disease came back to him months later in the form of a concerned telephone call from the editor of a Dallas newspaper who had heard rumors of King's bad health. King, momentarily forgetting his epistle to Mrs. V., was furious that someone was floating bad health rumors about him in Texas. King said later his "rare, incurable disease" was the aging process.

April 30, 1982

A. Williams, C.T. Verrill, and V. Herring
The Viking Press
625 Madison Avenue
New York, N.Y. 10022

Dear Uncle Alan, Cousin Chuck and Sister Vicki:

Gee, gang, I truly want to thank all who had a hand in the wonderful *Newsday* book promotion bash yesterday. It was good for my humility.

Never mind that the limo driver got lost and we were thirty minutes late; it all went downhill from there.

We were supposed to speak 15 minutes each. Mr. William Attwood, touting his book about Middle Age—though he seems to be safely past it—spoke for twenty-one minutes. What he said of middle age as I understood was that you are likely to get thicker, have weak eyes, and probably grandchildren if you have not been careful earlier in life. Mr. Attwood himself found himself amusing, pausing to wheeze and giggle at his best lines while around him was the sound of much silence.

Ms. Bette Bao Lord has written a novel called *Spring Moon* about a Chinese woman. She spoke for twenty-seven minutes about Chinese women, including, largely, herself. Her speech was a mixture of what she assumed to be high-flown imagery and a hot attack on Red China. I was very much uninspired throughout.

Next a woman who—sad to say—is a Viking writer. She droned on thirty-two minutes. Though her book is about childhood in the Bronx she chose to spend much of her time telling about being molested by dirty old men, including relatives, as a child. She managed to make even this uninteresting, and at great length.

I did my bit within the required time limit—12 minutes by the clock—and had 'em laughing and rocking and rolling, and now we go out to an anteroom to sign and sell our books. To 1,200 people.

Mr. Attwood sold about 300. The Chinese lady sold about 100. Diana Trilling, who was not there but was represented by her book, sold exactly 37. I do not know how many the Viking lady sold, as I could not see through and around Mr. Attwood's line of folks, but I am certain she did better than yours truly. At least, on the way out, she pinched me and said, "Good luck. Looks as if you'll need it."

I sold nine books.* I shit you not. Count 'em. Nine.

I would have sold only eight, had I not bought one myself. True. How that happened was a sleazy-looking guy told me all about how he had founded the Rocky Point Volunteer Library—2,500 volumes— and lured me into congratulating him on his civic-minded good work. Then the clever rascal asked me to donate one of my new books to said library. The lady selling the books would not give me one free. I had to pay the full price everyone else did: $16.03. (Incidentally, four of the eight persons who bought my book griped that it cost more than the $14.95 price on the dustjacket. I had no defense and had to stoop to apologies.). . .

When you receive my itemized expenses, you will note it cost us about $50 for every book sold. Including the one I bought. I do not think that will look very good on the ledger. . . .

*The Whorehouse Papers.

October 11, 1982

Dear Willie:

As history clearly shows, yours truly and Dean Faulkner Wells (the beer thief) got the Ole Miss Rebels off to a 2-0 season during my visit. We then entrusted the team to you and Larry Wells, with, I fear, disastrous results. You have now lost 3 1/2 games counting the 0-9 second half you miscoached during the final half of the game with Southern Mississippi. I feel, therefore, that I have no recourse but to reclaim the coaching duties. Unfortunately, the press of bidness prevents my return to Oxford in person and my co-coach, Dean Wells, is busy with her beer theft duties. Therefore, I must ask you and Larry to see if you possibly can accurately relay the following instructions to the Rebels. If they will obey them to the letter, they will win their remaining games just as they did when Dean and I had command:

1. Knock down any sumbidge not wearing a shirt the same color as yours.

2. Score touchdowns in preference to field goals, and field goals in preference to safeties.

3. Run faster, hit harder, kick it and catch it better than the opposition.

4. Do not flang a pass to anybody wearing a different-colored shirt than yourn.

5. Do not never drop it without picking it up.

6. When and if it ever is fourth and long, punt it.

7. Always make at least one point more than them others in different-colored shirts. . . .

Larry (Bear) King

March No. 24, 1984

Dear Dr. Shrake:

Thankee for the packet of clips. I do think as my P. R. man, however, you should speak to editors of the Austin newspaper about more careful preparation of the headlines used over stories about my Glorious Excellency: "Larry King Goes To Work" makes it sound like I been on Welfare a long time. . . .

Speaking of plays, I think that whining maggoty ass what shat on yours* ought not to be forgiven by you. Don't meet him for no "lunch, dinner or happy hour" without you intend to poison him. He wrote the bitchiest, most jealous petty review I've read in many moons. He did one of those knee-jerk Liberal numbers—reviewing your ties to what he considers the Austin "establishment" rather then your work—and now he wants to recant in private what he done publicly. . . . You ort to mail the shitass' weasling letter to the *Texas Observer* and put him in deep shit. As for his comment on "the moody circumstances under which I composed the review of your play," ask him did somebody have a gun to his head. . . .

Pancho Villa's Wedding, produced by Austin's Zachary Scott Theatre.

April 24, 1984

Dear Lanvil and Glenda:

All remains as serene at Chez King as babbling young 'uns, ringing telephones, and household helpers will permit. This morning we had here three mothers, two nannies, a housekeeper and five kids — for a "play period"—and as I wrote against deadline (for a *MacNeil-Lehrer News Hour* piece) Barbara suddenly pushed Blaine into my office and told me to watch him awhile. I still have not figured out how I got nominated and elected without choosing to run. Or what all that "womanpower" was doing—though I was paying two of them and feeding three—while I was drafted to kiddie-set. Blaine helped by typing something like Xj4xcx%P across a statistic I had called Dallas to obtain information(about voter registration); I had tossed away my handwritten note showing the scrawled figure and, naturally, in an uncharacteristic show of efficiency, the housekeeper had grabbed it within seconds, sacked it, and put it in the trash—tied up—waiting next Friday's collection. It seemed easier to call Dallas again than to hack and sift through orange peels, tea bags, egg shells and so on—so I did. Pray for me. Wish me six weeks of solitary on an Island where there ain't no dogs, alligators, lightning storms, kiddies, mothers, or nannies. Or overly-efficient housekeepers.

The *News Hour* piece I am doing—to be illustrated by Pat Oliphant cartoons—is to air sometime before the May 5th Texas primary and deals with the changes in Texas—what the candidates may expect to find—of recent years. I like the first draft, which will become a second draft demanded tomorrow A.M. by MacNeil-Lehrer. They will, of course, futz with it for days then call with suggested changes. We will film it. They will say it is wonderful until two hours before Air Time, requiring emergency last minute scramblings, and after much noise and pain and aggravation they will air a piece about 30% as good as I originally had it. S.O.P. for T.V. I'll let you know, assuming they let me know in time to (a) make the inevitable repairs and (b) call you, when it is to be aired. . . .

June No. 20, 1984

Dear Roy Blount:

Protecting your valuable privacy, Esther Newberg's* office said I was not qualified to receive your home address even to send you this puff-piece about yourownself from yesterday's *Washington Post*. I told 'em I had knew you since you was but a barefoot bumpkin and had saw you commit sex crimes and other felonies—indeed, had hepped you in a couple of bank heists and so on—but they said no dice even when I told 'em we exchange quotes for one another's dust jackets. I am glad you are becoming such a Star I cannot even contact you direct any more, for no sooner had it happened to Willie Nelson than he got richer than I can describe. I assume the same is happening or about to happen with you.

I got chure new book** when it come out and laughed about the dust jacket, where they had powdered and painted you and blowed your hair dry even though they left you in the same old ratty out-at-elbows jacket you had posed in for the cover of *Crackers*. A boy who has not been thru what I been thru would not understand how they could of convinced you to whisper behind your hand and grin silly. But one time I done a piece for *Esquire* and they talked me into wearing a powder-blue tuxedo while *barefoot* and holding a bottle of bourbon in a brown sack. They said it would take three minutes and would be done at night in front of Elaine's drinkery in Manhattan. It took two hours. I stood out there barefoot and otherwise well-dressed and looking silly—getting vicious man-eatin' diseases on my feet from the cruddy sidewalks—while everybody I knew in N.Y., including then-mayor John Lindsay, came by to cat-call and hoot and make wisecracks. The only reason I done it was because *Esquire* promised I would be on the cover, which despite my personal antipathy toward

Personal Publicity I done so as to assist Art, and the bastards claimed the pictures had turned out too dark to print and didn't even print a Kodak snap of me in the magazine's innards. . . .

*Writer Blount's literary agent.
**What Men Don't Tell Women.

July 28, 1984

Mr. Aubra Nooncaster
2321 Aspen
Pampa, Texas 79065

Dear Coach Noon:

Got a letter today from Keith Gregory, Associate Director of TCU Press, wanting to publish a collection of my work (including the piece on you from *Parade*) and he said the following which I thought might enlighten and/or amuse you:

"I had Mr. Nooncaster for senior English in Pampa. I liked him, enjoyed his class, and even listened to the poetry he read while most of the students smirked. But he never knew I listened. I even pretended not to. I don't think I ever gave the slightest hint that I was learning anything or that I was getting excited about some of the material he presented or about the extra reading I did secretly at night or about my increasing ability to write somewhat coherently. Remaining silent, I left him alone in front of that unappreciative class. I will always be ashamed of that. I am glad that one of his students spoke up. Thanks."

Damn, high school kids are philistines! How did you ever stand us, Coach?. . .

August 7, 1984

Mr. Herming Galloping*
Vice-President & Sr. Editor
Simon & Schuster
1230 Avenue of the Americas
New York, N.Y. 10020

Dear Mr. Gollop:

I like the tone of your letter of July 30, 1984, better than the one you wrote me a year ago cussing me out for sending you a friend's manuscript and asking why I troubled you with such "shit." For years, many of my friends—and myself—have been waiting for you to lose your natural arrogance and go back to being the sweet fellow you once were when you begged to buy me drinks and get my autograph. We all agree that humility becomes you, you having so much to be humble about.

It is not true that I am going to be a visiting professor at the Texas Agricultural and Mechanical College** next year, though if I had to work at A&M at all I would much prefer to think of it as mere visiting.

Here is what you may say that I say of the new book by one D. Jenke. (I did not have to read the bound gallies you sent, having read the book in typescript while freeloading off Dan and June as houseguest recently):

"Ol' Billy Clyde Puckett or Dan Jenkins ain't either one lost a step. *Life Its Ownself* is their funniest and best book."

Then you can add how Dan is better than Shakespeare and different ones if you wish.

From one who knew you when, and hardly believed it, I am, with highest regards to my ownself. . . .

*Herman Gollob.
**Gollob's Alma Mater.

September 13, 1984

Senator Carl A. Parker
One Plaza Square
Port Arthur, Texas 77642

Dear Carl:

Lawyer Warren Edsel Burnett is putting it out that you have been charged with the making of smutty materials, operating a whorehouse and fibbing outside of barrooms. Do you reckon there's a musical comedy in it?

I do not for a moment believe any such slanders against you, but when the legal crisis has passed I would appreciate any interesting films or books that might happen to be introduced as evidence.*

Hello to Tootsie, Bubbles and April. . . .

*Charges against Senator Parker, which he had labeled as "purely political," were soon dropped.

October 11, 1984

Dear Ol' Willie:

In connection with my book on writers & ritin'* I have been reviewing dog-eared, yellowed old correspondence and ran across love letters from Barbara Howar; it occurs that you should trot yours out and we'll publish them in a book. I think Ms. Howar would consent provided we promise a split of the profits to her. You better have a bushel of letters, though, because I only have two! (She didn't love me very long). Or maybe we can make some up. . . . Damn, reviewing old letters seems to warp my mind. . . .

Dan Jenkins overnighted here twice late last week and was an honored guest in the Willie Morris-Chuck DeGaulle Memorial Guest Room on the thirdmost floor. We had a chicken-fried steak dinner for him here—honest—with everybody Texans except Leslie Stahl and she is a Texan-by-marriage. Cast included Jim (PBS-TV) Lehrer & wife Kate, Rep. Goodtimes Charlie Wilson and young big-tittied date,

Lynn Coleman & wife Sylvia, Joe Christie, and a couple of other Texas couples I don't think you know. Had young Ben Herring come over to do the bar-tending honors; he done good and didn't break anything valuable. . . .

*None But A Blockhead.

December 4, 1984

Dr. Stanley Walker, Jr.
and
Mr. Gordon Cooper
1005 Eason Street
Austin, Texas 78703

Dear Dr. Walker and Mr. Cooper:*

This is to acknowledge receipt of your fan letters of September 12, 1984, to the distinguished author Dr. Larry L. King. We get to these letters as quickly as possible, but as Professor King is so popular we cannot always answer in a timely fashion.

I am sure Mr. King will be appreciative of your letters. We just wish we could fill your request for a lock of his hair as a token of remembrance, but he is currently in short supply. We will try to honor your request when he has grown additional hair. We expect a good crop by spring.

It is nice of you to invite Mr. King to Austin to take a trip through West Texas with you. However, since his personal reformation Professor King no longer consorts with rowdy persons. He has given up drink because his liver was decomposing and his asshole falling out, and he has given up the chasing of nookie due to being extremely frightened of his stern lawyer-wife and the spread of herpes. He has not even molested a boy child since the outbreak of AIDS. All in all, we find him as dull these days as a Republican banker and not a fit companion for people of your ilk.

Dr. King inquires of you, Mr. Cooper, as to when you got back from the moon? He suspects you found Dr. Walker there on an earlier journey and brought him back in a sack of moonrocks. . . .

Yours in Dr. King's and Jesus Christ's names.
(Miss) Bubbles LaTour ·
Private Secretary

*Stanley Walker, Jr., the son of noted Texas newspaper man Stanley Walker, was a well known Austin gadfly and barfly.

December 4, 1984

Dear Cousins Two:

This morning I was reading *New York* magazine's recent issue. Letters-to-the-editor. The writer Anthony Burgess was protesting in one letter that critic John Simon had treated him unfairly. I finish that, then am reading along in Simon's response—reading innocently, if that is possible in my case—and stumbled upon this sentence from Simon: "But it is disheartening to find a distinguished author declaring that something or other 'worked'. . . and that in the theater, that is all that matters.' I would expect that from the authors of *The Best Little Whorehouse in Texas* and *Sugar Babies*." Ain't critics *pricks?* I mean, we didn't really rape a baby! We just wrote a play Mr. Simon happened not to like. But to reach out, these years later, and smite us in passing—well, I know it's of no import but, goddammit, it has put my teeth on edge. Screw critics. That is not an original thought, of course, but a deeply-held one. . . .

Recent conversation at hearthside:

Lindsay:* "Da-Da, you will die before I will, won't you?"

Da-Da: "Yes, many, many years before."

Lindsay: "Oh, Goodie!"

Da-Da: "Thanks very much."

Lindsay (Frowning): "But will you die before Mommy?"

Da-Da: "Probably. I'm twenty years older."

Lindsay: "Okay, then. Go draw a map to the candy store. Mommy and I don't know where you buy those good chocolate mints!" . . .

*King's then five-year-old daughter.

"The Play's the Thing"

May 29, 1985

Dear Doctor Querry:

My markings and curt instructions ain't as fatal as they look, though of course you will originally shout "That sumbitchin' coke-sackin' Kang has ruint my work and don't know his ass from his elbow and can go suck a goddamn lemon" and then you will cry awhile and threaten never to write again and fantasize of killing me slow while a collection of your friends and loved ones watch and cheer. Fine. Just when all that is over with, read this letter and the painful markings and suggestions with which I blighted your near-perfect manuscript and then go sullenly to the typewriter and do as I say, within reason. . . .*

Your story is here, it just must be carved out and you must take a little more care with your prose. Not so much rambling: if it doesn't move the story along *cut it*. Conversely, don't rush past things that are important: you gave me four or five pages on meeting your dog Lefty (good stuff, I have no quarrel with it) *but* about 2 pages on meeting, courting and marrying Miss Elaine! Son, that's what is known as out-of-balance. I want a *whole chapter* on the meeting, courtship and marriage. I want *dialogue*. There ain't 10 lines of dialogue in your manuscript. Dialogue brings people *alive* in writing and gives them personalities the reader must otherwise guess at. . . .

Remember at all times your main story is the conversion from academic to cowboy; the giving up of one way of life for another. Point out the contrasts: there is very little of that in your manuscript. . . .

I know by now you probably feel abused and will be discouraged. Don't be. I've seen many manuscripts in much worse shape that went on to be pulled together, published and made good books. It ain't easy to get a flow, but you've gotta work at it if you want it. I find it easier to satisfy myself pretty much sentence by sentence, then paragraph by paragraph, and finally page by page—not leaving a page until I'm truly satisfied with it—so I won't have a whole discouraging gob of shit to re-write at once. That may, or may not, work for you but I'd like you to try it awhile to see if it puts things in clearer focus, heightens your awareness of the need for pruning, pertinent details, and sticking to your story.

Go get drunk and curse me if you must, let Miss Elaine comfort you with a back rub or whatever, but then get back to that typewriter. When you're comfortable with a hunk of it, send it along. I'll be eagerly waiting. . . .

*Ron Querry's manuscript of his first book, *I See By My Outfit,* published in 1987 by the University of New Mexico Press and reprinted by the University of Oklahoma Press in 1994, with a foreword by King.

May No. 31, 1985

Dear Doctor Peeler:

Lordy me, yes I recollect when we got all drunk up in Odessa in 1953 and painted [Bill] Shoopman's house in about 47 minutes. Indeedy. Some of the windows was a mess on account of they run out of window-trim paint, but me and Carlisle* solved it by trimming ours in what was left of the barbeque sauce Mary Shoopman had provided. It looked okay in the dark but Miss Mary wasn't plumb took with it when she discovered it in the daylight. Two or three years ago I seen at Edsel Burnett's house one 8 x 10 photo taken that night in which me, Carlisle and the Distinguished Banker Joe Hodges was giving the stiff middle-fanger to the camera. If you will send them old Phoots up here I will promise to return them soon in good condition. I have forgot what we all looked like young, both the quick and the dead. . . .

*Brad Carlisle, later city editor of *The Nashville Banner.*

June 12, 1985

Dear Coach Noon:

Whoops! Sorry I slipped up on the "Fatherhood" piece in *U.S. News and World Report.* My good intention was to send you one, but you know what the road to hell is paved with. That thing happened quickly—blip blip blip—when I was busy with my *Hank Williams* play and I guess my Shipping Department facilities caved in under pressure. The magazine called me on a Wednesday morning to ask me to write the piece, took pictures of us that afternoon; that night and Thursday morning I wrote the piece; it was picked up by messenger on Saturday early evening. I went back to *Hank Williams* and forgot about it. . . .

All this reminds me that when I first began publishing in 1964 my literate cousin Lanvil Gilbert asked me to apprise him of everything I had published. Because—he said—"J. Frank Dobie wrote so much, and didn't keep track of it, that many of his literary tracks have been forever lost." I said well, I would never write that much. So my cousin pressed his case until I promised that, yes, I would always notify him of when and where I published. I did it for awhile, then quit doing it regularly, then quit doing it at all. And, sure enough, a year ago some Ph.D.—apparently with little else to do—wrote me for "your complete bibliography" and when I sent him what I had, it turned out *he* had compiled a more complete list than had I. He wrote me back to complain of "careless irresponsibility" (which I found redundant). . . . I take the position that it is probably good for whatever long range assessment may be made of my work—if any—that some things *remain* lost. But, it's funny, occasionally in old files I will find short pieces and book reviews carrying my by-line that I have absolutely no recollection of having written. . . .

October 25, 1985

Mr. Mike Nichols
Carlyle Hotel
35 East 56th Street
New York, N.Y. 10028

Dear Mike:

Had a first reading of *The Night Hank Williams Died* at Actors Studio from 4-7 P.M. Wednesday (including a critical session of a half-hour afterwords) and, by God, that sumbitch rolled. Actors Studio folks voted before we left the building to fund a full scale workshop of

15 to 20 performances. Timing will depend on availability of Henderson Forsythe and Pete Masterson (directing); Pete hopes to do it in February; if not, it could be as late as May. Maybe April. Anyhow. I'll keep you posted and want you to come see it if you can. I learned a few things: some cuts, a place or so where it sags, and that I can eliminate two characters (and one actor) without hurting a thing. That means six actors could do the play. I don't know if you've had a chance yet to read it; I suspect you're still *Heartburning*. But wanted to tell you, Mike, I think the damn play is stronger than I thought. And I'd already had the temerity to tell you I thought it as strong as dog breath. . . .*

*After several postponements because of Masterson's or Forsythe's unavailability, King, in a fit of pique, withdrew his play from the Actors Studio. Mike Nichols, who had said good things of the *Hank Williams* script, never got involved.

November 18, 1985

Dear Dr. Querry:

Norman Mailer was doing some workshop scenes from his new play-in-progress about Marilyn Monroe (called *Strawhead*) at Actors Studio some weeks ago and—as I got the story—he had a scene where he permitted Miss Monroe to be dorked on a motorcycle and Ellen Burstyn and Shelley Winters and some others attacked him and said Marilyn was a sensitive, marvelous person and he in his male-chauviness-pigism had insulted her and her memory and *he* allegedly responded, "I don't intend to be dictated to by a bunch of Stalinist dykes." Which I thought was wonderful and wrote him congratulating him and got a letter from him today that he was troubled because he had said "*Stalinoid* dykes" which he meant to indicate a totalitarian state of mind whereas "the other would have been mere Red baiting." Oh. Catch me trying to compliment *him* again. . . . Anyhow, he also said that *Strawhead* is to be done in full at Actors Studio in January and invited me up, and I'll be there with bells on. . . .

December 15, 1985

Dr. Willie Morris
P.O. 682
University, Mississippi 38666

Dear Dr. Morris:

Memphis State University is to do a production of *The Best Little Whorehouse In Texas* April 18-27. Keith Kennedy, Director (an old Lamesa, Texas boy of my vintage), has invited me there to attend opening night and has agreed to pay me money to talk to the drama-literary students that afternoon. Here is my scheme:

I would like to fly into Memphis on Wednesday, April 17th, and have you and a delegation of Oxfordonians of your choice meet me at the Memphis airport whooping and cheering. A band is optional. Then I am inviting myself to go to Oxford to spend the night and we'll collect a troop of disciples and go out yonder and eat catfish. Then the next day, Thursday, you and I (and maybe Larry Wells & the Beer Thief, if they can be persuaded) will motor back to Memphis State so I can talk to the young 'uns. Then, to improve your cultural level, you will join me in seeing the opening performance of *Whorehouse*. After which we will rape and pillage, at the cast party and elsewhere. Fair enough?. . .

We might be able to arrange for a symposium on the subject "Why I Am Such A Great Writer And Nobody Else Ain't," starring a panel to be made up of Norman Podhoretz, Bob Silver, Jason Epstein, and Susan Sontag. Just as an added bonus, you understand. . . .

December 30, 1985

Mr. Buck Ramsey
2212 Hayden
Amarillo, Texas 79109

Dear Buck:

To comment on your comments about *The Night Hank Williams*

Died. You—and others—have insisted that my protagonist (Thurman Stottle) must be more sympathetic. To make him so would destroy such message as I have in my play: that even the most soiled and the least of us, whatever our faults or weaknesses, deserves to be judged more kindly than we usually are. We did a three-day workshop performance of this show at Memphis State University recently; all through rehearsals I had to fight the director, the actor, and several volunteer critics who insisted—as I saw it—on "sanitizing" Thurmond. I wouldn't let them; the role played like King Kong, as did the play, and the audience wasn't put off a bit by the fact that Thurmond had warts. The central preachment of the play (that too many people superimpose their own dreams or ambitions on others, when the object of their attentions might be better left to his own devices) would, I believe, be hurt by the sanitization of Thurmond Stottle. I did not set out to write a "pretty" play with a happy ending, but to show the boredom and meddling and craziness and injustice of life—particularly small town life—and I think I caught it to the best of my ability. It is a thing I have wanted to say for a long time but couldn't find the format. Now I think I have. . . .

Forgive me if I am wrong and falsely accuse you, but I think I hear echoes of Burnett in your comment re: the "Childress" voice.* Burnett seems to think that I follow Childress around, take down his wisecracks and sell them as my own; that seems to be the extent of my "art" in the Burnett mind. I am getting a bit sensitive to the charge, I guess. Sure, I've used some one-liners from Childress—he's good at it and I once paid him $1,000 to be taped about minor league baseball for a novel I haven't yet written—but I'd like to think that other people, including myself, have the ability to crack a few. (Among them yourself, Burnett, my late Daddy). And I'd like to believe that one must take the cracks, from whatever source, and then make something of them in a story with plot and characterizations. If it were simply a matter of writing down Norman's one-liners, I would assume that Odessa by now would have produced many novelists and playwrights, though I can think of none other than myself. And I believe if you'll think about all the old cowboys and barflys and lawyers and waitresses and country gentlemen and newsmen you've known in Texas, quite a bit of "Childress talk" goes down. I must admit that I wondered, before our Memphis production, whether there was too much of a sameness to the speech of some of the characters; it seemed not to bother the Memphis audience, though I don't know how New York audiences or other audiences will respond. I have done a great deal of spot rewriting throughout the play since you read it, and hope that situation has been improved as a problem—if, indeed, it is a problem. Hell, I know it ain't a perfect play and I'm sure as we rehearse in NY I'll be making changes—that is what rehearsals are for as much as to drill the actors. Anyhow, keep your fingers crossed for me. I may be deluding myself, but I believe *Hank Williams* will be around in modest productions here and there for years to come. And, hell, if it ain't I'll write another 'un. Hope springs eternal. . . .

*Norman Childress of Odessa had been a former minor league baseball player and car salesman known for his wild tales and funny one-liners. He went to that great cocktail party in the sky in the early 1990s.

April 22, 1986

Dear Cousins:

Things went well at my speaking-M.C. duties at the Literary Lions Awards Festival in Dallas (about 500 who paid $25 each for tickets). I also accepted, at Larry McMurtry's request, his award and $1,500 check (but didn't get to keep them, although I remarked on receiving them that if I changed just half my name I might get away with keeping them). Saw a lot of old familiar faces—A.C. Greene, Bill Porterfield, Bryan Woolley, Lloyd Olds (publisher's rep who drove me around West Texas 20 years ago as I promoted *The One-Eyed Man*), T. R. Fehrenbach, Darwin Payne, Grossblatt of Grossblatt Books in Dallas, and Bill Gilliland. (Who is, yes, still in the book business: he and McMurtry are partners in a rare book store in Dallas much like the one McMurtry has here in D. C.)

Shelby Coffee of the *Dallas Times-Herald* presented the McMurtry award, and had talked on the phone to McMurtry—who was on a speaking tour and couldn't attend the event—and passed along a good story. The day McMurtry won the Pulitzer for *Lonesome Dove* (but before the announcement thereof) he arrived in Uvalde and put up at a Holiday Inn, where the marquee read:

> Welcome Larry McMurtry
> Author of
> Terms of Endearment

A few hours later, the Pulitzer is announced. Larry is fielding phone calls while looking out his motel room window. He sees a man with a ladder scurry to the Holiday Inn sign and begin to take down the letters, from the bottom, and he thinks, "Oh, that's nice. They're going to put up something about the Pulitzer Prize." He gets another phone call, finishes it, and looks out to the sign. And now it reads:

> Today's Special
> Chili Burger and
> Strip Steak

Peace and love to you both. . . .

June 3, 1986

Dear Cousins:

Returned last night after three nights and two days in Eastland County. Had a good time seeing old friends, eating country food, listening to country music, and playing dominoes until 2 A.M. three consecutive nights. Real down home stuff. About 240 Scranton ex-students and teachers attended the Sunday shindig, and perhaps 30 Putnamites and several of my cousins on both sides of my family. Cousin Al Purvis was full of life and cheerful bullshit; he took a run to Atwell—his birthplace—Sunday and asked me along, but I felt obligated as "guest of honor" not to leave the Scranton gathering. . . .*

Carl William Bailey, old boyhood chum and grandson of W. B. Starr—on whose farm, you'll recall, Sheriff Ed Earl Dodd caught the "little greasers" barbequeing a goat in *Whorehouse*—returned from Denver and although we hadn't seen each other in 44 years, it was almost as if we'd never been away. Carl has just retired from 30 years government service and he'll now spend 3 or 4 months each year on the old W.B. Starr place. I went over there Saturday morning and we sat around drinking coffee in Mr. Starr's old study. Carl gave me a book *I Was A Share Cropper*, by Harry Harrison Kroll, published in 1936 (first edition) and signed to Mr. Starr by A. F. VonBlon, a San Antonio book dealer in those years, who visited Starr frequently to talk literature; Mr. Starr in 1965 signed the book to his daughter Ethel Starr Bailey Black (Carl's mother), who in 1975 signed it to Carl, and then Carl signed it to me as one "who knows what it's like to be a share cropper—and understands the power of the written word." Neat gift, and I was touched. Carl also let me select any book I wanted from Mr. Starr's library—in addition to the sharecropper book— and I took a socialist book (Mr. Starr was a socialist, even though the most successful capitalist farmer ever in Eastland County!), *The Workers of the West* by Walter A. Wyckoff (a Princeton professor), published in 1899 by Scribners. I chose that one because Mr. Starr had underlined many passages and had written brief marginal comments throughout. . . .**

Carl also, Saturday night, brought by two big rocks from the W. B. Starr farm—now in my office—and two jars of home-made plum jelly from thickets on the place, which had been put up by his mother Ethel. (She died in February, while I was in Alaska). Carl saw the Alexis Smith company of *Whorehouse* in Denver and said he was so "shocked and pleased" when the W. B. Starr line was given by Sheriff Dodd that he "bawled and sniveled" through the rest of the scene and missed most of what the actors said. It was a real nostalgia trip. I sat at the table in the kitchen where on Monday night, December 8th, 1941—while staying the night with Carl William—I heard radio reports of more about the Pearl Harbor attack; I recall so clearly Lee Starr—then about 20—saying, as Carl and I made kiddie comments about the Japs, "Don't you little boys worry about the Japs. Let *us* take care of them." I saw Lee this trip and reminded him of that comment—which he didn't remember making—and then he grinned and said, "And after all that bragging, I turned out to be 4-F!". . .

Would you believe Putnam is booming? Has a new barbeque place, plus two new restaurants—Hugh Shrader, Carl William and I had a damned good Texas hamburger at one of them Saturday noon—and three or four other going concerns besides its liquor stores. Whiskey has revived Putnam! There was more action downtown than we found the same afternoon in Baird. 20-odd cars on the Putnam streets! Shades of the old days! Visited the "Bear's Den" in Baird, where I played as a fourth grader for the Putnam Panthers (moved to Scranton after the football season late that year) and where Hugh Shrader played his junior and senior years in high school after his Dad took a job in the Baird school system. Drove by the old Harwell Place farm where we lived south of Putnam and, of course, the vacant lot that once held the house [in town] where I was born. Well, I could bore you forever about my nostalgia trip, but will end it with one comment indicating what I believe to be a statistical rarity: of the 275 people or so attending Sunday, five—*five*—were 90 or older! Maybe I should move back to Eastland County. . . .

Off to Nashville Friday to speak at annual banquet of *Nashville Tennessean.* Then, thank God, I make no more "public appearances" until Corpus Christi opening of their version of *Whorehouse* on August 7th and a Saturday night roast of Warren Burnett in Odessa two nights later, August 9th—which will be the 40th anniversary of my being sworn into the U.S. Army.

The Night Hank Williams Died goes into rehearsals in N.Y. August 15th. I'll be in N.Y. during the weekdays for all rehearsals, and return home only for weekends, until the opening is past. . . .

---

*King had been imported to speak at the 1986 reunion of the rural Scranton school, which he attended, 1939-1942.

**W. B. Starr wrote for agricultural publications and was "the first real professional writer" King met.

July 9, 1986

Mr. Edward Bennett Williams, Attorney
839 17th St., N.W.
Washington, D.C.

Dear Ed:

Just read in the current *Sports Illustrated* your comments about Zeke Bonura,* and feel prompted to pass on my experience with Zeke of 35 years ago:

In 1951 I was a 22-year-old sports writer on the *Midland* (Texas) *Reporter-Telegram* when Zeke came to town as a player-manager of the Midland Indians of the Class D. Longhorn League—than which there was no lower place to play allegedly-professional baseball. Early in his Midland tenure, Bonura inserted himself at first base one night. I was official scorer as well as the newspaper's reporter—gaining an additional and much-needed three bucks per game for that service—and, when Zeke waved at several balls thrown to first base as if wishing them Godspeed on their journey, not moving one inch to touch them, I charged him with errors. Gave him five and should have given him two more. Zeke shook his fist at the press box after each call and bellowed that he hadn't touched the ball. I took over the P. A. to brashly announce that he should not only have touched them, but caught them. My newspaper story the next morning began, "Even in his salad days, former Major Leaguer Zeke Bonura couldn't have caught a fat bear in a phone booth. . ." and went on to describe Zeke's playing first base "as if both feet were buried under anvils." About an hour after the paper appeared on the street I heard a great roar and looked up to see a 260-pound Zeke Bonura charging me and roaring "I'll teach ya I can catch a *sportswrita!*" Using all available desks and the bodies of newspaper colleagues, I fended off the stout Zeke until he ran out of breath, and I thus escaped relatively unscathed. . . .

I hadn't heard Zeke mentioned in years, didn't know if he was still on the planet, until I read your *S.I.* comments. Just wanted you to know he never changed the way he played first base from the way you recall it, even in his twilight years in the low, low minors. . . .

*A first baseman for the Chicago White Sox and Brooklyn Dodgers in the 1930s and 1940s.

23 July 1986

Mr. Stephen C. Byrd
Issues Section
Democratic Congressional Campaign Committee
430 South Capitol Street
Washington, D.C. 20003

Dear Steve:

No, you haven't in any way offended me. Lack of contact on my part is explained by days being limited to twenty-four hours, and I can't get everything done I want or need to get done even if I sleep but five or six of them. I appreciate that you like and read my books, and your comments on them, and that you have several times invited me to lunch and such good things. But, as I have tried to indicate in the past, I am an aging fellow with miles to go before I sleep and the sleep will be eternal. So I have to be pretty tough-nutted about my time. So you won't feel that I am picking on you, or am crassly unappreciative of your attentions, just consider the following:

I get about 75 letters per week, almost all requiring some action or response. Many, as you do, send me stuff they have written to read, pass along to editors or whatever. I unfortunately have a telephone, and it is the life and joy of goddamned mankind to ring it 30 times each day. I have two small kiddies and a wife to attend, and all the headaches of maintaining a home. I travel a lot on business, promotion, and speeches. I have to deal with lawyers, editors, agents, accountants, and goddamned tax men. I am solicited to judge contests, attend luncheons or dinners, fund raisers for this candidate or that cause, read books and give quotes for them, place manuscripts, babble on the goddamned radio or television. Why hell, Steve, you'd think I was a goddamned Congressman so many folks want so many things!

None of the above, of course, helps me get any *writing* done. I am currently writing a novel, plotting a new play, negotiating a production contract on a second play and, in connection with that, getting ready for days of auditions and weeks of rehearsals. I am finishing one magazine article, and have four more lined up. I am a *writer*, you see: it is what I want to do and without it I am miserable. That is why most of my lunches and dinners are business ones: the goddamned business end eats me up and takes away from my writing time. So don't feel I am picking on you or go taking my inattentions personal. I just have to have a list of prorities, that's all, and my priority is to reserve such time as I can to work.

It was nice of you to send me the $30 check for having read my last two books without buying them, but I wouldn't feel right about accepting it and here return it. But thanks for the thought.

I'll pass your article along to Grant Oliphant at *American Politics*. You probably saw my name listed on their Advisory Board. The deal there is they asked and I said, "I'll serve if I don't have to give any advice or attend any meetings. If you want to use my name, fine, but that's the extent I'll participate."

Quit writing me long-winded letters and go elect us some goddern Democrats!

Best and peace. . . .

January 20, 1987

Mr. William Styron
c/o "Styron's Acres"
Roxbury, Connecticut

Dear Bill:

The enclosed first-edition of your *Lie Down in Darkness*, featuring a picture of you when you were 12 years old, belongs to my friend Jack Kent Cooke who also owns the Washington Reskins, the Chrysler building, the world's largest thoroughbred horse farm, and possibly Albania and Mexico. As well as downtown Phoenix. In other words,

Jack is likely to get through the winter without help from either of us.

How you *can* help him, however, is to warmly sign *Lie Down* to him and return it to his digs in your native state via the enclosed stamped, pre-addressed envelope. One of Jack Kent Cooke's few weaknesses is that he is more a devout Styron fan than a King fan, but then nobody's perfect. Seriously, I will appreciate your good services in this regard and so will JKC. For God's sake don't lose this book or steal it. Jack permits me to sit in his box at all Redskin games—which, as you might expect, is not in the end zone—and I would not wish to forfeit that.

Next time you come South to read poetry, run rabbits and bark at the moon give me a call and I'll get Jack to buy us a hot dog, a Moon Pie and a Arya-Cee Cola.

As we say in the Ivy League, I have just wrote another play. *The Golden Shadows Old West Museum.* Protaganist is an 88-year-old former cowboy who makes life difficult for all who run the Golden Shadows Senior Citizens Home in Leon, Texas. Am clean-typing it now and will afflict you with a copy soon. . . .

August 27, 1987

Dear Jim:*

Q: Whatever happened to the trooper's kid who lost the eye in the kick-the-can game?

A: He changed his name to Jim Lehrer and became a semi-star on semi-TV, and then the smartass began writing books and plays by the carload and lived happily ever after until a scraggly bunch of free-lance writers, whose wives kept holding Lehrer up as a good example, got enough of that horseshit and formed a mob and killed him in a slow and most horrible way. . . .

Yours in Christ. . . .

*Jim Lehrer.

October 13, 1987

Dear Dr. Shrake:

Tell Susan Walker to let me know in writing, as she promised, when I am to be there to get my Star put in the Austin sidewalk* and where is my plane ticket and all? She promised me all the info and expenses and ain't did shit. I imagine they are trying to trick me. They know that, despite my aversion to personal publicity, I would probably go to Paris, France or Rome, Italy or the smallest town in Georgia to get my star in the sidewalk and once I get there they don't intend to pay me. . . .

If we get to make speeches at the Star-in-the-Sidewalk ceremonies I think I will just quote what you wrote in your letter, and sit down. What you wrote, in case you forgot, was with respect to me, you and Jenke: "Drinking and doping ourselves practically to death in pursuit of our craft and our determination not to ever get a real job, but always to live as if we were rich, we three scrappers are the Texas myth in the flesh."

*In the fall of 1987, Gary Cartwright, Dan Jenkins, Bud Shrake, and King had "stars" placed in a sidewalk on Austin's 6th Street, joining those of Darrell Royal and Willie Nelson.

December 30, 1987

Dear Rev. Doctor Shrake:

Your Holy Excellence, His Worship thanks you for the card celebrating the birth of Baby Jesus. Which reminds me of a recent occurrence at our house. Lawyer Blaine set about reading the Nativity story to 5-year-old Blaine King one recent bedtime and he fidgeted and scowled and then delivered himself of the following utterance: "Read me something else. Everywhere I go people want to read me that Baby Jesus stuff and I'm tired of it. I don't believe in God and I don't believe in Baby Jesus and I don't like Baby Jesus and I'm glad old Jesus got *nailed!*" I think the Baptist recruiters may be wasting their time on that young 'un.

Wal, I am fresh back from Noo Yawk where we auditioned a bunch of folks who spoke in Brooklyn, Boston, London, and Shakespearean accents under the mistaken impression it might get them cast in my play*. . . . Despite all the horribly misguided folks who showed up (one lady read for Nellie Bess's religion-crazed Mama in her native Cockney accent), we wound up with a damned good cast after two weeks of auditions here and the two days in Gotham. Got my bartender Gus in N.Y. and Nellie Bess there; got the Thurmond I wanted, who played the role to a turn in Memphis two years and many scripts ago; and got the Sheriff, Moon and Nellie's Mama here in D.C. All are Texans or Tennesseans except Nellie Bess, who spent some years in North Carolina. The more we heard folks with strange accents (there was one guy, I swear to Christ, who had a thick German-Jewish accent and a Mennonite beard who auditioned to play Moon, the old lay-about beer-drinker who drives a bread truck) the more we realized how desperately we depended on authentic types if we wished to avoid staging an unintended comedy.

You would never have heard of any of these actors except possibly Gus (Kevin Cooney) and probably not him (he was saw in the movie *A Trip To Bountiful* as the agent of the small town bus station where Geraldine Page passed the night) but all have worked a lot and are good. We'll have to age Kevin Cooney about 10-12 years by a whisker stubble or two, three days growth and other tricks but I think we can get by with it. He moves old, and that helps.** (Of course, the role of Gus was wrote for Hank Forsythe, the Broadway Sheriff in *Whorehouse*, but he's playing General Marshall or somebody in a 13-part TV series about our World War II leaders and couldn't finish the shooting in time. Sometimes I believe God don't like me. Maybe it's because I have an atheist five-year-old son.)

I have already caused to be fired a set designer who brought sketches making an old West Texas beer joint of the 1950s look like a fern bar, and who thought it would be peachy to write in a bar-maid on roller skates. (I shit you not.) The *new* set designer appeared entirely rational when I told him about the old wood, scruffiness and so on but today I hear he wants the old bar to have once been a church so he can use some stained glass in it. We are going to have to have a talk soon. Sometimes I wonder if I am cut out for Show Biz.

Through my twisting arms we have done sold out nine of our 35 performances before even going into rehearsals (which commence January 8th)*** and I think I have two more about lined up, plus a "Special Benefit Preview" at $100 per seat for rich folks who want to feel like they are in on things, that $12,500 evening unfortunately being for the benefit of New Playwright's Theatre rather than for the old playwright hisself. Got Texas State Society to take two nights (the second one of which you good Austin folk will attend), U of Texas exes one night, shamed my Alcoholics Anonymous friends into buying two nights (I love the irony of all them old drunks spending two hours watching folks on stage sop up beer in a beer joint) and got outfits like the Capitol Hill Staff Club (which I sold by pointing out that I, myself, was once a Capitol Hill Staffer) and the Administrative Assistants Association (same deal), and made Barbara make her law firm buy a night, and my lobbyist friend Craig Raupe a night, and Washington Women in Government Affairs a night (they just sort of happened by and I grabbed 'em) and so on. Think I'll land R. J. Reynolds Tobacco Company for a night (I told 'em Gus would smoke whatever kind of cigarettes they want him to during the run, *not* just for that one performance) and now I'm working on a beer lobbyist for a night on account of there is much beer drinkin' in the play. Maybe I should have bought me a gray flannel suit and went into huckstering on Madison Avenue. (Naw. I would of jumped off something tall and splattered the street long about 1971.)

As adverse as I am to personal publicity, I consented to write a 3,000 word piece about the show ("Getting On the Boards") with pix of me and the Director looking artistic over scripts at the theatre, and so on, for *Washington Dossier* mag, which will come out four days before we open, and which is read by richies who pretend to the arts. What is amazing is that Lawyer Blaine persuaded the mag to pay me $1,500 for what amounts to an eight-page ad, since they also are running a side-bar interview with me bragging on myself at wholesome lengths, as well as two pages from the script itself, selected by me. I dearly wish I could just do my Ort and not get caught up in sales and publicity, me being so shy and modest and all, but can I help it if I am indispensable and no person on earth but me can do them things? No. I cannot. You will be one of the few people who understand this, Doctor, being a genius yourownself. Jenke**** probably would understand it, too, though not as well as you and me. I always thought Jenke was only about a 97% genius whereas there is no quarrel about me and you being 100% geniuses. (Though when I am with Jenke sometimes I promote him to 100% genius and make either me or you only a 97% genius. Usually you.)

Of course I ain't wrote shit of my re-writes lately on the novel, *War Movies*, being all wrapped up in this Show Biz stuff. About all I have did useful is play Santa Claus again, but I am getting tard of that job after having did it more or less constantly now for 35 years. Sometimes, however, I wish Santa Claus would be left alone by others to do his job as he sees fit: my mother-in-law sent Blaine an electric guitar that plugs into a workable microphone and his Ort thus may be heard from my house to Baltimore when he is trying good. He also got a portable radio-cassette player and had owned all that stuff a good three minutes before discovering that should he turn the radio-cassette player up to maximum volume *then* hold it up to the microphone, and sing along with it, his broadcast range increased to take in Philadelphia. This in the house where I work. The little farts have been off for the holidays for about 10 days and do not go back to school until about 10 more days. I am thinking of getting a teacher's certificate so I will not have to be around kids so much.

Wal, that is about it except *National Geographic* has decided that piece on Anchorage, having laid around in their bins to ripen for two years, now qualifies to be published in their February issue. I also got a piece in the February *Texas Monthly* about cheatin' songs, though it pisses me off they changed my original title from "Music to Fornicate By" to something much more pallid. No guts. . . .

*"*The Night Hank Williams Died*," set in the mythical West Texas town of Stanley.
**Cooney withdrew for a better-paying stage role in New York.
***At the New Playwrights Theater in Washington, D.C.
****Fort Worth writer Dan Jenkins.

May 20, 1988

Dear Doctor Shrake:

My asshold publishers [Viking Krestel Books] sent me the dust jacket of my kiddie book, *Because of Lozo Brown,* saying about me (allegedly): "Larry King lives in Washington and has an all-night radio talk show on Mutual Broadcasting Network." I ain't been publishing with the shitass Vikings but 19 years, so no wonder they didn't know who I was. Boy, it makes a man feel like he is ever on their minds and is going a long way in The Organization. I calt up and taught 'em some new cuss words. They are now fast destroying dust jackets and starting over. . . .

Yours in Christ,
His Worship

September 27, 1988

Dear Mr. Winokur:*

You ask, "What do women want?" Answer: money, power, love, sex (until they get married), adulation, children, and control. Of these, children cause the most trouble. Women also want equal rights and equal pay for equal work, and I agree with them 100%. Though on some days it is hard to figure how a species that controls 97% of the money and *all* the pussy can be downtrodden.

All-time worst date: I had lusted after Dora for years. We dated in a time when nice girls didn't go all the way, so we didn't, but several times there we went 97% of the way. She married another. Years pass. I see her infrequently with the simple-minded asshole she chose over an obviously superior person. My lust continues. More years pass. Then I am in her city and learn she has been divorced by her husband. Didn't I tell you he was a simple-minded asshole? I call "their" home and cleverly ask for her former husband, expressing astonishment when she tells me the marriage has gone kaput. Ever-so-casually I ask her out for dinner. I bathe, powder, deodorize, dress in my best, walk the hotel lobby looking at my watch every ten seconds, alternately growling away old friends who want to chat and thanking

Sweet Jesus for my chance at Dora. A hump-backed old dowager approaches, carrying one of the books I have authored. I unsling my trusty pen, bark "I'm-meeting-somebody-and-I'm-in-a-hurry-how-do-you-want-this-signed?" And the bent old crone says, "How about love and kisses to Dora?" Things went downhill from there. . . .

<hr />

*Jon Winikur, a writer doing a book about "the battle of the sexes"; he queried King and many other male writers.

Editor's Note: In the fall of 1988, King and producer Drew Dennett were preparing for the New York production of *The Night Hank Williams Died*. The preparations included giving the young director a weekend tour of far West Texas and eastern New Mexico.

October 27, 1988
Thursday noon

Dear Cousins:

Arrived home Tuesday night. Had very successful trip to West Texas so that young North Carolina native to direct at WPA Theatre in New York—Christopher Ashley—could get the feel and flavor of Stanley country. Drew Dennett, who never thinks small, chartered a small jet at a cost of $1,000 and at 9 A.M. last Saturday we flew from Austin to Abilene, rented a car and drove West so that Chris could get the feel of decreasing foliage and great distances the further we went. From Midland on—where, in my mind, "Stanley country"* begins—we drove around the town and engaged the locals (though not the Midland Kings) in conversation: beer joints, restaurants, a garage sale in Wink, a "B" team football game (Wink vs. Marfa), a country-music band in Jal, N.M. Saturday night (we couldn't find such a band in Kermit, Wink, or Monahans: what is West Texas *coming* to?); *church* Sunday morning in the non-denominational church in Mentone. We got a bonus there: remember Newt Keene, who owned the only restaurant-bar in Mentone, and his feud with Sheriff Punk Jones? (Basis for Sheriff-Gus feud in my play, really). Well, as we

were in church Sheriff Punk Jones came in, handcuffed and took
Newt's 30-odd-year-old son off to jail with the aid of a black highway
patrolman. The Keene son, a Vietnam Vet, had been reportedly acting "crazy" for a couple of days because—according to locals, who
delighted in filling us in—he refuses, periodically, "to take his medicine for his nervousness and then he sort of goes off haywire."

Chris Ashley's eyes got as big as saucers; he scribbled frantically in
his notebook. Drew—who of course believes in, among other things,
reincarnation, astrology and such—felt that a "higher power" had
arranged for that scene: the last time I was in Mentone, 1971, Punk
Jones and Newt were having a face-off over Punk having turned Newt
in to the Liquor Control boys for being open a few minutes past closing time (see "The Lost Frontier" and the play dialogue) and almost
the instant we arrive there is the arresting of Newt's son. Shades of the
Hank feud being handed down to the next generation! Newt, by the
way, closed his restaurant-bar two months ago and moved to Andrews
so we didn't see him. Did peer inside at the leavings: old juke box,
stacked chairs, a couple of cases of beer and so on.**

Saturday we visited Midland, Odessa, Monahans (including
Monahans Sand Hills State Park, where Thurmond and Nellie Bess
made out and caused local gossip), Wink, Kermit and Jal (at night).
Came back and stayed in a scruffy old motel in Kermit that night.
Sunday morning, took a swing through Wink and discovered the
garage sale early; I pointed out homes where, likely, Thurmond lived
with his Mama; where Vida Powers lived; the house, with a rose garden, where Thurmond stole the rose from "old lady Livingston's garden"; a decayed old house Gus had bought on the theory he would
marry Vida, which he rented out for years once she married someone
else; the best house in town, by the city park, which obviously
belonged to Tood Brandon, and so on. Chris and Drew both
enthralled; much scribbling by Chris; Drew began to check out where
we'll keep the cast when we make the *movie* on location in Wink!***
Then on to Mentone and happenings there. Then to Pecos, Barstow,
Monahans again, brief tour of Odessa and Sunday night spent in the
good hotel in Midland. Sunday night I drove the boys around

Midland—including by the house where I lived with the folks while in high school, and saw a light in Estelle's bathroom, but God forgive me, did not stop. Chris scribbling in notebook all the way. In Odessa he said, "Do people realize how *bad* it is out here?" In Kermit he said, "Why do these people *stay* here?" And when I asked him what he thought of the area in general he said, from the heart, "I couldn't have imagined it would be this bad!" So I think we served our purpose, in that he got a sense of what everyone in the play is trying to escape from, and that can only be good when it comes to his interpretations to the actors and his directing.

Midland and Odessa looked *closed.* I tipped a bellboy in Midland handsomely, then asked how many rooms vacant in the hotel last Sunday night. He said, "It's easier to say how many are occupied. Sixteen." And that's a 250 room hotel! (And three were occupied by us.)

We flew back by commercial airline to Austin about mid-morning Monday. Street traffic and hotel traffic showed a slight upsurge, but not enough to approach "normal." Real depressing. Noted that the plane we *left* on was two-thirds full, but that two planes *arriving* while we were at the airport disgorged but a handful of people. Pointed this out to Chris, who scribbled in his notebook again. ****

Must start going to New York soon for early casting looks. All fine here, and much saner than Austin moments! Drew in New York now doing pre-production stuff.

> *Stanley is the mythical Texas town in King's *Hank Williams* play.
> **Newt Keene, whom King wrote about in his *Life* piece on Mentone.
> ***Options were taken on King's play, and he wrote the movie script but it was never filmed.
> ****The Midland-Odessa area then continued to suffer from the 1986 oil crash.

December 5, 1988

Dear Stanley:*

I am not at all sure I could write of my mother as I did of my father. I do not know the reasons for certain—they are complex indeed—but my feeling for him was somehow deeper, at least from about the age of 20 or 21 on, and at bottom I think (may I be forgiven the judgement) he was a more selfless person and without certain characteristics of emotional manipulation and manipulation of events that I saw in my mother and which, I fear, caused pain to myself and others. Not that I never caused *her* pain, not that she was without good qualities, not that she didn't love me or wish me well by her own guidelines. But her goals were not mine, and that conflict was always there, and when I did not accept her goals but insisted on my own she was not above collecting a tax of guilt and knew how to *raise* the taxes, yes indeed. All, of course, "for my own good" and I'm sure she honestly and sincerely had my "good" uppermost in her mind. She would have died for me, I have no doubt, but when it came to *life,* well . . . but perhaps I judge harshly. It is my wont in most things; grand irony that, since it's what I accuse my *mother* of! I think it may be summed up better than I can say it by something she once said, in my 20th year when I was freshly home from the Army and had liquor on my breath: "I wish I had kept you on that farm and you'd never gone anywhere or learned to read or write!" The twain had a tough time meeting after that. Perhaps we were too much alike, about different things. . . . We simply lived in different worlds and had trouble understanding the other's world or why anyone would insist on living there. . . .

This oddity just in. A friend of Barbara's from Yale sent along a thermofax page of the new Webster's Dictionary giving me credit for its third-preferred definition of the word "rote," to wit: "a joyless sense of order . . . and commercial hustle." Wonder what I must do to work up to 2nd or 1st preference? . . .

*Cousin Stanley Gilbert, a brother of Lanvil's.

December 13, 1988

Dear Cousins:

Opening night* we are taking Elaine Kauffman (of Elaine's), Dan and June Jenkins, Kurt Vonnegut and wife Jill Krementz, Mike Arlen (*The New Yorker*) and his wife, Alice, screenwriter (co-credit on

Silkwood and *Alamo Bay*), Lynn Coleman and Sylvia de Leon from here and Charles Simpson (ex-Charlie Wilson and Lloyd Benson aide, now a lobbyist) and wife Louise. Invited the David Halberstams, but they're going to be in the Carribean that week. Invited Norman Mailer and Norris Church Mailer, but he must be in California (talking movie deal); however, Norman and Norris are going to see the show with us on Saturday night the 28th. Other nights, Barbara and I are going to see other shows; she's going to work the full week out of her firm's New York law offices, and then gad about the theatrical world at night.

We've made a deal with Mort Cooperman, owner of the Lone Star at 5th Avenue and 13th in the Village—where we held Off-Broadway opening night party when *Whorehouse* was at the Intermedia—to have the cast party after opening night performance. We're reserving his second floor—balcony—for our party of about 125, while regular patrons use lower floor. Cost: $3,000, which ain't bad. Drew is calling Susan Walker to see if Jerry Jeff can come up and play a set for the party. . . .

*January 24, 1989 opening of *The Night Hank Williams Died* at the WPA Theatre, New York.

February 14, 1989

Dear Coach Noon:

Thought I had given you a report on *Golden Shadows* earlier. In any case, it went extremely well, both as to the audience reaction and reviews (see enclosed). And I was gratified that Arkansas Repertory gave it a truly outstanding production. They do good work there. As a result of the reception and reviews there—and I'm sure, because of the New York reception of *Hank Williams* as well—we've had contact from theatres in Fort Worth, Houston, Florida, Georgia, Tennessee and New York. . . .

You are not the first—among those to have read and/or to have seen *Golden Shadows*—to find it more "compelling" (or "better" or "stronger" or "funnier" or "more moving") than *Hank Williams*. Indeed, I'd say 90% who have some familiarity with both plays take your position. I have mixed feelings about that. I'm glad people respond to it—and, oh boy, do they—but, in a personal sense, I feel like a parent might if told someone preferred one of his children to the other—when the parent in his heart preferred the *other* child. That is, I feel closer to *Hank*—have put more into it in many ways—than to *Shadows*. It is more from my bone and soul. But I ain't knocking *Shadows* or people's reaction to it, Lord knows. Maybe as I spend more time with it I'll feel closer to it myself. . . .

February 20, 1989

Dear Reverend Doctor Shrake:

Things still going along better than could be expected with *Hank* up yonder in Gotham. Selling out all the time. We end at the WPA on Feb. 26th and move into the Orpheum (347 seats) on March 6th. Take about 10 days to get the set in, do all technical rehearsals, re-block the show due to stage configuration, and such. Expect we'll be back in action, playing at preview prices, on March 16th and have official Orpheum opening March 21st. We gonna low key it: already had our cast party and good reviews, so no big deal. Probably take the cast to dinner along with some of the folks we've flim-flammed into investing $400,000 and that's it. . . . We'll need to spend a ton of money advertising when we re-start—having lost our momentum—but we're buying a couple of big quote ads in the *NY Times*, got some articles set up in papers, more TV and radio interviews and such, so I think it'll all work out. . . .

I'm still running back and forth betwixt Noo Yawk and Washington City, and will be until the theatre move is made and all is running smooth. Then I hope to get settled down to new work. I ain't wrote shit in a year, getting *Hank* and *Golden Shadows* started. Sure time consumin'. . . .

May 20, 1989

Dear Ol' Willie:

Grand news that you have finished *Taps!** I know you must be proud, relieved and strangely shorn in the same instant. (What a weird life we lead, Willie!) Hummin' Gollob told me some weeks ago that you were working hard and that you were doing excellent work. I can hardly wait to read it. Be sure Hummin' sends me galley proofs.

The other day, dressed in my usual "out of work cowboy" clothes, I was humping along the street downtown and I heard someone sing out, "King, you're *overdressed* as usual." And I looked up to see Hodding Carter, impeccably attired as always. I sang out, "Fashions by Willie Morris!" and we both laughed and kept on our merry ways.

Well, la-de-dah about you breaking bread with George Bush. George ain't seen fit to extend an invite to me, even though we once attended weekly meetings of the Midland Jaycees together. (George because he apparently wanted to, I because the *Midland Reporter-Telegram* inflicted the torture of covering one weekly civic luncheon on each of its reporters.) George did have me to his Vice-Presidential residency for a Christmas party in 1981, but I must have et with the wrong fork or maybe it was breaking wind at the table that caused him never to invite me back. I hoped you washed your feet and put on fresh underwear before going to the White House.

I had to scoot to the Big Cave** on short notice awhile back and do 17 performances in *Hank Williams* on account of Darren McGavin insisted on leaving to make a TV pilot. Had fun and got good notices, but that's tiring work and I'm glad it's over. The problem with having a success in Show Biz is that suddenly you're always talking other "deals," having to promote, being called or visited by every sumbitch who has a scheme, dream or project to sell and so your private time and writing time becomes almost non-existent. I've been hustling *Hank* a long time now and I'm weary of it. We're in rehearsals (another time-gobbling process) here now for *The Golden Shadows Old West Museum*, which opens at American Playwrights here in D.C. on June 8th; it then goes to Theatre-on-the-Square in suburban Atlanta.

Hank companies are opening in Phoenix and San Francisco later in the summer. . . .

*A novel set in Mississippi in the Korean War years, not yet published.
**Willie Morris' term for Manhattan, used in his memoir *North Toward Home*

December 20, 1989

Dear Doctor Querry:

Well, hell, I'm sorry you got another of those we-love-your-novel-but-fuck-publishing-it-here letters. I know how very damned frustrating that must be. It probably won't help the way you feel but I say again it is a good sign—those letters stressing your work as being worthy if not-quite-now-and-here—because to me if you keep on keeping-on you're gonna publish novels. What I like best in your letter is your angry declaration that you post-scripted: "Mark my words . . . the sumbitch *will* be published—by *some*body!" I believe that, but—more importantly—you believe that. As long as you keep believing and keep working, you are going to make it happen. . . .*

A few weeks ago I got a bitter letter from the writer Paul Hemphill about his publisher only printing 10,000 copies of what he saw as his "big" novel—*King of the Road*—and he was threatening to quit and take up slopping hogs or something. I wrote him a buck-up letter about how no matter how foolish his publisher was, he had written several very fine books, including that one, and that I believe he would not be better off slopping hogs. This very day he sent me a letter full of bubbly joy: *King of the Road* is being bought for the movies by Ring Lardner, Jr., and Otto Preminger's son and Hemphill may get to write the screenplay. He gave me a lot more credit than I deserved for my buck-up letter, but I meant what I wrote him at the time and mean it now. If a man works hard and is good, then odds are something good will come of it one day. . . .

My friend Bud Shrake is writing the as-told-to book of Barry Switzer . . . and he thinks he's gonna have a hell of a book. He said when he and Switzer were going in front of different editors at different publishing houses to peddle their wares—it was a bid situation—Barry asked him how he should act. Shrake told him, "Every little 120-pound editor you see fantasizes about being a football stud like you, and every *female* editor you see fantazies about fucking one or marrying one," and he said Switzer took that cue and charmed the ass off everybody. He also said that Switzer can "cry on cue, like a good actor" and at every editorial-sales pitch meeting they had, Barry teared up and bawled for 'em when he told of his wretched childhood. Wish I could have been a fly on the wall!. . .**

*Querry ultimately wrote a well-received novel, *The Death of Bernadette Lefthand*, published in 1994, and in 1998 a second novel, *Bad Medicine*; he continues to be a working novelist.

**The book Shrake wrote for former Oklahoma University football coach, *Bootlegger's Boy*, became a bestseller. Switzer went on to become the controversial coach of the Dallas Cowboys for several seasons.

8

"Bungee-Jumping" Through
the 1990s

L ate in the decade Larry L.
King confided to his friend
Bud Shrake, "I feel like I've
been bungee-jumping through
the entire 1990s. I leap out with a great exuberance, then suddenly get
pulled back by some invisible string short of my goals. It's a little like
being repeatedly smacked in the head with a baseball bat." Indeed,
King's mood swings long had been recognized. Bill Brammer, in the
early 1970s, once told him, "You remind me of the Great Pumpkin."
[Brammer's private nickname for LBJ]. "Half the time you think yourself to be Sole Ruler of the Universe and half the time you think yourself to be the biggest flop, failure or victim since Lucifer fell."

Despite many demonstrated successes during the decade and many
wickedly funny letters, King's dark side and dissatisfactions reveal
themselves more often than not. He appears almost obsessed with a

fear of aging, dwells on the deaths or lost vigors of old friends, what he perceives as his own slippage, and decries '90s developments in technology, celebrity journalism, and political correctness, all of which he feels have undermined what he terms "this old writing game." Nearing seventy, he appeared to feel a new sense of urgency to complete projects before it is too late, fears that he may be about washed up, but at the same time teeming with new ideas for plays, books and stories he still hoped to accomplish.

The spectacular failure of *The Best Little Whorehouse Goes Public* in 1994 would have given pause to any writer, much less one as closely in touch with perceived rejection as Larry L. King. By this time, King was very much in the habit of forwarding packages of his current correspondence to the Southwestern Writers Collection, and sitting there in San Marcos reading months of letters leading up to the train wreck that "HoHouse II" became was a morbidly fascinating experience. King's brilliant analysis of the Broadway flop in his Friday the 13th letter to Lanvil and Glenda should be required reading in every theater course in the country.

Another disappointment was the rejection of his minor-league baseball novel, *Breaking Balls*, a project that he had dusted off after a dozen or so years. This reaffirmed his image of himself as coming up short as a novelist. Another "back-burner" project had a more viable life, his darkly comic take on Presidents Johnson and Nixon, in the 1995 stage play, *The Dead Presidents' Club*. In the fall of that year, Southwest Texas State put on a mini-festival of King's work, with a theatre department production of *The Best Little Whorehouse in Texas*, readings of some of his letters in the writers collection, and a very successful staged reading of his new play, with G. W. Bailey reading Nixon and Barry Corbin reading Johnson. The big surprise of the play, being when God is revealed to be a black woman, brought down the house.

For the evening in the writers collection, I had mounted a career retrospective of King's work from his first *Texas Observer* piece on Brammer to just-off-the-typewriter drafts of *The Dead Presidents' Club*. Before G. W. Bailey read a bit of the letters, I introduced King, who, tongue-in-cheek, remarked that the exhibit was quite nice as far as it went. He, however, had something more grandiose in mind, say like the recently unveiled statue of J. Frank Dobie, Roy Bedichek, and Walter Prescott Webb, located in front of Austin's Barton Springs. This continued a theme present in King's letter exchanges with Bud Shrake about "their statue" and the quest for the East Pole. Funny stuff, yet King was obviously concerned about the "lastingness" of his literary reputation. While he welcomed the genuine affection and respect that his new work found in Texas, what he saw as a corresponding decline as a national literary figure depressed him. The fact that there has been in America a regionalization in almost all of the viable arts throughout the last decade appeared to be of little comfort.

The Dead Presidents' Club received a fine Live Oak Theatre premiere production at Austin's State Theatre in May 1996. Directed by G. W. Bailey, it starred Bailey as Nixon and a fine Oklahoma actor, Dennis Letts, as Johnson. Letts' uncanny resemblance to LBJ's appearance and speech and Bailey's brilliant turn as the paranoid Nixon made for an entertaining evening of theater, and King was encouraged about setting up productions back in what he still calls the "Mystic East."

Even as other non-theatre projects lagged, the decade was marked by King's successful entry into a new form—the short story. "Something Went With Daddy" was published in *Story* and found a happy afterlife as a performance piece at the Dallas Museum of Art's literary series Arts and Letters Live. It was published by the museum in one of their *Texas Bound* volumes, and along with three others in King's 1996 collection, *True Facts, Tall Tales & Pure Fiction.*

The death of cherished friends, such as his Viking editor Alan Williams, put King, naturally never too far from it anyway, into a thanatoptic frame of mind. Any perceived slippage on his part is not perceived by others—his 1998 performances both at the "Evening With Larry L. King" in Dallas and his reading of two letters at the Jan Reid benefit in Austin won him enthusiastic new fans. For the future, we are looking forward to King confronting the Computer Age. Having a closetful of manual typewriters and ribbons and proudly maintaining his reputation as a West Texas Luddite, he has spent his entire writing career on the same 1920s technological plane as one of his heroes, H. L. Mencken. I can testify that riding in a car with him driving in Washington D. C. is a riveting experience and that he thinks nothing of jumping out to trade seats when it comes time to parallel park. We can only look forward to his encounter with "word processing" and what I am sure will be great new creations as he sails into cyberspace.

—Richard Holland

February 16, 1990

Hon. John Culver*
Washington, D.C.

Dear John:

. . . . I'm reminded of another Harold Young story. One he told me about the writer Edna Ferber, who wrote *Giant* (a book and movie that pissed off many Texans because they said it grossly parodied Texas and the oil/cattle business). Anyhow, Harold says that when Edna Ferber was traveling Texas to research *Giant*, someone directed her to him and he (Harold) showed her around Dallas for a couple of days. Some years later, Harold said, he was in some city—I can't remember what one—and saw in the paper that Edna Ferber was in that city, lecturing or making a speech, and was staying in a certain hotel—which Harold, too, was staying in. So he said he rang her room, got her on the line and said, "Mrs. Ferber, I'm Harold Young from Dallas, and I'm registered here in the hotel tonight and would like to buy you a drink." He was in the midst of further identifying himself as the man who had escorted her around Dallas but she cut in saying, "I'm sorry, Mr. Young, I have never been to Dallas but once in my life and then briefly" and hung up. A few minutes later, according to Harold, *his* telephone rang. "Oh, Mr. Young," Edna Ferber allegedly said, "I'm sorry I was rude. My secretary reminded me that you were the nice man who escorted me around Dallas while I was researching my book *Giant*. And I'd be happy to accept your invitation for drinks." And Harold swore he said, "I'm sorry, Lady, I've never been to Dallas in my life!" and hung up. And when Harold told that story—I must have heard it a half-dozen times—his great belly would shake with laughter. I don't know if it is true or just another "Piss Wilson" story, but I always enjoyed it. . . .

There is an obscure book in my possession, *My Name is Tom Connally* (Thomas Y. Crowell Company, New York, 1954), by the late Senator from Texas, in which he gives himself very much the best of it in an exchange with Henry Wallace during hearings (chaired by Senator Connally) on the bill that would establish NATO. I must tell you that I knew Senator Connally in his later years and he was a bit over-blown in describing some of the events of his time. (I own and now live in the house that Senator Connally owned and lived in during most of his time in Washington and the Senator claimed to have written a lion's share of the U.N. Charter in the office that was his and is now mine. I have not put up a plaque.)

*John Culver, former U.S. Senator from Iowa and a Washington lawyer, was writing a book on former Vice-President Henry Wallace and had quizzed King about King's Texas friend Harold Young who had worked for Wallace.

April 14, 1990

Dear Terry:*

The remark in the *Hank Williams* preface about the play dealing with my family meant [son] Brad and my late Mama. Mama saw Jesus all the time. He walked right through her bedroom wall ("purty as you please") Mama said, and sat down on the edge of her bed and talked about Heaven and her Loved Ones already there and—quite pointedly, Mama made clear to *me*—some who might never experience Heaven's ecstasies unless they changed their sinful ways. The old woman nearly drove me crazy with that shit, and I paid her back by reincarnating her as Vida Powers, Nellie Bess's purse-mouthed and Jesus-seeing mother. Gus, the beer joint owner, is an amalgamation of my Dad's character (he uses my Dad's speech patterns too) and mine.

Mine is the part in Gus that lectures Thurmond about getting off his ass and amounting to something. Dad's is the kinder part beneath the rough exterior. . . .

Yeah, I knew Sheridan Taylor** real well. We were very, very close friends. He faced his death with courage I couldn't believe. Just weeks before he died I went home with him from a party for me in Fort Worth—hell, he shouldn't have even been there given his condition—and all night long, in his sleep, I heard the poor bastard make the same long groans I had so long heard from Rosemarie. It was a long night. But I knew it was the last time I would ever see him, so when he decided to leave the party I left with him and we went to his house and sat around—just the two of us—bullshitting for a couple of hours; he never once mentioned the state he was in. And the next morning, when I was about to make an awkward last goodbye, dreading it like hell, he sensed it and jumped up and said, "Listen, you gotta get your ass outta here, I got things to do," and ran and called me a cab and almost shoved me out the door the minute it drove into view. And I was grateful for that. He saved us both some pain that morning. . . .

*Terry Pringle, West Texas novelist and memoirist.
**A Fort Worth attorney.

April 11, 1990

Dear Doctor Shrake:

The birds are tweeting and friends are grinning rightchere in the Mystic East, on account of Ann Richards beating that scurvy asthold Jim Mattox. *Washington Post* has a story longer than Joe Louis's dick about it today, but there is a lot of negative stuff about Ann. Such as how people were disappointed she engaged in mud-slinging herownself, that she goes into the race against [Republican] Clayton Williams "bruised and broke" and so on. I don't know whether those perceptions are accurate, but if so it seems to me Ann should begin working on getting her image back of being witty and saving the state money and being sort of a Good 'Ol Girl, (there's a *song* in that!). You may pass this intelligence on.

Jay Milner wrote the other day, "If Ann Richards is elected Governor, will that make Bud Shrake First Gentleman of Texas?" If that happens, maybe you should market T-shirts and buttons saying "I'm a Friend of the First Gentleman." I will take 37% of the profits for this nifty idea, and will promise to buy a T-shirt or button myownself.

Last I heard tell Ann had a 56-44 bulge about the time Mattox conceded. Hope it didn't slip down past 55%, and it would be wonderful if it came close to 60%, as I think that would help her down the line. But maybe that is giving the public too much credit for remembering. Probably, in the warp and woof of daily living, they couldn't tell you by noon tomorrow if she got 75% or 50.1% without being reminded. Those of us in "public bidness"—politics and writing and so on—probably think we're on the public mind a hell of a lot more than we are, though I personally know a little old lady in Des Moines who cannot hardly sleep at night for dwelling on my prose and career. I am sure you got fans like that in Chicago and Waco yourself.

I do not really know no news as I am still chatting to myself at this infernal word machine about eight or nine hours each day and do not see nothin' or hear nothin' that ain't in the newspapers or on television. I keep thinking I should bestir myself and live a more well-rounded life and all, but ever time I try I just want to come home and eat peanut butter and crackers and put on my jammies. I console myself by saying "Oh well, Lawrence, Doctor Shrake ain't been to town at night in nearly three years." I have purty much put in a rule that if I ain't *paid* to go to it, I ain't going to it. And even when I am paid it is usually an ordeal.

May the sweet ghost of Jesus haunt you in tender ways throughout the Easter Season. Hugs and stuff,

His Worship

May 9, 1990

Dear Terry:*

Well, this old dog has learned a new trick. I sold my first short story, "Something Went with Daddy," to *Story* magazine couple of weeks ago. You remember *Story?* It published a lot of early work by future-famous folk; Mailer sold his first yarn there while at Harvard, before WWII; Truman Capote got there with his third or fourth story. Anyway it was revived a year ago, about, as a Quarterly, and I saw an ad and subscribed. And so recently after reading the Spring issue I thought "Shit, I believe I'll see if I can do that"—first time I'd tried a short story in years—and, to my surprise, it sort of wrote itself, as they say, and I mailed it in and sold it. Got a zinging $250—*Story's* one-and-only price right now as they struggle—but will be glad to see it in print. (This is another example, incidentally, of my straying from pro-jects at hand when I am swamped with deadlines to do something not on the schedule. I think I am pathological about it. Maybe it is a reac-tion of resentments of deadlines, I don't know.). . .

*Terry Pringle

January 15, 1991

Dear Hank:*

I'm glad you wrote. I've missed hearing from you. And I, too, have a sackful of regrets about your never being in *Hank Williams* and wish I could re-make some decisions. But . . . the past can't be changed. Sometimes I wish I had never written that damned play. It caused more grief and disappointment than anything I've ever done. Great review in *New York Times* and various awards made me think it was headed for a commercial success, but in truth the investors—mostly my friends—lost most of their $400,000 and Drew Dennett lost about $50,000 himself. There was a Samuel French sale, yes, but nobody much has done it from that source. Drew couldn't afford to mount a tour, so that went to hell. Movie sale, yes, and I think I wrote a bet-ter screenplay than the play and it is supposed to start filming in the upcoming year (I mean 1991) but I hear little from Drew or the Silvers and have come to the conclusion they ain't levelling with me about money. In short, I believe they have not been able to raise it. But they leave me wondering and guessing. . . .

Stevie Phillips got in touch with all of us who created *Whorehouse* a few weeks ago to suggest a sequel. I thought she was flogging a dead horse. But she had some good ideas. We all met—Peter, Carol and I— and actually came up with a pretty good plot. So we have agreed to it, though contracts may not be easy to fashion. Terms are being discussed. Universal is again interested. So is Tommy Tune. Lots of details to work out. I want to bring back Ed Earl, of course. Pete originally said he didn't see a place for him. I think I've persuaded him otherwise. Ed Earl will allegedly come to Nevada "to go hunting"—he claims—but he really has come to see Mona. Ed Earl has always got to have somebody or something to cuss and stomp about, so he decides Mona is getting interested in another man—haven't worked out just whom—and hangs around to bust up the romance; eventually, he'll discredit the rival suitor, of course. Pete is now making an outline to turn over to me; Carol is writing the first song. I've said I won't work until we get contracts, and that's where we stand right now. Stay tuned.

On the personal front, I just had cataract surgery on my left eye as of ten days ago. Still kinda sore, but I can already see better and am told in about six weeks more it should afford good sight. I was just about blind in that eye until the surgery. . . . I remember fussing at you about three years ago when you were brooding about being "old" and now I am feeling the same way at sixty-two! . . . .

*Actor Henderson Forsythe, who won a Broadway "Tony" as the cussing old Sheriff Ed Earl Dodd in *The Best Little Whorehouse in Texas*.

February 22, 1991

Dear Reverend Doctor Shrake:

This letter is an unabashed endorsement of the mood-modifying drug Prozac—that's P-R-O-Z-A-C—which I was put on by medical science exactly eleven days ago, and is to be read aloud by you and Miz. Judy (Courtnay) Gent* wherever two or more people are gathered, night or day.

You will recall I had not been able to write nothing for months, and wanted to stay in the bed of a morning, and hide under the bed in the afternoon, and in the evenings thought a lot of jumping off tall bridges and the blessings of oblivion. And since taking the wonder drug Prozac for eleven days I am so light-hearted as to laugh long and loud at broken bones and/or death and taxes.

In eleven days I have wrote four scenes (26 pages) of *Whorehouse II*, a 3,000 word introduction to an upcoming TCU Press book, *Crazy Water*, by Gene Fowler, and a 3,000 word preface to my play *The Kingfish*, which SMU Press is publishing this fall, plus I have wrote about 200 letters and wrote—in my mind, anyhow—a 54,000 word oration I got in mind making at the U. N. I ain't had time to type the U. N. Address, though it is a fine one dealing with the burning issue of why do we need two Dakotas in the United States, on account of I been too busy outrunning deer, barking at rabbits, doing pushups, grinning at strangers, and singing Christmas Carols each noon hour at the intersection of Wisconsin and M Streets in Georgetown, which you would be surprised how good "Rudolph the Red Nosed Reindeer" sounds with a Reggae beat and bongo drums and hummed through a comb.

The only thing that slightly bothers me is Prozac makes me feel exactly like Speed did back in '65-'66 when my body was semi-virginal as to drugs, but then after two years of them little "diet" pills exploding in my head I got the amphetamine poisonin' and laid jangling and sweating and crying for several weeks before kickin' 'em. But, what the hell, at this juncture if I can have two good manic years of production I will trade it for another few weeks of sweating and whimpering, wouldn't you? Medical science tells me they ain't no side-effects to the wondrous drug Prozac except that it can make you sleepy *(hah!)* and be careful about driving cars or operating machinery; them is minor penalties, especially since I got so much energy I can move faster than cars. I figure anything this good is bound to have serious consequences eventually—there not being no free lunch—so probably my pecker will fall off in two or three years, but what the hell, sword-fighting ain't as important as it once was anyhow. Well, I got to quit and write some more on *Whorehouse II* and I am thinking of learning to speak German and got this urge to perfect my pole-vaulting technique. . . .

Happily,

*Shrake's assistant Jody Gent.

March 11, 1991

Dear Ol' Willie:

I think *New York Days* will be great. I've read your prospectus and I can't think of anything you've left out. I believe you have a good lock on what the book should contain, and great faith that you will execute it in the incomparable Willie Morris style. This should be a book that you'll find fun to write, as well as a valuable addition to the literary history of our period.

You might, in touching on your initial impressions of New York as a young man, want to hark back to other young writers—especially Southerners—and their first encounters with The Big Cave. Like Thomas Wolfe, Faulkner, maybe Tennessee Williams, Styron and others. There's some good stuff in Joseph Blotner's *Faulkner: A Biography* about when Mr. Bill first went to NY and stayed with Stark Young, working for awhile in a book store run by Elizabeth Prall, who later married Sherwood Anderson. In the up-dated one-volume Blotner that I have, that is chapter 12, pages 104-109. This was just before Faulkner went back home to become the worst postmaster in the history of the U.S. Mail.

What I recall most about that period—when you were first in New York and climbing the ladder, on through when you were Editor-in-Chief and I was writing for you—is the sense of excitement and of unlimited possibilities. And the energy—God, the *energy*—that we had. We vibrated with it, *shined* with it. I couldn't be still.

When flying into New York from D. C. I would be so revved up about seeing you and the others, of drinking and talking writing and spinning yarns, I could hardly contain myself. And I remember Jay Milner, when he was teaching at TCU and SMU in those years, telling me how everybody—students and faculty—could hardly wait for the next issue of *Harper's* because they knew it would be filled with the best writing of the time, issue after issue. And on the road, on assignment whether with Louie Armstrong or Nelson Rockefeller or Brother Dave Gardner or Harold Hughes—whomever—being so in tune as an observor, wanting to see and feel and capture and record everything. *Everything.* It was a heady time. . . .

November 16, 1992

Dear Rev. Doctor Stroke:

Thank you for that 1919 photo of you and Jap [Gary Cartwright], with Blackie Sherrod lurking in the background. I shall send it to the Southwest Writers Collection, along with many admiring notes wrote to me by Mark Twain, Harry S. Truman, Cecil B. DeMille, Robert E. Lee, Marilyn Monroe, Gorgeous George and Mrs. Rutherford B. Hayes. You will go down in History as one who knew me personal. Purty good for an old Paschal Boy, eh? . . .

Tall tap-dancin' Tommy Tune has now consented to meet with his artistic inferiors—myself, Pete Masterson, Carol Hall—on December 1st, 2nd or 3rd (whichever proves most inconvenient to us) about the *Whorehouse II* project; he will indulge in his usual eyebrow lifting, shrugs, and incomplete sentences, I am sure, and then—the next time we meet—express astonishment that we so failed to understand him. Tommy's favorite ploy is to shrug, raise eyebrow, wink, twitch, and say "Oh you *know* what I mean!" And when one of us—usually me—says, "Naw, Tommy, goddamnit, I *don't* know what you mean!"—we are treated to more twitches and shrugs and maybe the occasional *moue.*

Meanwhile, them ast-holds in Hollywood keep on sending stupid memos. I bet I could write stupid memos with the best of 'em, so how come they won't hire me at outrageous sums to do it? Personally, I think they are bigots when it comes to redneck farm boys. Just because we romanced heifers ought not to disqualify us artistically, should it?

I wisht I could have been a fly on the wall when you were out yonder in Tinseltown pitching them 12-year-old TV and movie executives. Never shall some twains meet. As for Bill Broyles being shocked at turning 48, fuck him and the horse he rode in on. Ast him how he'd like 64, which I turn on January 1, 19-and-93, assuming Jesus don't call me in the interim. It has happened far too fast. Ever since I turnt 60, and especially since I turnt 62, I cannot open my junk mail without being addressed as "Dear Senior Citizen" in pitches trying to sell me burial plots, exotic insurance, discount subway tokens, catheters, prosthetics, memory courses, wigs, tomes on How To Enjoy Sex Though Far Past It, and nostalgia items dating back to Theodore Roosevelt. God knows what shall be wrought once I reach 65—which, sob! sob!—am only one year and six weeks away—but I would reckon it to include discount cremations and pleas to leave my vital organs to Medical Science. Occasionally, though, I get the odd left-handed compliment, as when my 10-year-old son Blaine, recently said: "A lot of kids say it's bad to have an old Dad like you, but I don't think so. Most of the time. . . ." This was uttered after I pled fatigue when he wanted me to play a game of soccer in the back yard, and then join him in climbing several trees.

Yeah, I seen that yours and Harvey's *Little Red Book* is selling its ast off. Do you—hopefully—get some good royalties, or did you do a stupid and take it for a flat fee?. . . *

His Worship

* Shrake and Austin golf teacher Harvey Penick's golf instruction book became the best-selling sports book ever, and Shrake did not take a flat fee.

Editor's Note: At the request of Judith Martin ("Miss Manners") Larry L. King wrote a formal letter to Washington's exclusive Cosmos Club recommending John Daniel Reaves for membership. Reaves, a Washington attorney/actor, several times played Huey Long in *Kingfish*. King was asked to speak to the category "known to be cultivated."

June 30, 1993

Admissions Committee
Cosmos Club
2121 Mass. Avenue, N.W.
Washington, D.C. 20008

Dear Ladies and Gentlemen:

It may seem passing strange that someone who has written a musical comedy entitled *The Best Little Whorehouse in Texas* should presume to recommend a candidate for membership in the Cosmos Club in the category "Known To Be Cultivated." I would plead that I have also written more serious and decent plays and books, was a Nieman Fellow at Harvard and held endowed teaching chairs at Princeton and Duke Universities.

The candidate I recommend is one John Daniel Reaves, a lawyer who also studied drama while at Auburn University. Mr. Reaves is a native, I believe, of Camp Hill, Alabama; I cannot vouch for the cultivated qualities of Camp Hill, only of Mr. Reaves.

Mothers, girl friends, and at least one wife in the past remarked to me that they wished I had the cultural qualities of Mr. Reaves, his politeness, his courteousness, his gentleness and general *savoir faire* and *savoir vivre*. But I like him anyway.

Beyond knowing John Daniel Reaves as a friend, I know him best as an actor and writer. I directed him in the title role of my play, *The Kingfish*, in 1979; I saw him perform as H. L. Mencken in a one-man show he also authored; I have good reviews of his performances in *Molloy* at Nantucket Theatre. I know Mr. Reaves not only to read books, but to talk of books intelligently. It would not surprise me to learn that he is an *aficionado* of opera, though I have never been positioned to catch him committing opera. It could be that he speaks Latin; certainly he dresses well, performs civic chores and church work. He is good to his family and pays his just debts. He tells funny stories well and is good enough to laugh at mine.

What more could one ask of a cultivated man? . . .

October 23, 1993

Dear Dr. Holland:

Can't recollect if I wrote you about the big bash for Willie Morris at Elaine's. I was astounded by the Old Fart quality of the gathering; apparently I am the only one who has remained youthful and handsome. Everybody else was old and withered and as ugly as Oink Jones. Men and women I once knew well flang themselves on me with glad cries, in most cases calling me by my right name, and I had to read name-plates through my bi-focals to have any idea who was slobbering on me. Among those I did not recognize at first blush were Jules Feiffer and Gloria Jones. Styron, whom I had last seen two or three years ago, looked truly old and about half-deef. I saw folks yawning way past their bedtimes and staring off into space without purpose. It was, to tell the truth, a bit depressing—especially since the P. R. ace Bobby Zarem, whom I have known since the Battle of David and Goliath, kept slapping me on the back while calling me "Charlie." I can only surmise his eyesight has went. Of course, I must confess to a gaff or two of my own: I called Howell Raines "Mike" three different times, until he rather churlishly properly identified hisself. And I addressed Jean Stein as Jean Vandenheuvel for fifteen minutes until she pointedly said she had been divorced from Mr. Vandenheuvel for almost 20 years. Finally I became one of them what slipped into a corner chair and stared off vacantly into space. . . .

Couple of nights later I went to a dinner party at a restaurant in Virginia for Willie—mainly Mississippians in these parts—and the party so needed livening up that I stood and publicly sang "Jesus On the Five Yard Line," a thing I had not done in concert ever before when sober. The applause was gratifying.

Tommy Tune and his entourage are getting a bit hard to take during the *Whorehouse II* rehearsals. There is no doubt that Tune flirts with genius at what he does, but now he thinks he is a genius at everything and stamps his pretty little size 13 tap-dancin' foot if and when questioned by his inferiors, which he makes pretty clear is all of the rest of us. My goal is to get through these next two weeks of rehearsals without slapping his cute little jaws. I have won one verbal decision over him and scuffled to a draw on two others, which puts me miles ahead of the rest of us no-talent folks. Even to *question* his autocratic decisions earns dark looks and mutters and frosty receptions from his ass-kissing entourage. . . .

Do good works for God and Country, Doctor.

November 9, 1993

Dear Frank and Alix:*

Sorry I didn't deliver on my promise to get you two invited to a run-through of *The Best Little Whorehouse Goes Public,* but a mutiny occurred among my collaborators when I turned in your names as my guests. Tommy Tune and the "Tunettes"—as I call his hangers-on and yes-men—had conniptions, claiming it would give nervous breakdowns to the cast. (The only exception being Phil Ostermann, who was afraid to tell Tommy but told *me* he thought they were nuts: "How many playwrights or producers could get those two to attend a workshop performance?") Peter Masterson pled the same "nervous cast" defense; Carol Hall thought I was crazy because she was afraid the performance wouldn't be good enough. Stevie Phillips was actually for your being there, but wouldn't fight Tommy about it and he is, as you know, the 800-pound gorilla where Universal-MCA is concerned. I was really pissed and so announced my state of mind but felt if I insisted and you *did* come and then things somehow went wrong I would be blamed from here to eternity.

Nothing went wrong as it turned out. In fact, last Friday's run-through was little short of a triumph. Within minutes of the presentation the two big shots from MCA and Universal officially signed on, releasing the big money. Had about 300 people there, who whooped and roared all the way through it. Joel Gray couldn't be effusive enough; Keith Carradine said it was good to see "next year's big hit this early." But the main thing was people laughed where they were supposed to, loved the score—by far better than the first—and the performers came through. My wife, Barbara, thinks it's much better as a theatrical piece than the first *Whorehouse*. I feel good about it, though three or four scenes need some work—mainly my book, I must confess—and we're getting back to work on those scenes shortly after Thanksgiving in order to go to rehearsals again at the Nederlander on February 28th for five or six weeks.

I think things went better than I would have anticipated although I find life among tap-dancers to be even less fun than formerly and *never* will do another musical. Just takes too much time out of my life: three years on this one to date, with several months to go, and I have neither the energy, need nor desperation to go through it again as a man about to be 65 years old come January 1st. I want to finish my play *The Dead Presidents' Club* next, then finish my long dormant baseball novel, maybe publish a collection of short stories and then I think I'll take it to the barn. . . .

Phil Ostermann said when I called my collaborators together to tell them I would be inviting you two, that they "kept waiting for the punch line. They thought it was a joke." Then, when they realized I was serious, "their faces suddenly looked like bunched fists." I wound up rather half-liking Ostermann, though I know his main job is to spy for Tommy and report what he hears. I frankly used this: when something did not go to suit me, I threw fits for Phil's benefit. He then ran and told Tommy, who then came to me in a more conciliatory mood than would have been the case otherwise. Usually I won my point.

Trying to confront Tommy in person doesn't work as well: he hates
confrontations—read: anyone who disputes him—and usually goes
off to pout. Somehow, with Phil acting as the go-between it worked
out better than I might have imagined. . . .

*Frank Rich and his wife, Alix Witchell, both of *The New York Times.*

November 9, 1993

Dear Brother Hemphill:*

Hoo Boy, if you think selling books is tough just try to get a play
produced:

Yeah, I got lucky with the original *Whorehouse*—how it all came
about was a fluke—and because of the success of it we are now bringing out a sequel, *The Best Little Whorehouse Goes Public* and I've just
returned from a workshop production of it in New York. Universal
Pictures has put up the money now for a commercial production. . . .
and if it works, will bring it to Broadway. But those are *musicals.*
Getting straight plays produced isn't easy and they don't really make
any money in most cases even when you get them produced, unless
your name is Neil Simon, Wendy Wasserstein, Chris Durang, or a
half-dozen others.

In the enclosed copy of my play *The Night Hank Williams Died* you'll
find, in the Preface, some of the glitches and problems quite common
to getting straight plays produced. *Hank* went on to a pretty good life
and still gets the odd production here and there, but despite rave
reviews—including in the all-mighty *New York Times*—my producer
and investors lost about $300,000. I made about $50,000 most of
which came from the Samuel French Company which publishes acting versions of the plays and then takes a piece of royalties of all future
productions. But since *Hank* didn't do all that well for Samuel French,
they have not bought my other plays. . . . Still, I consider myself a
"lucky" playwright in that all of my plays have been produced and
that isn't true of 9 of 10 playwrights. In short, it's a tough market and
a tough process.

To answer your questions: no, there generally is no up-front development money. There are exceptions: a given theatre might be interested in a given playwright and offer him or her development money. Or a commercial producer might put up development money if (1) he thinks the play or the playwright has a chance to make money, but these are rare indeed. I got only a $6,000 advance for the new *Whorehouse* and have worked three years to date!

In short, almost all plays are written on "spec." Then you have to find either a commercial producer to put up the money or more likely, find a non-profit theater or a regional theatre, in which case you may be competing with dozens or even hundreds of other scripts and most such theatres only do four to six or eight plays per year, tops. If you get such a production you won't get more than $1,000 in front money— and that will be charged against any royalties the play earns; the playwright's royalties range from six to 10 per cent, depending on how good a deal you can make. A production at a small theater—and most non-profits are small, seating from 125 to maybe 350—running, say, for four or five weeks probably would not return royalties much above your original $1,000 front money. If the play gets good reviews in its original production, and does good business, then perhaps it will be picked up by a commercial producer as happened with *Hank* after productions at small non-profit theaters here and in Austin.

Or it may not: my play *The Golden Shadows Old West Museum* had good runs in Little Rock, Austin, Washington and is scheduled for a production soon in Fort Worth and another in Houston, but thus far not a glimmer of an interested commercial producer is to be found. (Commercial producers put up, or raise through investors, the money necessary to produce a show which includes paying the cast, backstage crew, technicians for lighting and sound, costumes, set designer, insurance, theatre rental and the playwright. Even a four or six person cast can wind up costing $250,000 or more to mount—and that does not include money for advertising, merely the bare bones—in a commercial theatre Off-Broadway. Maybe a bit less in commercial theatres elsewhere, but not a lot less.) All of my "straight" plays have received good notices—see quotes on the three enclosed—and got published as well as produced. And, to the last in number, they lost money for their commercial producers. . . . Frankly, the only way I can afford to write "straight" plays is because (1) my wife subsidizes me during the long writing and production process with her lawyer's career and (2) *Whorehouse* made me a "known" theatrical commodity and producers are more willing to bet on me than they would an unknown. But, still, it ain't easy. . . .

If your connections in Atlanta and Seattle like your play and come through for you, then something might happen to keep the play alive: i.e., getting productions at other theatres or even the bonus of finding a commercial producer. Lightning *can* strike, but to be honest it rarely does. One of the problems is that there is no central place a playwright can make his work known or get his play read: you have to send them out on a one-shot basis, willy-nilly to many theatres, where—because of a lack of money to hire people to go through the plays and read them; or because theatrical folk seem to be badly organized—your manuscript might gather dust for six months or a year or forever without your ever hearing a word. And often, I've found, the first-readers are kids just out of school and what they know about plays could be stuffed in a thimble and still have room to rattle around.

If you know somebody in a drama department at a college or university, you might get some help in having a live reading of your play—this can help you hear it and understand the difference between how something reads and how it sounds—or even a workshop production of it. No play ever has been written that didn't require rewriting somewhere in the rehearsal process—unless maybe ol' Willie Shakespeare got his lines right the first time—and workshop productions are ideal for this. I used Memphis State University, where the head of the theatrical department was an old friend from Texas, to develop both *Hank* and *Golden Shadows*. The latter got its first production at Arkansas Repertory in Little Rock, because we persuaded their artistic director to come to Memphis State to see a performance during our workshop.

Don't let this report discourage you: go ahead, write your play, and see what happens. I *love* writing for theater and think you probably will. Send me some of the work later on and I'll give you my comments if you'd like, with the understanding that I might be wrong as hell. (One of the things you'll find is that everyone who reads your play will tell you something different.) I just wanted to let you know you'll be in for hair-pulling frustrations. But I ain't saying don't do it. Go for it!

Just called the bookstore and they have your *Leaving Birmingham* so I'll pick up a copy tomorrow. . . .

*Paul Hemphill, an old friend of LLK's, is a Georgian who in Atlanta and San Francisco was a successful newspaper columnist; he has written award-winning nonfiction books, novels and many magazine articles.

December 17, 1993

Dear Stevie:*

Okay, I ain't ever worked on Madison Avenue but I think we might do well in our Print Ads to stress a little more than the semi-nude showgirl in her cowboy boots. Could there not be something hinting at Washington and/or Wall Street? The script deals with much more than S-E-X, and while I know everybody sells everthing from cars to toothpaste with at least subliminal doses of pussy, I ask the musical question—as did Peggy Lee—"Is That All There Is?"

I'm afraid we may be hoisting ourselves, commercially, on our own sex-oriented petard, and I'm afraid this may make not only the asshole critics but the hoity-toity and Limousine Liberals curve their mouths into permanent sneers—as well as those who have the notion from our first show that we are outsider Freaks or Accidents—and to think of us as a Carnival and not a Legitimate Show. *And we are much more than that, this time out!*

So come on, give us a bit of variety! This ain't a one-note show and should not be advertised as a one-note show. I ain't saying it's opera or ballet, no, but it's more than we're telling people—and that, I think, can hurt us at the box office and with the Tony folks and others. Think about it! Talk to me! And to others!

Somewhat grumpily Yours,

*Stephanie Phillips produced both *Whorehouse* musicals for the stage.

March 30, 1994

Dear Doctor Shrake:

Speaking of you and Gov. Richards,* we talked on the phone a few days ago and she pretended to write down on her Calendar the Broadway opening date of *Hohouse Two*—which is May 10—and claimed you two will be there. . . . Don't let her book a speech to Meskin Field Workers or the Alliance of Lesbian Dog Trainers or something in her insatiable search for votes, if it's gonna mess up yawl's attending our opening. Only thing I hate about the opening is they are calling for "Fancy Dress" which means Tuxes for us pecker-owners and I reckon $5,000 gowns, jewels and baubles for them that ain't got none. I have grew so fat I don't know if my Tux still fits. If it don't, I may buy a larger cummerbund or whatever it's called and strop it crost my spreading belly just above Bluejeans heighth.

I just returned from your hometown, Fort Worth, where Circle Theater is doing a month-long run of *The Golden Shadows Old West Museum.* They booked me on every damn TV and radio talk show in the Metroplex Triangle or whatever they call it. They expected me to talk about *Golden Shadows* but mainly I tried to sell tickets to *Hohouse II* on account of they cost more and I get a bigger dollar than I do with *Golden Shadows* tickets. As has been proved many times, I will do nearly anything for Ort. In my spare time I drove around Fort Worth staking out places I think that your statue should be established, and done so many I run plumb out of stobs. (You understand, of course, each Statue will show you polishing my shoes; I stand upright; you stoop. And since your head is down, looking at my shoes, you might be hard to identify. But it's the Thought that counts.)

After my Cowtown adventures I flew out to West Texas, rented a car and drove to Odessa to see my 80-year-old brother, who is in a home for the decrepit. And he surely is. He went from reality to wild fantasy and blank looks—again and again—during my three-hour visit, which was all of it I could stand, what with old folks singing a backup concert of gurgles, screams, coughs, cries, hollars, chants, and giggles. Surreal. (Though probably a glimpse of our future, Doctor, without we jump off of something high while we can still climb.) My brother does not know, or refuses to remember, that our two sisters are dead. He also told yarns of having driven himself to Brownfield, Seminole and Hobbs, N. M. recently. Unlikely, since he weighs 86 pounds and has to be lifted from bed-to-wheelchair. You'd think if he was gonna make fantasy trips he'd go to better places. . . . My, my, my, what grim jokes God plays on the old! Kinda weird to go straight from two performances of my play about people in an old folks home to the real thing. I don't wanta see nothing but Young 'Uns for the next month! . . .

P. S. Blaine King, age 11 1/2, just romped in showing me an item he sent to *Zillions* magazine a few weeks ago and damn if they didn't *print* it! The little shit! I sent stuff to magazines my whole childhood and didn't nobody print squat. I now see him as a writing rival. He is in for a rough year.

*Ann Richards, then Texas governor, a close friend of Bud Shrake. After she assumed office King and his other friends began referring to Shrake as "The First Guy."

April 29, 1994

Dear Cousins:

No, I haven't fallen into some black hole. Last Friday—week ago today—I was working away on my novel, about 1:30 P.M., when Producer Stevie Phillips called with panic in her voice and said she needed me "immediately" in New York. I asked if Tommy Tune was agreeable and she said "He wants you here *now*. He *needs* you. Can you be here for tonight's show and then meet with the creative team the minute the show's over?"

So I threw some ragged jeans in a suitcase and headed out. Problem was some of our "book" scenes had been revamped—without my being consulted—and we had long stretches of "dead air." Also, I think, some ill-considered acting approaches in one scene. Made a bunch of notes—mainly first act stuff—and at the meeting later (myself, Tune, Hall, Masterson, Phillips, Jeff Calhoun and Associate Director Phillip Osterman) in the Marriott Marquis across the street from the Lunt-Fontanne I reported on what I'd seen wrong with what Tommy Tune called my "fresh eye." ("We've been so close to it so long we can't see the forest for the trees," he said.) What I said was accepted by all, though Pete Masterson seemed a bit less than enchanted. (Was told later by another at the meeting that he had told Phillips and Tune I "wasn't needed," for reasons I can only guess: one being that he somehow hates change once he decides he likes something.)

Anyway, I was a virtual prisoner in my hotel room—except when across the street at rehearsals from 1 P.M. to 5 P.M. each day—rewriting parts of three first-act scenes, working on one scene in the second act, cutting the odd line here and there, writing new lines here and there. We put the new stuff in at rehearsals on Monday and Tuesday, using it the same nights. Tuesday night's preview performance went wonderfully well, though I recommended a few cuts in our Senate Hearing scene—perhaps getting into it later, as the opening parts tell us only what we already knew—and they began putting that in yesterday. Tommy, Jeff and Carol and Stevie said good things of what I'd done; Pete said little or nothing. Perhaps this was because I criticized—as gently as possible—some of the direction and staging in a couple of books scenes. I'm sorry if it hurt his feelings, but I thought he had our I. R. S. Director (Kevin Cooney) playing too broadly too soon and recommended that he bring the performance down.

I don't know what to think about the show at this point, only a dozen nights before officially opening. Much of it is very good, some of it is less than good. We are increasingly getting better crowd reaction, but those who don't like it—I'd guess about 10 per cent from observing in the theatre and circulating among patrons at intermission and after the show—*really* don't like it. What is puzzling is that during our workshop production last fall and early in previews, we were getting excellent word-of-mouth in the show biz community; now we are getting some slams. (Although I sat behind the cast of *Guys and Dolls* last Monday night when they had the night off, and they whooped and cheered and truly seemed to like it.)

I think some of it may be the "artsy" folk looking down their noses, some may be that we have an "outsider" producer who isn't noted for friendly communications, some may be our p. r. man is not well-liked in the theatrical community and some may be that we aren't as good as we thought. On the other hand, I think the show is now tightened and better than when good things were being said earlier. Who the hell knows? To counter balance the *Guys and Dolls* folks' good reactions, I sat by Carol Channing and her husband one night—them having no inkling of who I was—and they snorted and fumed against the show throughout. Carol Hall may have said a perceptive thing when we talked on the phone yesterday afternoon—at least I *hope* she did—when she said, "It's like the last time, Larry. The theatrical community didn't like us then, and the public did."

Bad sign: we have only sold a bit over $400,000 in advance tickets where the Tune revival of *Grease* has sold about $3 million in advance. Good sign: Though we are only in Previews, the Outer Circle Critics—critics from New Jersey, Pennsylvania, Connecticut, and New York outside of Manhattan—have nominated us as "Best New Musical" and Dee Hoty as "Best Actress in a Musical." It's like that up and down the board: good signs, bad signs. I have a notion we may get slammed by David Richards of the *New York Times*—he hated first *Whorehouse* [when at the *Washington Post*] and *The Kingfish* and was mild about *Hank Williams*—and I simply have no idea what Clive Barnes of the *Post* (loved first *Whorehouse*) or Howard Kissell of the *Daily News* (despised *Hank Williams*) will do. John Simon? Hated first *Whorehouse*, was o.k. about *Hank* and loved *The Kingfish*. Go figure.

We have this big damned white horse—"Snow"—that Dee Hoty and Scott Holmes ride on for curtain call (Scott, a New Jersey boy, hating and fearing horses, provides amusement to us by his obviously uneasy manner) and the crowd goes ape-shit. Okay, Tuesday we changed the curtain call drill, but *no one thought to cue the horse or the horse's professional handler.* So when the handler pushes the horse forward, backstage to get it started, it comes on stage and sees that *things are different!* It had been trained to come onto an empty stage and now it sees the whole cast running off stage and it thinks *No! I'm not supposed to enter here!* So it stopped, dead. Dee Hoty made the mistake of digging it in the ribs. It shyed, almost reared, and Scott Holmes' eyes got big as saucers. And the horse simply wouldn't go on to its appointed place at center stage, hanging back out of the spotlight. Well, the horse handler cursed us and screamed because no one had remembered to tell her and let her re-program the horse. So on Tuesday, after Pete and I were on TV on that American Theater Wing thing, and I was leaving to catch a plane home, he said, somewhat grumpily, "Now I've got to go rehearse the godamned horse!" I broke up. They've rehearsed him ever since, and Carol Hall said yesterday he is getting better but still a little uncertain. Apparently not having the right cue disordered the horse's mind!

Ain't no bidness like show bidness, for sure!

Well, enough. Seems I am leaving a thing or two out I meant to relate. Will write addendum if I think of 'em. . . .

P. S. Just remembered one thing I left out. Packing hastily for New York last Friday, I did not exercise due care. On Tuesday, 15 minutes before I was to go to the theatre for new put-ins, I was dressing after my shower and suddenly found my only remaining blue jeans—the others having been sent to one-day laundry service two hours earlier—so small I couldn't get two legs in them. Close inspection revealed they were Barbara's. So there I sat, no britches, due at the theatre in 15 minutes. Frantic call to son Brad. He found it hilarious, but dutifully rushed out and bought me a pair that would fit. I was only 10 minutes late, thanks to his quick assistance. Weird feeling to be in Manhattan naked in the middle of the day! (Without a *Partner,* anyhow!) Ah, Show Biz!

May 3, 1994

Dear Cousins:

For the record—though I would hope you'd keep it to yourself until the votes are in—this is the day when I faced the fact that *The Best Little Whorehouse Goes Public* is likely to be a flop. Last night—the first preview night our Producer failed to "paper the house" with 500 or so freebie tickets, we had a theater only 2/3rds full, I am told, and not a good performance by the cast. I think they feel a lack of enthusiasm and hope—most of our publicity being negative and about our slow ticket sales—and they also may be influenced by the word in the theatrical community that our show won't last. Last night's tepid performance, I am told, was matched by a tepid reception from the audience: our first, in point of fact, but that is not a good sign considering that we open one week from tonight.

Yesterday I was interviewed by some guy from the newspaper *USA Today* and he wanted to talk about two things: our disastrous "Infomercial" ad campaign, and whether, in this age of AIDS and safe sex, we are not being foolish in doing another show about a whorehouse. Much the same several days ago when I was interviewed by a reporter from *New York Newsday,* except he also got into the L. King-T. Tune feud. There has yet to be one positive story in any publication and I see none on the horizon. In fact, the two interviews just referred to will appear on the weekend just before our opening. We've already had negative yarns re: advertising and sagging ticket sales in *N.Y. Times, Wall Street Journal,* and *N.Y. Post.* These are self-fulfilling prophesies, I fear. If everyone writes that the sky is falling, then more than likely the sky will fall. We are at the point where we can be saved by only two things: (1) great or at least very good reviews and (2) positive word-of-mouth. I much doubt we will get the former and certainly we are not getting the latter among Show Biz types; problem is, we can't get good word-of-mouth from the masses unless the masses show up, and it does not look as if they will.

I am still having a hard time rhyming the usual audience reaction to the show—ranging from good to excellent for the most part—with what is happening commercially and in the publicity. They are almost at opposite ends of the pole. But those who don't like the show hate it as much or more as those who do like it love it. And while I'd guess that at only 10%, the fact is that the antis are more vocal than the pros. I guess I will be awhile in sorting all this out in my mind—how we went from such great enthusiasm in the Show Biz community during last fall's workshop to being slam-dunked by the same folks, more or less, here in the time when it really counts. I ask myself "Have we glitzed the show up too much, have the cuts in the book hurt us, did Tommy Tune make a mistake in several times saying publicly 'I have never had a Broadway flop and I don't intend to start now,' is the bad advertising campaign and the miserable publicity (by which I mean lack of it) campaign done us in? Or is the show simply not as good as we thought? Or is it good but has no shot because of factors mentioned above and those enumerated in my letter to you of a few days ago?"

I can't tell you the "whys." I *can*, unfortunately, tell you I feel a small death coming on. And I wanted to prepare you for likely bad news, just as I intend to tell my gathering family in New York, not to be shocked if and when we fold our tents and try to silently slip away. . . .

Friday, May 13, 1994
(An appropriate date for this letter!)

Dear Lanvil and Glenda:

Hoo, Boy! Let the record show that on May 10th I opened *The Best Little Whorehouse Goes Public* and Willie Nelson got busted for pot. Willie got better Press than I did, so apparently my crime was the larger. And that young kid who got his ass caned in Singapore? He took his licks in private; I was caned as publicly as it can be done.

Few of the critics may be accused of human kindness (understatement of the year) to me or anyone else in the show but I took a couple of licks undeserved. Example: *USA Today* personally blamed me for a fart joke that actually was a lyric in one of Carol Hall's songs, the joke being complicated by Tommy Tune's having a bunch of Cowboys and Cowgirls fan their hats to drive away the fumes. I don't know if that one got pinned on me out of vitriol or carelessness, but the bottom line is it doesn't really make a damn since our canings were so universal and blame assigned to all, in general.

First review I read, shortly after dawn in my room at the Marriott Marquis across the street from the scene-of-the-crime Lunt-Fontanne Theater, was by David Richards of *The New York Times*. Mr. Richards accused me of a "jerry-built book . . . a series of stillborn sketches . . . lame jokes." I was about half-pissed off at him until I read Howard Kissel in the *New York Daily News*, who opined that Pete Masterson and I took "quite promising material" and from it "concocted cliched skits" in which "much of the humor may have been gathered from comedy writers' wastebaskets, since it is not funny enough for prime-time" and said our story was "crudely told, with pathetic interludes in which a Vegas emcee tells feeble jokes." *That* almost inspired me to call David Richards and say, "Hey, Old Pal, come on over for coffee!" Linda Winer of *New York Newsday* (who wanted me put in jail for having written *The Night Hank Williams Died*) stopped just short of calling me a child molester this time, her tender mercies including a crack about "what we'll euphemistically call their 'work'"—meaning yrs. trly and Masterson—and going on to find us "idiotic" and "pretentious." Clive Barnes—who liked the first *Whorehouse*—wrote—under a headline saying OH, BROTHEL! THIS IS AWFUL! that the book is "a curiosity wrapped in a cliche." After that, he got nasty. If "misery loves company" then I must be overjoyed, because we *all* got pasted except for Dee Hoty and Scott Holmes—Tune, Jeff Calhoun, Carol Hall, comic Jim David; say a name and likely the owner was fetched at least one blow.

It's not just that we received "bad" reviews, Cousins; it's as if the New York critics were so angry and hated us so much they decided to kill us by sticking the dagger deep in all hearts. Bill Goldman, the screenwriter and novelist, told Pete Masterson, "I have a long memory but it's not long enough to remember an outpouring of vitriol like this." And in his Broadway column in today's *New York Times*, Bruce Weber did us the honor of calling *HoHouse II* "the most universally reviled

Broadway show in memory." (This means we will become a running joke, like such spectacular failures as *Moose Murders, Breakfast at Tiffany's* and *The Three Musketeers*—each of which ran one performance and lost millions; after I am dead, probably, bad reviews will begin "Not since *The Best Little Whorehouse Goes Public* has such a sorry mishmash shown its face on a Broadway stage," etcetera.) Skip Hollandsworth, in and out of N.Y. during the past two weeks while writing a piece on the show for *Texas Monthly*, called me yesterday and said "Godamighty! I've never seen such uniformly bad stuff! I may be as crazy as the JFK conspiracy theorists, but it almost seems as if the critics got together in one room and plotted to assassinate you." Except for them all gathering in one room—unless it was in the Lunt-Fontanne!—I think he's right. And after talking with Pete and Carol and others—though not Tommy Tune; he didn't speak to me the last five days I was in New York and I think I was the only member of the Creative Team and the Production Team that he did *not* invite to his apartment for a late party after the official Opening Night party—and after thinking on it with some introspection, I believe I know some reasons why we were belabored with such glee. (This may take awhile, so go refill your iced-tea glass, Lanvil.)

When we did the workshop production last fall in New York, we had many from the theatrical community cheering us and going ape; the word went out that we were on the way to being the new big hit. Joel Gray, who had tears running down his cheeks during the "It's Been Awhile" duet by Dee and Scott, turned so far around that when he attended a Preview about a week ago all he said was "Loved the curtain call white horse!" and then scurried away like his britches were on fire, with—I am told—"a little smirk" on his face. And I think that typified our going from being a rumored hot hit to a certain flop in the minds of theatrical types even though they were seeing the same show dressed up. The question begging to be answered is "Why?" I think there are several answers, and they are as follows:

(1) I believe our unfortunate half-hour Infomercial did us in. Or at least started the slide that led to the avalanche. I think it was not a bad *idea* by Stevie Phillips—trying to find a new way to sell tickets—

but it was badly executed. It stressed only one thing: the sex in the show. And did it in a cheap and gaudy way. I complained, Barbara complained, Carol Hall complained, Peter Masterson complained. But Tommy Tune did not complain; he liked it. It could have been made more acceptable had they cut out and substituted for some four or five minutes in the film, and that would have been easy enough to do; indeed, Stevie Phillips finally *said* she would do it. But she didn't. By the time she realized it was both an artistic and commercial disaster, and pulled it from the air, the damage was done. The "Theatrical Community" was offended, thinking we had tainted all—not just ourselves—and that's when the bad vibes and revisionist thinking began. The shame is, we did it to ourselves.

(2) When the Infomercial failed to sell tickets in great lots, the rumors of a "disaster" started and the hounds were quick to pick up the scent. Thereafter, most of the pre-Opening feature articles began—or somewhere included—a line something like this: "Advance sales are only $300,000 and should be around two million dollars;" when advance sales reached $500,000 suddenly we should have sold three million or four million. The revival of *Grease*—the writers pointed out—had sold $3 million in advance, *Beauty and the Beast* $8 million, and so on. All of that was accurate—except maybe for arbitrary figures being manufactured as to how much we *should* have sold—but the point is, anybody reading that people were determinedly not buying tickets were *not* likely to prove themselves fools by rushing out and buying a batch.

(3) Because Stevie Phillips had poured $350,000 into the making of the Infomercial—plus the $150,000 or perhaps more that it cost to air it—our advertising budget was crippled. Full page ads cost $56,000 in the Sunday *New York Times* and we could afford but a couple. And *they* didn't say much about the show: tried to exploit the sex-and-Tommy-Tune connection only. Stevie did *not* hire an ad agency— unheard of!—and thus we had no professional outsider's touch. She *did*, unfortunately, hire a p.r. man who neither pees nor rrs with much effectiveness: one whom, I know by the authority of Frank Rich, cannot get his telephone calls returned by most in the theatrical depart-

ment at the *New York Times*. Two weeks ago he did not even have Press Kits available (authority: Skip Hollandsworth, *Texas Monthly*) and the day after our disastrous opening they were *still* not available! (Authority: Carol Cling, writer-critic of the *Las Vegas Review-Journal*). At a time when Sondheim and his new show, *Passions*, and *Beauty and the Beast* and *Grease* were getting a lot of ink, one could hardly find a *Whorehouse* story that didn't dwell on the negative sales. I personally got *Texas Monthly*, *The Washingtonian*, *Las Vegas Review-Journal*, *The Dallas Morning News*, and *Playboy* to attempt features; all reported no cooperation from the P. R. guy and a pictorial in *Playboy* was flat turned down by the powers that be. My reward for taking the bull by the horns—when no one in authority even saw the goddam bull—was a charge from Stevie Phillips that I had created "a sense of panic" about our show. Curious. Even more curious: we were the only show on Broadway *never* to put up a large poster in Shubert Alley in the theatrical district . . . or anywhere else. In short, we had a terrible advertising and p.r. campaign.

(4) I believe all this made it easy for theatrical writers to take an easy leap forward to strike a blow against the reigning Broadway King, Tommy Tune. Tommy shot himself in the foot—or at least gave the theatrical writers and critics ammo to shoot him—by saying in every interview (and in the dreaded Infomercial)—"I have never had a Broadway flop and I don't intend to start with *The Best Little Whorehouse Goes Public*." Well, shit, is that a challenge or what? It was the first time I had seen Tune's private arrogance be allowed to go public—he has been very good, in the past, at hiding his dictatorial chickenshittery behind a sweet-guy public facade and has done it charmingly and well—and the results accumulated as another piece of the disaster pie. It was fatal to him, and to the show, as evidenced by the clubbings he personally suffered from the critics: the first time that had happened to him. (He called Carol Hall the day of the shitty reviews with the plaintive wail: "Why do they *hate* us so? Why all the *anger?*" Perhaps I should send him a copy of this letter by way of answering his questions!) The critics decided to kick his ass, in short, and he helped by not being *consistently* good in his choreography: that,

too, was something of a first. Oh, he had a couple of good production numbers, but several were mediocre—for him—and at least one truly in lamentable bad taste even for me. (Fat, balding dancers jumping around grabbing their gonads during the "Telephone Sex" number.) I think Tommy had aroused the not-too-latent jealousy of the critics by a string of successes and winning all those Tony awards—most ever in Broadway history by one individual over a career—and once he permitted his private arrogance to go public he was a dead man long-overdue for a burial, in the critics' eyes, and they obliged.

(5) For reasons I cannot understand, the New York Theatrical Community fears and hates the "Hollywoodization" of sacred Broadway. Why should it matter that West Coast money comes to be spent in the East? Indeed, should that not be a *plus* if one really *cares* about Broadway? But for the past few years, theatrical writers have been pissing and moaning about the "Hollywoodization" of Broadway being some sort of threat while—on the other hand—crying of the dearth of new, original American musicals. It seems obvious to me that this "dearth"—and it is a real one—is because big musicals cost so much now that investors fear to risk the losses. Example: original *Whorehouse* had a weekly running cost of about $100,000; *Whorehouse II* has a weekly running cost of $412,000. Takes no genius to figure that in the former case one can let the show build slowly, on word-of-mouth, while now successes must come quickly or you must fold your show tent to stop serious financial hemorrhaging, and fold it early, because you can drop a couple of million very quickly. If we close the show next week—a good possibility—then Universal Pictures-MCA will be out *at least* $8 million bucks, perhaps more, and nothing to show for it: obviously, if you can't tour a show long enough to make its name a household word—and if your reviews are as bad as ours have been—then the movie rights become worthless. And movie rights are why they put up the money in the first place.

These elemental facts seem somehow beyond the elemental grasps of theatrical writers, so they worry about "Hollywoodization." (The *real* danger of "Hollywoodization," I think, escapes the critics: and that is the turning over to one person of the creative team—in our case Tommy Tune—*all* power so that no meaningful input gets into a show from other sources; stars and directors have that unhealthy power in movies, and now they are trying to bring that to Broadway with largely disastrous results.) Anyhow, fear of "Hollywoodization" caused theatrical writers to piss on Disney's *Beauty and the Beast* in pre-opening stories and reviews. And when the public *ignored* that—having seen the successful movie—and stuck it up the theatrical writers' and critics' bungholes by buying $8 million worth of advance tickets despite the wails—then they turned on the next Hollywood group to come in, Universal and *Ho'house 2*, with a special fury. And we were vulnerable for reasons heretofore mentioned and more to come.

(6) The critical anger and hate—like a feeding frenzy—seems to me curiously misspent. We ain't talking life or death here (except in the case of the poor old playwrights who've worked nearly four years for nothing!); we ain't talking war or peace. We're dealing with a *show*, with mere *entertainment*. I just fail to understand how folks who have nothing personal at stake can get so aroused and exercised and mean. But they managed it quite easily, it seems. Some of the anger, I think, is that we had the audacity to try another musical about a whorehouse in the time of AIDS. I understand, and sympathize with, the fact that many young theatrical talents have suffered and died from that fatal and incurable disease. I am not opposed to the many shows on and off-Broadway dealing with the misery of AIDS, and the pain and young lives it has cut short. But does that mean that a *musical comedy* cannot be done, just because AIDS exists? We had many meetings and discussions about how to handle that problem; we were not insensitive to it. We decided—over the original and curious objections of Tommy Tune, who didn't want even to *mention* it—to (1) have Miss Mona warn the girls to insist on "safe sex" with all customers and say "adios" to any customer who wouldn't go along and (2) to use a "Telephone Sex" number to indirectly comment on the dangers of promiscuous *physical* sex. Apparently that wasn't enough for the critics.

(7) "Political Correctness" was a factor. This is a humorless time, Cousins. We had a line about Congressional hearings that included

something like "The truth doesn't always win out. Anita Hill isn't even in jail!" Since the line was uttered by the IRS Director, who had earlier been established as a dim-witted reactionary bumbling bureaucrat, it represented *his* point of view and therefore showed *our* sympathy for Anita Hill and women in general: a point of view, we thought, consistent with our sympathetic treatment of women in a political and career sense. The audiences, however, cringed or hissed and booed: so we killed the line. They obviously misunderstood it! The critics went even further astray: our *numerous* preachments about how shitty women are treated in general, and politically—not only in the book but in certain of Carol Hall's lyrics—were interpreted by critics as a shameless attempt to excuse our musical about whores by "pandering" to women. Go figure that out! We modeled our Senator A. Harry Hardast on Jesse Helms, our dumb-assed bureaucrat on Dan Quayle and our President on Bill Clinton and got slammed for dealing in cliches. Well, ain't Helms and Quayle, at least, true life cliches? All we did was depict them, and parody them. Bad thing to do, apparently, in this time of "political correctness." (Of course, the political *knowledge* of Broadway critics may be as under-developed as Tommy Tune's: Carol Hall wrote one of the funniest political satire songs I've ever encountered—hell, *the* funniest—"The Smut Song" for our Senator A. Harry Hardast. We *all* loved it, except Tommy. He insisted it wasn't funny. That's when he and I had the first battle in our war. When I was defending it, he said to Carol—as if I were not there—"Don't pay any attention to him. He doesn't know what he is talking about." Quite naturally, that pissed me off. And I said, diplomatically, "Fuck you, Tommy! I know more about politics and political satire than you'll know if you live to be a thousand!" And he said, "Well . . . maybe about *that!*"—as if "that" was a minor bit of knowledge, indeed—and from that moment on he was *determined* to kill the song and did, so that Carol had no choice but to write another, lesser version and that is the weakest point of her otherwise *very good* score. So chalk up another step-in-shit for Tune!

(8) I really didn't understand Tommy Tune's attitudes—or work—this time around; it seemed he was blinded by his own power and ego, indeed, that his instincts had left him save for here and there. He

insisted from scratch that no character except Miss Mona should be in this show from the old show. Pete, Carol, and I all argued against that; he remained adamant. I *begged* him to give me Sheriff Ed Earl Dodd, in retirement and jealous of Mona's affections for Sam Dallas, so we could use that salty Texas humor. He said "No." Stevie Phillips backed him up. I wrote a scene using Ed Earl anyhow; I said when I submitted it that it was only a first draft scene, and I hadn't found how to use him exactly, but that I *would*—we had time to "find" him at that point—but Tommy got in a snit, stamped his tiny feet and refused to let me explore it. Then, kiss my ass, two or three weeks before opening night Tommy insisted that I come to New York—after having had me banished most of the time—and both he and Stevie lamented that I had not come up with "those good Texas humor lines" in this show. I asked them then—and ask you now—"How can I do Ed Earl humor, and that is what you are talking about, without Ed Earl?" Tommy waved an impatient hand and said, "Oh, just put those lines in someone else's mouth!" Easier said than done, but I tried. I gave Sam Dallas some Ed Earl lines. They used them in one preview, said they "didn't fit him"—surprise! surprise!—and threw them out, probably wisely. In early drafts, Pete Masterson and I invented a young IRS agent, sort of a young Jimmy Stewart type, to assist Terri Clark (the young IRS woman) and to provide a romantic angle. Tommy insisted on killing that character because, he said, "the love interest seems obligatory and forced." I think he meant, really—and I'm not being homophobic—"heterosexual"; he apparently not only fails to understand such relationships but to understand their importance. Weeks ago, Barbara said—after watching a run-through—"Larry, Tommy Tune is cutting the heart out of the show." And last Saturday night, after a preview, she said, "The show is technically smart and seamless. But it simply doesn't have the heart of the old show. You can't care about the people as you did in the first *Whorehouse*." I didn't want to believe her at the time, but now I admit she was right on both counts.

So our show wasn't "perfect" or anything like it. *Still* . . . Carol Hall's score is better than the first time around. It's a prettier show, a flashier show. Despite what the critics think, our political satire was good. Tune's choreography was, yes, disappointing—but better than many shows I've seen, even if not credited with being. As we've all said to each other, in some bewilderment during the subsequent three days—and, my God, it already seems like a month—"If our show was *that* bad, what the hell were people laughing and cheering about all during previews and opening night?"

The frustrating thing is that one gets absolutely no sense of any audience acceptance in the reviews earlier referred to. Vincent Canby, in the upcoming *New York Times* this coming Sunday, did so; but in a way that sort of seemed to *apologize* for liking the show in the face of the vitriol of his writing colleagues: "You can't honorably lambaste a show after spending so much time laughing out loud at the jokes and the sets, being amazed by the glitzy costumes and being stunned by the leggy showgirls who almost don't wear them. That's more or less my position in relation to *The Best Little Whorehouse Goes Public*". . . and columnist Liz Smith actually said, "The audience goes wild! I had a perfectly wonderful time. Dee Hoty and Scott Holmes are big talents and just terrific!" Well, thanks, Liz, but I fear it's too little and too late. But I think her comment certainly gives the lie to Bruce Weber in today's *New York Times* in his Broadway column, in which he makes the astonishing statement that our show was disdained even "by many of the opening-night invited guests." What horseshit! I was there! It didn't happen like that. But, apparently wanting to be certain we are dead and buried—on the day the Tony voters actually mark their ballots—he managed to get in three kicks to the prone body, one of which was a knock that we may be guilty of "the most egregious instance ever of product placement on Broadway. The clear plastic television set that spends several minutes of the show front and center has, for no easily discernible reason, a recognizable brand name on it. The reason is this: the brand is made by Matsushita, the Japanese mega-manufacturer, which in 1990 bought MCA, the Hollywood film company that owns Universal Studios. The entire capitalization for the $7 million show came from MCA/Universal." So? We're supposed to have used a *competitor's* TV set? *What?*

So much for analysis, speculation, and guesses. The rest is a personal report: Had a great visit with Alix and her friend Martha, Kerri and my grandson Chad, and son Brad; it was the first time all five of my children had been together; we'd had four of them several times, but someone—either Alix or Brad—had always been missing. We got pictures of that "historic" event at the cast party and otherwise.

Anyhow, my blood brood enjoyed the show hugely and the big cast party: Universal did it up right, several hundred people, tables of ten, great food and wine, a superior dance band, all offset by nice decorations and a generally convivial atmosphere. And on Saturday, Sunday and Monday nights I'd taken the family out to dinner at three different restaurants, we'd spent time in my hotel room, and so on. Lots of laughs and remembering when. I had to fake some of it, knowing that we were going to take some critical hits, though not suspecting *nearly* enough bad as it turned out.

At the party, those of us show-connected began—about eleven o'clock —to sidle up to each other and say "Heard anything?" meaning, of course, reviews. We knew that at 10:ish Stevie Phillips had repaired to a private suite to receive reports from spies and flunkies sent to various papers and TV stations, and that the New York Times would have its first reviews off the presses about 10:40 P.M. (John Kent Cooke of the Washington Redskins, one of my guests, said "I always thought waiting for the reviews the same night happened only in the movies!") When no reports filter down by 11 o'clock we know that Stevie ain't got nothing good to report. Carol Hall's agent, Larry Weiss, slipped out and bought a New York Times; he and Barbara sneaked off and read the dismal words of David Richards; they also heard reports of a bad review on some television channel. They made a decision not to tell anyone. But shortly thereafter Masterson tiptoes up and whispers "I hear the Times review is terrible." I ask, "Just plain terrible, terrible terrible, or *shitty* terrible?" He laughed like a man would climbing the steps to the gallows and said "I don't know, but probably all three!" Shortly thereafter I see that Barbara—who normally drinks just enough to stay alive—is gulping wine. *Zoom!* went my antennae. *That woman knows shit she ain't telling!* Sure enough. We leave the party around 11:40 and, once we are disengaged from the others, she tells me in the privacy of our room that our asses belong to the gypsies. We talked until 1 A.M., conditioning ourselves—we thought—for critical blows to come. "Who'd have *thought*," Barbara said, "that at this point we'd be praying for *mixed* reviews?"

And, of course, our Prayers went unanswered even though I was smart enough and careful enough to Pray under an assumed name. After a semi-sleepless night I got up at 6:30 A.M. and went downstairs for the papers. Gathered the armload, rushed back, and tried not to waken Barbara but apparently uttered one too many long moans and "Oh, shits!" It was *ever* so much worse than we had imagined it might be. By 7 A.M.—when our pre-ordered breakfast arrived—we had damned small appetites.

My visiting "adult" kids slept late; but by about 9 A.M. they began to call in with truly shocked reactions to the angry notices. I had perhaps ill-prepared them: not wanting to spoil their trip or the show or cast party, I had asked Barbara and Brad not to show their own reservations and/or guilty knowledge. And the poor innocents, after seeing the show and the rousing audience reaction, after attending a cast party where everyone wore bright faces, went to bed thinking Daddy had another big hit. So their shock was at least double mine. (Several guests of ours—and guests of others connected with the show—had run up to me all night to bestow hugs, handshakes, kisses. . . . and all I could do was grin and say thanks and then escape them as quickly as I could decently do so.) As you know, Cousins, I had as early as May 3rd written you of the likelihood that something was rotten in Denmark and had privately thought it even longer: not based on the show so much as on the perceived hostility from rumors and pre-opening stories.

Anyway, I told the shocked kiddies to keep stiff upper lips, that I would take a few days to grieve and bury the dead and attend my wounds, then put it behind me as best I could and the best way would be to work hard on my baseball novel, *Breaking Balls*, and my nonmusical play, *The Dead Presidents' Club.* Told them, "I've been through worse than this in my private life, and *you've* been through worse than this. Ain't nobody dead or plumb outta work, so suck it up and forget it." They held up o.k. around me. But when I talked to Brad last night he said that yesterday, while he was showing Alix and Martha around the city on their final day in New York, Alix burst into tears three times. And yesterday morning, when I called Kerri at her office in Dallas, she burst into tears on hearing my voice and said Chad had cried in the cab on the way to the airport and cried himself to sleep that night. No matter how bad an experience, there is always a bottoming point and I guess those reports were the worst for me. And a few minutes ago I got by Federal Express a touching letter written by Chad saying not only that he *loved* the show, but he loved me and thought I looked nice in my Tuxedo! I guess the old dude in the country song had it right when he invoked God's blessings on "old dogs and children and watermelon wine" because even Buster still licks my ears in adoration!

Lindsay and Blaine took the big flop better than the big kids, but in all fairness they'd had fairer and more complete warnings; that did not, however, keep Blaine from muttering "those bastards" and "that son-of-a-bitch" as he read the crappy reviews. Perhaps I should have warned Alix and Kerri; I *thought* I was doing the right thing by not doing it, but maybe I made a bad choice.

We left New York Wednesday on a 12:40 p.m. train; Barbara and I tried to read but the words wouldn't connect with our brains, so we spent a lot of time staring out windows and sighing and muttering to ourselves. We were certain that the show would close this Saturday night—the cast and crew must be paid through this week, according to union rules—and figured that the meeting Stevie Phillips was having Wednesday morning with Sid Shineberg, President of MCA, was a mere formality from which would be issued the closing notice. We got home about 5 p.m. and when I called Stevie's office I was told she was at the theatre, talking to the cast between the afternoon matinee and the night's performance; figured she was giving the formal closing notice. To my astonishment, it turned out that Sid Shineberg had said he loved the show, he thought it a good show, and fuck the critics, he intended to keep it running if at all possible. He would put more ad money in the pot, he was hiring a big ad agency in New York, sending in Universal's marketing chief with orders to "make this thing fly," and new commercials—featuring the cast—would be shot beginning at 8 A.M. yesterday. Which, indeed, they were.

So we cheered Sid for walking the last mile with us. Barbara, indeed, was preparing to send a fax to Stevie and Sid thanking them for their stubborn and brave efforts yesterday afternoon when Stevie called to say well, er, ah, Sid *still* loved the show and *still* wanted to keep it running but, ah, unless the Tony folks nominate us for "Best Musical" on Monday he'll have to close it soon because even MCA-Universal can't hemorrhage $300,000 per week. I called Barbara and said "Don't send the fax. Sid ain't walking the last mile with us after all, he's walking more like a hundred yards." Because, frankly, I don't think we have a Chinaman's chance to get that nomination—especially do I think that now, following today's overkill comments by Bruce Weber in his *New York Times* column. And just moments ago, Stevie's office called to ask that we forfeit or defer any royalties due past this week—the cast, crew, director and so on have agreed to salary cuts—in an effort to keep the show open *if* we get the nomination Sid demands. I told Barbara to make the decision, since she handles the bidness end, but I think all that will become moot when the Tony folks utter their nominations on Monday. Don't look for us among the quick, but among the dead.

Well, shit, this letter has went on and on. I'll keep you posted as to our fate—which I think we'll know probably by the time you get this letter—and, in due course, when all the other anticipated throat-cutting reviews are in I'll send copies of the ugly goddam things to you and a few other friends with strong stomachs. I hope, after that, that you will hear damned little from me about *The Best Little Whorehouse Goes Public*—funny how quickly I've grown to hate the name!—because, as Nixon didn't want to "wallow" in Watergate, neither do I wish to wallow in this, the most painful and unpleasant experience of my writing life. I've work to do, and I hope to be smart enough and tough enough to get on with it. . . .

August 30, 1994

Dear Doctor Holland:

This letter is in the interest of your Literary Education. This morning I had a 50-year-old (I'd guess) plumber come by to check out leaking pipes. Coming into my office to present the bill and await his check, he looked around at the mementoes in my office then pointed to a poster re: my play *The Kingfish* and said, "You the one that wrote *that?*" I blushed modestly, and admitted it. He said, "I'm old enough to remember that from television! Say, was them real niggers?" At which point I realized he thought I had written "Amos 'N Andy." I said, "Uh, well, yeah, pretty much. Why do you ask?" He said, "Somebody told me white men played niggers on that show, but later on I learnt they was talking about radio, not teevee. Was that true?" I said, truthfully, that I had not written "Amos 'N Andy" for *radio,* so I couldn't say. "But them *was* real niggers on teevee, right?" he asked. I assured him they were real, indeed, and he left happy. I try to spread joy wherever I go. . . .

May 1, 1995

Dear Rev. Dr. Shrake:

Wish I could have attended the Billie Lee Brammer Memorial Beer Drink,* though it probably would have been depressing to see how old my youthful companions have become and how badly their faces and bodies wear the years. Thank God a lifetime of clean living spared me and you from time's ravages. Most of them others look like shit. I would have loved to see the extent of the manuevering twixt Mrs. Brammer 1 and Mrs. Brammer 2—Nadine and Dorothy—or was there any? That was always a pretty democratic and forgiving bunch when it came to folks bedding others down and falling temporarily in love and what not.

I swan, as Mama said, who'd of thought back yonder in '61 that *The Gay Place* would still be celebrated in 19-and-95 and already has lasted 17 years past Billie Lee's being bugled to Jesus? Ol' Billie Lee got a lot of mileage outta writin' just one book. If he had wrote two books, he might be celebrated until Jesus comes back. That was a good piece by Shelby Brammer in the *Observer* and I appreciate your passing it on.

Now, Doctor, I know you invented the spinning wheel, birth control, nitroglycerin and—when drunk—several different languages, but I believe that Billie Lee and I invented "Famous Arthur" on account of I have read that we did in print several times and I got a high degree of faith in everything I see in print except what Burt Reynolds writes. Speaking of which, I can't find no lawyers willing to sue him even though it looks to me like we got a lay-down case against him. They all hum and haw and give me lots of reasons why it would be risky but what it boils down to, I believe, is that they collectively and individually think I am too sorry to be libeled. This does very little for my self image. . . .

Have you read Mailer's *Oswald's Tale?* Critics are here-and-there as to its worth. I think it is worth a great deal. It is the first book I've read that makes Oswald more than a cardboard cutout; he has a personality for the first time beyond just being an ogre. And I believe that is a service to our time and a service to history. Now and again Nawmin' went in to fanciful flights and maybe a little suspect philosophy but I found it an *informative* book—especially about the Russian years, though not exclusively the Russian years.

I missed seeing Willie Morris when he was here flogging *My Dog Skip* on account of I was down in Collidge Station learnin' them Aggies some Anglish. But, you are right, every review I have seen credits ol' Skip with all the virtues and talents Willie claims for him, including driving a car and going shopping by hisself and playing wingback on the football team and always scoring on the Statue of

Liberty play. Funny you should mention that your old dog Prince used to beat Ben Hogan at golf. My dog Buster—who will not be four years old until day after tomorrow—speaks French, batted .409 in Little League last year, instructs in ballroom dancing and is being considered by Bill Clinton as the next Surgeon General unless they find out about the abortions he has performed. Quite a remarkable group of dogs, I'd say. Lassie, Asta, Sandy and such movie and stage play dogs can't hold a candle to 'em. Please don't tell anyone about Buster's brilliant accomplishments; he is so much smarter than any of the current Democrats that I fear they will try to draft him as National Chairman, and I want him to associate with a better class of people. . . .

In Jesus' sweet name, I beg to remain,
His Former Worship

*A party at Scholz Beer Garten to celebrate the new University of Texas Press edition of Brammer's classic *The Gay Place*.

June 7, 1995

Dear Doctor Hoot:*

Don't worry about pain during "deep cleaning" of your rotten miserable old teeth. They shoot you so full of deadening stuff that, while it sounds like they are breaking up a concrete bridge with sledge hammers in there, you don't feel nothin' a-tall. That much numbing dope, of course, does leave one unable to eat, smoke or talk right for several hours. If you have it did, do not try to talk to little children or young ladies in tight shorts with whom you feel a need to communicate, because all you can do is make grunting noises and waller your tongue in a swol jaw, so that kids and girlies alike will run screaming tales of sexual attack, and the more you wave your arms and point to your disfigured jaw by way of explanation the louder they hollar. It does not help in such a circumstance to be fat, bearded and old, but since you are only the latter of that trio you might not come off as threatening as I. They gave me pain pills, claiming I would hurt some once the deadening dope wore off, but I never got around to hurting beyond sensing it would not do to bite into a Milky Way that had been in the freezer since last November.

The worst part will come later—July 11th in my case—when the learned Doctor Tooth Fairies sit down to cluck over the x-rays now that the deep cleaning has revealed how *truly* rotten is the ivory in one's old head and tell you this 'uns got to be pulled, and that 'un needs a root canal job, and the other 'un is so bad it'd pay to yank it out with pliers and knock its neighbor out with a crowbar. . . .

I am a little down in the dumps since, about eight hours ago, I sat down to prune three pages out of the first act of *The Dead Presidents' Club*, it running a tad long, and I cut and slashed and changed things and when I finished a half-hour ago I realized my "pruning" had made it five pages longer. And now I got to retype the whole sumbidge, because every page is so marked up and struck through it looks like an exchange of letters between me and Jay Milner. I am going to type it at the length it now is, screw it, and them what find the first act too long I shall accuse of small bladders. . . .

    *Shrake.

May 19, 1996
The Holy Sabbath

Dear Reverend Doctor Shrake:

No need to apologize for not showing up at Joe Christie's brunch [in Austin]. Had you been there, we would have been harder pressed to find a writer we could say condescending things about, such as "He does the best he can with his limited gifts" and "I *do* believe he's a little better than he used to be, though of course that's speaking relatively" and "I tried to read his last book but could never make it past page three."

Actually, I appreciate your disappearing into the Austin maw after the Friday night opening of *The Dead President's Club* at Austin's State theater* and know that you did so as to allow me to shine on a stage where your own brilliant light might have obscured my lesser laser. It worked. I was besieged by autograph hounds, followed around by the applauding masses and offered much young stuff. None of this would have happened had you been present to eclipse me. So I am in your debt.

Had a long meeting with Dr. G. W. Bailey before leaving town, suggesting a few changes in the production that I thought might make it play a little better, though of course I was greatly pleased with his overall production. The one part of the show that doesn't play as well as the rest—the "sentencing" by God—is my fault because the trouble lies in the writing. I can't get repairs done in time for the Live Oak production, but *hope* to find and correct what is wrong by the time a second production is done, whenever and wherever that may be. Had a breakfast talk with Dr. Wittliff** on Tuesday last that I think will prove helpful. He gave me simple but good departure-point advice: "Think of your definition of a benevolent God and start from there," which was pretty good, and "Think of God as a football coach ranting at his trailing team at the half, but then building them up before sending them back into battle," which was even better. I have not yet found the strength and time to get with the re-writes, but am mulling it and will commence when ready.

Anyway, I think G. W. was brilliant as Nixon as I knew he would be from last October's staged reading at LBJ Tech in San Marcos; where he also impressed me was wearing not only the director's hat but the producer's hat—meeting with lighting, sound, set, and costume folks, hell ol' Dr. Bailey done everything but work the concession stands. My hat's off to him. Dennis Letts was a damn good LBJ and by the time the run is over will be even better; he is an actor who learns and is not afraid to change if it will help the role and the show, and them kind don't grow on trees. God is, in my stage directions, "part Barbara Jordan and part Pearl Bailey"; what we got was part Pearl Bailey and part Aunt Jemimah; she just ain't by instinct or training good at the "dignified" part. The crowd loved her, and that's good, but I think the actress left half the role out. Maybe some of that was my fault in the writing, so I'm giving God another look in upcoming repairs. Overall, however, that was a damned strong cast for Austin. I was very much enamored of our Truman [Thomas C. Parker] and our Heavenly Bureaucrat [Corky Williams]. Coolidge started out well, but he increasingly seemed to think that the poker scene was about his cigar; kept removing it and pausing before delivering his lines, or trying to talk around it. Coolidge did not smoke, to the best of my knowledge, but that aside all the goddamned cigar did was cause too many pauses when Cal's lines are best delivered rapid-fire while the lines that set up his *bon mots* still hang in the air.

Just got in the mail a copy of *Texas Studies Annual*, Vol. II, 1995, which came in a plain brown wrapper. Guess some "good friend" wanted to make certain that I did not miss an article by Tom Pilkington, who in praising Larry McMurtry decided to bolster his case by saying that McMurtry has "outlasted and outstripped and out-written the Billy Lee Brammers and Larry L. Kings of this world." I do not think he ought to have picked on Brammer, who is dead, or myself, who is old. Uncle Tom also throwed in a paragraph saying I got off to "an excellent start" as a writer but then "found it necessary to move on to more remunerative literary occupations" and surmises that I ain't been worth a shit since. Ruint by money, I reckon he is saying. Not satisfied with them pokings, ol' Tawm then allowed it is "somewhat shocking to survey the corpus of King's work and to note how slight and evanescent it is. This is, in its own way, almost as minuscule a quantitative yield as Katherine Ann Porter's collected works." I believe Dr. Pilkington teaches over at John Tarleton, so next time you are in Stephenville I shall expect you as a loyal friend to drop by the campus and kill him for me. Let me know when this has been did, so I can send flowers like Mafia hitmen do to the funerals of their victims.

Sure enjoyed having you and Guv Richards at the Opening Night stuff. Tell Miss Ann I grinned every time I heard her booming laugh, which was—blessedly—often. And thankee, Sire, for your kind words about my new opus. Ought to motivate you to renew your efforts for my Statues at the East Pole. . . .

*The opening of *The Dead Presidents' Club*, which set box-office records at the State Theatre in Austin during its premier production by the Live Oak Theatre.
**King friend and scriptwriter Bill Wittliff.

April 15, 1997

Dear Reverend Doctor Shrake:

Well, I am reaping a few letters from other writers and old frens bragging on my U. of T. Press book, *True Facts* and such. However, there have been a couple of exceptions. One was my father-in-law's opinion—never mind I dedicated the book to him—who told my daughter, Lindsay, while counseling her about college choices, "I liked most of it, but I didn't like the last part. Those short stories. I will never understand why Larry insists on writing dirty stuff about Black hookers, oilfield trash and drunks." I told Lindsay she should have responded, "Well, Dad once was *two* of those and may not be entirely innocent of past associations with the third. . . ." She laughed.

And an alleged old friend, in Midland, wrote that my plays and books would be "much better if you *tried* harder." He, of course, has never wrote shit and so has little or no idea how hard one tries—every time out—or how difficult it is to do that which he has not tried. This same ast-hold has wrote me that about another or two of my works, which I think I earlier reported to you. I reckon it proves he ain't lowered his standards. . . .

Doctor, it now looks as if "Poot" Shrake may not be immortalized in print after all. The senior editor at W. W. Norton, who wanted to buy it* for big money, finally confessed that he was the only editor in the house who likes the book; his 26-year-old "contemporaries" said the book is (1) old fashioned, (2) has already been written and (3) makes too much use of "politically incorrect" language such as nigger, pussy, cunt, and such. This in a time when one can turn on TV and find women licking one another's snatches, and boys playing with one another's dangles, and what not. I do not understand the respective values. I do think much of my novel is hurried and not all that carefully wrote—and you yourself said it is a bit wordy, which crime I confess—and I would not be against running much of it through the typewriter again. But it having been thumbs-downed now by 5 or 6 publishers, I wonder if the game is worth the candle. Do I forget it, or what? If you got any suggestions as to repairs, I would appreciate their

being stated, you having been through this shit yourself and therefore
a expert or at least having a clue. . . .

Lemme know what you think. Honestly. . . .

   *King's baseball novel *Breaking Balls.*

April 25, 1997

Dear Reverend Doctor Shrake:

Wal, Hail, when you come down to it I guess I've gotta conclude
that I have proved—once again—that I ain't no novelist. The only one
I published was a piece of shit, which I realize more as time passes; I've
had one other one I finished rejected by Viking years ago,* I have
started at least a dozen and ran out of gas anywhere from page
three—mercifully—to page 200-odd. And now *Breaking Balls* ain't
working, so what the hail. Back to the drawing board. I reckon my fictional outlets will, hereafter, be on the stage and in the short story.
And I'll keep doing non-fiction as I can and must. Bah humbug. Don't
know why Jesus don't want me to write novels.

I was absolutely astonished to learn about that "Bingo Long's
Traveling All Stars" plot. Thought I had hit on one nobody in the
world had thought of. Alas. . . . What is embarrassing about my novels is that I think they're good and got potential until about twenty
folks tell me they ain't. Rap my knuckles if I ever say I am gonna write
another 'un. . . .

I am wingin' it to Austin on Sunday, May 4th, to preen myself and
try to sell copies of the new U. T. Press book.** Sign books at 7 P.M.
at Book People store. Monday is give-over to radio and TV and
maybe a newspaper simpering; Tuesday me and a buncha other hacks
signs books from 8 to 10 P.M. at Scholz Garden for the Barnes &
Noble folk. I know them events is all past your jammie time, but
maybe in the daytime once we can eat a Meskin. I'll call. (Now that
you been warned you have plenty of time to skip town or claim that
you did.) Nearly ever time somebody calls to tell me they are in
Washington, or about to visit, my first reaction is to commence claim-

ing illness, family deaths and week-long funerals, unavoidable trips and so on. What's embarrassing is to give your excuses and then be told "But I haven't even told you when I'll be there," which I once was told after my premature eagerness to avoid having to go out. . . .

I been trying to write a *Parade* magazine article for two months—counting the research—on account of they pay me $10,000 and Lawyer Blaine wants the money. It is how life in America differed a hundred years ago, from now, both them times being near turn of the century. Halberstam says I should turn it into a book, and is much more excited about that notion than am I. He *loves* the kind of ditch-digging research that would be required by such a book, while I rate such labors with eating broccoli and cauliflower and asparagus and other stinky vegetables. I am having hell's own time just getting the *article* did, on account of it ain't nothing a man can put much poetry to. In my next life I am going in the roofin' bidness. . . .

*War Movies.
**True Facts, Tall Tales & Pure Fiction.

June 20, 1997

Dear Onkle Jake:*

To answer your questions about how University Presses work, I say with full confidence: "Slowly." But, hail, so do them in New York. I have never turned in a book that ought to take the Publisher over an hour-and-a-half to have it in the stores, but you would be surprised how many months and months they can sit around thumbing themselves and other people's manuscripts, turning deaf ears to our curses, mutters and threats. I think there is some Editors Union Rule that lightning bolts will strike any who assist a writer to publication short of his fullest desperations.

Do *not*, for God's sake—as I recently have—threaten to die before your book is published, on account of this will encourage the Editor/Publishers to say, "Oh, goody-goody! Once he has died we can make up quotes from him from his deathbed such as 'Despite my being half-addled from a stroke and my tongue lolling and a little bit of drooling going on, I desperately hope to see this—the best book I have ever wrote—did justice by . . . .'" Or the publisher will write on the dust jacket, "This book tells many frank tales the late author was too timid or cowardly to tell during his lifetime, but him having went to Jesus we now can reveal the full and sordid details of his exciting if sorry life." None of this will advance your pub date. What may be more effective—and I intend to use this in an effort to get a quick publication of my next book—is a direct threat to visit the publishing offices in possession of many lethal weapons and as bent on destruction of all hands as Charles Whitman. (Be sure, however, if your editor is under 45 he/she won't have no notion of who Charles Whitman was!) If that be the case, forget Whitman and just threaten to kill all them that ain't of a age to draw Social Security; this should strike fear in the hearts of all.

Hail, yes, I will give you a quote for the dust jacket claiming you are almost as handsome, talented, and hard-peckered as myself. Hail, I will even write a "Foreword" saying much the same, giving you the nod over everybody except me: Shakespeare, Salinger, Shaw, Shrake, Jap, Jenkins and all them. What more could a man ask?

Yours in Christ and for instant publication, I beg to remain, Longer than I probably will. . . .

*Jay Milner, who was writing a reminiscence of his friendships with King, Bill Brammer, Willie Nelson and others titled *Confessions of a Mad Dog* (published in 1998 by the University of North Texas Press).

June 9, 1997

Dr. Stanley Gilbert*
4830 Crooked Lane
Dallas, Texas 75229

Dear Stan:

Thanks for the postcard of those wretched-looking farmers standing on barren Texas ground. For a moment I thought it was an old family photo that I somehow never saw around the King house. And thanks, too, for your good words about my most recent book. I am getting good reaction from many indivduals, but am puzzled that five weeks after official publication date only two reviewers have passed judgment that I know about. Never have I started that slowly out of the gate. All I can figure is that most reviewers these days—like New York editors—are about 26 years old, never heard of me and don't care to.

Lanvil sent me a copy of your letter to him about the review in *Dallas Morning News* by the Stephenville academic, Tom Pilkington. Mr. Pilkington, whom I may have once met years ago at some Texas Institute of Letters to-do, early in my career wrote several times that I was a whiz-bang good writer. Increasingly, however, he pokes and jabs me; couple of years ago he wrote in some stuffy academic journal that he had been "shocked"—on reviewing my work—at "how little" of it will prove to be "lasting." Well, who knows, he may be right. But except for sneering at *Whorehouse* he never has mentioned any other of my plays and this leads me to believe he is not a theatrical type and figures stage work not to be "serious." Thus he likes to leave the impression that I am somehow an idle writer, one who lolls about, perhaps, on welfare rolls or engages in profitless studying of belly-button lint. A peculiar judgment, since he—about my age—has produced but one co-authored book, to my knowledge, and several pieces in academic journals during which he sighs and laments the sad state of Texas letters and those who make them. When not toiling there, he boxes us in our creative regions in newspaper reviews such as you supplied Lanvil and he, in turn, supplied me. But at least Dr. Pilkington liked three or four of my short stories—surprise: so the day was not totally lost. A couple of years ago I commissioned my friend and fellow-writer Edwin (Bud) Shrake to motor from Austin to Stephenville and kill Dr. Pilkington slowly and with great relish. (The problem could be that I did, indeed, meet Pilkington at some TIL event and didn't bow deeply enough. Them academics, I have learned—at Harvard, Duke and Princeton—are pretty-much born pucker-brows and don't appreciate those who do not recognize their serious intents. Not many approve of fun, which I think probably accounts for Pilkington's grumblings about my "comic" pieces.)

I reckon I ought not to let such fellers bug me, but—dammit—they *do*. Every writer I have ever met—and some I have only read about—never derive total satisfaction from their reviews. Most of us, given the nod over Shakespeare, Shaw and Salinger, would brood in our beds that we had not, after all, been favorably compared with Jesus. (And I *know* I must have been a cuter baby than Jesus, but guess who got all the publicity?). . .

I have been swamped with end-of-school parties and proms. Son Blaine (soon to be 15) graduated from Middle School to Upper School at Sidwell Friends. Daughter Lindsay, soon to be 18, attended not only the Junior-Senior Prom at Sidwell but also at Landon—another fancy private school—because the momentary love of her life is a Senior there. I am going broke chipping in for limousines, pre-Prom dinners at fancy restaurants, graduation gifts and what not. Wasn't like that in the public schools of Putnam, Scranton, Jal—or even Midland—somehow. I also had to drop Lindsay off for the Sidwell Friends Upper School Graduation—she, as a Junior, was an invited guest—an hour before President Clinton spoke at commencement and there were so many Secret Service and other cops—park police, city cops, highway patrolman, federal marshals—that they screwed up traffic 10 blocks from the school in all directions.

Sometimes I think if the Secret Service didn't *do* all that—just would sort of *sneak* the President in with minimum hub-bub—security might actually be better. But they make such a to-do of it a *blind* assassin could find the man. (Last night, for example, the Vice-President—who lives but three blocks from me—attended a party across the street from our house and for two hours we had cops on foot, on motorcycles and in cars and what looked to be weapons carriers running up and down, making noise, talking on radios and so forth until at first I had the notion that this rich neighborhood had undergone a sudden crime wave.) I *refuse* anymore, to go to *any* party where the President or V. P. will be: having done it several times, all I get for my pains is chaos including metal detectors, hard looks from guys with radio wires in their ears and a general buffeting. . . .

Well, hell, enough. Except that my play *The Dead Presidents' Club* has been jumped forward from a January production to a September one at Ford's Theater here, provided my lawyer-wife and the theater's lawyer can get the contract negotiated without fatalities; right now they are doing much screaming and finger-pointing on each side, but that is S.O.P. and probably lawyers do that just for practice. We are beginning rehearsals about August 20th, open to a week of previews on September 23, and have an official Opening Night on September 30th. Contract calls for four-week run, with option of theatrical folk to extend to a fifth, sixth and maybe even a seventh week if box-office business justifies it. Ford's Theater folk also asking an option to move it on to New York—Off-Broadway—in partnership with some New York money if all goes well here. . . .**

*King's first cousin, one of Lanvil's two brothers.
**King and the person who runs Ford's Theater never arrived at a contract satisfactory to both. Negotiations ended when King asked, "Where is John Wilkes Boothe now that I need him?" Barbara Blaine told her husband his remark had not been helpful.

November 21st, 1997

Dear Adrian & Miss 'Niter:*

I had a ball attending the Midland High Class of 1947 50th reunion; first one I *ever* had been back to. Which means, of course, I missed the big 40th when *everybody* came back; during the ensuing decade, a lot of the classmates were called to Jesus (or maybe Lucifer) and I always regretted not having attended. I didn't even know they were having a 50th until Royce Higgs called from Ohio, Jack Cox called from Houston and Gilbert Seviere called from New Orleans, all saying *they* were going and ordering my ass to attend. Glad I did, too: it amazed me how quickly and easily old friendships were picked up with people I had not seen *since* high school or not many years thereafter. We had 159 members of the class of '47; about 75 were in attendance for the 50th. (I was only technically a member of that graduating class; went into the Army in 1946, got my GED in the Army and was issued a Class of '47 diploma by MHS.)

We had a full three-day schedule of cocktail parties, lunches, brunches, a banquet at Green Tree Country Club and so on, so that I really had little or no free time; when not at events, I rode around town with a few old ex-Bulldog football and basketball team mates, or sat around the motel bullshitting with them, so that I wound up not getting in touch with anybody other than that group. It was really great, though I was startled when a hump-backed little old lady wearing hearing aids in both ears ran up and kissed me and it turned out to be someone I had dated in high school and recalled her as young, stacked and sexy. Ah, well. . . .

There was, indeed, sort of a "Twilight Zone" feeling to the trip: several of us, in two cars, drove around looking for old landmarks and our old homes—many of which were where parking lots or office buildings now are, or [the houses] are caved in and vacant—or, in my case, at 1010 North Whitaker—much reduced below even the modest circumstances when I lived there, being filled now by Meskins who keep broken-down refrigerators on the front porch and old cars propped up on blocks in the front yard. I said to my companions, *"I'm* home but *home* ain't." About the only thing left of my old days in Midland, downtown, are the courthouse—and *it* has a facade over it—and the Petroleum Building and one or two other office buildings, long overshadowed by taller ones, though in "my day" they *were* the tallest! Still, I'm glad I went. Maybe, who knows, it was my last goodbye to the old home town. And if that proves to be the case, it was a damned good farewell.

*Bud and Juanita Lindsey, Stanton, Texas.

December 8, 1997

Dear Ben Z.:*

. . . .Believe me, I surely can identify with your frustrations about getting published. I have been very lucky—13th book being worked on for publication, seven-of-eight plays I have written coming to life on various stages—but still, I must face the fact that I am not as "popular" as I once was, not as "in demand," no longer a "budding" star but one blinking out, where New York and its current attitudes are concerned; my consolation is that in *Texas*, at least, I am still both socially and professionally accepted as a writer and even, maybe, a little bit venerated. And there is no way to say how *important* that is to me, from the standpoint of personal ego and my "writerness" and my feeling of worth. I have been goddamned lucky in this old word game, and so it ill-becomes me to whine—though I often want to—because I should, really, be on my knees thanking such powers as be that I began to write and publish in a time much freer and easier than now, before the goddamned conglomerates took over publishing and the Money Men dictated the bottom line. (Do you know that one's past "sales record"—i.e., *lack* of it—now is so ruling that many agents are having their often-very-good veteran writers submit their book manuscripts under *nome de plumes* so that fucking computers can't say: "Stop! This asshole won't make you a dollar!" Sad, but all too true. . . .)

I really feel sorry for young folks trying to break into publishing now. At least you and I have had some few moments and you have forged a distinguished career as legislator, lawyer, judge. Think of *that* when what Winston Churchill called "the black dog" is barking at you. (Can you imagine *Churchill*, a man writ large in History, being *depressed?* But we have his own testimony that he often *was!*)

I feel that my career is *limping* along right now even though U. T. Press is working on my letters book, three theaters in D. C. have expressed varied degrees of interest in doing my *Dead Presidents' Club* play (which I am spot re-writing, due to recent revelations in newly released Nixon Tapes), the Dallas Museum of Art is having an "evening" honoring me and my work next May 7th—G. W. Bailey and I will read from it, and I hope you will come—and I've just been asked to Emcee the Texas Book Festival for the third consecutive year, which is how old it is, and I'm speaking at the National Press Club on January 16th . . . and Reader's Digest Books is paying me $12,000 plus for a week of promotion of a new book on "old folks"—in which I have a piece along with such writers as Arthur Miller, John Updike, Bel Kaufman, Carl Sagan, Dan Wakefield, Willie Morris, Roy Blount,

Jr., Dr. Ruth Westheimer, William Kennedy, many others—*so why ain't I got a better attitude?* I dunno: beats hell outta me! Could it be as simple as that I have gotten too goddamned *spoiled?* That is probably part of it, though not being able to place my long-in-progress baseball novel anywhere in New York, the big failure on Broadway of *Ho'house II* musical four years ago (almost) and no reviews outside of Texas and a few other places of my most recent book makes me aware of slippage. And, too, face it—as the old "September Song" says—"The days dwindle down/To a precious few" . . . my way of saying that, yes, unbelievable as it may seem, I will be 69 years old come New Year's Day and . . . well, hell, ain't nobody put up a *statue* of me yet and don't nobody seem to be *clamoring* to . . . but, more seriously, I ain't sure of how many more productive years I'll have as a writer except to know at rock-bottom and in the central core the answer surely is "not many." . . .

*Judge Ben Z. Grant, King's collaborator on *The Kingfish.*

May 22, 1998

Dear Cousins:

Hell has frozen over. The needle was found in the haystack. And Chicken Little was right. Larry L. King, you see, is buying a computer. . . .

Not that I really want to, but technology has whupped me down. My old typewriter repairman died a couple of years ago, and my surviving typewriters are themselves about to croak, all having at least one or two things wrong. Ribbons are hard to find; I can't find carbon paper up here, as you know, since you—and Shannon Davies at the University of Texas Press—have been supplying me with it for the past year. I feel like Dad once said of his being forced out of the blacksmith business: "Then the car come along and I was blowed up." So, not yet ready to give up this crazy word game despite advancing years and mysterious machines, I had to face up to surrendering to the new technology—which, as Barbara points out, isn't all that new except to me and a handful of other die-hard coots. For several years she has been urging me to convert but I fought it as hard as I fought conversions to Jesus in my youth. She has claimed that my manuscripts are so old-fashioned in appearance that young editors automatically will consider me an old relic on his last professional legs even if only subconsciously. And perhaps she is right. Anyway, she's buying me a top-of-the-line Mysterious Apparatus and getting an instructor to give me lessons.

At least I won't have to take off a typewriter ribbon and re-wind it by hand eight or ten times per day, as I am doing now with this the *best* of my ancient typewriters. . . . Ah me. . . . pray for me. . . .

I suppose my grousing about technology that most people not only accept, but take for granted, is another sign of Old Fartism along with the belief that hardly a decent magazine exists in America any more. They either are Celebrity-driven or partisan organs that stoop to the worst sort of tabloid journalism with just no leavening humor—with rare exceptions such as P. J. O'Rourk, Roy Blount, Jr., and Molly Ivins—and their intellectual or informative content would cause Thomas Paine and Mencken to revolve in their graves. I think the Celebrity horseshit has been the ruination of magazine journalism. I couldn't sell my article about the inner workings of my jury duty— "Seeking Justice"—to *Atlantic Monthly, Vanity Fair, Parade* or *Esquire*, among others—even though, when it appeared in my UT Press book *True Facts*, etc. it received good critical comment from reviewers, lawyers and judges. They don't want substance any more, just entertainment. (David Halberstam was so taken with that piece, when I sent it to him in manuscript form, that he called to say how "compelling and spellbinding" it was and told me he had recommended it to some woman who buys movie materials. When the movie lady called, her only question was "Does it have a celebrity angle?" Puzzled, I said, "No, quite the opposite. It's about a rape case involving two ghetto Blacks, one claiming assault and one claiming not to have assaulted her, and how a mixed jury of whites and blacks, with very different cultural experiences, viewed the case and the principles." She lost interest as quickly as had I said, "No, it is a piece about how to make ice cubes.")

But for all my rantings in recent years against goddamned "celebrity journalism" I didn't know the half of that crime until a front-page article in the *New York Times* several days ago. Jesus Christ, many magazines now permit Celebs—or their image-makers—to select or control photographs to be used of the Celebs, demand—and usually get—the "right" to see the writer's copy before it is published and, of course, to make "corrections" when deemed necessary. Otherwise, the image makers and their Stars threaten, they will not give an interview to Magazine X but will shop it around to "competitive" magazines Y and Z! And to the shame of my craft, the gutless magazine editors are *agreeing*, by and large, because "If we don't have a celebrity on the cover, our magazines won't sell." Christ-on-a-stickhorse! What the hell has happened to journalistic integrity and what kind of blathering idiotic readership wants pap bullshit of the old ass-kiss false-story Movie Magazine tradition of the long ago? (Remember when Joan Crawford was represented as a wonderful mother, Rock Hudson as the quintessential Macho Man, John Wayne—who never served a day in the Military in his soft, fat old life—was the To Be Admired Super Patriot? That sort of horseshit now is being peddled in once *respectable* journals. Where are the gonads of current magazine editors? Or writers? The heart? The committment? The *caring*? The *pride*? Well, in the words of the old 1960s anti-war song "Gone like flowers, every one"—or goddamned close to it. Bah, humbug! Fie fie and a pox on the fuckers!)

Rant over.

To some extent, the same happy horseshit is happening on Broadway. We see more musical revivals—or imports from England—than not. Glitz and glitter prevails, though far be it from me to claim that Broadway musicals ever, in the aggregate, carried "social messages"—with the exception of a spare few, including *Finian's Rainbow* of the 1940s—an early preachment against racism—and, though I beg your pardon, the original *Whorehouse* about shameless politicians

and sensational tabloid journalism techniques and the natural hypoc-
racies of both the pols and the alleged newsmen! So musicals are,
really, and I think increasingly so, merely to entertain the same mind-
less sons-of-bitches who rush out to buy shitass celebrity-driven magazines.

Second rant over.

Third rant: "Serious" plays rarely make it to Broadway any more.
Which reduces the promotional "Tony" Awards each year to what
truly is "The Best Disguised Pap Award"—excluding Wendy
Wasserstein's work, the occasional but not always Stephen Sondheim,
and the occasional Arthur Miller revival—while, conversely—a
bright spot—Off-Broadway, and the Regional Theaters, continue to
offer the best of American playwrighting. But, alas, to small audiences. I believe it was Edward Albee who once estimated "serious"
theater-goers in New York as "about 40,000" and then—after box-
office realities of his own good plays set in—reduced his estimate by
about a third. And I think he was right. And we are talking about an
extremely talented playwright in Mr. Albee. But the masses rally not.

Now leave us piss on New York Publishing Houses—now owned by
Giant Conglomorates, who consider them as little more than nui-
sances who don't carry their own weight as measured against the
manufactures of Miracle Drugs, Gas-reducing Fart-Helper medications, Tobacco, Booze, Vitamins, Health Foods or other profitable
scams—few of which have proved themselves beyond the claims of
vast Advertising and Promotional schemes. Any day now, we will see
Ads in print and on TV and maybe even in the neglected Art of
Radio—the best media ever, in terms of one's exercising one's brains
to paint a personal picture of what one *heard*—claiming that Cancer
is Good For You in that it reduces death by sudden heart attack or
strokes, and therefore is a greater Aid to the Dying than is marijuana
which, as all of us Scientists know, eases death and brain seizures and
helps one cross to The Other Side, never mind what the chickenshit
Republicans claim. There is nothing in the world worse than Partisan
dolts, a thing known to all of us Free Spirits who believe in low grade
smokin' dope, women's rights to have an abortion on demand and low

taxes for us millionaires. At least two-thirds of that is what Made America Great!

Anyway, what I am doing next—though I have not decided in what order—is (1) a play about Adam and Eve in the Garden of Eden, (2) some sort of Washington-based "thriller novel" and (3) a retrospective, non-fiction, about writers in my time and place. Other than that, respondant sayeth not.

Yours in Christ (and perhaps near the End of The Trail.)

Simply, a writing man,

Larry L.

May 27, 1998

Dear Cousins:

All signs portend aging, loss, attrition and death. Witness this *New York Times* obit of a week ago today of my dear friend and editor Alan D. Williams. Was glad to see that today's *Times* had the "in memorium" ad from Viking-Penguin and with respect to ADW quoted Aeschylus, "No, I will never tire of telling you your gifts." Quite appropriate, I think.

Alan Williams edited five of my books and, with the possible exception of Willie Morris, was the best editor I ever worked with hands-down. Wry, funny, educated, caring, sprightly, a punster, an entertained and entertaining observer of the world's mock shows. I recall sitting with A. D. in his Princeton home—he in a robe after the daily commute from Manhattan, relaxing with a few scotches—and his laughing, uproariously, at Richard M. Nixon's mock show on television: the one where Nixon spoke near a huge stack of "White House Transcripts," the President telling us the whole truth about Watergate was in there and, yessiree, that Watergate should now be put to rest and such. Of course, the next day all the nation's newspapers called attention to the many "expletives deleteds" and "indistinguishables" and such, and of course, it was perfectly obvious that nothing like the whole truth had been contained in those "White House Transcripts." What I recall most is Alan's pure enjoyment of such a straight-faced mock show as Nixon managed to give us. "Checkers Two," he called that speech, as it occurred, with satisfied chuckles. And he was right.

Alan loved a few sociable drinks—though nothing like the stupid drink-til-dizzy-or-puking technique I favored—and his yarns, puns and observations gave me a moveable feast each and every time we lunched, dined, popped into a bar for post-work drinks, visited in his home or my apartment in Princeton. He loved talking about writing and politics and of the human comedy. I'll miss him.

I regret only a couple of things about my relationship with Alan D. Williams—and they are my fault, not his. One, I never finished that LBJ biography he went out on a $100,000 limb for and, two, I did not talk to him the last three months of his life. Did write him a long letter—shortly after the last time we talked—but, by then, he apparently was in pretty bad shape although the obit says he worked editing Aleksander Solzhenitsyn's "November 1916" until about three weeks before his death. (Did you know that Alan Williams was an Airman at Midland Army Air Base in 1945? That came out in one of our many rambling conversations. He remarked that with "a paucity" of things to do, he attended a number of Midland High School football games—and I played in them! What were the odds that a young soldier sitting in the stands and a teenager on the field in that desert wasteland would become dear friends, and one would edit the other?)

Well, hell, a lot of my old editors are dead—A. D., Brad Carlisle, Jim Scott, Wick Fowler—or retired (Herman Gollob, Berry Stainback, Eric Swenson) or semi-retired—Arthur Kretchmer, Steve Gelman—writing more than editing (Geoffrey Norman, William Broyles, Willie Morris) or agenting, like Chuck Verrill, or doing God knows-what such as Bob Gutwillig. And those are only a few who immediately leap to mind; I am sure that many others are gone, or forgotten, who worked at any number of magazines—Helen Gurley Brown pops to mind—themselves perhaps now defunct. And they all, of course, have been replaced by 26-year-olds, except in Hollywood where they are 14-to-22 if in charge of much. . . .

Working now on final chapter of Letters Book with Dick Holland. (He has more than that to do, but I'm very close to finished with my part.) Negotiations still going on about the two-company 20th Anniversary Tour of the original *Whorehouse* and Lawyer Blaine sees no insurmountable obstacles. Meeting in about a week with Ethan McSweeny, the hot shot young director palpitating to direct *The Dead Presidents' Club.* Hear from a third party—Chuck Conconi, columnist for *The Washingtonian Magazine*—that McSweeney wants my stage Nixon to be a little more "complex." I thought he was, but will listen to what the kid has to say. . . .

Some time soon, please send this letter, along with Alan D. Williams obit, to the Southwestern Writers Collection. I want what The *New York Times* and I said of A. D. "on the record." A small payment for all that I owe him.

Peace. . . .

August 9, 1998

Dear Fat Ben & Miss 'Niter:

Twenty-four years ago today Richard Nixon resigned for having tracked mud on the Constitution; 52 years ago today the United States Armed Forces attained an all-time strength-and-readiness state due to 17-year-old Private Lawrence Leo King—RA 18271471—being sworn into the Army Signal Corps at Goodfellow Field in San Angelo, Texas. I leave to History which of these acts was the most momentous. . . .

I am not surprised that *you* were surprised to find that I have become a Computerizer. Daughter Lindsay said "I never expected you to become obsessed with a dog or a computer but I have lived to see both!" I don't yet love this Magic Machine as much as I love the faithful booger-and-bear dog, Buster, but after about six weeks of exposure I must admit to being a bit entranced—and to wondering why I spent twenty-odd years cussin' Computer Nerds. Plain ol' ignorance, I reckon, plus man's inherent fear of the unknown.

As to why I entered the 20th century here on the cusp of the 21st, it has to do with necessity being the mother of invention. See, I had been using the same old typewriter repairman for 20-odd years and he died on me two or three years ago. In the interim, all of my several ancient manual machines broke down in one way or another. For the last eight months or so, I had to remove the ribbon from my typewriter eight or ten times or more, daily, and rewind the sumbidge by hand. This not only hindered efficient production, it left one with perpetually grubby hands. Came a day when Lawyer Blaine discovered my hand ribbon-rewinding and uttered "Hold, Enough!" She and son Blaine then went out and bought this Magic Machine—said to be top-of-the-line—with all sorts of mysterious accessories, at a cost of "only" $3000-plus. It was quite frightening to a boy who never has understood exactly what drives a wheel-barrow, makes a radio talk or sing to him or how big old heavy airplanes can possible stay aloft—and who, in 1935 in the public school in Putnam, Texas, was taught to communicate by writing on a second-hand little slate with a nub of chalk.

I am already persuaded that converting was a good move, and not just because I have hands free of ribbon black, or that I couldn't find new typewriter ribbons and had to ill-repair holes in my used ones with Scotch tape. It also has saved me certain cultural embarrassments in that of late when I tried to buy carbon paper the "old" clerks laughed and the young ones did not know what it was.

But the real good has been the amazing uplift of my spirits; this Magic Machine has been almost as good as a triple-dose of Prozac in keeping me from wanting to stab folks or sulk under the bed. Glory Hallelujah, I want to *work* again! Visions of literary sugar-plums dance once more in my head; the brain reels with plans and plots to write new plays and short stories and maybe even try the accursed novel form again. Hell, I could get so carried away I might attempt a book of critical essays, passing hard judgements upon my fellow writers and lamenting the wasting of my valuable time through pursuing their inferior Ort. But, in truth, I am disadvantaged as a critical expert because I have actually written things and, therefore, might know what I am talking about—a clear disqualification.

On the other hand, once the new wears off I might revert to sour musings and dark prophesies and crawl under the bed again, never having been proficient at keeping blue skies smiling at me. Right now, however, I feel this new shot-in-the-arm might actually last awhile. And as Ol' Hemingway said in the tag line of *The Sun Also Rises*— "Isn't it pretty to think so?"

Enough. Best, old friends, from

L. Clatterbuck King

March 5, 1999
Friday

Dear Drs. Peeler & Peeler:

Well, I have seen more of "Doctors" lately than I truly enjoyed. Hit a brick wall about three weeks ago: gasping, wheezing, fighting for breath. Slept 36 hours. Woke, felt no better, slept another 10 or 11 hours and then dragged myself to my physician's office and he stuffed my ass in the hospital immediately—with a case of pneumonia and put me on oxygen and I. V.s and all sorts of tubings and I lay about half out of it for a week. Came home on Monday of this week. On five different daily medications and two inhalers four times daily each. Told to take it easy, and I'm trying to because I really tire quickly.

My old lungs—no surprise—are apparently about as tattered as 10-year-old sox. I have been bluntly told that I will live neither long, nor well, if I ever again smoke. They got my attention. I have quit. Among my medications are Wellbutrin—an anti-smoke pill—plus wearing a nicotine patch changed every morning. Actually breathing well now, and Lawyer Blaine flatters me with the observation that "Your fingernails and fleshtones are actually pinkish now—rather than slate gray." Gee, thanks, hunny. . . .

Think maybe I told you I was commencing a "funny" book for Crown Publishing Company of New York—about living in the Dee of Cee—but ain't did nothing since I got sick. Anxious to get back to it but don't feel real "funny" or creative yet. . . .

Latest political joke: Right after Bill Clinton beats the Impeachment

Trial in the Senate, Ted Kennedy goes to the White House, offers his congratulations, and asks "Mister President, I know you've been through a terrible ordeal. Is there anything I can do to help?" Clinton looks around, lowers his voice, claps Kennedy on the back and says, "Sure, Ted! Would you mind driving Monica home? . . .

March 6, 1999
Saturday, 9:05 A.M.

Dear Gilberts All:

I am a sucker for nostalgia—even the "bad times"—and articles such as the enclosed on FDR's "fireside chats" bring back old memories to share. (Which is what writers do).

Anyway, we didn't have a radio until Mother insisted on one following Pearl Harbor, but our neighbors "Uncle Tal" and "Aunt Ola" Horn did. Two things we always went to their house to hear, stumbling through the woods going and coming by pale lantern light: FDR's "fireside chats" and, of course, Joe Louis' fights—in anticipation that some "white hope" would beat him for us! I recall vividly how we all hung on every word of FDR's and the discussions afterward. I recall in general that each such "chat" somehow brought a vague "hope" of better days—and when hope is all you've got it is vital to have and to hold.

Mother idolized FDR. She always said there was one place she hoped to see "before Heaven"—and that was the White House. So when our daughter Kerri was born—February 7, 1955—I contrived to pretend a bigger need than we actually had for Mother's help in order to entice her to Washington. My parents and Estelle would not hear of flying, and so rode a day coach for three days and two nights—or maybe vice-versa—from Midland to Washington. They had to change in St. Louis, which of course scared them so I used my new Congressional influence with a railroad lobbyist to see that some functionary met them in St. Louis and got them aboard the proper train. I met them at Washington's Union Station and never shall forget how their eyes were darting nervously until they spotted me.

In those days—unlike now when it is a huge mass-production deal with limited access—one could actually get small groups a guided "Congressional" private tour of the White House. I arranged that. On a given morning at 7:00 A.M. in February of '55, I, Mother, Dad and Estelle—along with three other people getting the special tour—actually got into the Oval office (Ike probably wasn't up yet!) and rooms around it (long a no-no now) and when, near a fireplace, our guide pointed to a chair he said FDR sat in during his "Fireside chats," my mother looked, indeed, as if she had entered Heaven. As she stared at the chair I said, "Sit in it." She looked startled, but did, and I shall never forget how she ran her hands up and down the arms of that chair with the most complete look of satisfaction that I ever saw on her face.

Outside the White House, as we were leaving, Mother said "Lawrence, do you reckon it would be all right if I picked up a twig or a leaf or something?" I said, "Sure! Help yourself." She put several twigs, a few leaves and a couple of pebbles in her purse. And she kept them until the leaves—pressed in the heavy old Family Bible—finally crumbled. The twigs and stones we could never find after she died, although Estelle swore they were "somewhere around here."

I never did as much for my mother as I should have, but I do love recalling that day of her grand satisfaction—and the enclosed article let me re-live it again.

Love to all,
Cuz Larry L.

March 13, 1999

Dr. Keith Kennedy,
455 South Perkins (Apt. #2)
Memphis, Tennessee 38117

Dear Dr. Kennedy:

I have come to the realization that I perhaps celebrated President Willie Jeff's beating the rap in the Senate with excessive whoops and hollars. The "Jane Doe 5" thing—the alleged rape—has given me pause, especially since Clinton and his spokesmen are saying absolutely nothing. One would think that *anyone* accused of that crime would surely—if wholly innocent—be screaming and frothing at the mouth. Or is it that Willie Jeff, having already been caught in a peck of lies, figures that no matter what he says folk won't believe him anyway? I am bothered by the fact that virtually no one in politics or the media—outside the original Clinton-haters—seems disposed to even think about that horrible and serious charge. Clinton's pattern with women would seem, at this point, to inspire a little uneasy thought.

Of course, he *could* be wholly without blame in that case. No witnesses, of course; no evidence at all; only the word of the alleged wronged and I know little of her. The presumption of innocence should be there, yes, but. . . .

What damage has been done to our trust in all this mess! And not just on the part of the President. As chilling a thing as I have heard is about how the Impeachment "managers" pushed the private reading of the alleged woman's statement on Senators sitting in judgement *when it was no part of the official record and had not been considered in the House!* We hear, now, that several Senators voted to kick the President out because of that "undercover" statement. By God, five more votes and Clinton would have become the first man in history to be kicked out of the White House, and it all could have hinged on the underhanded tactics of the so-called Impeachment managers. Whom the hell *do* we trust?

Certainly not Kenneth Starr. As soon as *his* ox gets in the ditch, he asks the Justice Department to investigate his own spokesman for leaking to the press. As if leaking hadn't occurred all along, and as if Ken Starr didn't *know* it! Are we supposed to believe that Starr didn't read the papers or watch TV for those months and years that it was pluperfectly *obvious* materials were being leaked from the special prosecutor's office? And are we supposed to believe that when Monica Lewinsky was being terrorized (there is no other word for it) by Starr's staff investigators that Starr himself didn't *know* that? Horseshit! As a former police-beat reporter and courthouse reporter I know that "terrorizing" a witness who might deliver other heads is common practice. Prosecutors do it to "wrap up the case" and attain convictions. The penal institutes— and some graves—are full of people who were cajoled or tricked or threatened until they capitulated at the expense of their freedom and the freedom of others. For Ken Starr to pretend it wasn't done in this case is as big a lie as has been told by Willie Jeff or anybody else.

And of course the Media, the talk-show hosts and their guests with personal or partisan axes to grind conducted themselves shamefully. Everyone claimed to want to get to "the truth" when, in fact, they wanted to arrive at their *own self-serving* truth: for partisan gain, for money, for another headline, for reasons of hate and envy and to take their stances on their respective sides of the huge cultural divide.

I am not proud of one goddamned soul in this whole degrading mess. There has been damage done to our nation and our system— and surely more to come. One thing for sure: there is blame aplenty to assign, and to many sources.

As a writer, I know it is damned hard to write a book or a play or a movie without having a hero. But where's the hero in this story?

Enough. I grow weary. All best,

Larry L.

March 22, 1999

Dr. Stanley Gilbert,
4830 Crooked Lane,
Dallas, Texas 75229

Dear Stan:

Pat Oliphant (the political cartoonist) said to me at lunch on Friday, "Your career seems to go in cycles. Have you ever noticed that?" Well, yes, I have and thank Sweet Precious Jesus it is on an up-Cycle right now!

Oliphant was reacting to the fresh news that (1) The Executive Committee at Ford's Theatre has newly offered me their mid-January through February slot next year for *The Dead President's Club*; (2) Both *Texas Monthly* and *The Washington Magazine* e-mailed that they want

LARRY L. KING

to buy and publish excerpts from my Letters Book coming in October from TCU Press; and 3) that I am writing a "funny" book about living in the Nation's Capital for Crown Publishing of New York.

The Ford's Theatre gig is the most personally satisfying of these new adventures. Given the history of that theater, how could a more perfect venue be found? I'd like to think that maybe the ghost of Old Honest Abe Lincoln might drop in to see his stage Presidential descendents—LBJ, Nixon, Coolidge and Truman—defend their lives and records on Judgement Day. Having seen the show when it opened to great audience and critical reaction in Austin damn-near three years ago, you know how disappointed and frustrated I have been over being unable to get a second production. Houston's Alley Theatre took the position "It's been done in Texas and since we were not given first shot. . . ." Molly Smith, the new genius-in-residence at Arena Stage here—who has been getting a wonderful press for allegedly seeking out new stage works—has not responded to me or Ethan McSweeny the young D. C.—New York stage director who also sent her a copy of the play. The dude who runs the Kennedy Center has said for three years that he would love to do *Dead Presidents'* but has never gone beyond trying to get us to take a "Blue Sky" deal, meaning that all he really is offering is an opportunity for us to pay high rent in his 500-seat Eisenhower Theatre without his theatre participating or risking its own money. Which is, of course, no deal at all: I ain't looking for a landlord but a producing "partner."

And you know the hold-up at Ford's Theater has been because I refused to sign a contract permitting the woman who long has run the place to control it in future productions. Her story was that I was refusing her "standard deal" and she could do no better. But I was adamant that I would not sign such a desperation deal, which damn sure ain't standard with me or with any of the many other theaters where my plays have been mounted. The Executive Committee decided it wanted the play so badly . . . in the next Presidential election year that it will handle negotiations with us—along with the theatre's lawyer—and cut out the middleman. (Or "middlewoman" as it were). I am just delighted!

390

This is a weird business and somehow it does seem to be cyclic. Some of this is explained away by a writer's dropping from sight while crafting a new book or play or whatever; I liken it in my mind to a bear's winter hibernation. When that new project is out, or about to come out, then new opportunities are presented (as with the Letters Book leading to excerpts sales) or someone realizes that in Washington in a Presidential election year what better theatrical offering than a play about Presidents.

But some other things can't be explained so easily. Why, suddenly, are more people interested in doing the original *Whorehouse, The Night Hank Williams Died* and even the old 1979 one-man play *The Kingfish?* And why is New York interested in me again after years of indifference? And why are more places or people suddenly asking me to speak or read? All this after a long period when it seemed to me I somehow couldn't get arrested.

Well, I think I shall not examine it any closer; after all, I don't want to conclude it is my last hurrah and that's where excessive reasoning might lead! I'll just accept it and enjoy it and go on. And be grateful. I did want to share these musings with a reflective soul such as yourself, however.

Hope things are going better for you. You are in my thoughts. All best,

Cuz Larry L.

Afterword:
Portrait of a Man of Letters

by
Richard A. Holland

When Larry L. King visited the Southwestern Writers Collection during its dedication ceremonies in 1991, we met for the first time after many telephone calls and much personal correspondence. Later at the party following the event, he loomed over me, LBJ style, and said that he had "considerable old mail" squirreled away in the basement of his home in Washington. I finally had the sense to say that I liked to make housecalls and would he be agreeable to my coming up to look at it. He immediately pumped my hand and said "Well, hell, why do you think I mentioned it in the first place?"

I traveled to King's Washington home in late January of 1992. Larry and his wife Barbara Blaine and two teenagers live in a fine house they bought from the widow of Texas Senator Tom Connally, three stories and a basement. More than thirty years' worth of letters were neatly stored in large mailing envelopes down on the bottom level. King's system was to keep a box under his desk and after it was full of mail to him, and carbons of his own letters, they went into an envelope marked with month and year. These we packed into cardboard storage boxes, an operation that took approximately six hours. The bathroom scale registered a total of 243 pounds of paper. The other two days we talked or rather I listened, marvelling at King's encyclopedic memory and fabulous storytelling. Later I learned that many of the stories were contained in the letters.

Months passed in San Marcos as the King letters were slowly unpacked. Contrary to popular opinion, librarians for the most part do not have time to read the contents of their collections, but in the case of the King letters, I was irresistibly drawn to them. Thousands of personal letters, both to and from, Father's Day cards, birthday greetings, letters from anonymous fans and seekers of signed books, and lots of invitations to give money or time to certain organizations or causes.

Larry was in Austin several months later for a fund raiser, and I told him I had spent a lot of time, weekends for the most part, reading his letters: had he thought about us doing a book? He said "Goddamn Doctor Holland, I thought you'd never ask!" With that the die was cast. As to the "Doctor" designation, I had figured out already that King freely confers the honorary doctorate when he deems it appropriate.

Separating likely looking letters from the more routine mail left thousands to read. Several things soon became clear: first of all, letter writing to some extent was concentrated on certain days. It was almost as if King set aside a day every so often to communicate. When he had an important story to tell—say his big advance from Viking to write the definitive biography of LBJ or the falling apart of *Harper's* in the spring of 1971—he might write as many as six or eight versions of the story. Almost always the definitive version would be that written to Lanvil Gilbert and his wife Glenda. Other correspondents favored with in-depth letters might include Warren Burnett, Jay Milner, Ben Peeler, Willie Morris, Bud Shrake, and later, Frank Rich. A man's man in letters, King very seldom communicated with women unless it was related to the business of writing, publishing, or producing a play. I found only one letter to Rosemarie, his wife from 1965 until her death in June 1972, a period when he travelled constantly and might write twenty letters a week to friends.*

King pretty much stands alone as a Texas writer although he has been grouped with both the *Texas Observer* crowd that would include Ronnie Dugger and Willie Morris and with several close friends who eventually all ended up in Austin—Bill Brammer, Bud Shrake and Gary Cartwright. In New York his writing colleagues were the superb staff that Willie Morris assembled at *Harper's* during its great period—David Halberstam, Marshall Frady, John Corry, John Hollander, and contributors William Styron and Norman Mailer. What places King outside these companionable fellow writers was where he was from . . . and how far he had come.

Though only slightly older than his close friends Willie Morris and Bud Shrake, King's background made him seem much older in life experience. The former were both southern "town boys" born before World War II and raised in middle-class circumstances. Shrake went to a good Texas high school, Paschal in Fort Worth, was accepted by Yale and went to TCU. Morris left Yazoo City, Mississippi, and moved to Austin where he made his mark editing *The Daily Texan* at the university and became a Rhodes Scholar. Literary ambition for boys of their talent and backgrounds might have been unusual, but at least it was part of a more or less recognized way of being.

King, on the other hand, has the feel of an older time. Rural West Texas in the early 1930s was just beginning to develop paved roads, electricity in country houses and indoor plumbing, and as far as the world of the intellect was concerned could be considered almost preliterate. Farm life was little changed from decades before, consisting of backbreaking labor that brought little reward; it was dependent on the weather and on economic forces based far away. The Kings' house had a Bible and a reference book, both of which King had mastered by a relatively early age. A bookish boy in a bookless place, he sought and absorbed knowledge and by the time he was in high school encountered one of those great seminal teachers who make a difference—Coach Aubra Nooncaster taught poetry to the football team. When King returned to West Texas after army service, he worked for radio stations and newspapers and, although he was largely self-taught, he was drawn to men who were educated.

What King did share with Willie Morris, Shrake, and his other contemporaries from Texas and the South was an observant eye for the absurd and a taste for outsize practical jokes and parodies of formal language. Shrake obtained a fifty-dollar mail-order doctorate from the Universal Life Church in the early 1970s that not only instigated his honorary title in King's letters as the "Reverend Doctor Shrake" but also set loose an entire vocabulary of high church language in their correspondence. "Yours in Christ" became the common closing to their letters, and at some point King began signing his letters to Shrake "His Worship." This changed after the mid-'90s debacle of *The Best Little Whorehouse Goes Public* that closed after twenty-nine previews and sixteen performances. At this point King immediately began signing his letters to Shrake "His Former Worship." Combined with a taste for ecclesiastical or legalistic language was an exaggerated use of southern country phrases or bad grammar that reminded themselves and their friends where they had come from but also how far they had travelled.

The late cowboy storyteller, poet and singer Buck Ramsey once accused King of writing his autobiography a story at a time, and if that is true, it began with his early piece for *Harper's*, "Requiem for a West Texas Town," a portrait of Putnam, when King had gone back after a long absence. The most notable of these memory pieces is, of course, "The Old Man," written soon after the death of his father Clyde. It is simply one of the best essays in American literature written by a son about his father. From his father King picked up a booming Old Testament-sounding cadence in his speech that is often reflected in his prose.

For King, evoking his past was natural but only at a distance. Texas writers of his generation tend to follow a couple of different patterns. They leave and come back (Bill Brammer, John Graves) or they leave and stay gone (Terry Southern, William Humphrey). King left and appeared to come home just often enough to reconfirm his reasons for leaving in the first place. A pattern emerged where King would come to Midland and Odessa and stop by briefly to visit his parents, saying that he was between flights, whereas in actuality he spent more time drinking and hanging out with old pals.

Some of his friends became curious about his family, whom no one had met. Finally, after years of badgering, King took the attorney Warren Burnett by to meet his mother and father. The scene that Burnett witnessed was that of a grown son and two aging parents, none of whom could communicate with each other in meaningful terms, although each managed to express some dissatisfaction with the others—and the parents appeared totally oblivious to the presence of Burnett. They had arrived in Burnett's car, and when they left, he was silent. Five minutes or so down the road, Burnett, a master of the High Sardonic, finally said, "Lawrence, you're not doing your best work." Beat. "Tennessee Williams started with much less."

In 1964 King's estranged wife deliberately destroyed his copies of the sizable correspondence he had saved during the ten year period he worked in Congress for J.T. "Slick" Rutherford and Jim Wright. We were able to find a handful of original letters from these years in Lanvil Gilbert's garage, a friendly archeological site located in North Austin. These letters from the '50s reveal King working around the clock in politics while supporting a wife and young children, but always there is the desire to become a writer. The archive in the Southwestern Writers Collection picks up late in 1964 after King has drastically changed his life by leaving his job with Jim Wright and separating from his wife and children who returned to Midland.

Matching image and lifestyle, King immediately grew an Ahab-style beard, encouraged by his young daughter Kerri, who told him that if he was going to be a writer he should try to grow whiskers "like Mr. Hemingway." The first time he returned be-whiskered to Odessa he was also sporting a cape and tam-o-shanter, an outlandish costume aimed at impressing Warren Burnett with his new status. Thus outfitted, King parked his car and was spotted by the prominent West Texas attorney and judge Harold Young, who ran out from his office and said "My God, King, you look like you lost an election bet!"

Well over half of the letters in the King archive are from the period

1964 to 1972, the years in which he astoundingly reinvented himself. When he started he was a fledgling writer with a wobbly idea for a novel and no proven publishing record. Eight years later he had published a novel, written highly acclaimed pieces in the country's hottest magazine, produced books of his collected pieces, created friendships with the literary elite of New York, won a distinguished Nieman Fellowship to Harvard and was runner-up for the National Book Award for his book *Confessions of a White Racist*. These years also coincided with his marriage to Rosemarie Coumaris Kline, who worked in a congressman's office and was the young widow of a jazz musician. They were married in 1965, and only a few months later learned of the breast cancer that finally killed her in June 1972.

Letter writing is a two-way street, and Larry L. King has been blessed in the quality of his correspondents. Early on he was so taken with his cousin Lanvil Gilbert's letters that he very seriously encouraged Lanvil to write something for Willie Morris at *Harper's*. Among his Texas writer friends, Bill Brammer, Jay Milner and Bud Shrake all have brilliant contributions present in the King archive, with Brammer in the 1960s and '70s winning the prize for psychedelia. King's earliest literary champions in New York, Bob Gutwillig and Sterling Lord, both recognized the renegade energy and wit present in King's letters, and as early as 1965 commonly referred to a future day when his letters would be collected and published.

In all honesty there were times when I believe Larry and I both tired of what became a very large project. He has a documented impatience with delay and sometimes becomes testy when collaborating. I tend to take my time about things, believing that the phrase "all deliberate speed" are words to live by. Months on end there were stacks of photocopied letters on my dining room table; I read hundreds of them to my wife Cynthia, and gradually Larry and I got the selection down to a managable pile. What you have seen here is a distillation of a paring down that hits the high spots and I hope begins to do justice to the life and career of Larry L. King.

—Richard Holland

*King explains that when on the road he called home, rather than write.

Index

ARROGANTLY CONFIDENT

Letters Reflect success, failure, hopes,
anxieties, fears, dreams, angers + joys

LBJ SAID OF HARPERS "LBJ, MY HERO":
"A DAMNED DIRTY STORY."

Fights w/ Editor Gutwillig...
teases Bob G about   "   is
piece in 'New Leader'

HST VISITS WITH CRAIG RAUPE

JNO CORRY + DAVID H. got more Do...

LOUIS ARMSTRONG CAN'T STAND SQUARES

Joe Pool's WRECK - LETTER TO MAVERICK +
"Tex. Congmen rarely do..."

your "candid comments for British TV

Your FLIRTATION w/ 60 MINUTES

BILLY Lee BRAMMER - BUD SHRAKE
DAN. JENKINS

The HARVARD experience | The HARPER's
                          experience

Letter to HARVARD   ~ 11   Tom GUINZBURG
     HILARIOUS   Viking Press

H. Allen Smith Letters | Princeton Life?

Mo UDALL | FIRED BY New Times
             Why?, JON LARSON LTR:

you QUIT WRITING LETTERS IN 1977?

BOOK
TITLES
& Other...

BOBBY
BAKER: ESU
CROOKED BOOK

FAMILY:
BARBARA
LINDSEY; BLAI
KERRI-
BRADLEY +
Cheryl ANN CAL
Jean?

→ 'LBJ
WILL RUN
in '68

You + the
MAILER piece

INDEX
KANTOR, MAC

10 DEY
MACKINLEY
KANTOR)

Phil
Hemphill

You
BUBBER
BROWN
SAME
TIME

DOAD PROS IDENT
CLUB
TTONE